子連れ狼

LONE
WOLF
AND
子連れ狼 CUB

story
KAZUO KOIKE

art
GOSEKI KOJIMA

DARK HORSE MANGA™

translation
DANA LEWIS

lettering & retouch
DIGITAL CHAMELEON

cover artwork
FRANK MILLER with **LYNN VARLEY**

publisher
MIKE RICHARDSON

editor
MIKE HANSEN

assistant editor
TIM ERVIN-GORE

consulting editor
TOREN SMITH for **STUDIO PROTEUS**

book design
DARIN FABRICK

art director
MARK COX

Published by Dark Horse Manga, a division of Dark Horse Comics, Inc.,
in association with MegaHouse and Koike Shoin Publishing Company., Ltd.

Dark Horse Comics, Inc.
10956 SE Main Street, Milwaukie, OR 97222
www.darkhorse.com

First edition: November 2000
ISBN: 1-56971-504-1

5 7 9 10 8 6

Printed in Canada

To find a comics shop in your area, call the
Comic Shop Locator Service toll-free at 1-888-266-4226

THE FLUTE
OF THE
FALLEN TIGER

子連れ狼

*By KAZUO KOIKE
& GOSEKI KOJIMA*

VOLUME
3

A NOTE TO READERS

Lone Wolf and Cub is famous for its carefully researched re-creation of Edo-Period Japan. To preserve the flavor of the work, we have chosen to retain many Edo-Period terms that have no direct equivalents in English. Japanese is written in a mix of Chinese ideograms and a syllabic writing system, resulting in numerous synonyms. In the glossary, you may encounter words with multiple meanings. These are words written with Chinese ideograms that are pronounced the same but carry different meanings. A Japanese reader seeing the different ideograms would know instantly which meaning it is, but these synonyms can cause confusion when Japanese is spelled out in our alphabet. *O-yurushi o* (please forgive us)!

LONE WOLF AND CUB

TABLE OF CONTENTS

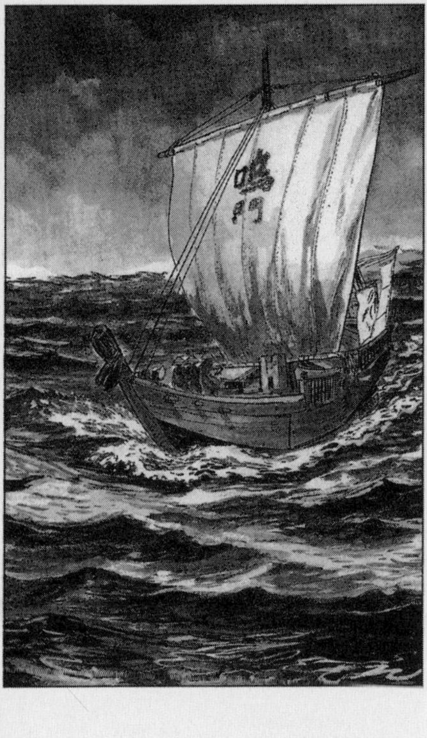
鳴門

the fifteenth

Flute of the Fallen Tiger

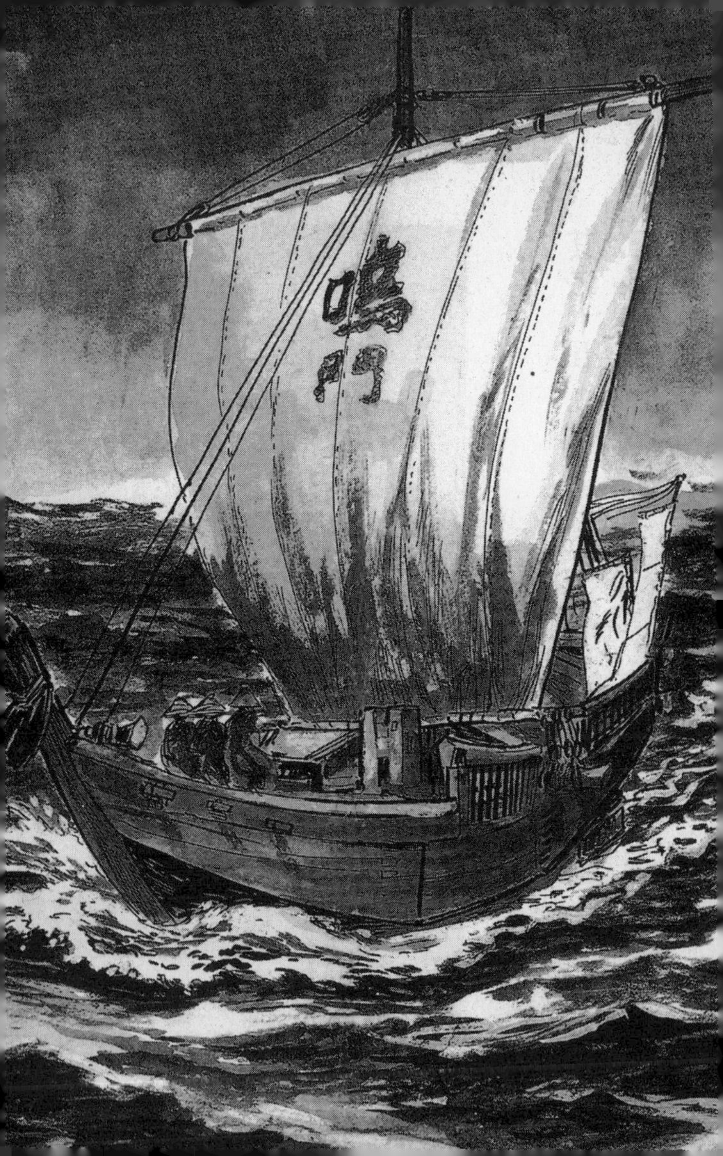
鳴門

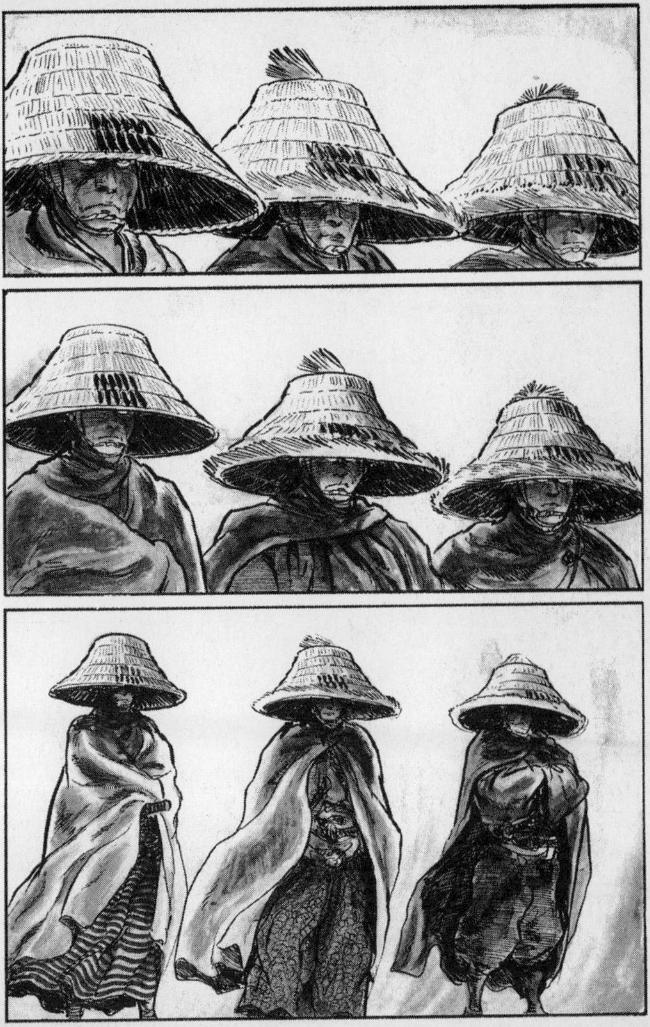

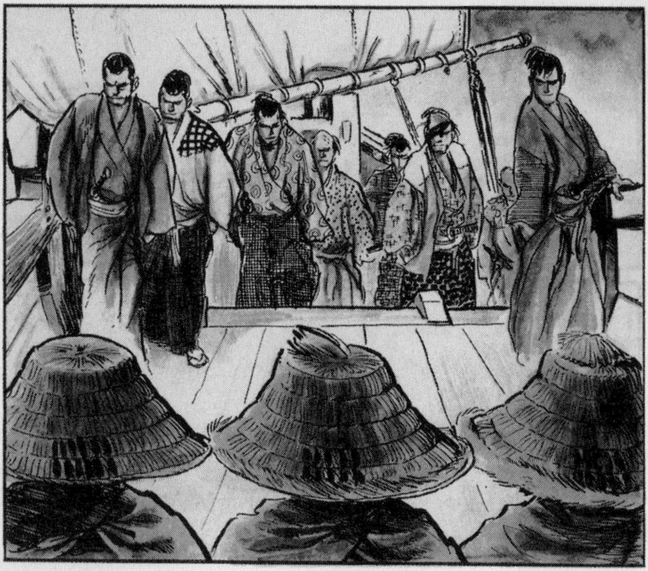

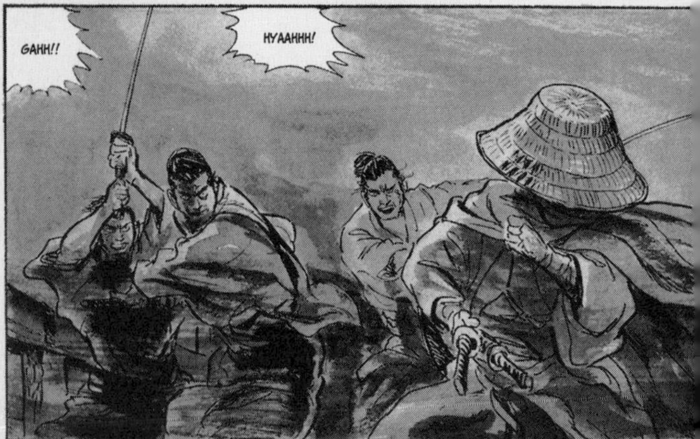
GAHH!!
HYAAHHH!

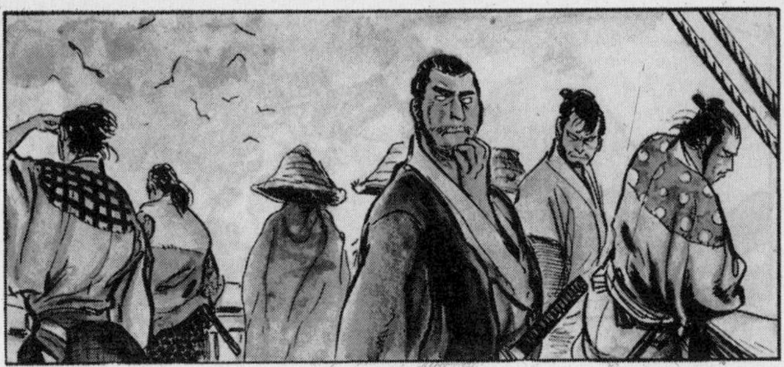

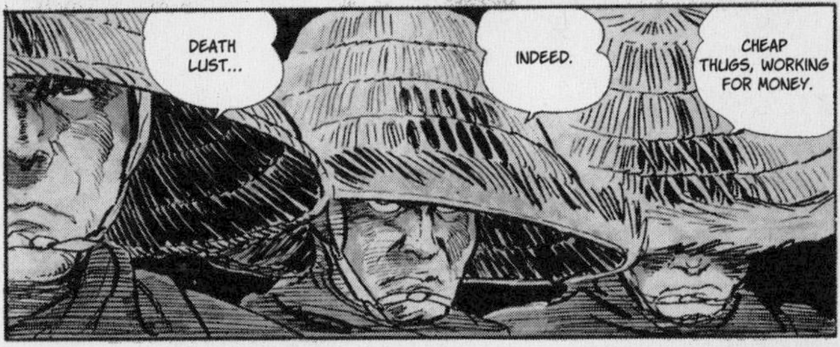
DEATH LUST...
INDEED.
CHEAP THUGS, WORKING FOR MONEY.

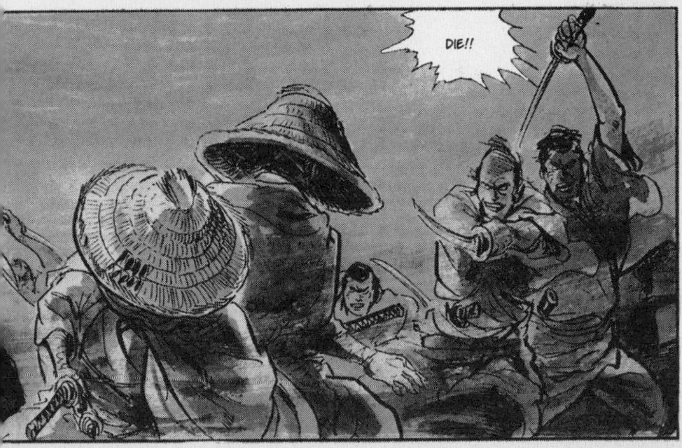
DIE!!

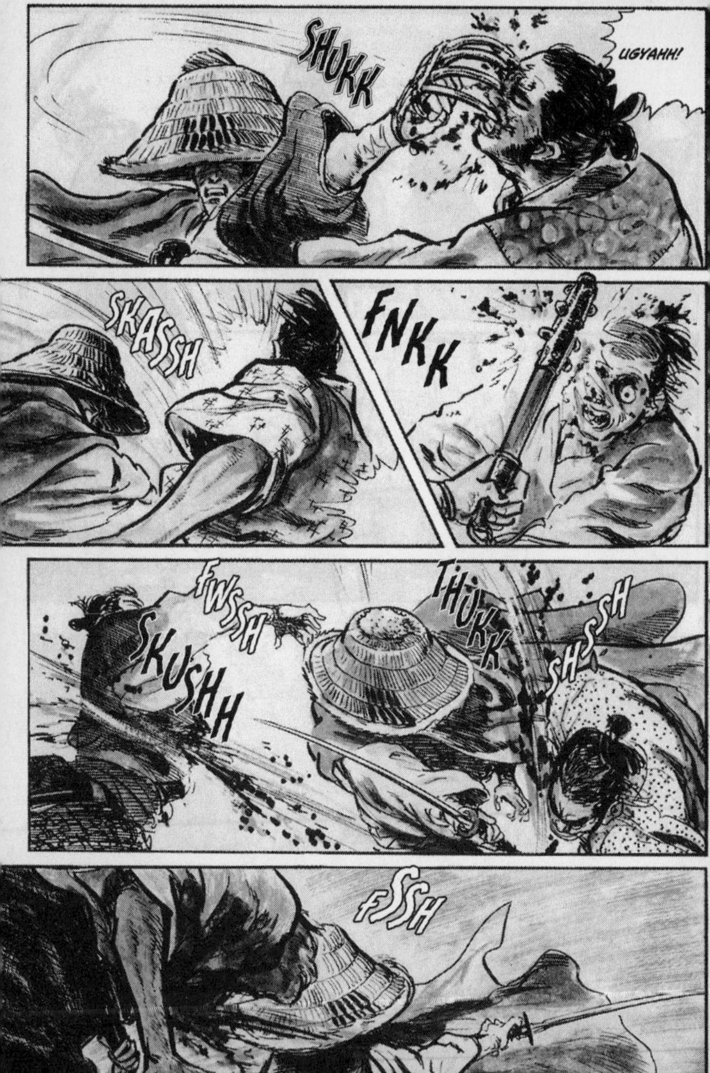
SHUKK
UGYAHH!
SKASSH
FNKK
FWSSH
SKUSHH
THUKK
SHSSH
FSSH

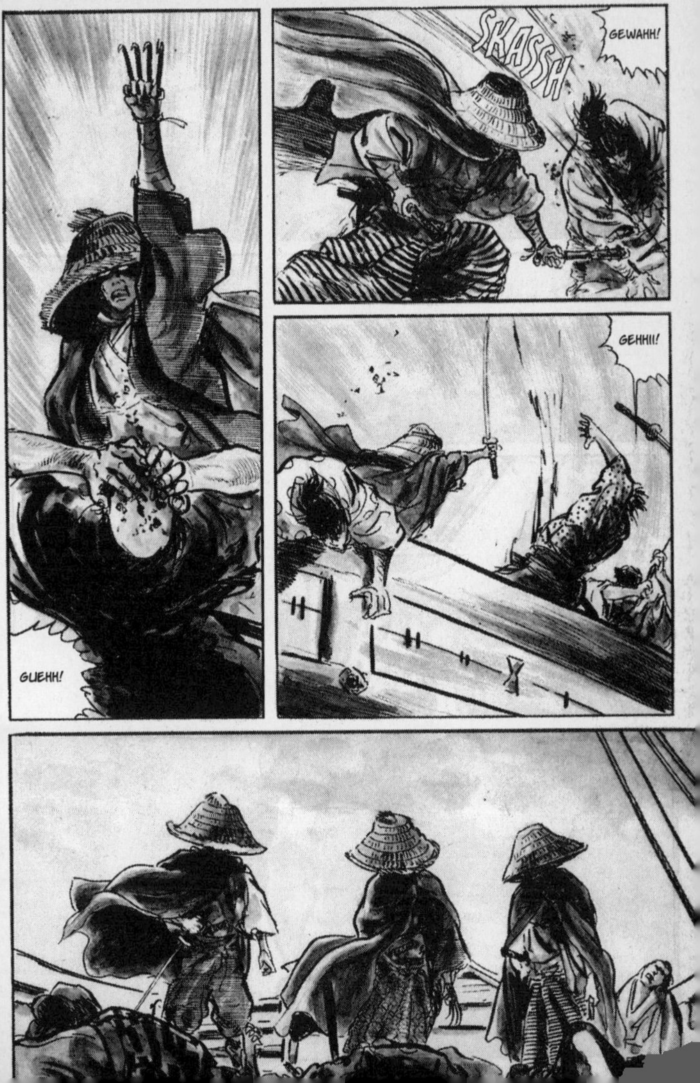
GUEHH!
SKASSH
GEWAHH!
GEHHII!

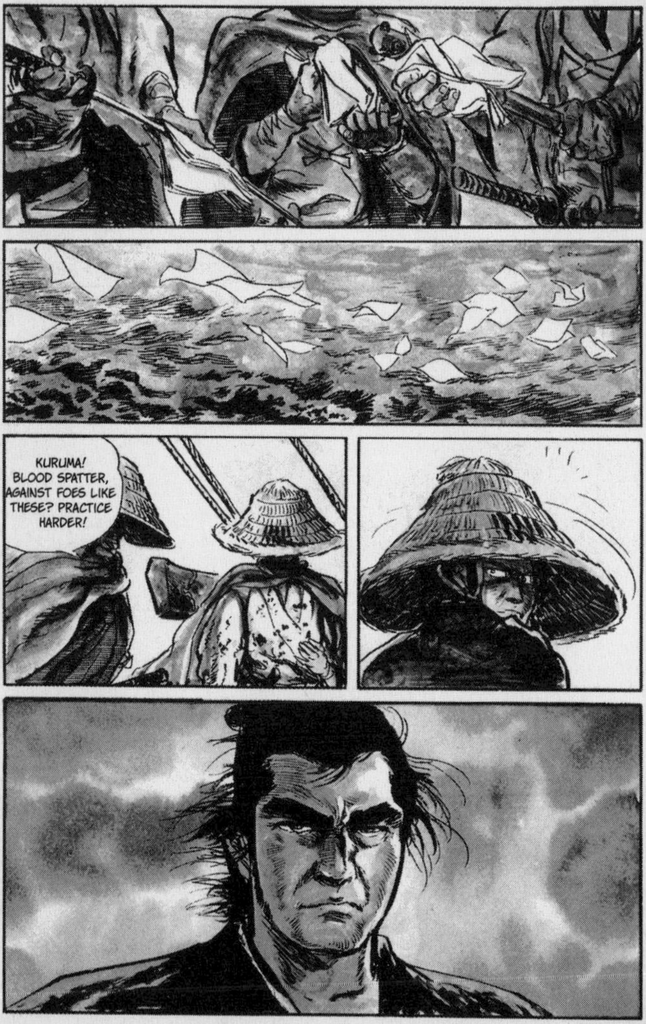
KURUMA! BLOOD SPATTER, AGAINST FOES LIKE THESE? PRACTICE HARDER!

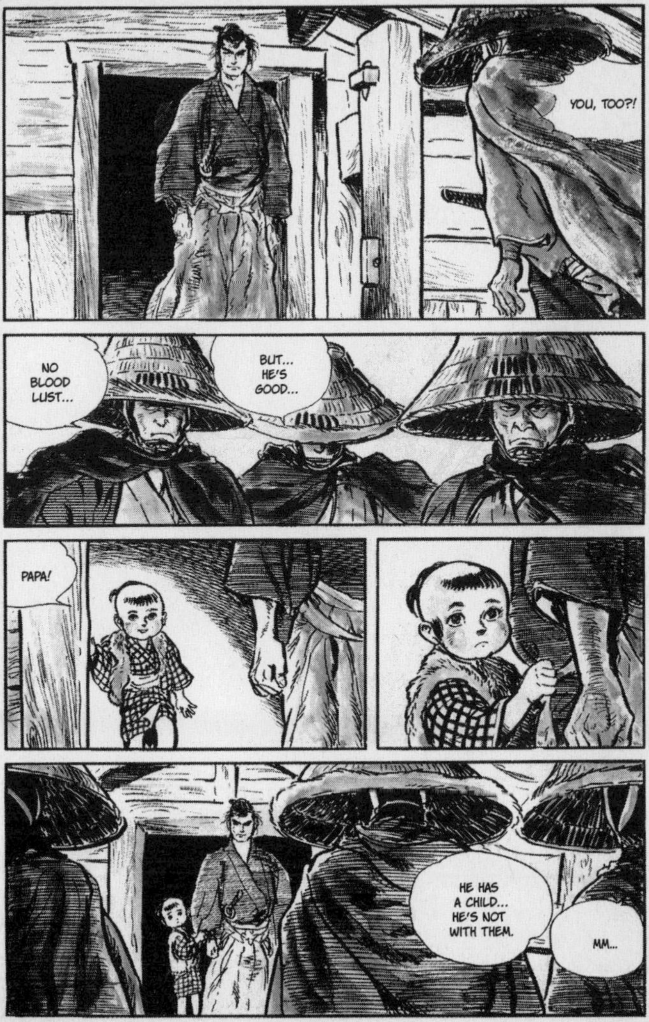
YOU, TOO?!
NO BLOOD LUST...
BUT... HE'S GOOD...
PAPA!
HE HAS A CHILD... HE'S NOT WITH THEM.
MM...

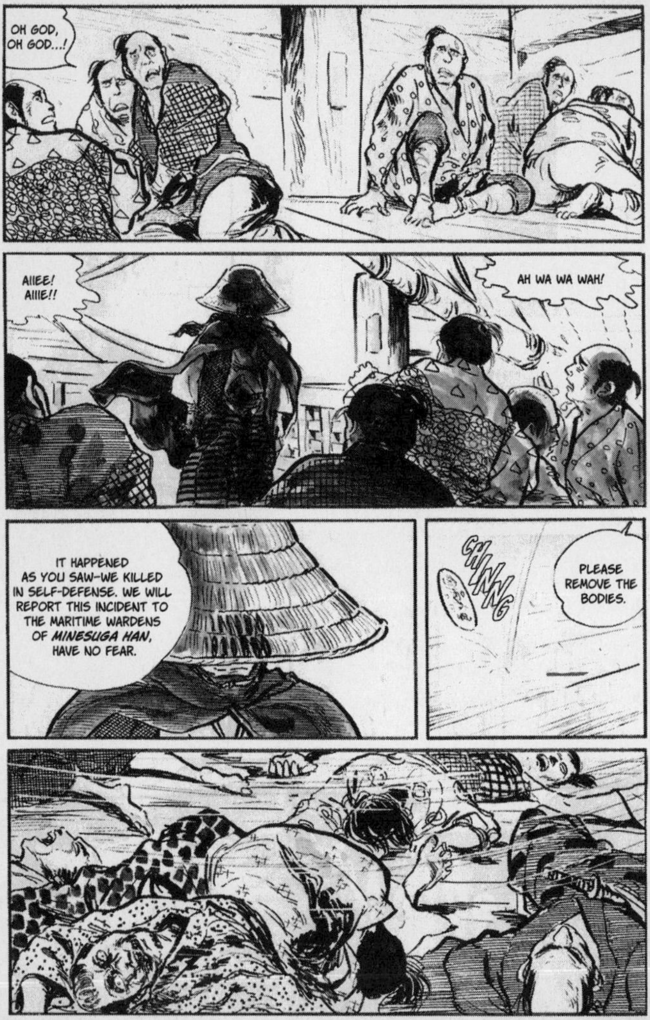
OH GOD, OH GOD...!
AIIEE! AIIIE!!
AH WA WA WAH!
IT HAPPENED AS YOU SAW–WE KILLED IN SELF-DEFENSE. WE WILL REPORT THIS INCIDENT TO THE MARITIME WARDENS OF *MINESUGA HAN*, HAVE NO FEAR.
CHINNG
PLEASE REMOVE THE BODIES.

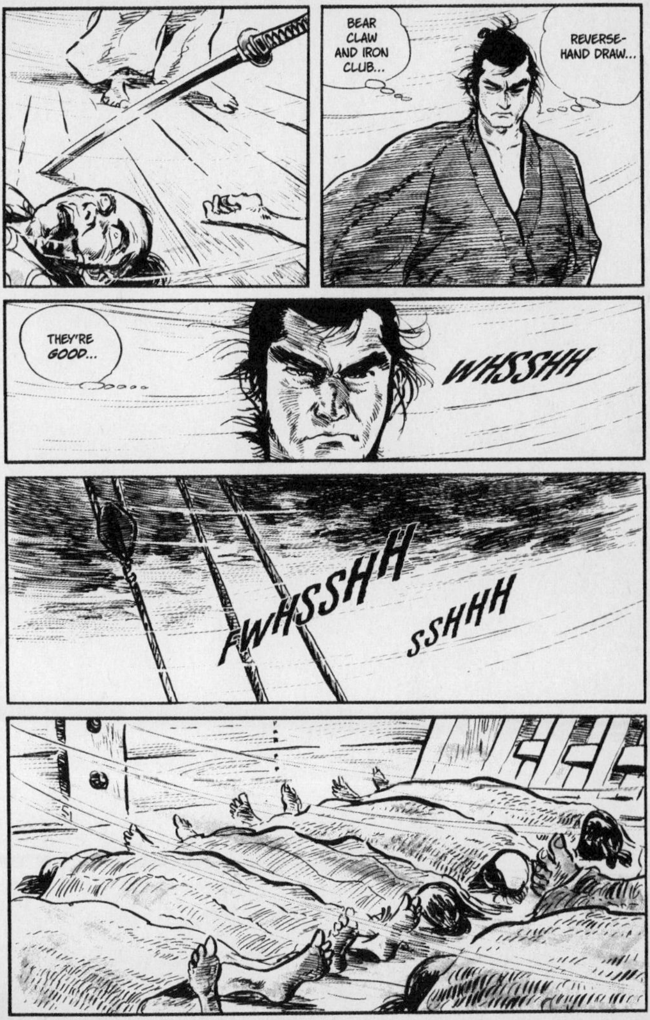
BEAR CLAW AND IRON CLUB...
REVERSE-HAND DRAW...
THEY'RE GOOD...
WHSSHH
FWHSSHH
SSHHH

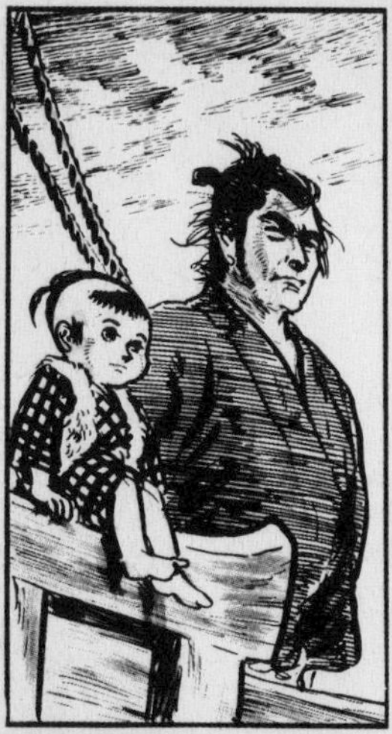

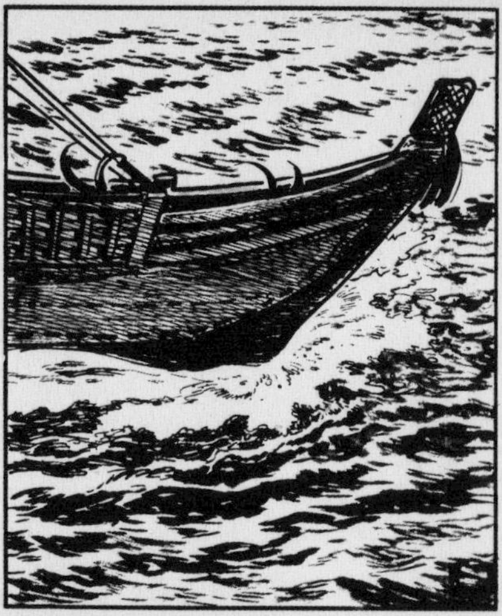

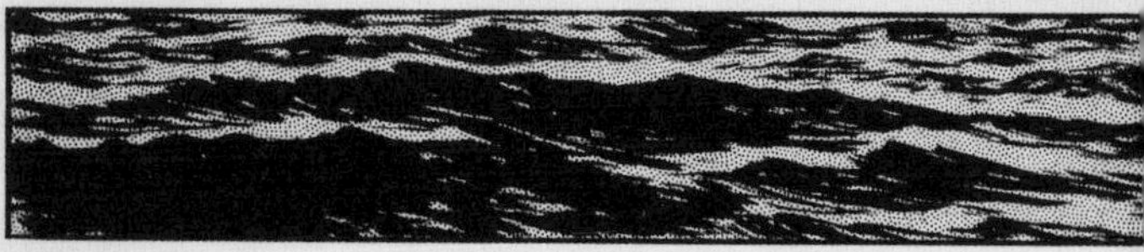

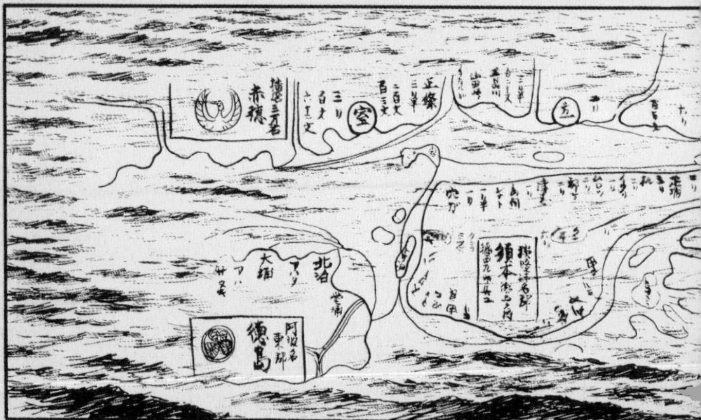

赤穂
室
正條
北泊
徳島
阿波名東郡

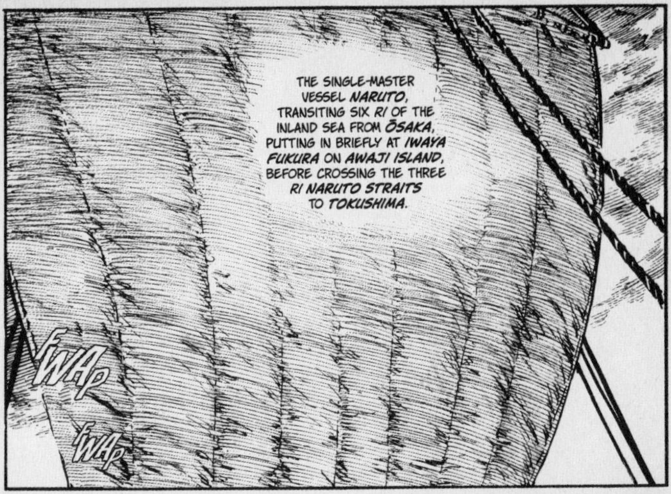
THE SINGLE-MASTER VESSEL NARUTO, TRANSITING SIX RI OF THE INLAND SEA FROM ŌSAKA, PUTTING IN BRIEFLY AT IWAYA FUKURA ON AWAJI ISLAND, BEFORE CROSSING THE THREE RI NARUTO STRAITS TO TOKUSHIMA.
FWAP
FWAP

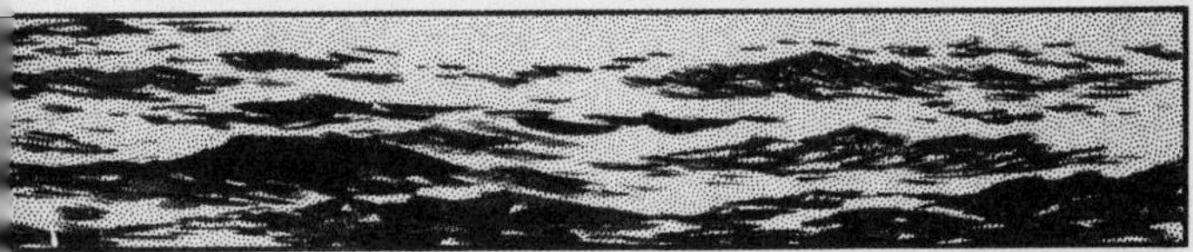

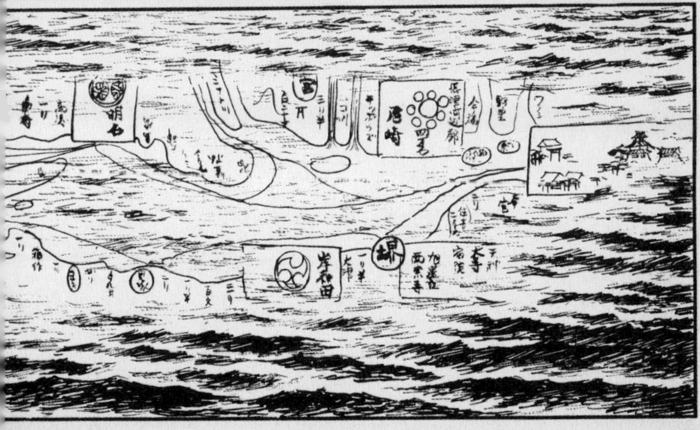

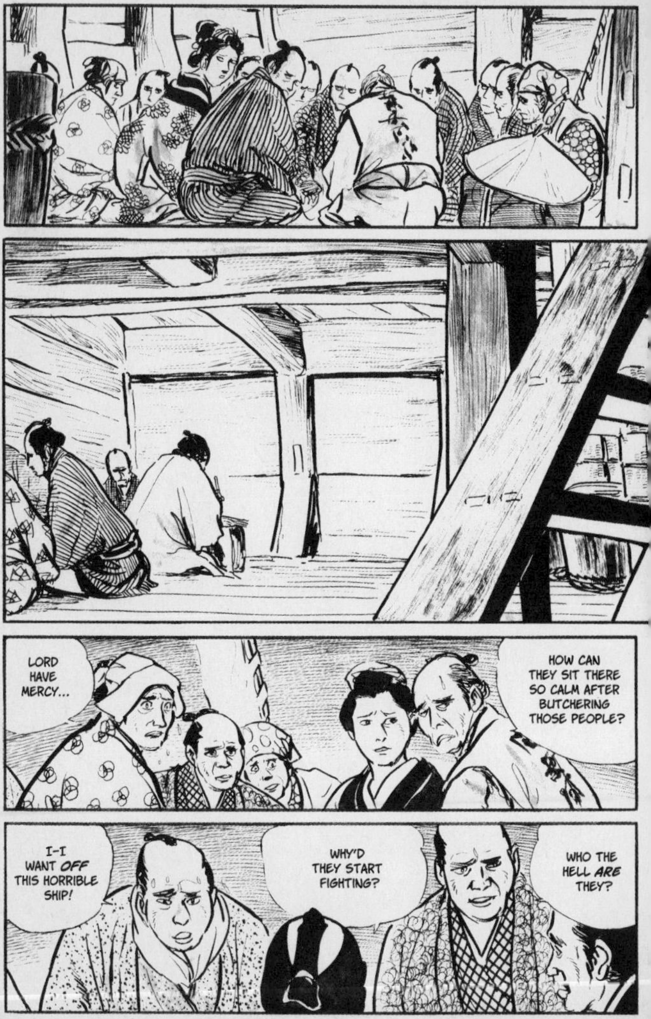
LORD HAVE MERCY...
HOW CAN THEY SIT THERE SO CALM AFTER BUTCHERING THOSE PEOPLE?
I-I WANT *OFF* THIS HORRIBLE SHIP!
WHY'D THEY START FIGHTING?
WHO THE HELL *ARE* THEY?

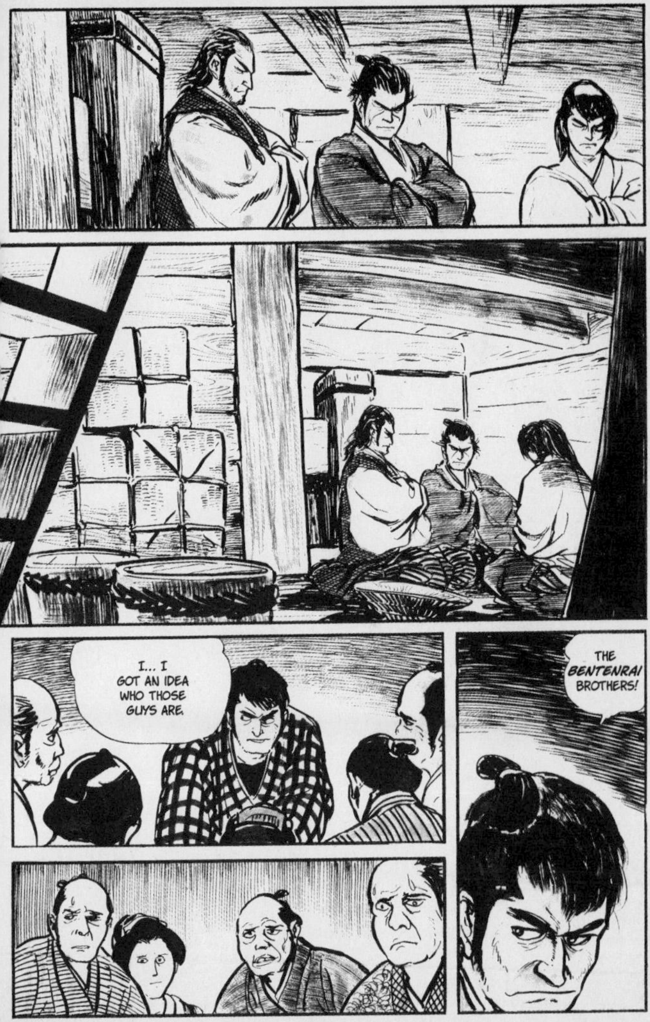
I... I GOT AN IDEA WHO THOSE GUYS ARE.
THE *BENTENRAI* BROTHERS!

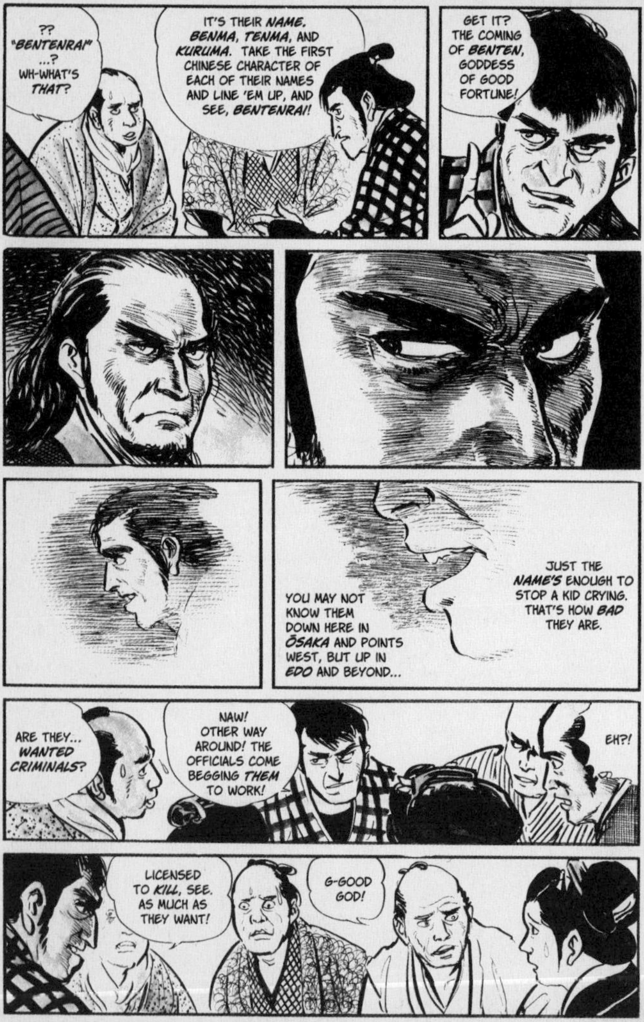

?? "BENTENRAI" ...? WH-WHAT'S THAT?
IT'S THEIR NAME. BENMA, TENMA, AND KURUMA. TAKE THE FIRST CHINESE CHARACTER OF EACH OF THEIR NAMES AND LINE 'EM UP, AND SEE, BENTENRAI!
GET IT? THE COMING OF BENTEN, GODDESS OF GOOD FORTUNE!
YOU MAY NOT KNOW THEM DOWN HERE IN ŌSAKA AND POINTS WEST, BUT UP IN EDO AND BEYOND...
JUST THE NAME'S ENOUGH TO STOP A KID CRYING. THAT'S HOW BAD THEY ARE.
ARE THEY... WANTED CRIMINALS?
NAW! OTHER WAY AROUND! THE OFFICIALS COME BEGGING THEM TO WORK!
EH?!
LICENSED TO KILL, SEE. AS MUCH AS THEY WANT!
G-GOOD GOD!

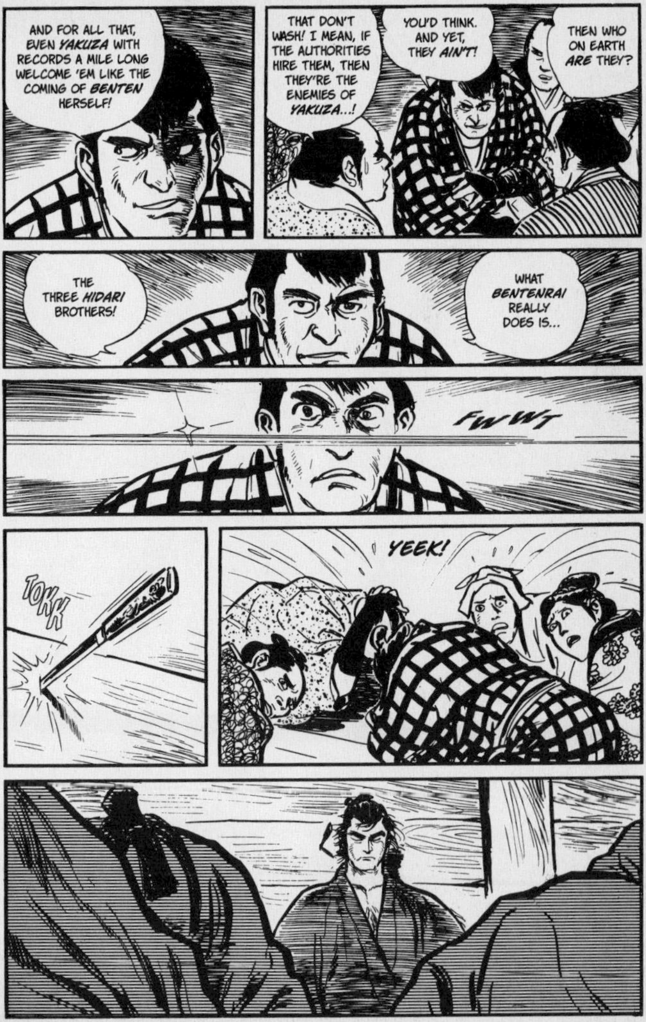
AND FOR ALL THAT, EVEN YAKUZA WITH RECORDS A MILE LONG WELCOME 'EM LIKE THE COMING OF BENTEN HERSELF!
THAT DON'T WASH! I MEAN, IF THE AUTHORITIES HIRE THEM, THEN THEY'RE THE ENEMIES OF YAKUZA...!
YOU'D THINK. AND YET, THEY AIN'T!
THEN WHO ON EARTH ARE THEY?
THE THREE HIDARI BROTHERS!
WHAT BENTENRAI REALLY DOES IS...
FWWT
TOKK
YEEK!

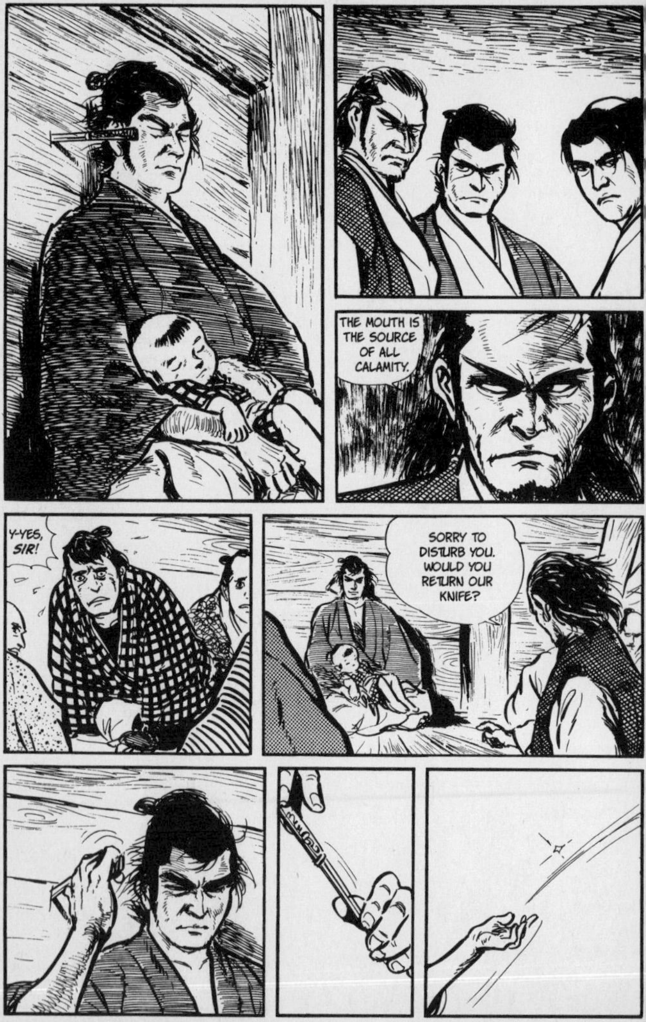
THE MOUTH IS THE SOURCE OF ALL CALAMITY.
Y-YES, SIR!
SORRY TO DISTURB YOU. WOULD YOU RETURN OUR KNIFE?

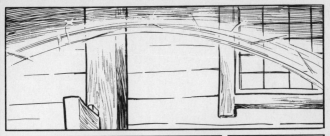

...THANKS.

AND SO, HONORED SIR. WHERE ARE YOU BOUND?

AWA NATO-GUN IN *TOKUSHIMA.*

WE TRAVEL TOGETHER...

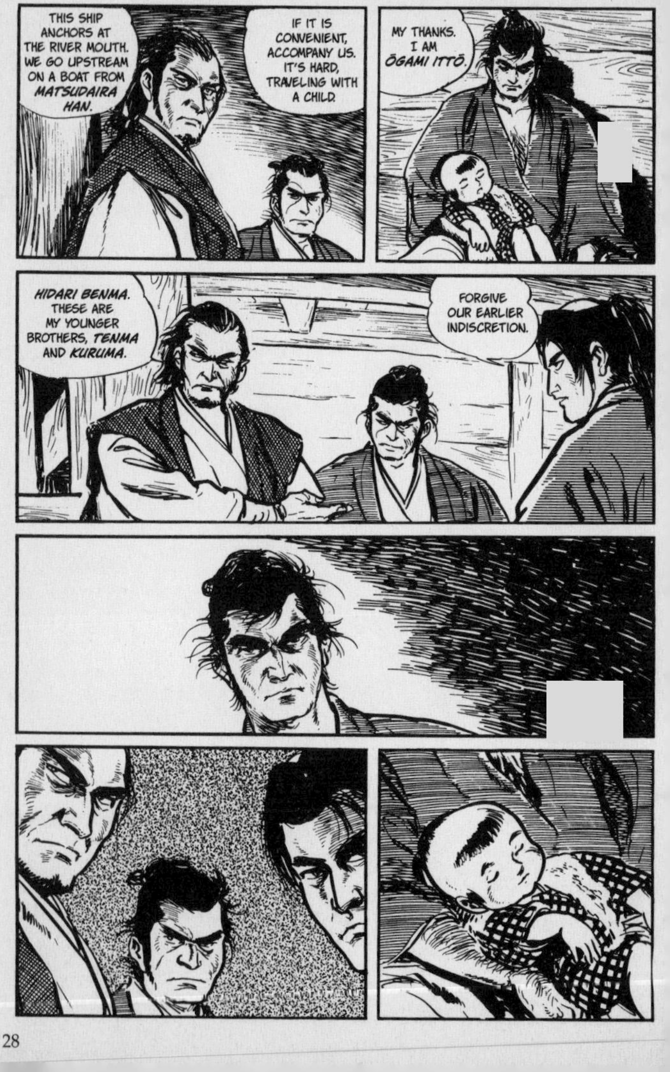
THIS SHIP ANCHORS AT THE RIVER MOUTH. WE GO UPSTREAM ON A BOAT FROM *MATSUDAIRA HAN*.
IF IT IS CONVENIENT, ACCOMPANY US. IT'S HARD, TRAVELING WITH A CHILD.
MY THANKS. I AM *ŌGAMI ITTŌ*.
HIDARI BENMA. THESE ARE MY YOUNGER BROTHERS, *TENMA* AND *KURUMA*.
FORGIVE OUR EARLIER INDISCRETION.

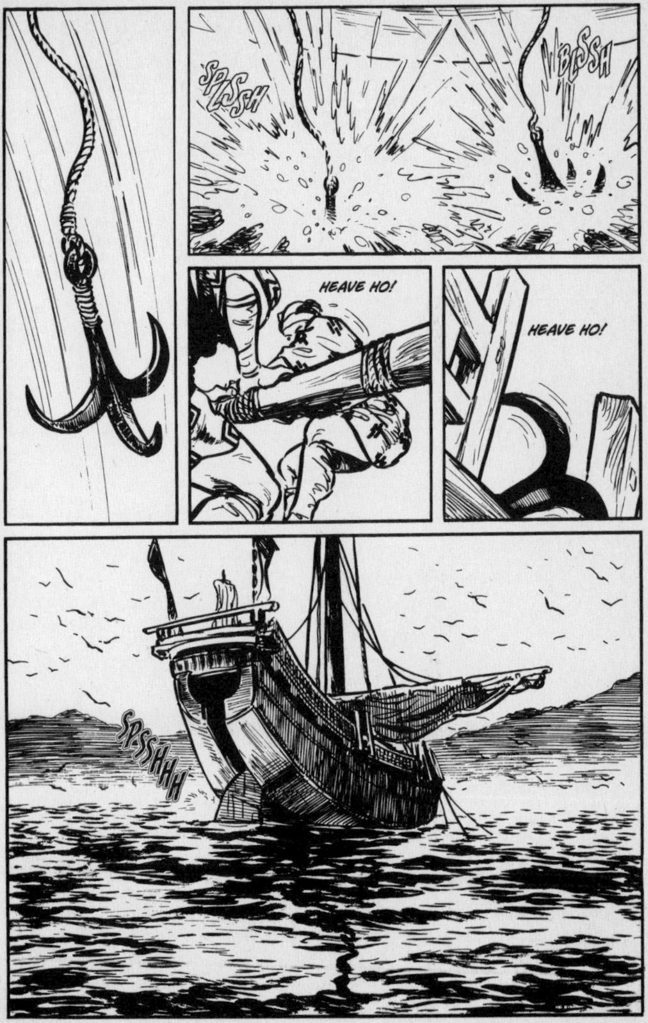
SPLSSH
BLSSH
HEAVE HO!
HEAVE HO!
SPSSHHH

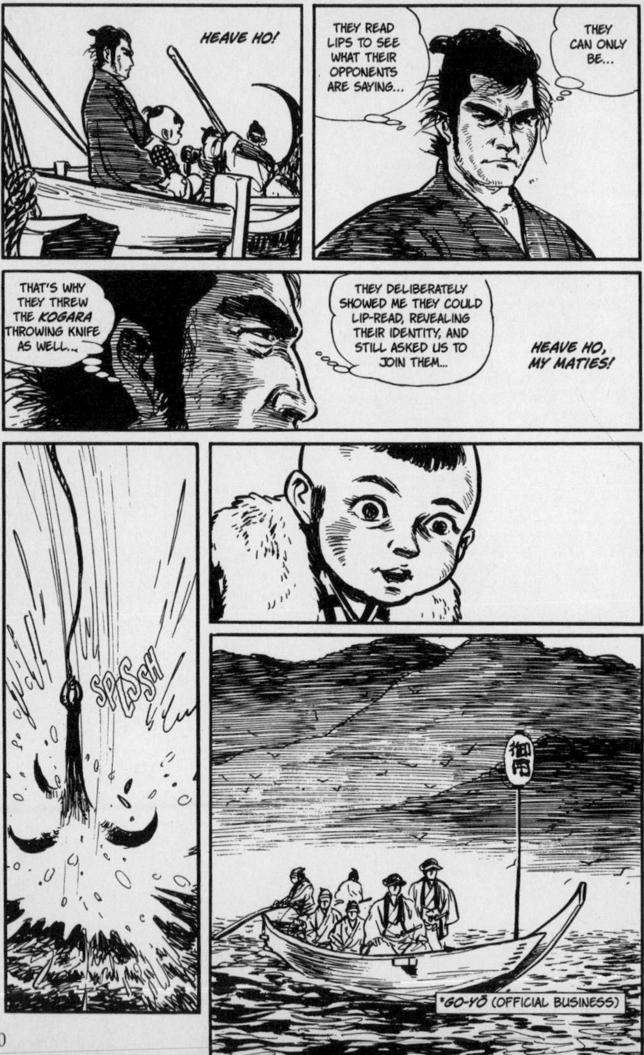
HEAVE HO!
THEY READ LIPS TO SEE WHAT THEIR OPPONENTS ARE SAYING...
THEY CAN ONLY BE...
THAT'S WHY THEY THREW THE *KOGARA* THROWING KNIFE AS WELL...
THEY DELIBERATELY SHOWED ME THEY COULD LIP-READ, REVEALING THEIR IDENTITY, AND STILL ASKED US TO JOIN THEM...
HEAVE HO, MY MATIES!
SPLSSH
御用
*GO-YŌ (OFFICIAL BUSINESS)

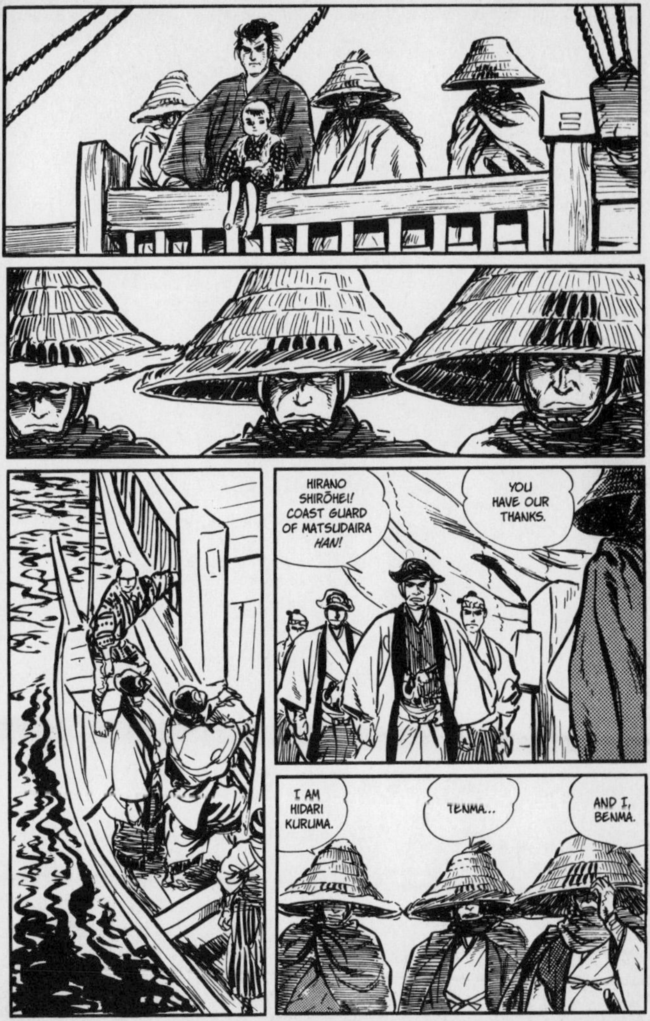
HIRANO SHIRŌHEI! COAST GUARD OF MATSUDAIRA *HAN!*
YOU HAVE OUR THANKS.
I AM HIDARI KURUMA.
TENMA...
AND I, BENMA.

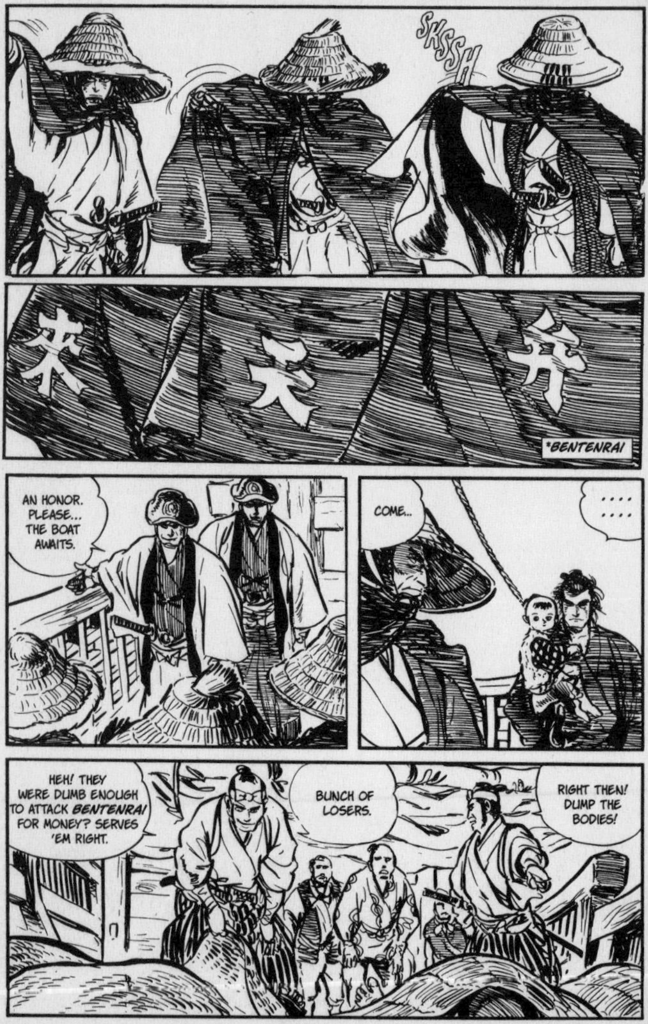
SKSSH
来
天
弁
*BENTENRAI
AN HONOR. PLEASE... THE BOAT AWAITS.
COME...
....
HEH! THEY WERE DUMB ENOUGH TO ATTACK *BENTENRAI* FOR MONEY? SERVES 'EM RIGHT.
BUNCH OF LOSERS.
RIGHT THEN! DUMP THE BODIES!

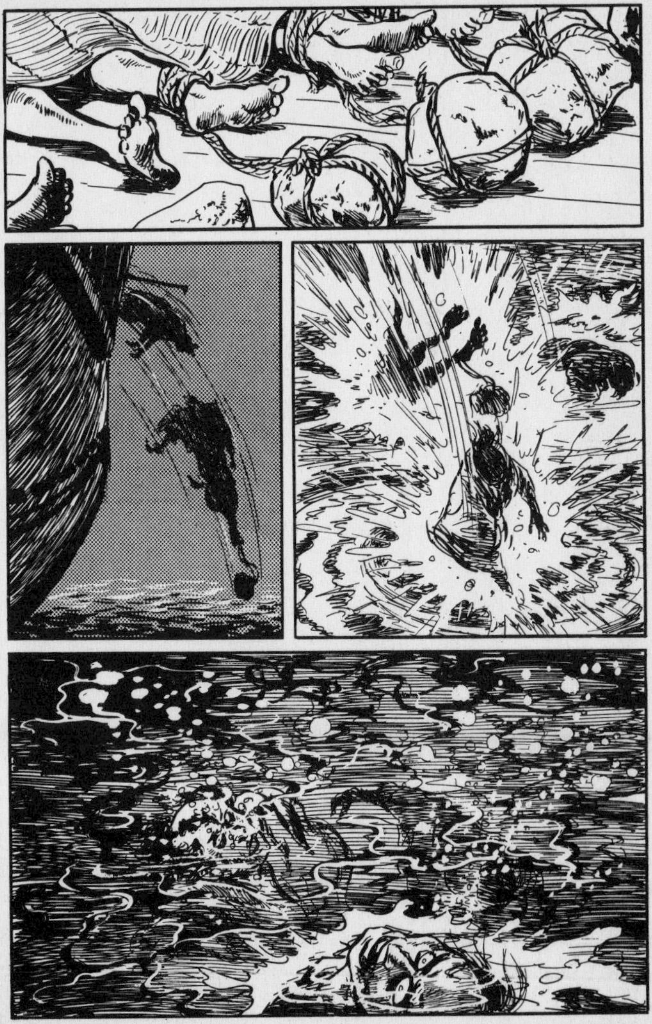

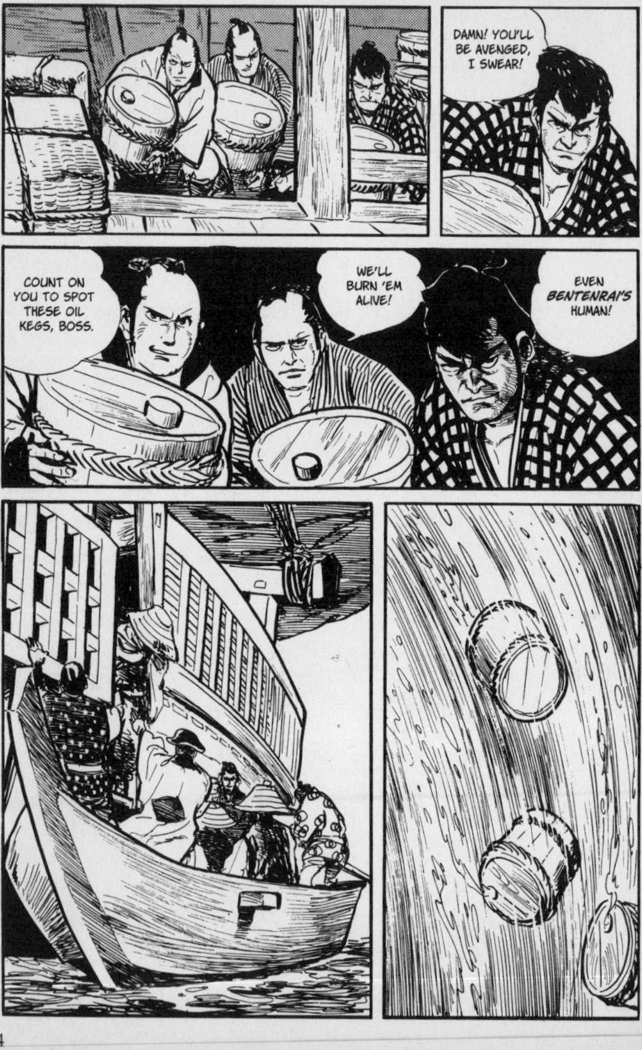
DAMN! YOU'LL BE AVENGED, I SWEAR!
COUNT ON YOU TO SPOT THESE OIL KEGS, BOSS.
WE'LL BURN 'EM ALIVE!
EVEN *BENTENRAI'S* HUMAN!

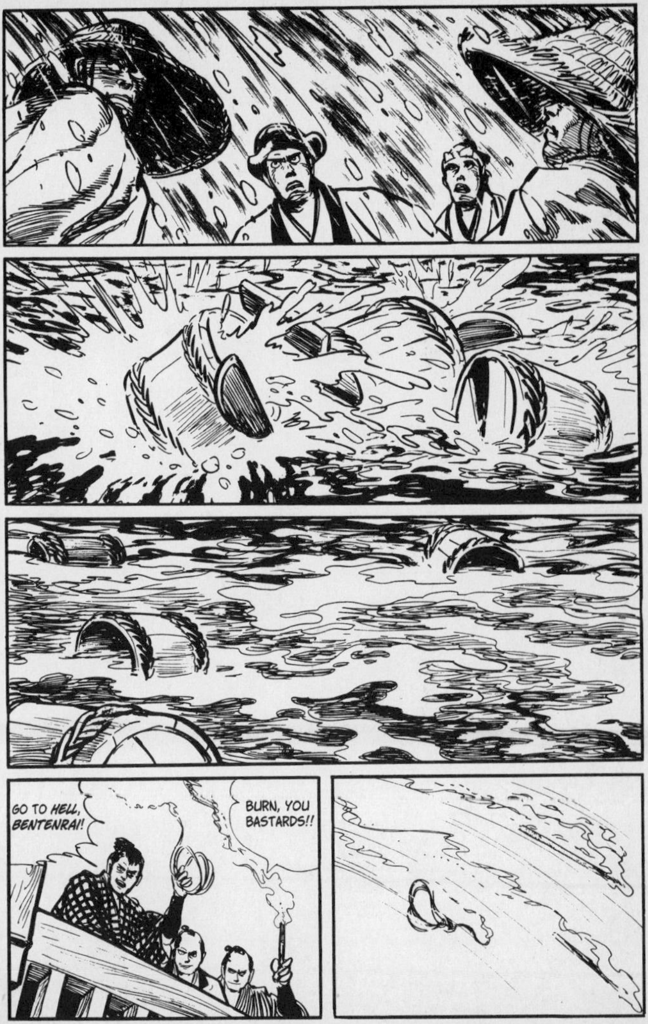
GO TO *HELL*, BENTENRAI!
BURN, YOU BASTARDS!!

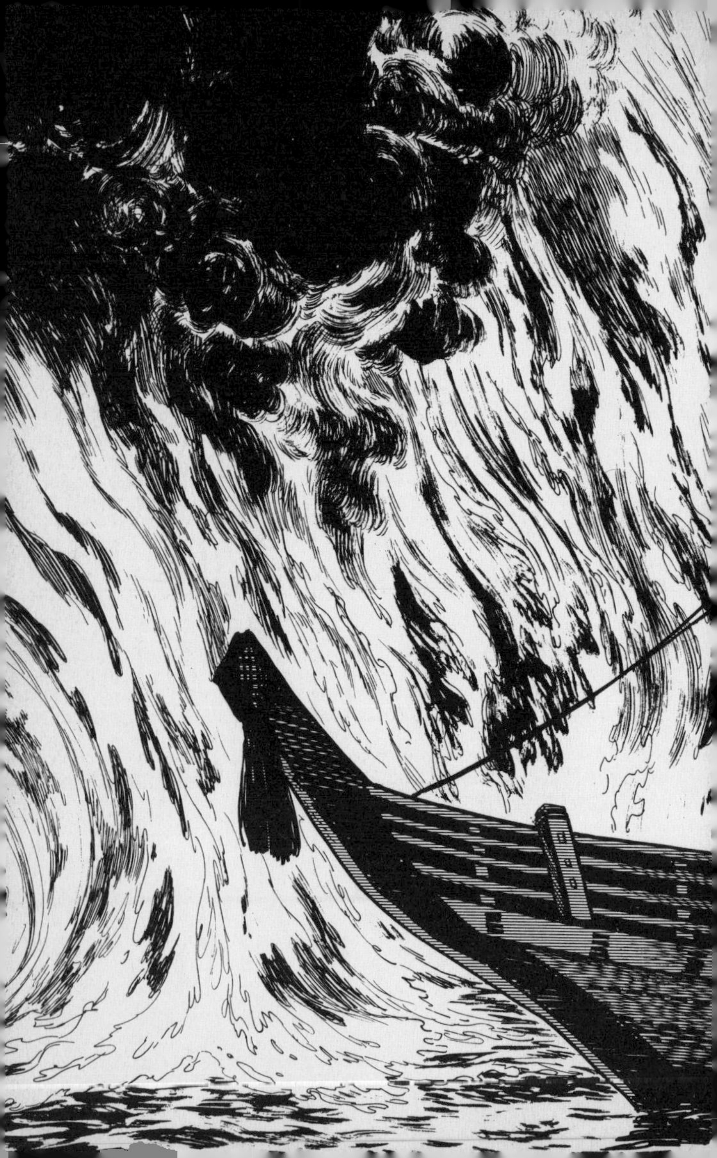

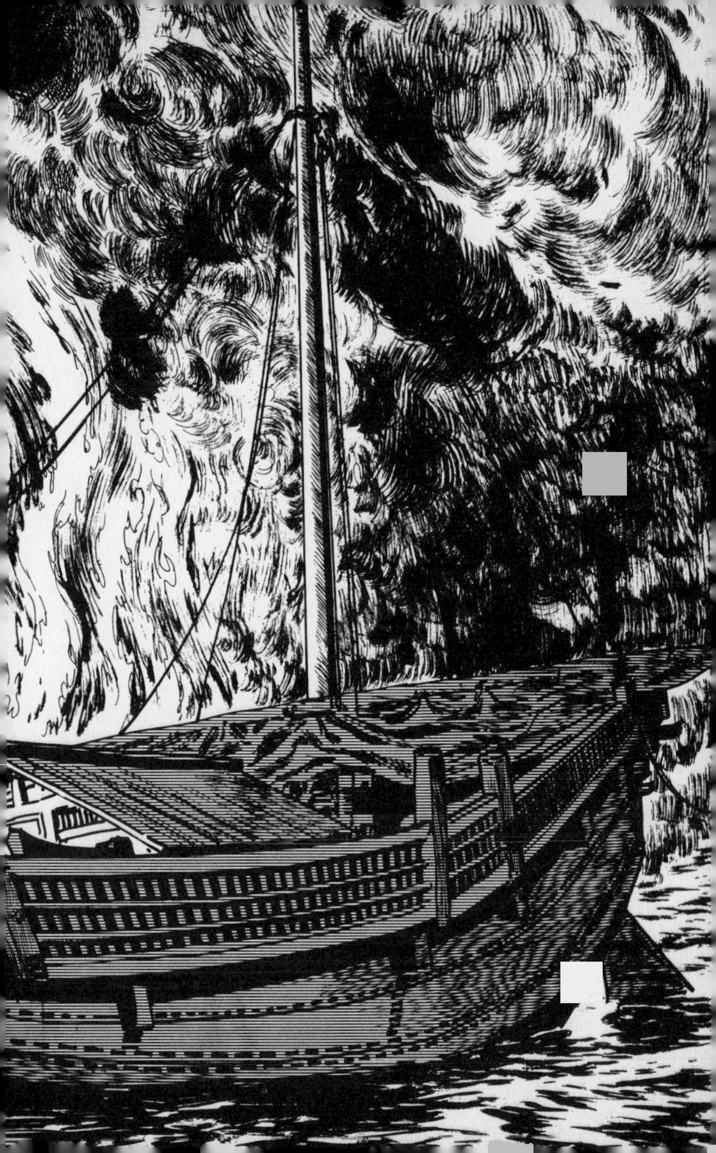

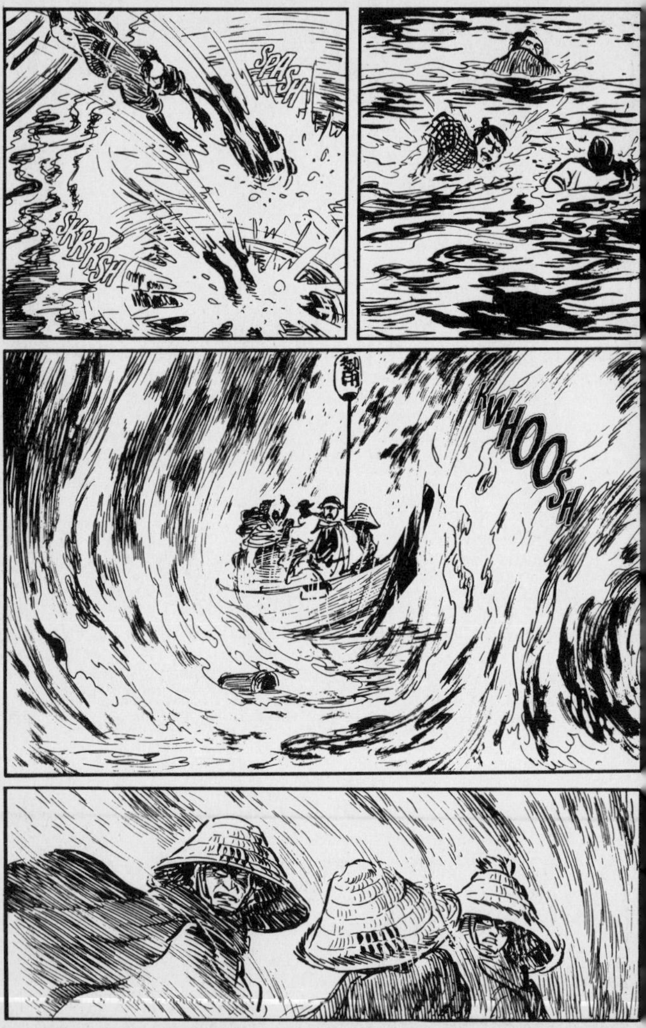
SPASH
SKRRSH
KWHOOSH

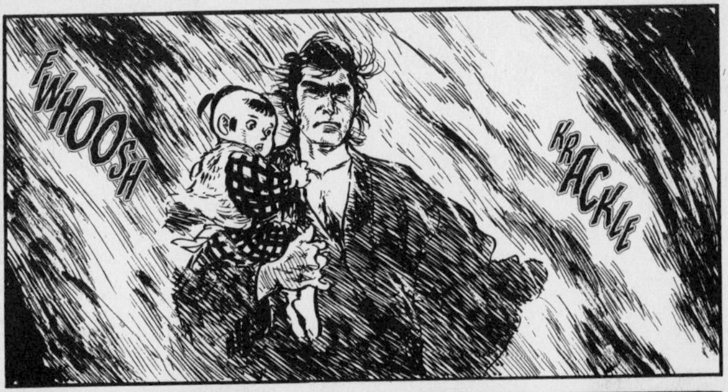
FWHOOSH
KRACKLE

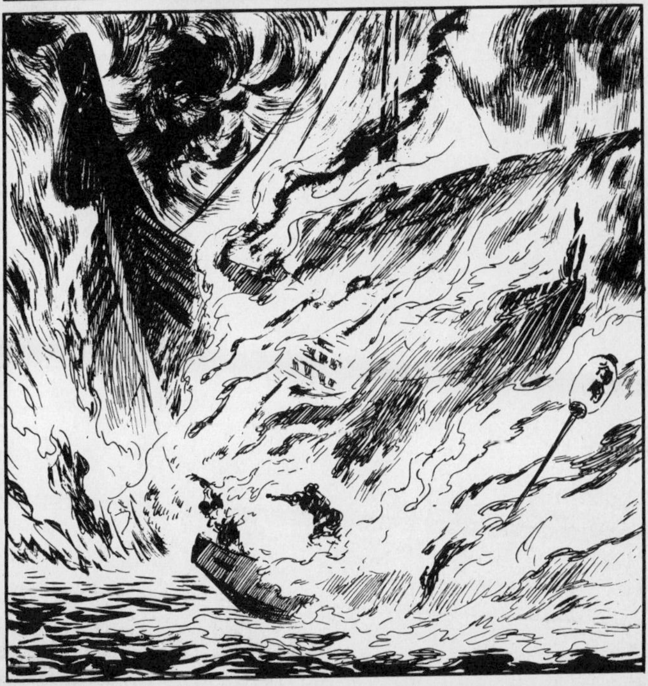

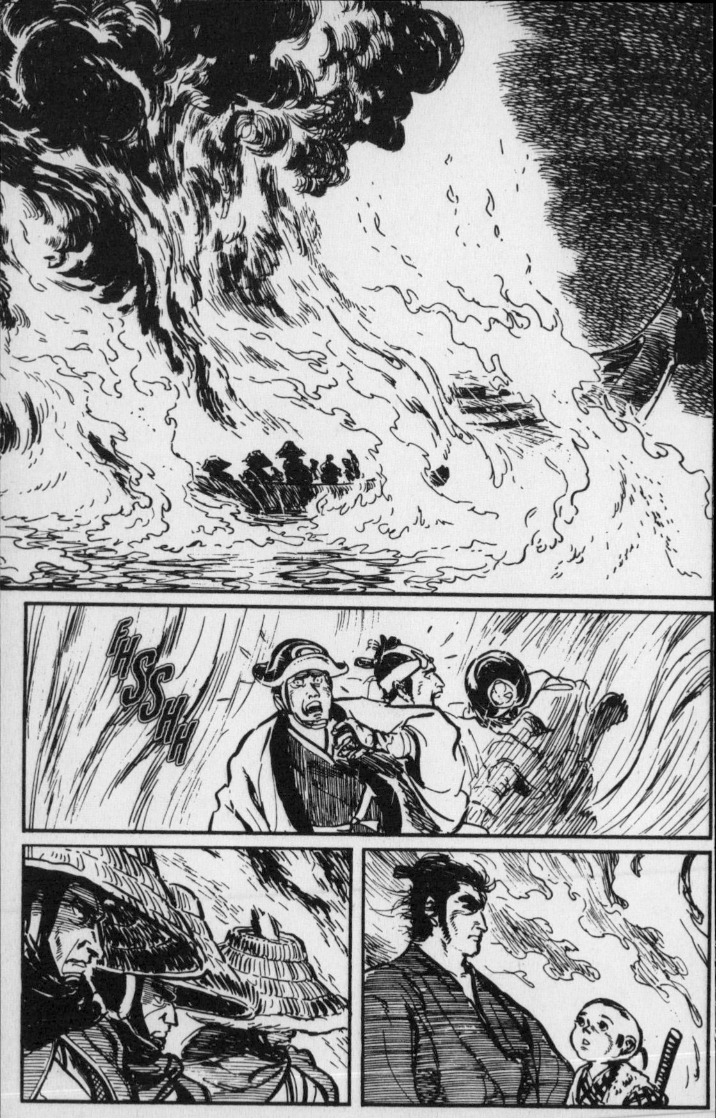
FHSSHH

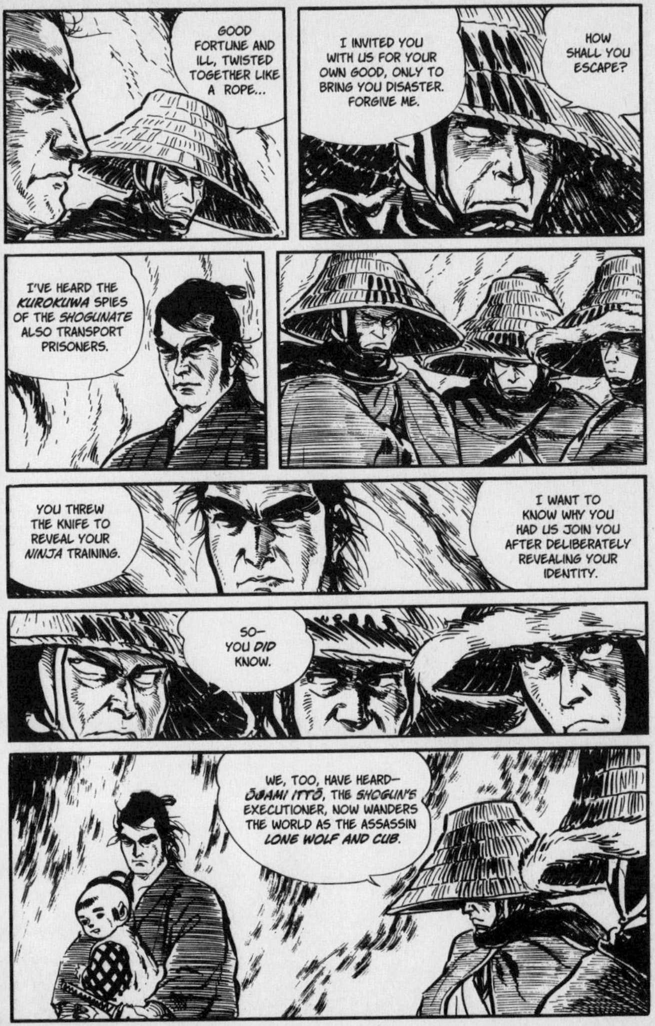
GOOD FORTUNE AND ILL, TWISTED TOGETHER LIKE A ROPE...
I INVITED YOU WITH US FOR YOUR OWN GOOD, ONLY TO BRING YOU DISASTER. FORGIVE ME.
HOW SHALL YOU ESCAPE?
I'VE HEARD THE KUROKUWA SPIES OF THE SHOGUNATE ALSO TRANSPORT PRISONERS.
YOU THREW THE KNIFE TO REVEAL YOUR NINJA TRAINING.
I WANT TO KNOW WHY YOU HAD US JOIN YOU AFTER DELIBERATELY REVEALING YOUR IDENTITY.
SO— YOU DID KNOW.
WE, TOO, HAVE HEARD— ŌGAMI ITTŌ, THE SHOGUN'S EXECUTIONER, NOW WANDERS THE WORLD AS THE ASSASSIN LONE WOLF AND CUB.

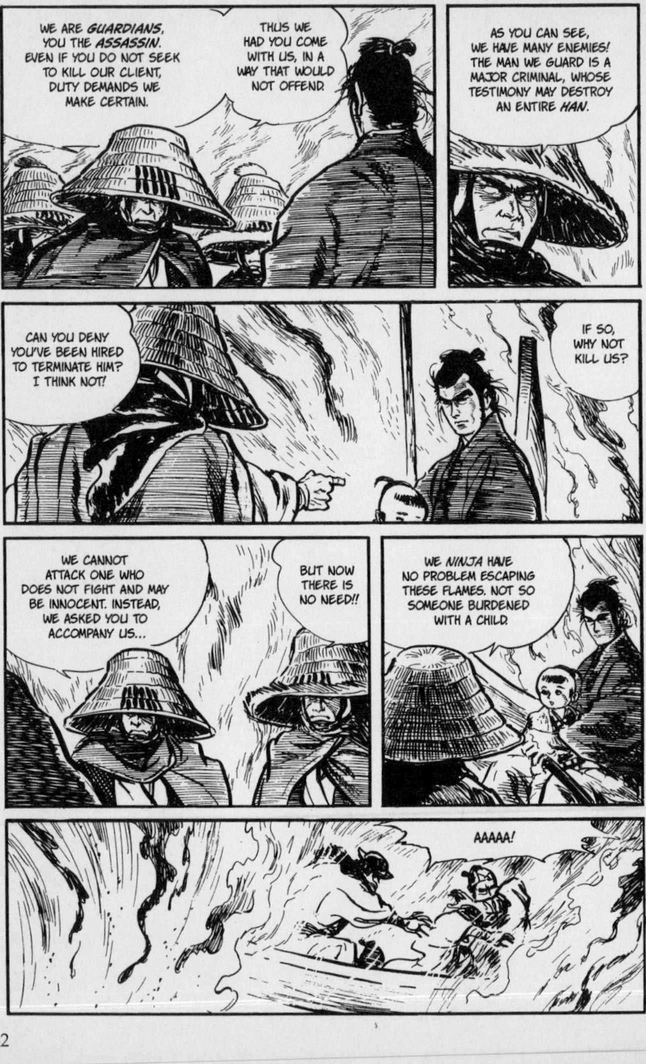
WE ARE GUARDIANS, YOU THE ASSASSIN. EVEN IF YOU DO NOT SEEK TO KILL OUR CLIENT, DUTY DEMANDS WE MAKE CERTAIN.
THUS WE HAD YOU COME WITH US, IN A WAY THAT WOULD NOT OFFEND.
AS YOU CAN SEE, WE HAVE MANY ENEMIES! THE MAN WE GUARD IS A MAJOR CRIMINAL, WHOSE TESTIMONY MAY DESTROY AN ENTIRE HAN.
CAN YOU DENY YOU'VE BEEN HIRED TO TERMINATE HIM? I THINK NOT!
IF SO, WHY NOT KILL US?
WE CANNOT ATTACK ONE WHO DOES NOT FIGHT AND MAY BE INNOCENT. INSTEAD, WE ASKED YOU TO ACCOMPANY US...
BUT NOW THERE IS NO NEED!!
WE NINJA HAVE NO PROBLEM ESCAPING THESE FLAMES. NOT SO SOMEONE BURDENED WITH A CHILD.
AAAAA!

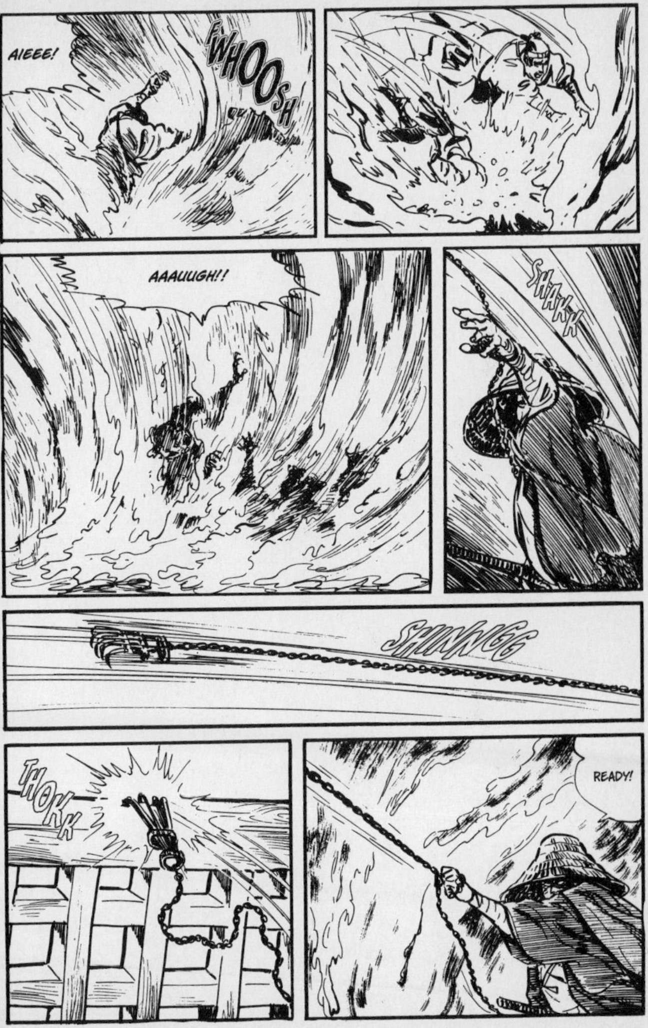
AIEEE!
FWHOOSH
AAAUUGH!!
SHAKKK
SHIINGG
THOKKK
READY!

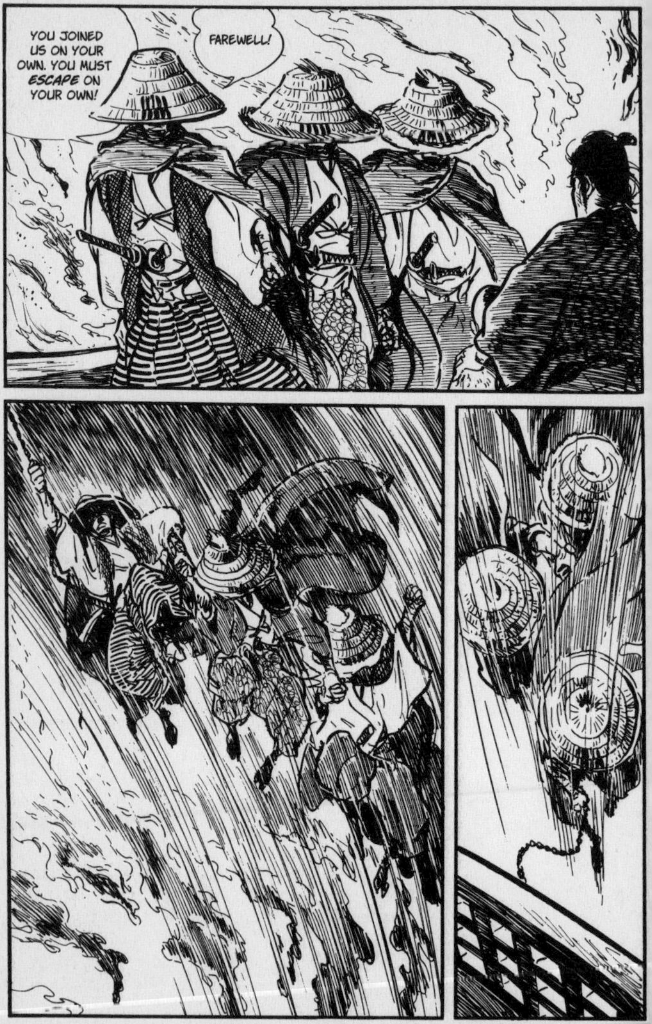

YOU JOINED US ON YOUR OWN. YOU MUST *ESCAPE* ON YOUR OWN!
FAREWELL!

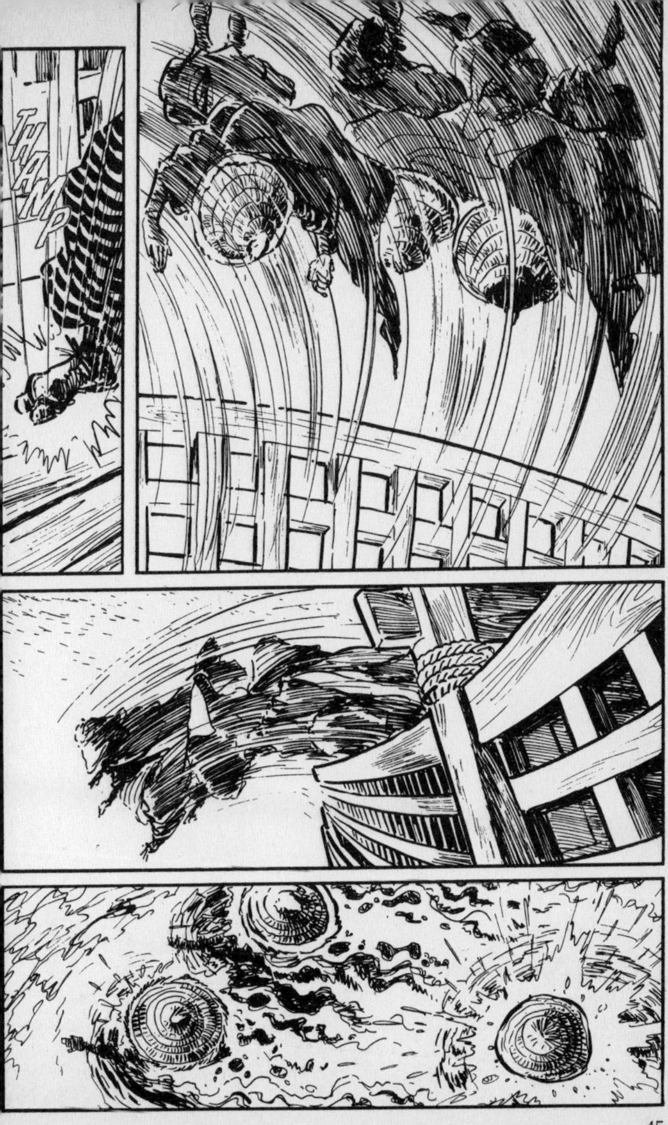
THAMP

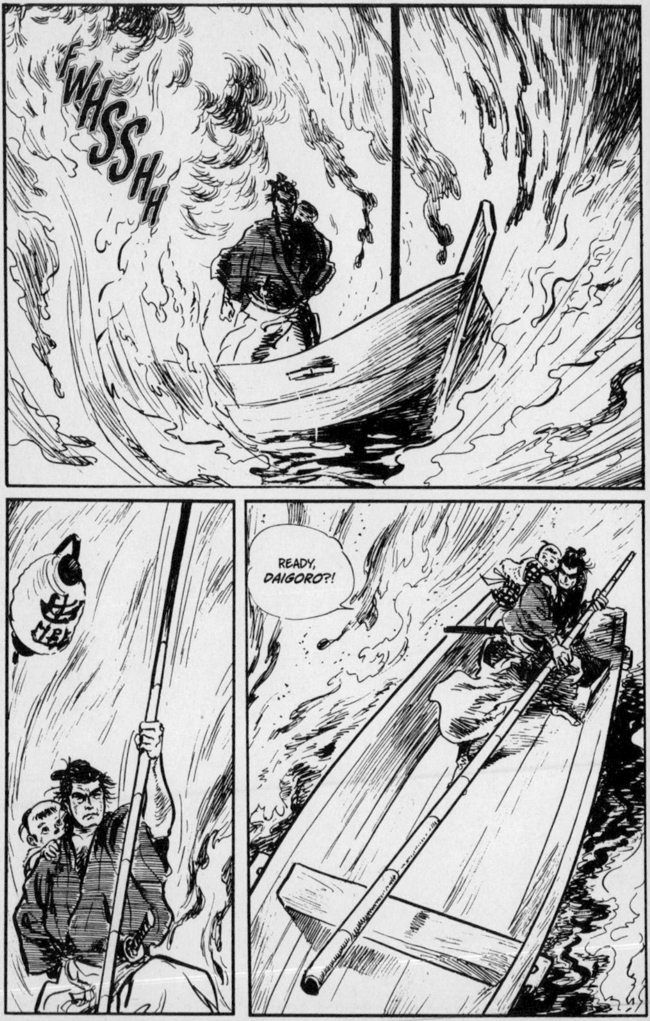
FWHSSHH
READY, DAIGORO?!

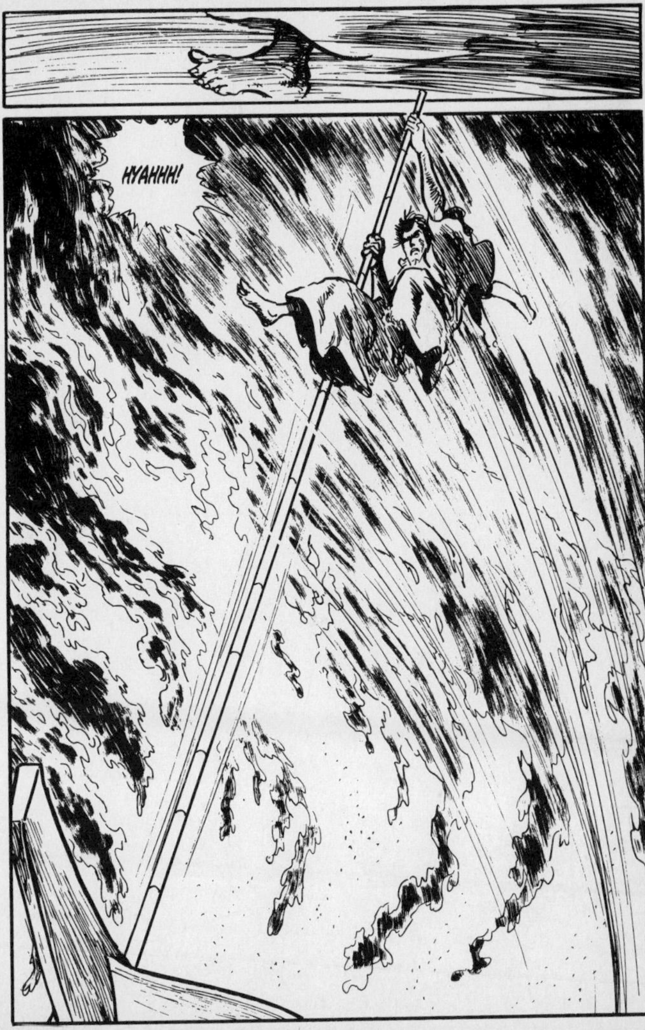
HYAHHH!

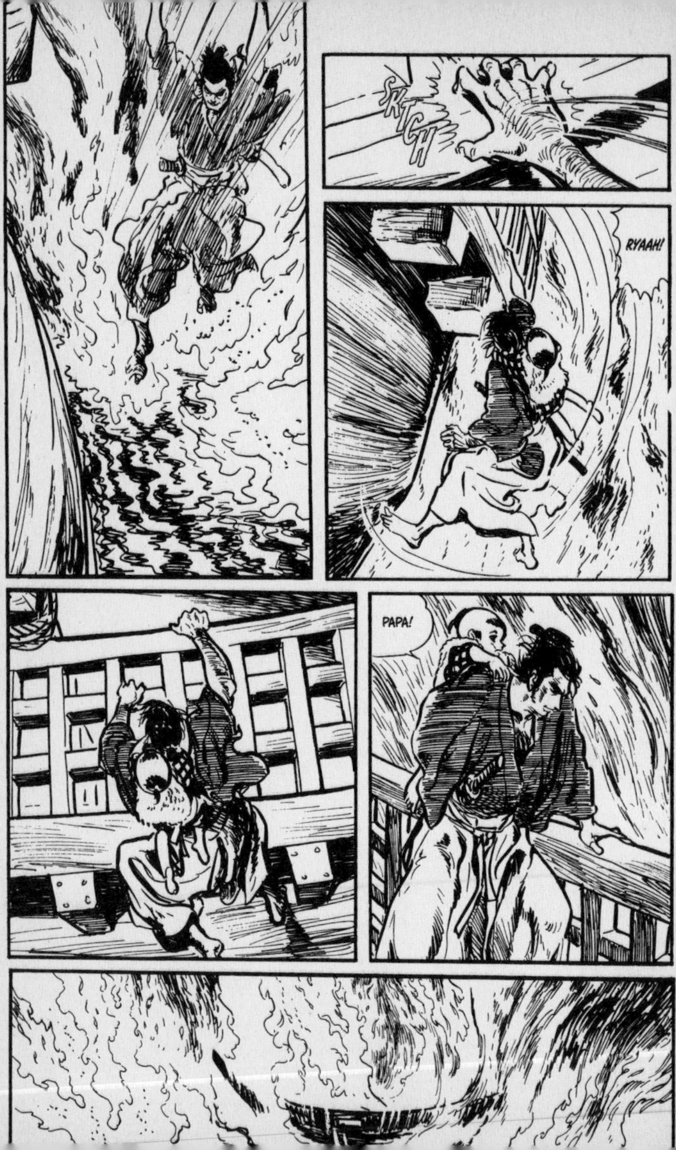
SKTCH
RYAAH!
PAPA!

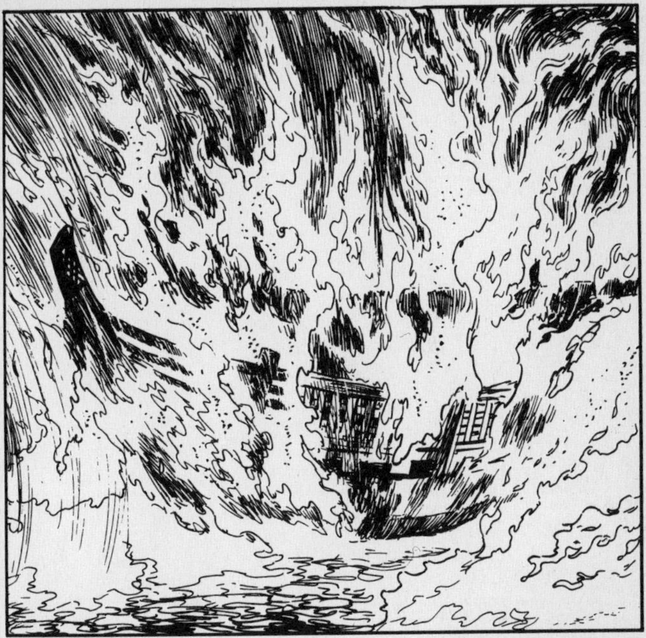

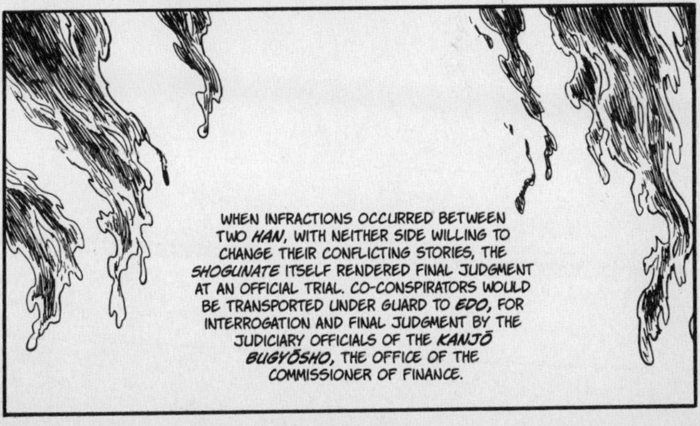
WHEN INFRACTIONS OCCURRED BETWEEN TWO *HAN*, WITH NEITHER SIDE WILLING TO CHANGE THEIR CONFLICTING STORIES, THE *SHOGUNATE* ITSELF RENDERED FINAL JUDGMENT AT AN OFFICIAL TRIAL. CO-CONSPIRATORS WOULD BE TRANSPORTED UNDER GUARD TO *EDO*, FOR INTERROGATION AND FINAL JUDGMENT BY THE JUDICIARY OFFICIALS OF THE *KANJŌ BUGYŌSHO*, THE OFFICE OF THE COMMISSIONER OF FINANCE.

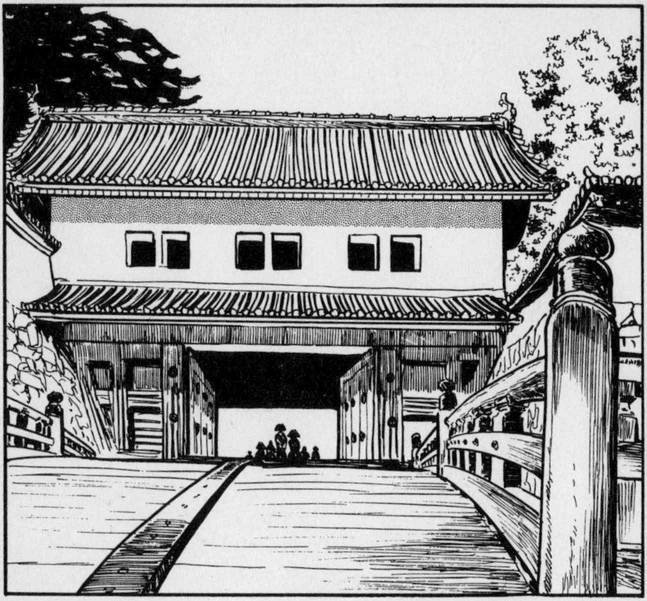

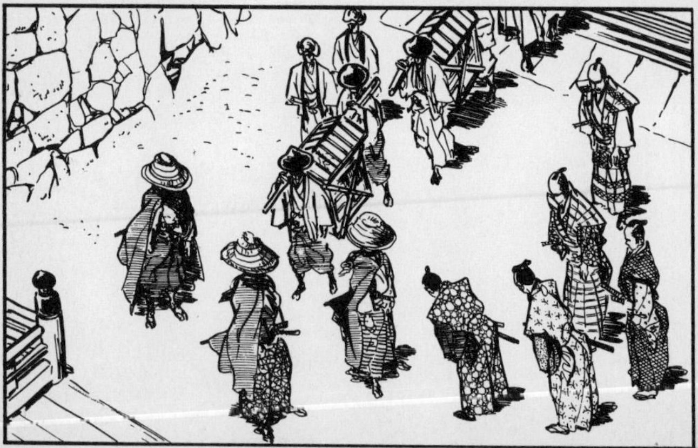

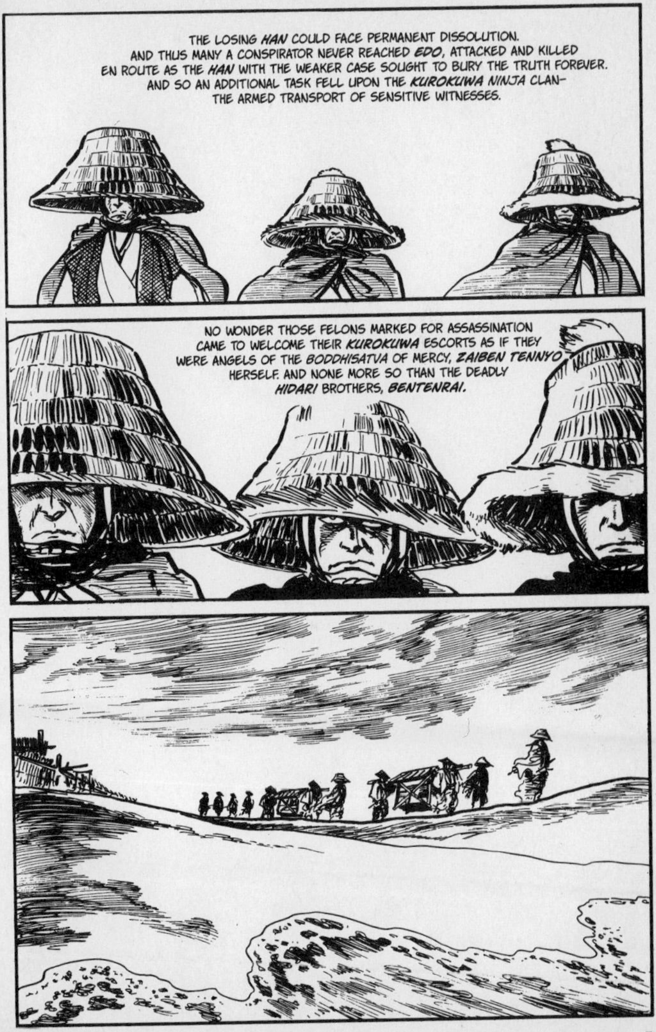
THE LOSING HAN COULD FACE PERMANENT DISSOLUTION. AND THUS MANY A CONSPIRATOR NEVER REACHED EDO, ATTACKED AND KILLED EN ROUTE AS THE HAN WITH THE WEAKER CASE SOUGHT TO BURY THE TRUTH FOREVER. AND SO AN ADDITIONAL TASK FELL UPON THE KUROKUWA NINJA CLAN-THE ARMED TRANSPORT OF SENSITIVE WITNESSES.
NO WONDER THOSE FELONS MARKED FOR ASSASSINATION CAME TO WELCOME THEIR KUROKUWA ESCORTS AS IF THEY WERE ANGELS OF THE BODDHISATVA OF MERCY, ZAIBEN TENNYO HERSELF. AND NONE MORE SO THAN THE DEADLY HIDARI BROTHERS, BENTENRAI.

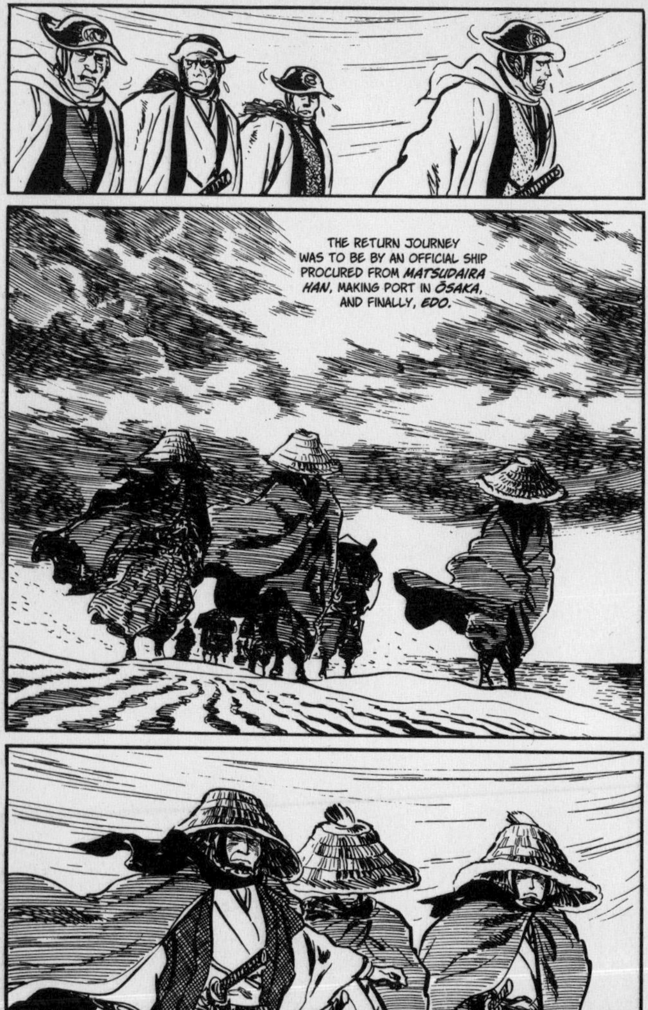
THE RETURN JOURNEY WAS TO BE BY AN OFFICIAL SHIP PROCURED FROM *MATSUDAIRA HAN*, MAKING PORT IN *ŌSAKA*, AND FINALLY, *EDO*.

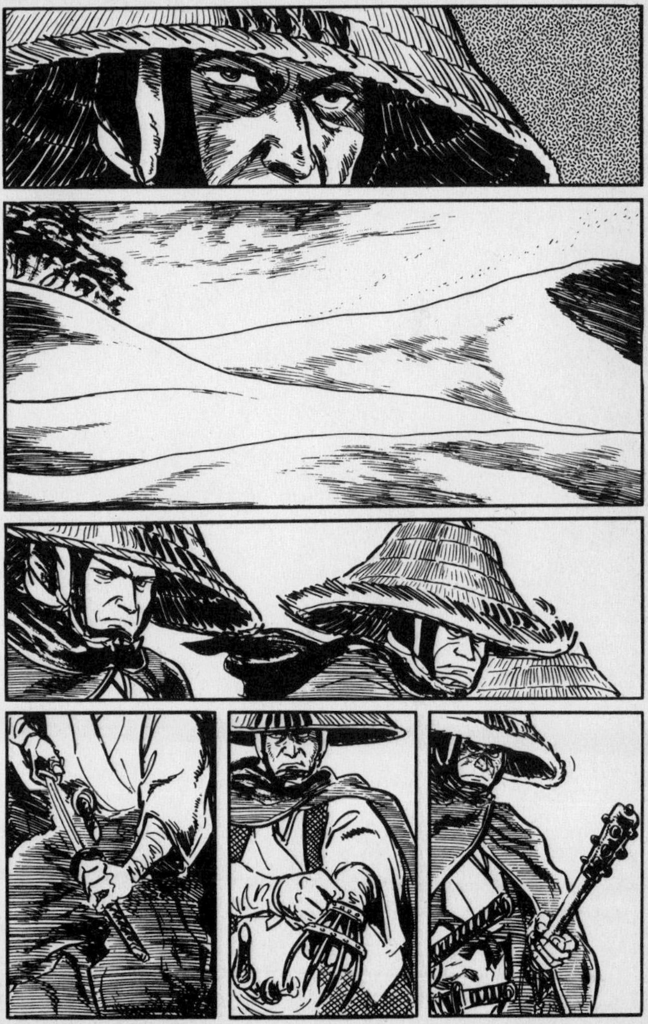

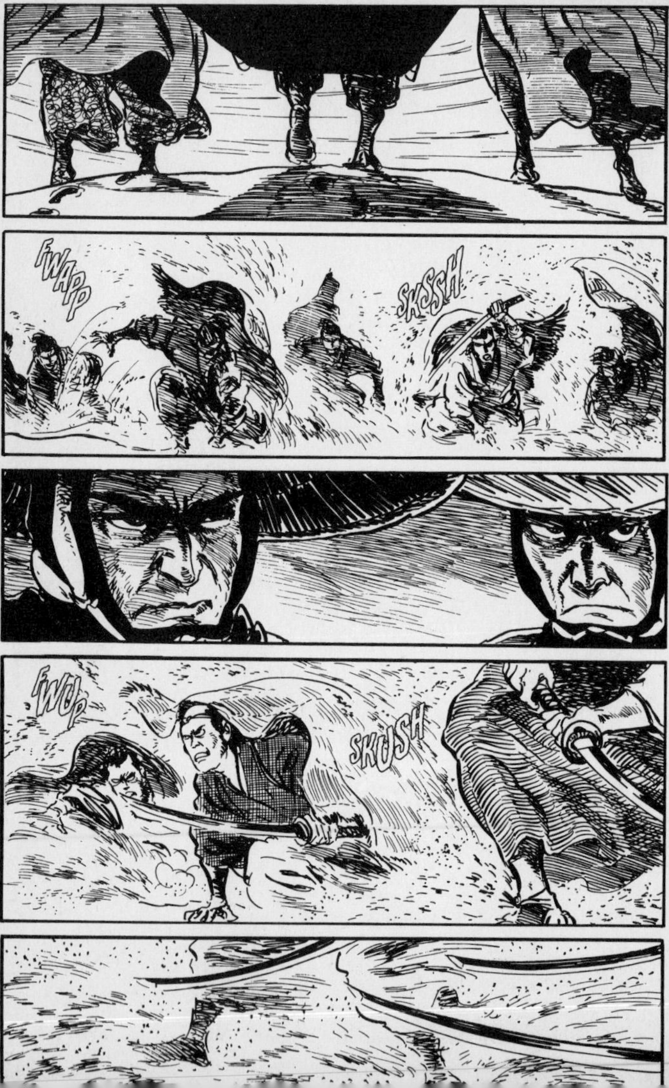
FWAPP
SKSSH
FWUP
SKUSH

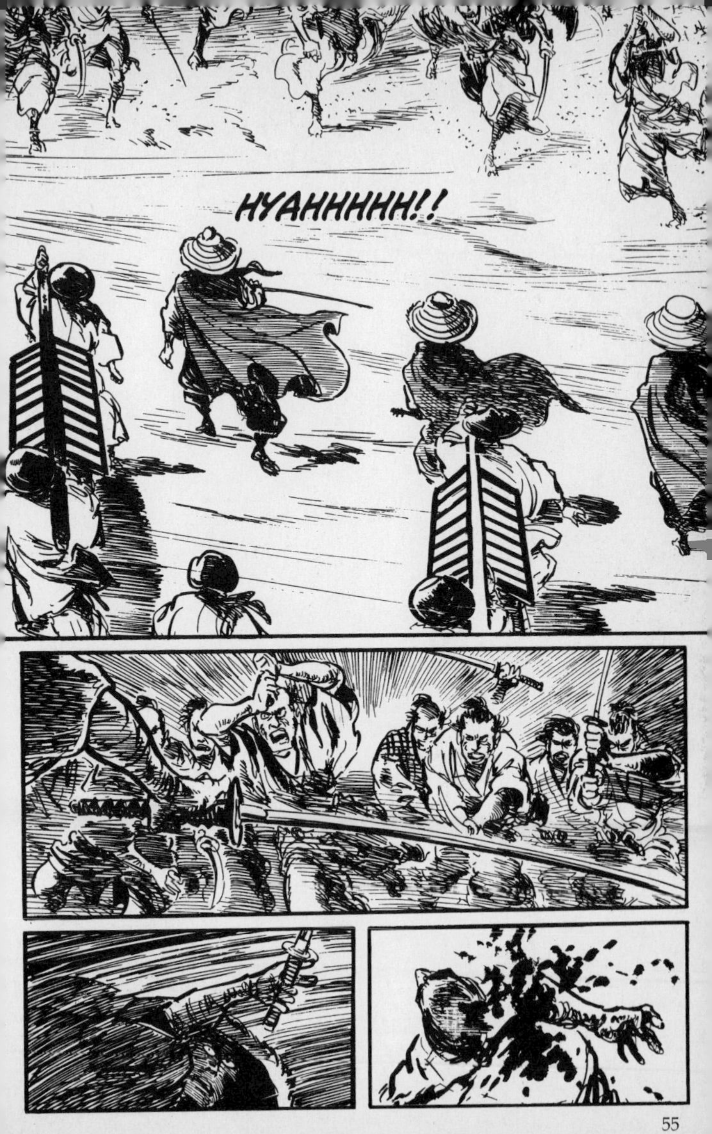
HYAHHHHH!!

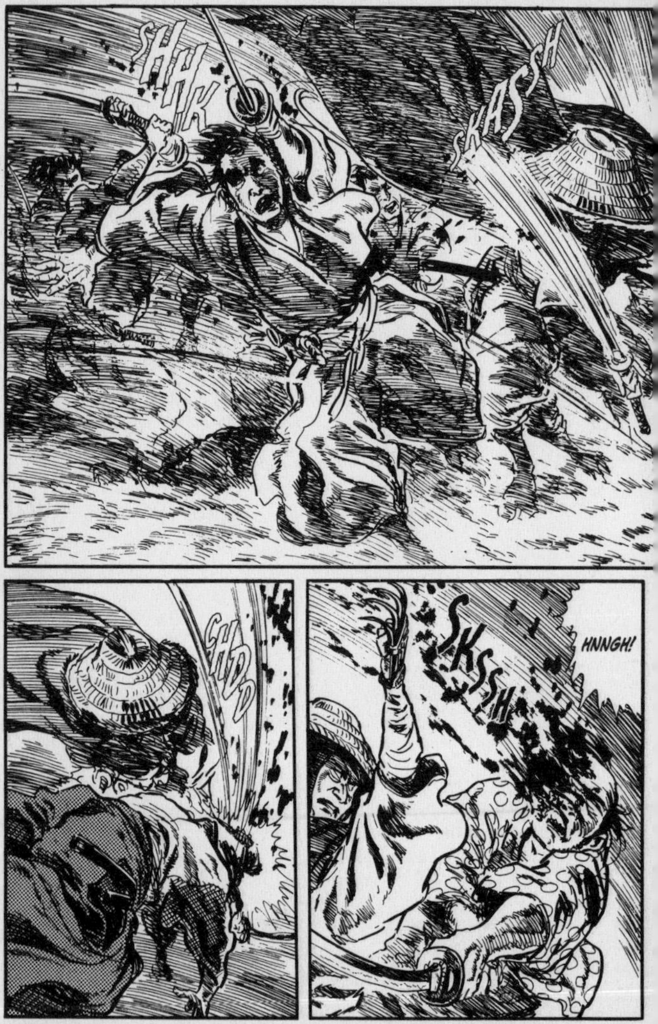
SHHK
SKASSH
CHDD
SKSSH
HNNGH!

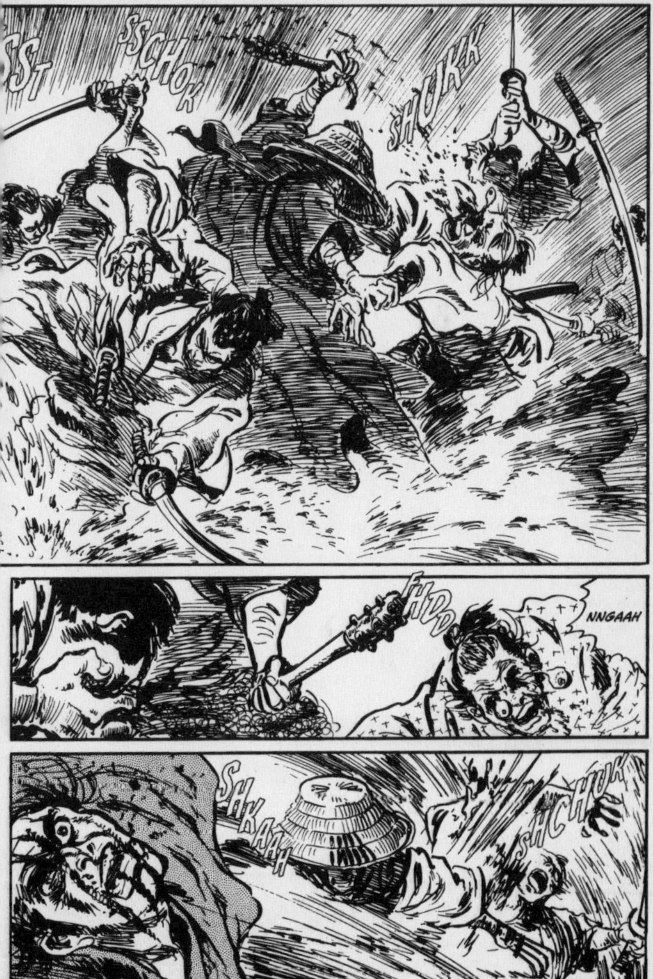
SST
SSCHOK
SHUKK
FHDD
NNGAAH
SHKAAH
SHCHUK

SHCHNK

UNGHAA!

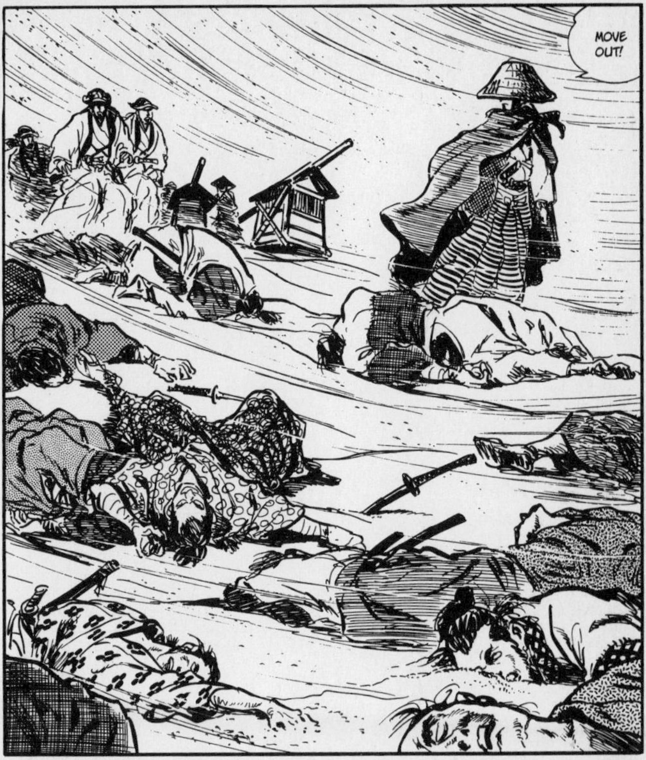
MOVE OUT!
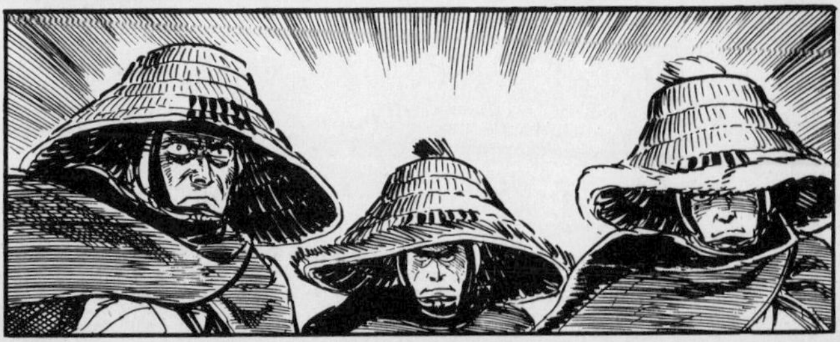

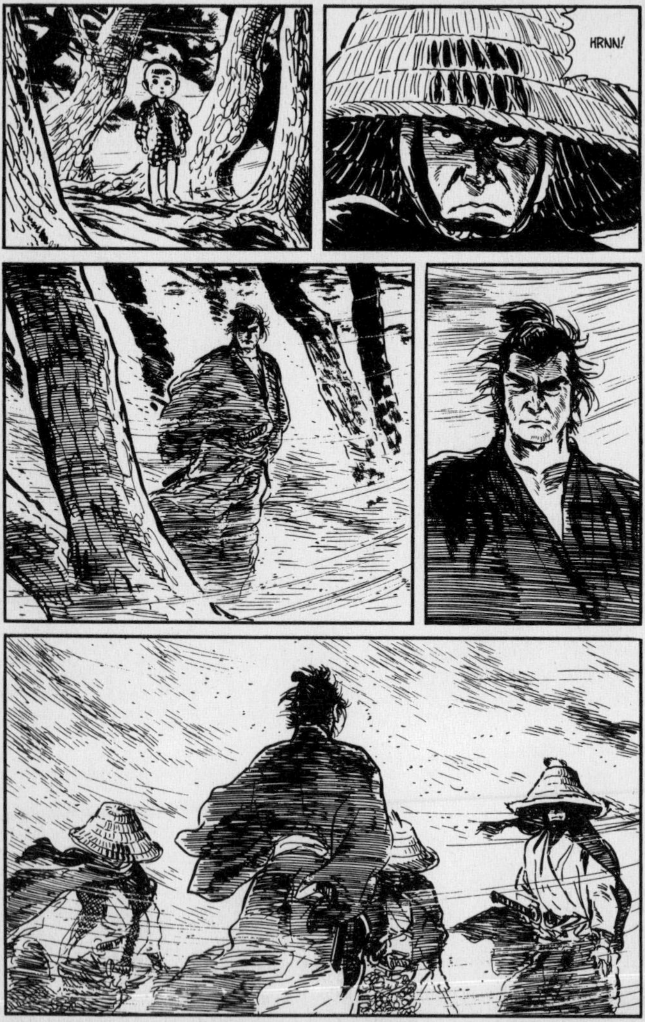
HRNN!

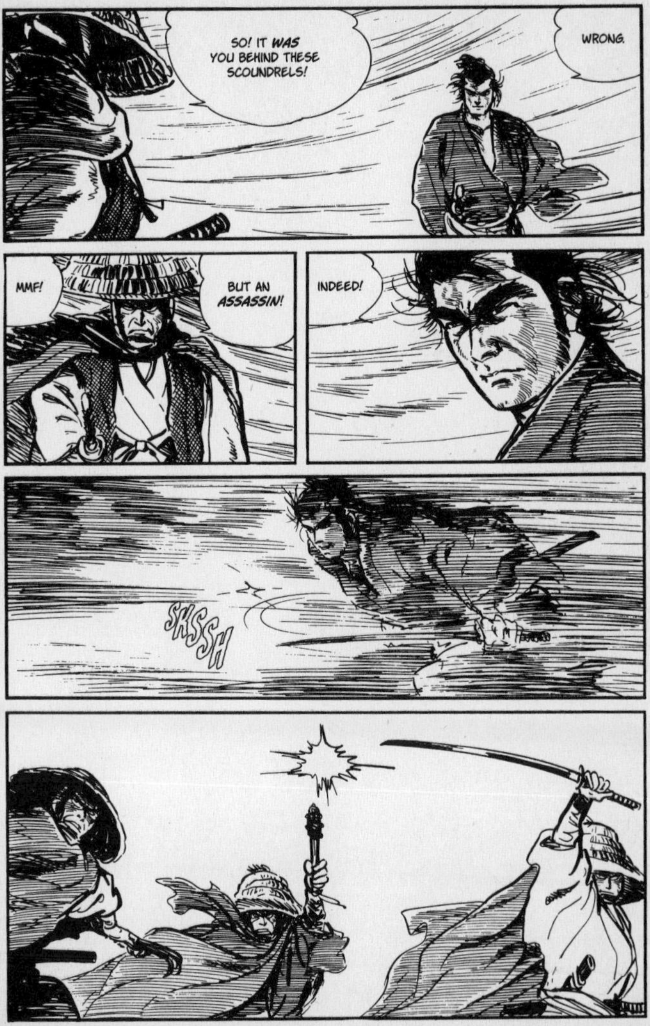
SO! IT WAS YOU BEHIND THESE SCOUNDRELS!
WRONG.
MMF!
BUT AN ASSASSIN!
INDEED!
SKSSH

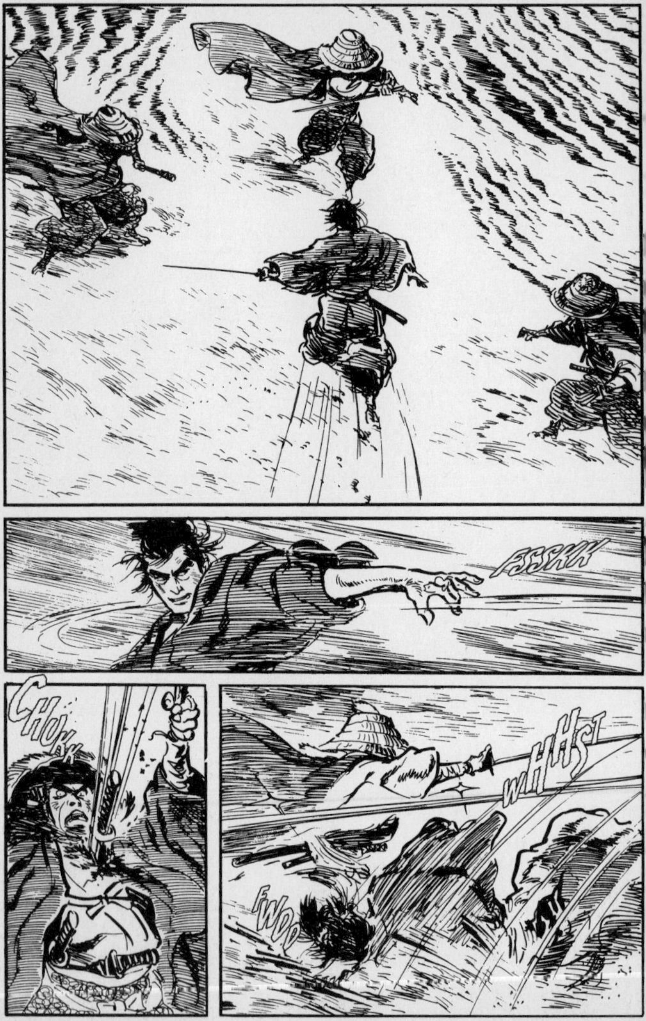
FSSKK
CHUKK
WHHST
FWOO

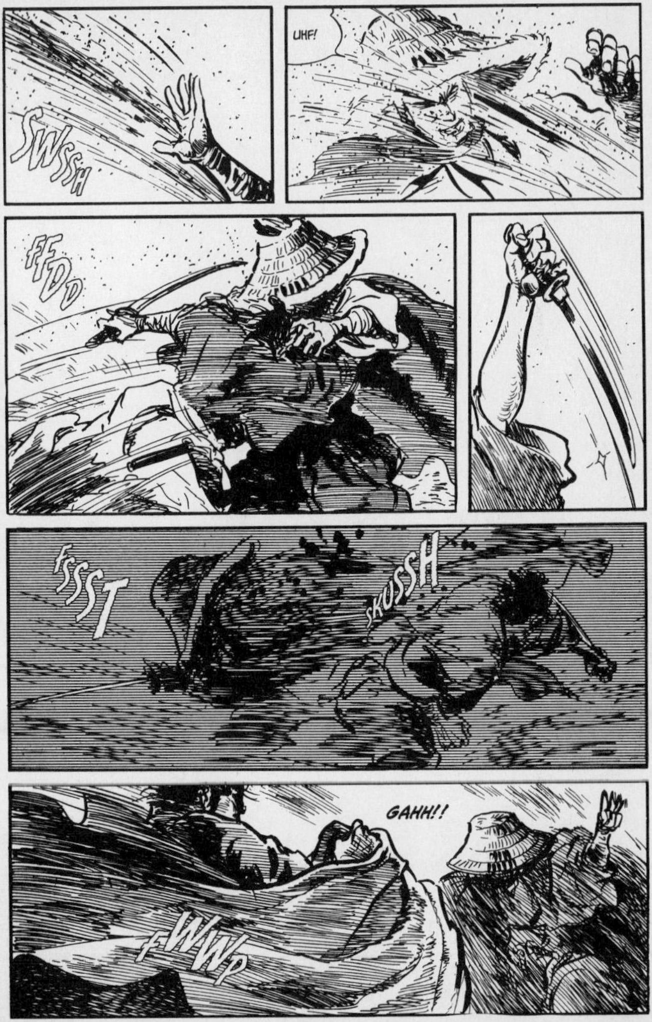
SWSSH
UHF!
FFDD
FSSST
SKUSSH
GAHH!!
FWWP

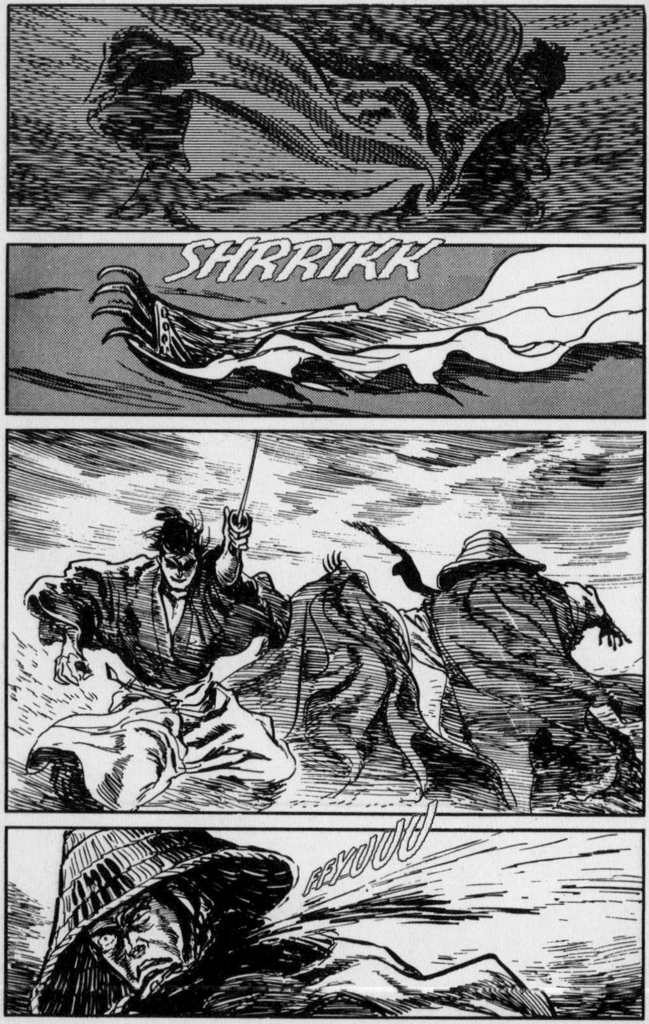
SHRRIKK
FFYUUU

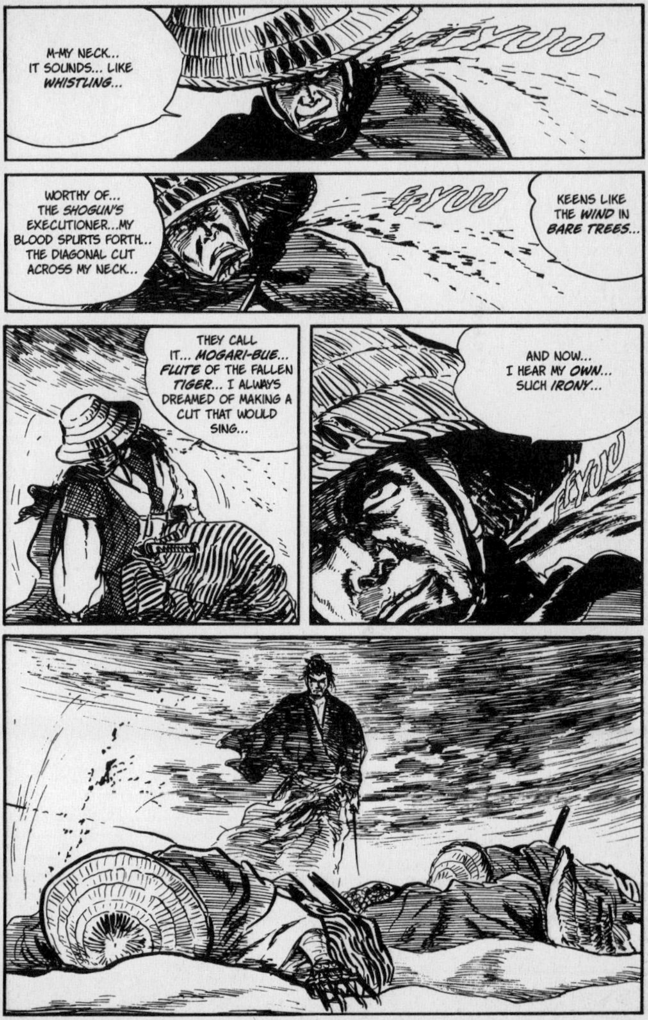
M-MY NECK... IT SOUNDS... LIKE WHISTLING...
FFYUU
WORTHY OF... THE SHOGUN'S EXECUTIONER...MY BLOOD SPURTS FORTH... THE DIAGONAL CUT ACROSS MY NECK...
FFYUU
KEENS LIKE THE WIND IN BARE TREES...
THEY CALL IT... MOGARI-BUE... FLUTE OF THE FALLEN TIGER... I ALWAYS DREAMED OF MAKING A CUT THAT WOULD SING...
AND NOW... I HEAR MY OWN... SUCH IRONY...
FFYUU

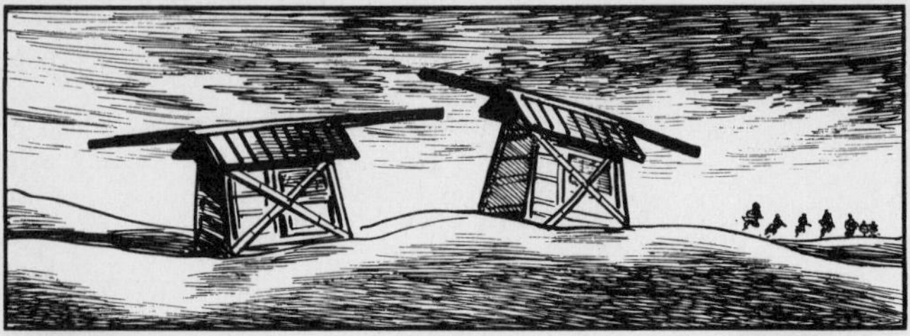

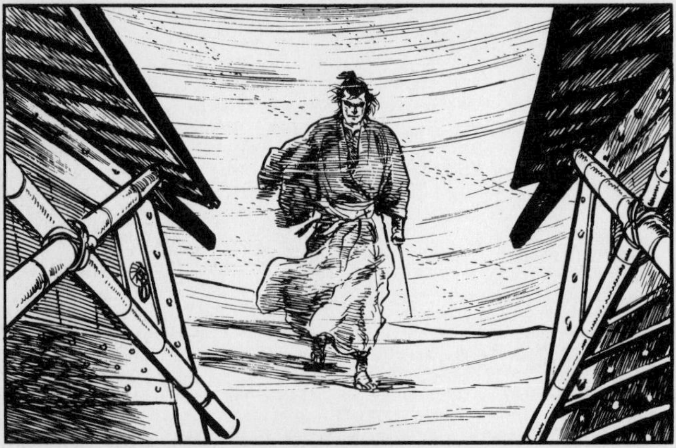

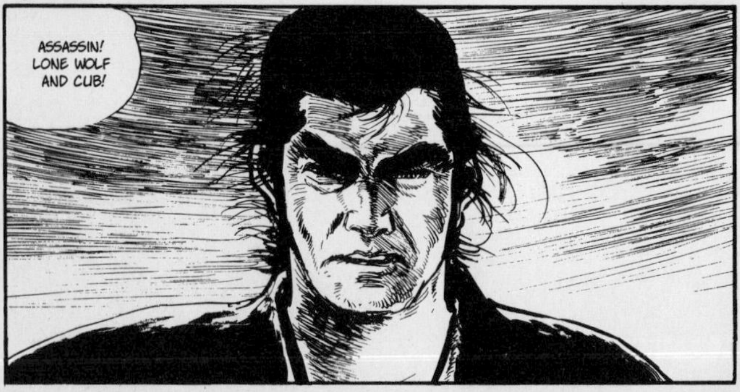
ASSASSIN! LONE WOLF AND CUB!

the sixteenth

Half Mat, One Mat, a Fistful of Rice

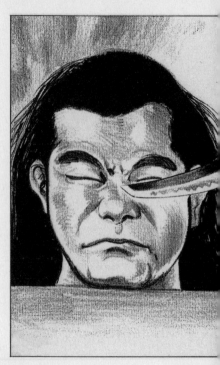

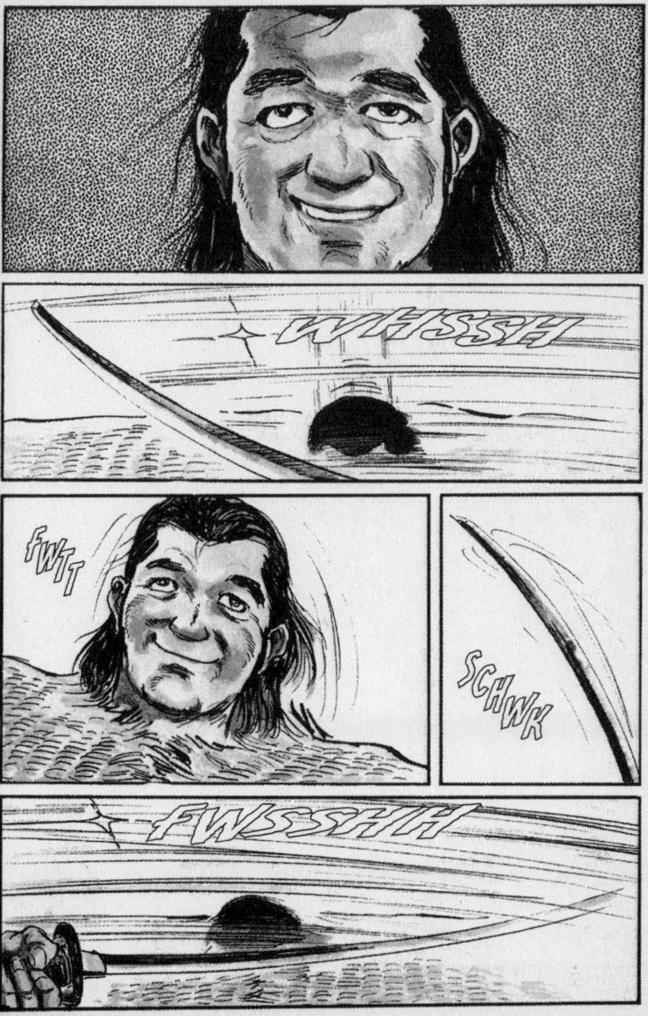
WHSSH
FWTT
SCHWK
FWSSHH

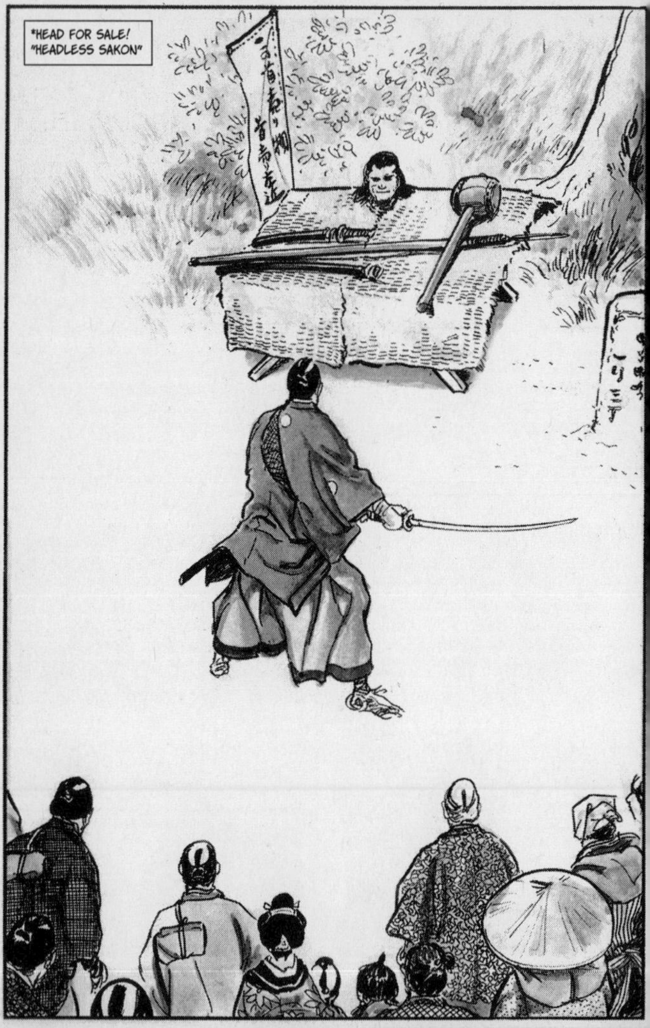
*HEAD FOR SALE!
"HEADLESS SAKON"

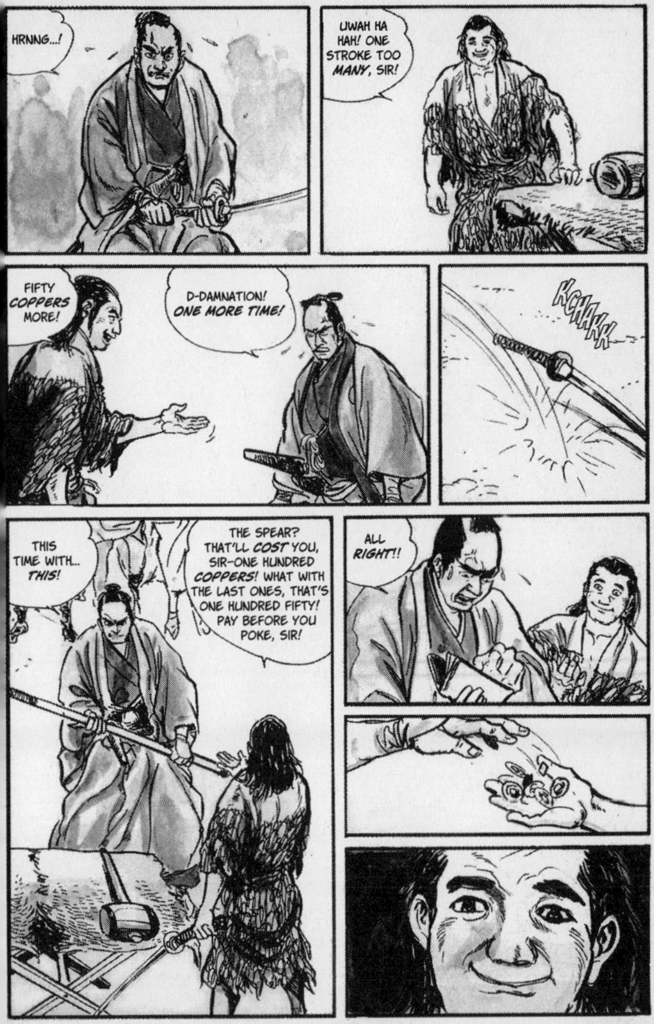
HRNNG...!
UWAH HA HAH! ONE STROKE TOO MANY, SIR!
FIFTY COPPERS MORE!
D-DAMNATION! ONE MORE TIME!
KCHAKK
THIS TIME WITH... THIS!
THE SPEAR? THAT'LL COST YOU, SIR–ONE HUNDRED COPPERS! WHAT WITH THE LAST ONES, THAT'S ONE HUNDRED FIFTY! PAY BEFORE YOU POKE, SIR!
ALL RIGHT!!

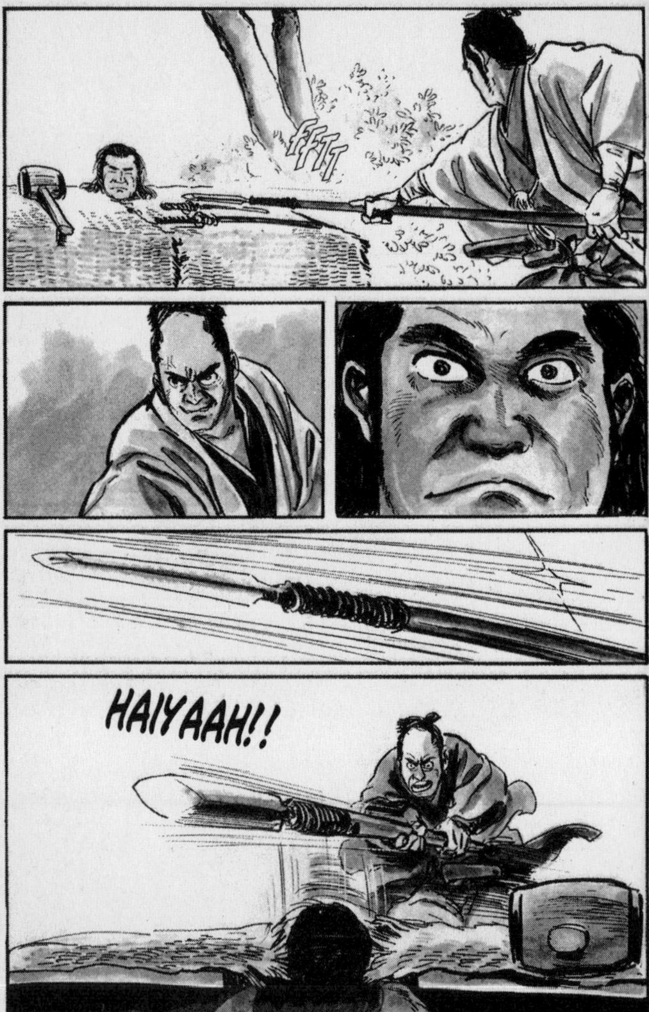
FFTT
HAIYAAH!!

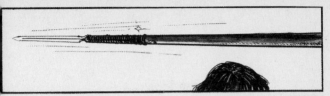

LORDY!

NEVER SEEN NUTHIN' LIKE IT!

LAND! GET COLD SWEATS JUST WATCHING.

SCARES THE WILLIES OUTTA *ME!*

KT KT KT

WAH HAH HAH! *PRACTICE,* GREENHORN!

HAH HAH HAH HAH!

STEP RIGHT UP! *STEP* RIGHT UP! NO ONE LEFT TO TAKE A WHACK?! CHOP IT, SQUASH IT, FIFTY COPPERS! A LIVE HUMAN HEAD FOR FIFTY COPPERS!

PICK A *SWORD!* PICK A *MALLET!* ANYTHING GOES! I PRAY TO *BUDDHA, YOU* SWING LIKE HELL! I PROMISE I WON'T BE BACK TO HAUNT YOU!

73

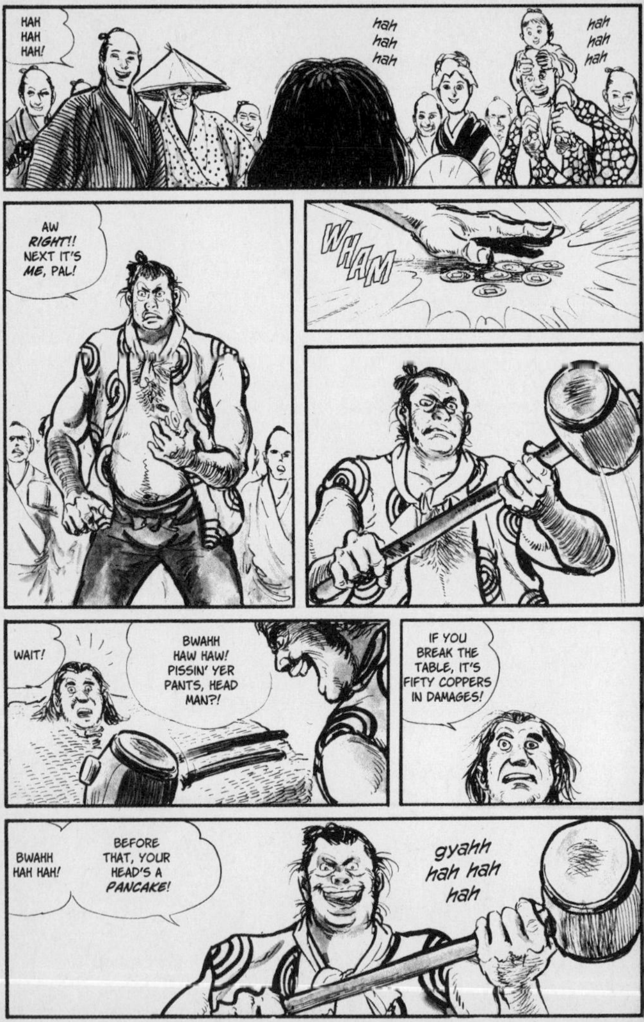
HAH HAH HAH!
hah hah hah
hah hah hah
AW *RIGHT!!* NEXT IT'S *ME*, PAL!
WHAM
WAIT!
BWAHH HAW HAW! PISSIN' YER PANTS, HEAD MAN?!
IF YOU BREAK THE TABLE, IT'S FIFTY COPPERS IN DAMAGES!
BWAHH HAH HAH!
BEFORE THAT, YOUR HEAD'S A *PANCAKE!*
gyahh hah hah hah

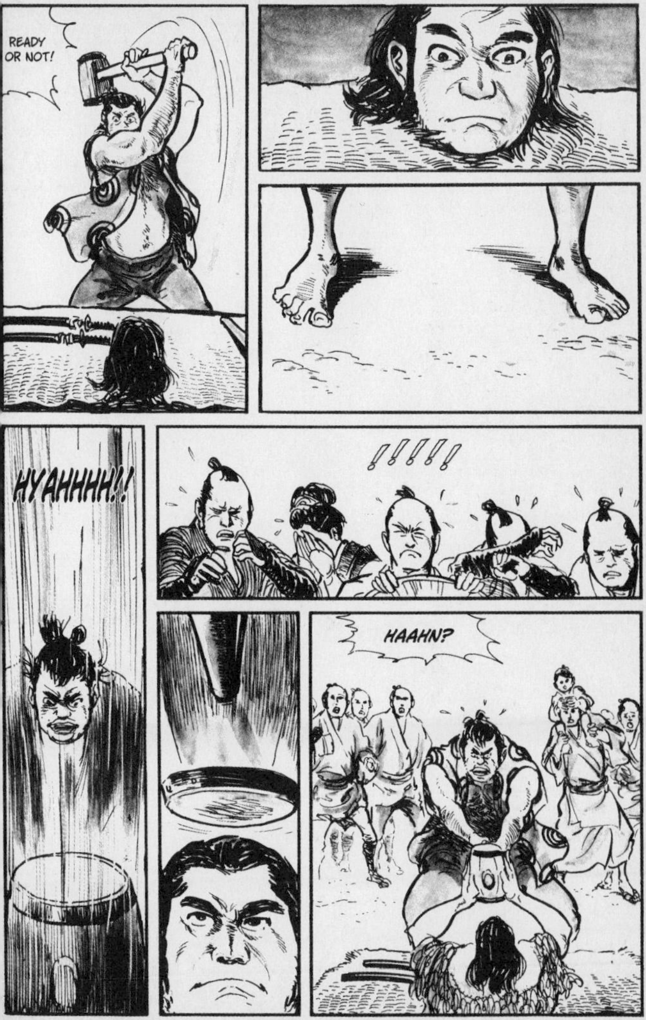
READY OR NOT!
HYAHHHH!!
!!!!!
HAAHN?

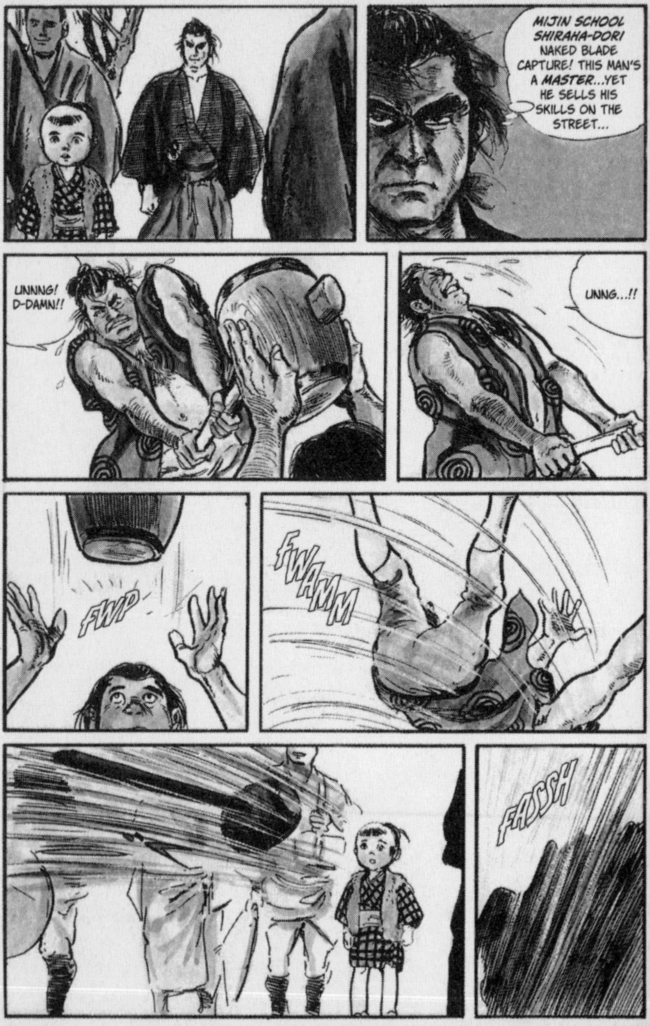
MIJIN SCHOOL SHIRAHA-DORI NAKED BLADE CAPTURE! THIS MAN'S A MASTER...YET HE SELLS HIS SKILLS ON THE STREET...
UNNNG! D-DAMN!!
UNNG...!!
FWP
FWAMM
FASSH

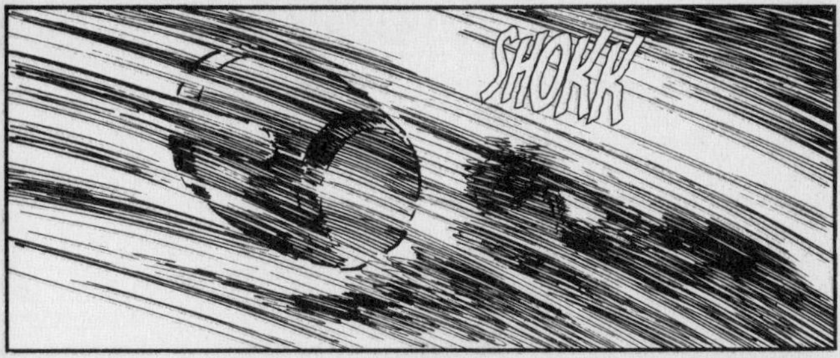
SHOKK
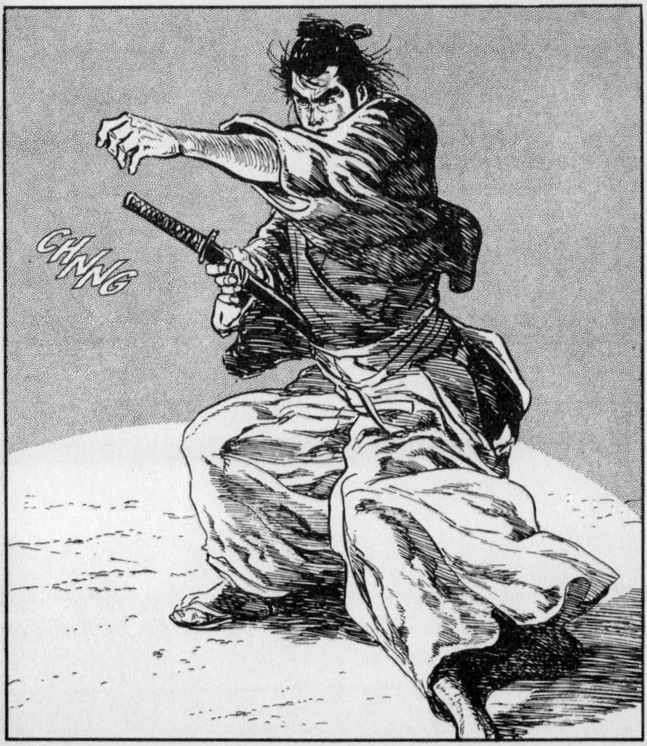
CHNNG

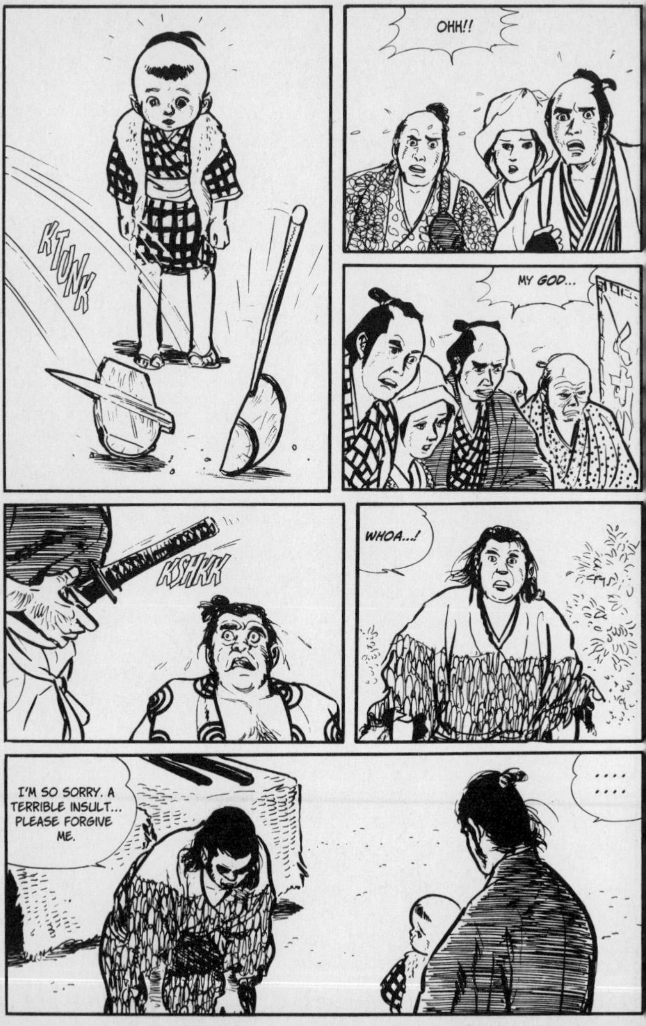
OHH!!
MY GOD...
KTUNK
WHOA...!
KSHKK
....
....
I'M SO SORRY. A TERRIBLE INSULT... PLEASE FORGIVE ME.

HERE—LET ME BUY YOU A DRINK TO MAKE UP FOR IT!

DON'T CONCERN YOURSELF!

NOW DON'T TALK LIKE THAT...

HOH! HERE'S A CUTE BOY! LET UNCLE SAKON BUY YOU SOMETHING NICE.

TO MAKE UP FOR THAT FRIGHT, OKAY?

THAT'S ALL, FOLKS! GONE FISHIN'! YOU RUN ALONG NOW!

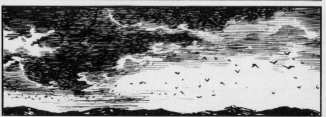

79

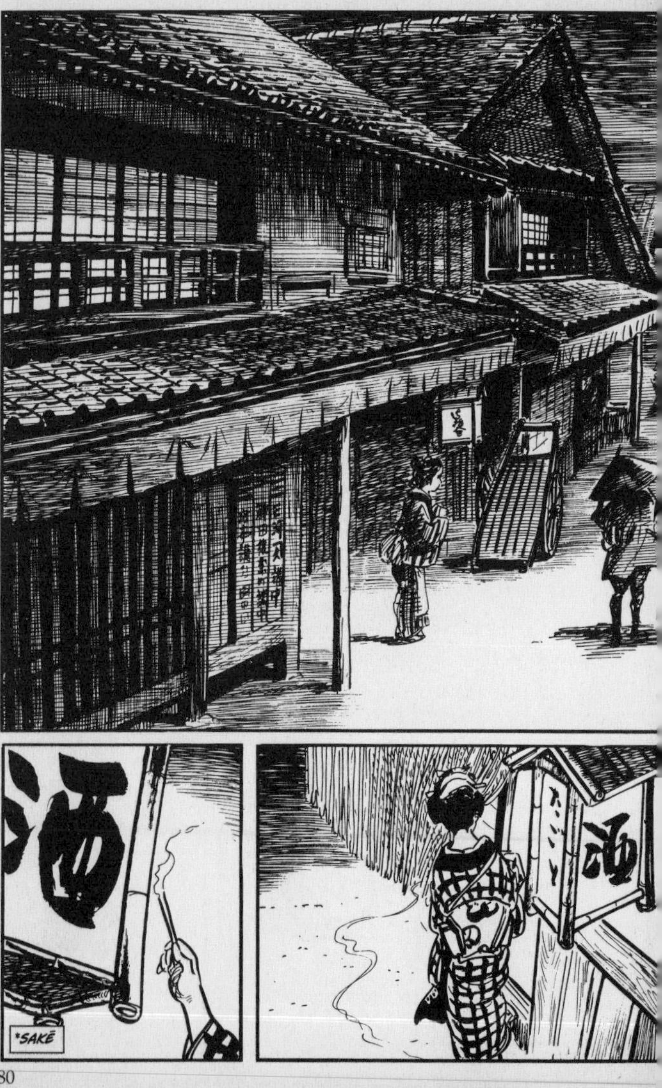
酒
*SAKĒ

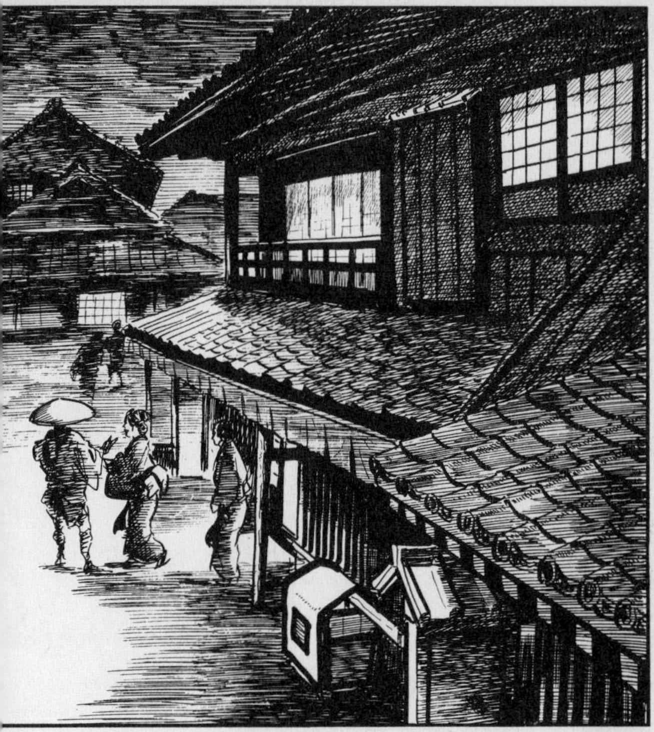

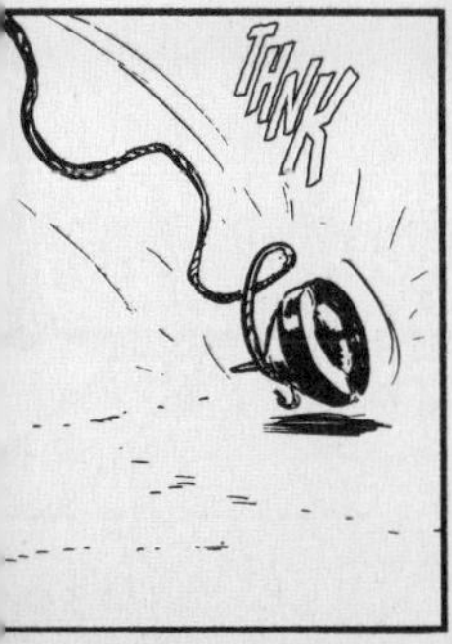
THNK

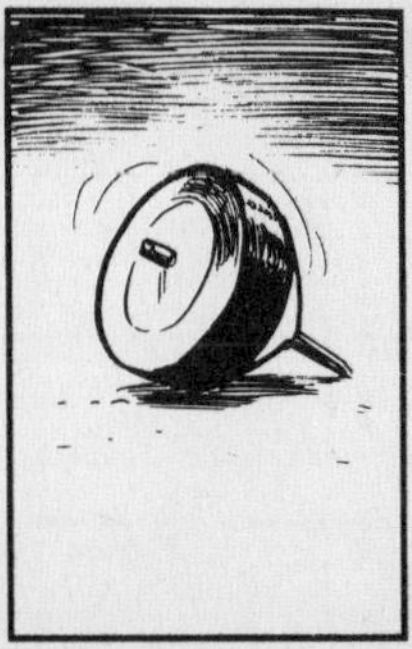

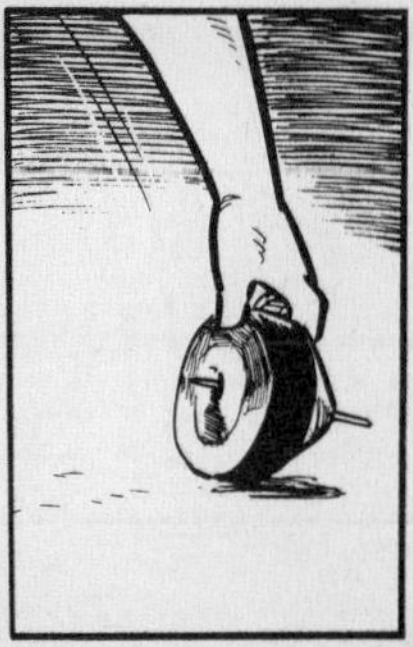

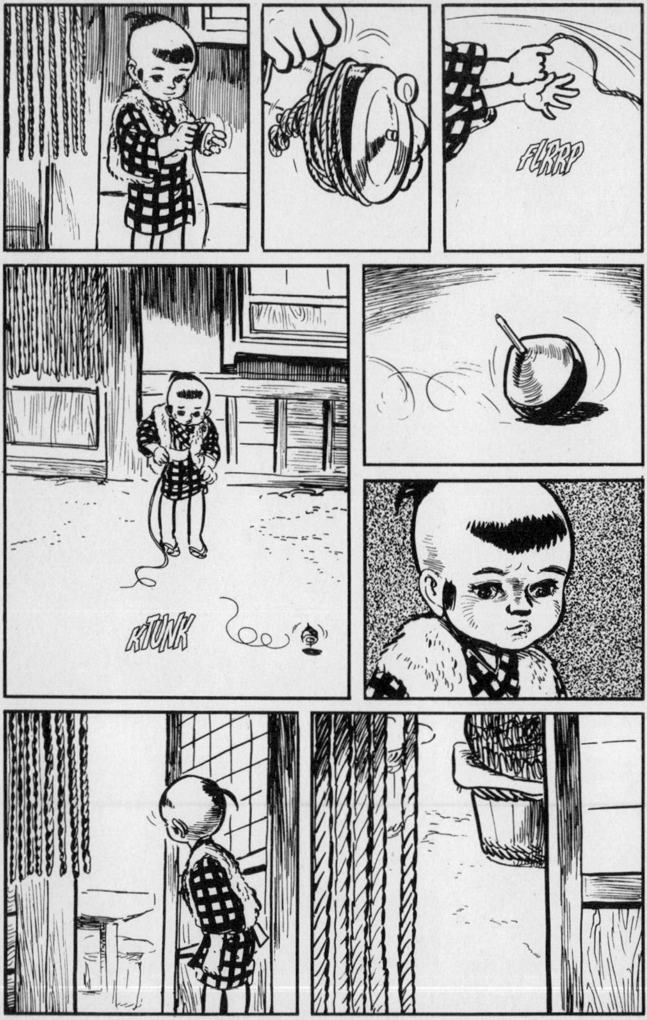
FLRRP
KTUNK

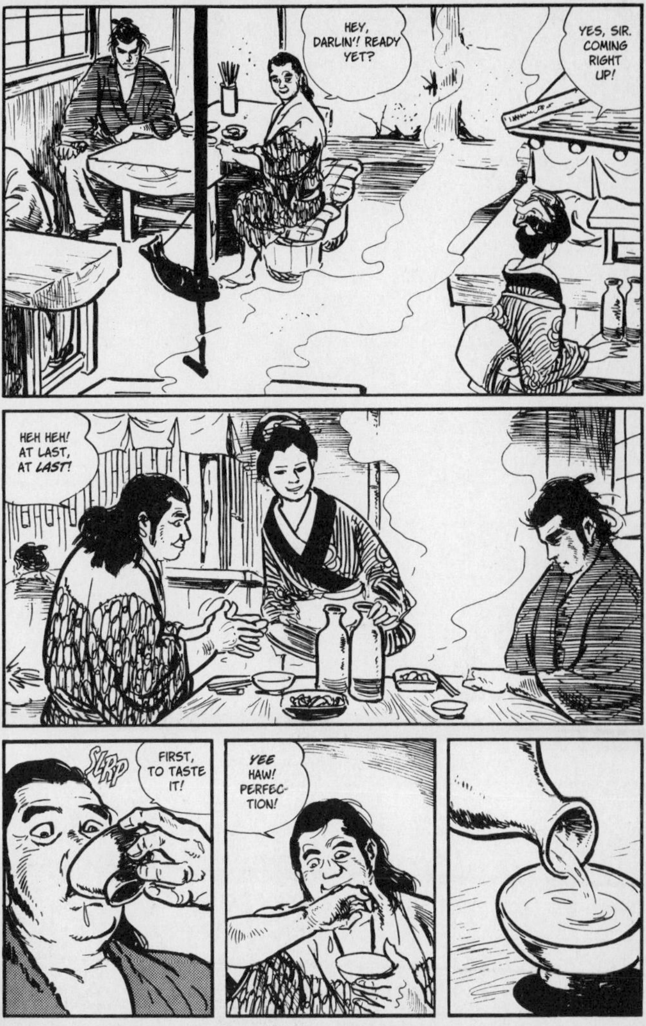
HEY, DARLIN'! READY YET?
YES, SIR. COMING RIGHT UP!
HEH HEH! AT LAST, AT *LAST!*
SLRP
FIRST, TO TASTE IT!
YEE HAW! PERFEC-TION!

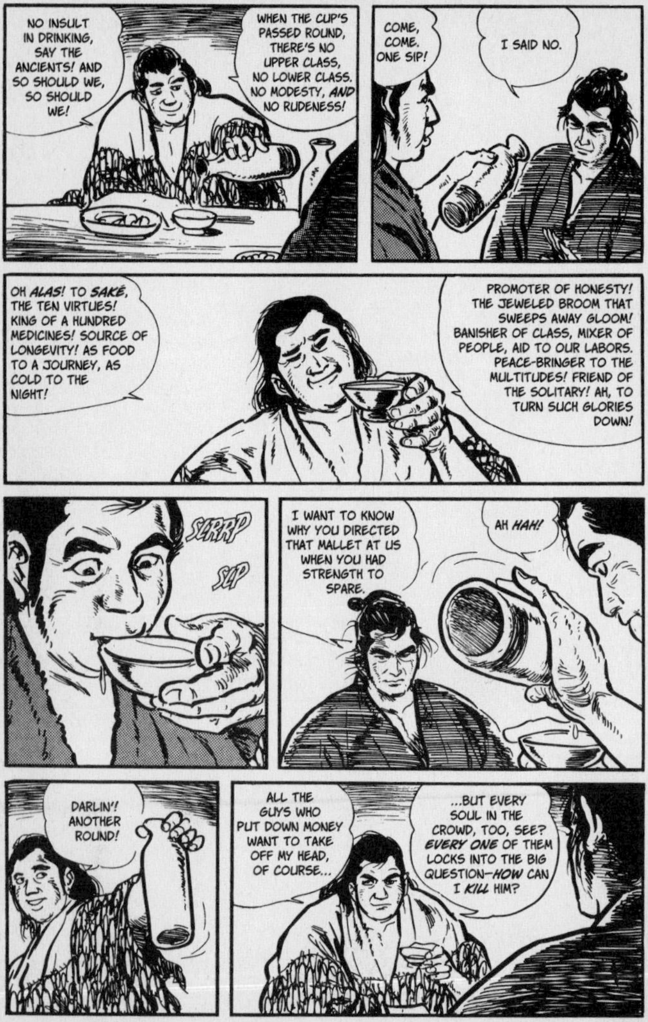
NO INSULT IN DRINKING, SAY THE ANCIENTS! AND SO SHOULD WE, SO SHOULD WE!
WHEN THE CUP'S PASSED ROUND, THERE'S NO UPPER CLASS, NO LOWER CLASS. NO MODESTY, AND NO RUDENESS!
COME, COME. ONE SIP!
I SAID NO.
OH ALAS! TO SAKÉ, THE TEN VIRTUES! KING OF A HUNDRED MEDICINES! SOURCE OF LONGEVITY! AS FOOD TO A JOURNEY, AS COLD TO THE NIGHT!
PROMOTER OF HONESTY! THE JEWELED BROOM THAT SWEEPS AWAY GLOOM! BANISHER OF CLASS, MIXER OF PEOPLE, AID TO OUR LABORS. PEACE-BRINGER TO THE MULTITUDES! FRIEND OF THE SOLITARY! AH, TO TURN SUCH GLORIES DOWN!
SCRRP
SLP
I WANT TO KNOW WHY YOU DIRECTED THAT MALLET AT US WHEN YOU HAD STRENGTH TO SPARE.
AH HAH!
DARLIN'! ANOTHER ROUND!
ALL THE GUYS WHO PUT DOWN MONEY WANT TO TAKE OFF MY HEAD, OF COURSE...
...BUT EVERY SOUL IN THE CROWD, TOO, SEE? EVERY ONE OF THEM LOCKS INTO THE BIG QUESTION—HOW CAN I KILL HIM?

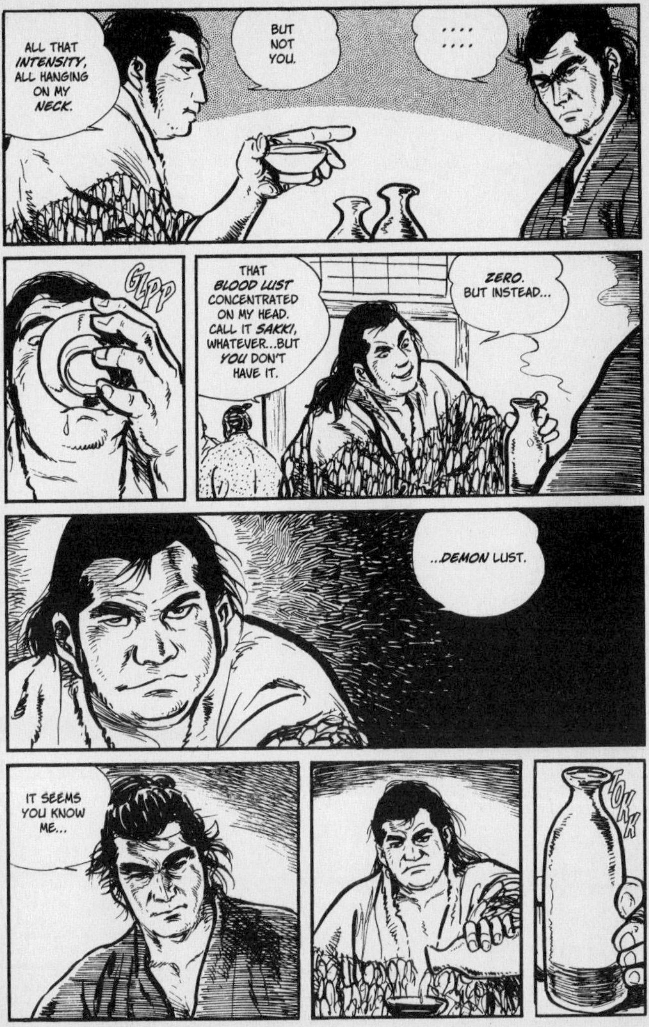
ALL THAT *INTENSITY*, ALL HANGING ON MY *NECK*.
BUT NOT YOU.
....
GLPP
THAT *BLOOD LUST* CONCENTRATED ON MY HEAD. CALL IT *SAKKI*, WHATEVER...BUT *YOU* DON'T HAVE IT.
ZERO. BUT INSTEAD...
...*DEMON* LUST.
IT SEEMS YOU KNOW ME...
TOKK

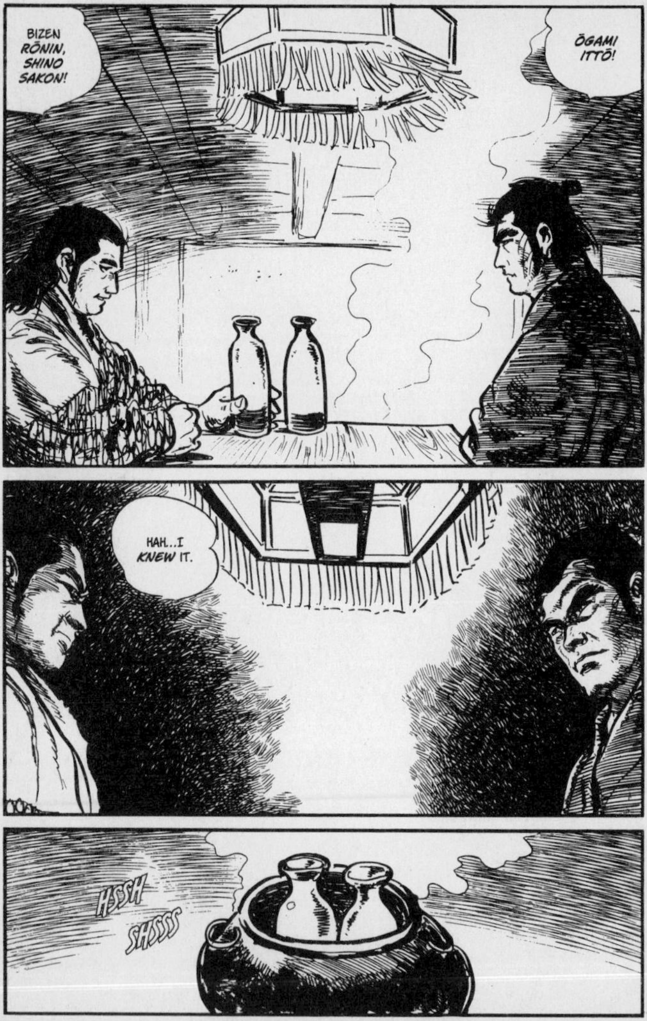
BIZEN RŌNIN, SHINO SAKON!
ŌGAMI ITTŌ!
HAH...I KNEW IT.
HSSH
SHSSS

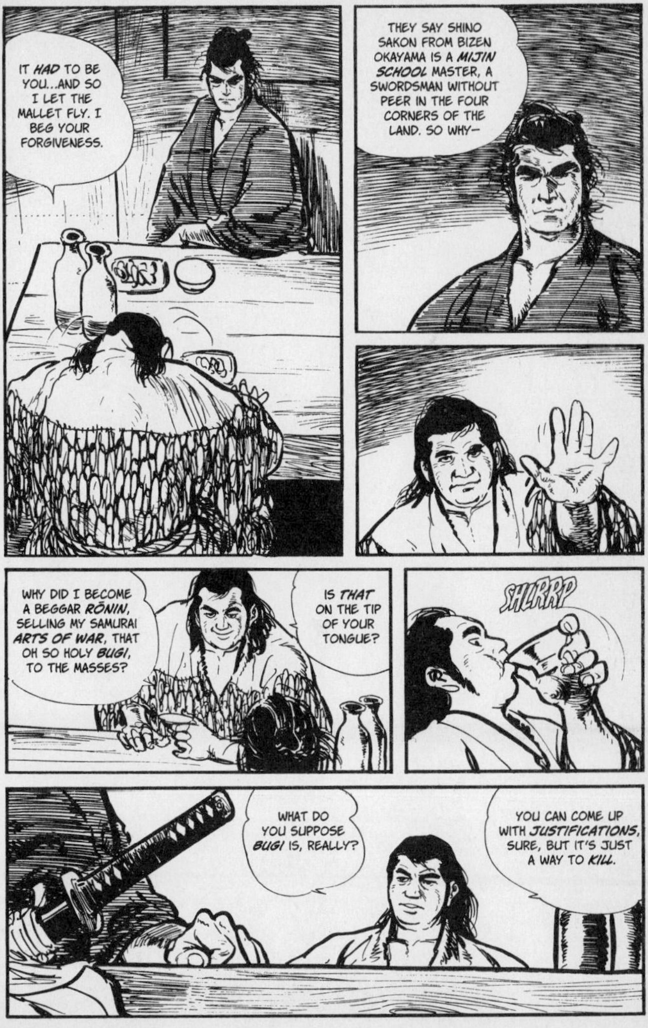
IT *HAD* TO BE YOU...AND SO I LET THE MALLET FLY. I BEG YOUR FORGIVENESS.
THEY SAY SHINO SAKON FROM BIZEN OKAYAMA IS A *MIJIN SCHOOL* MASTER, A SWORDSMAN WITHOUT PEER IN THE FOUR CORNERS OF THE LAND. SO WHY–
WHY DID I BECOME A BEGGAR *RŌNIN*, SELLING MY SAMURAI *ARTS OF WAR*, THAT OH SO HOLY *BUGI*, TO THE MASSES?
IS *THAT* ON THE TIP OF YOUR TONGUE?
SHLRRP
WHAT DO YOU SUPPOSE *BUGI* IS, REALLY?
YOU CAN COME UP WITH *JUSTIFICATIONS*, SURE, BUT IT'S JUST A WAY TO *KILL*.

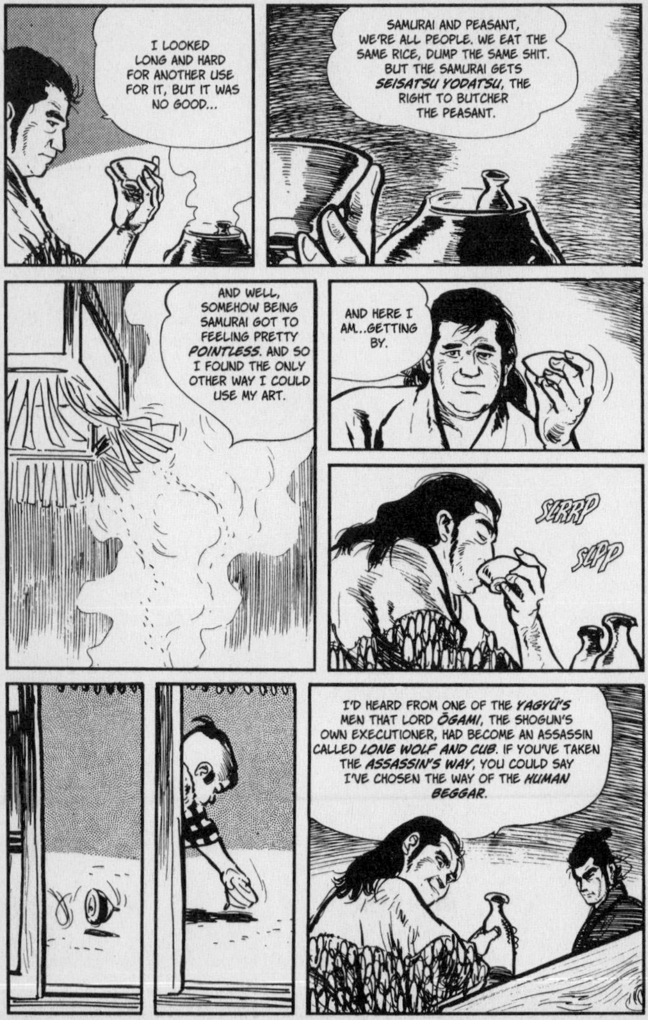
I LOOKED LONG AND HARD FOR ANOTHER USE FOR IT, BUT IT WAS NO GOOD...
SAMURAI AND PEASANT, WE'RE ALL PEOPLE. WE EAT THE SAME RICE, DUMP THE SAME SHIT. BUT THE SAMURAI GETS *SEISATSU YODATSU*, THE RIGHT TO BUTCHER THE PEASANT.
AND WELL, SOMEHOW BEING SAMURAI GOT TO FEELING PRETTY *POINTLESS*. AND SO I FOUND THE ONLY OTHER WAY I COULD USE MY ART.
AND HERE I AM...GETTING BY.
SLRRP
SLPP
I'D HEARD FROM ONE OF THE *YAGYŪ'S* MEN THAT LORD *ŌGAMI*, THE SHOGUN'S OWN EXECUTIONER, HAD BECOME AN ASSASSIN CALLED *LONE WOLF AND CUB*. IF YOU'VE TAKEN THE *ASSASSIN'S WAY*, YOU COULD SAY I'VE CHOSEN THE WAY OF THE *HUMAN BEGGAR*.

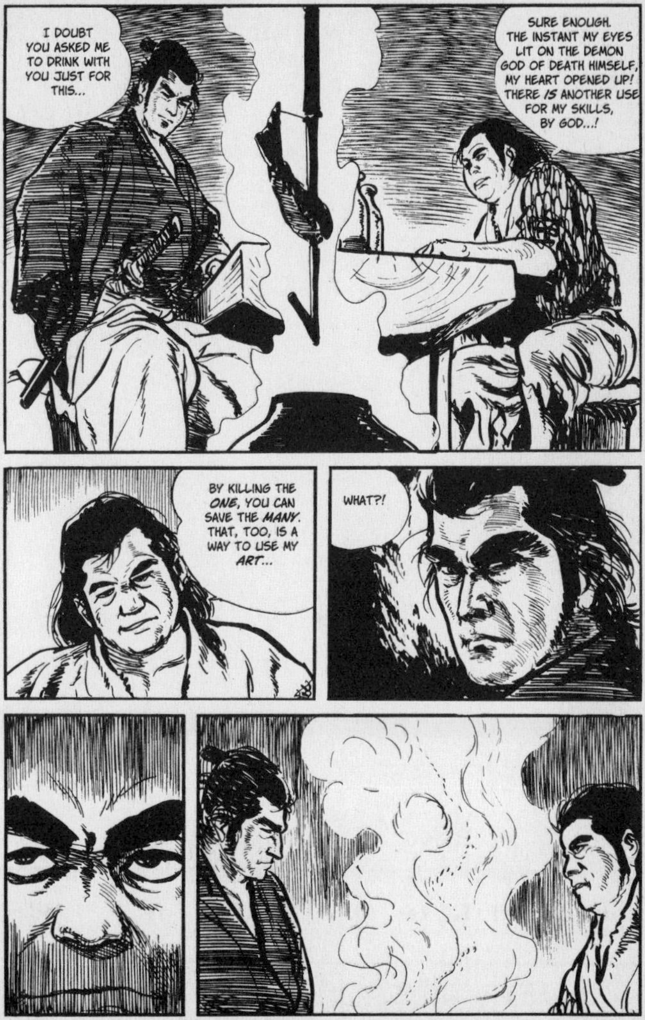
I DOUBT YOU ASKED ME TO DRINK WITH YOU JUST FOR THIS...
SURE ENOUGH. THE INSTANT MY EYES LIT ON THE DEMON GOD OF DEATH HIMSELF, MY HEART OPENED UP! THERE *IS* ANOTHER USE FOR MY SKILLS, BY GOD...!
BY KILLING THE *ONE*, YOU CAN SAVE THE *MANY*. THAT, TOO, IS A WAY TO USE MY *ART*...
WHAT?!

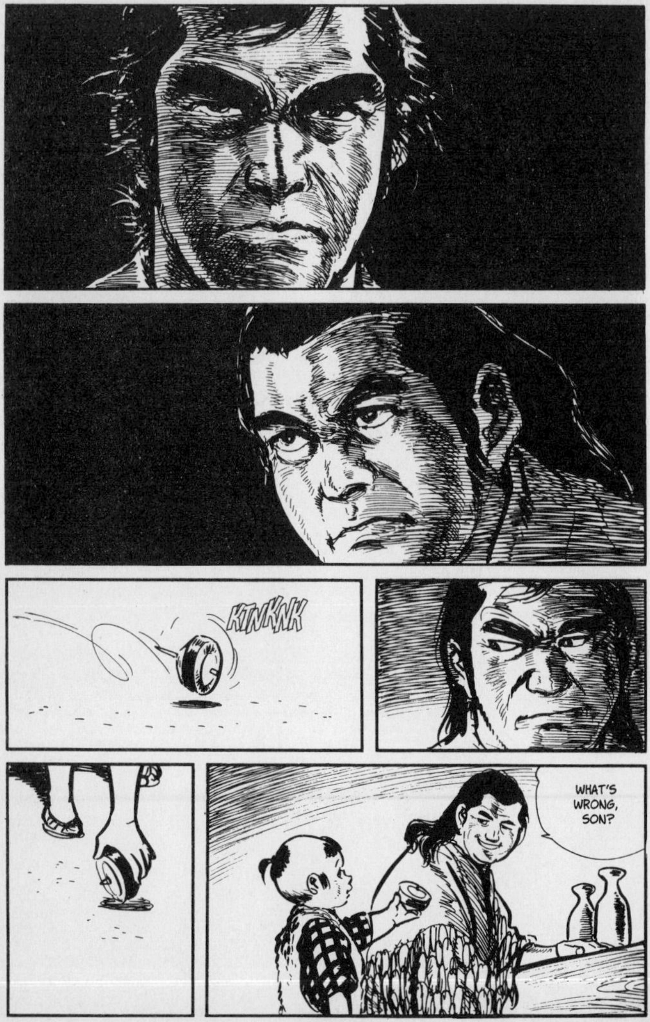
KTNKNK
WHAT'S WRONG, SON?

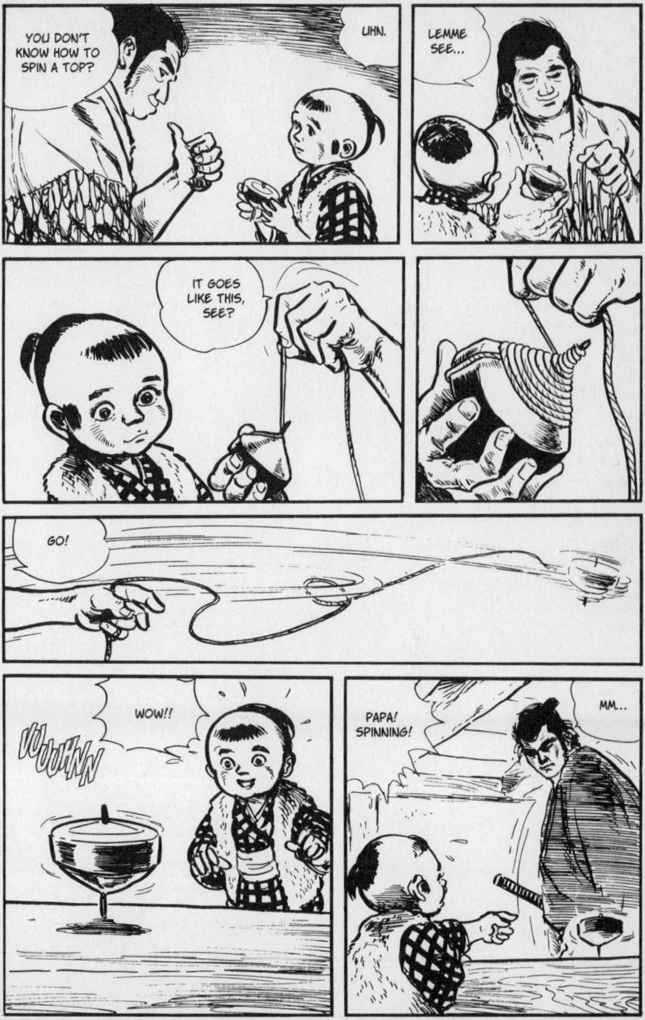
YOU DON'T KNOW HOW TO SPIN A TOP?
UHN.
LEMME SEE...
IT GOES LIKE THIS, SEE?
GO!
WOW!!
VUUUHNN
PAPA! SPINNING!
MM...

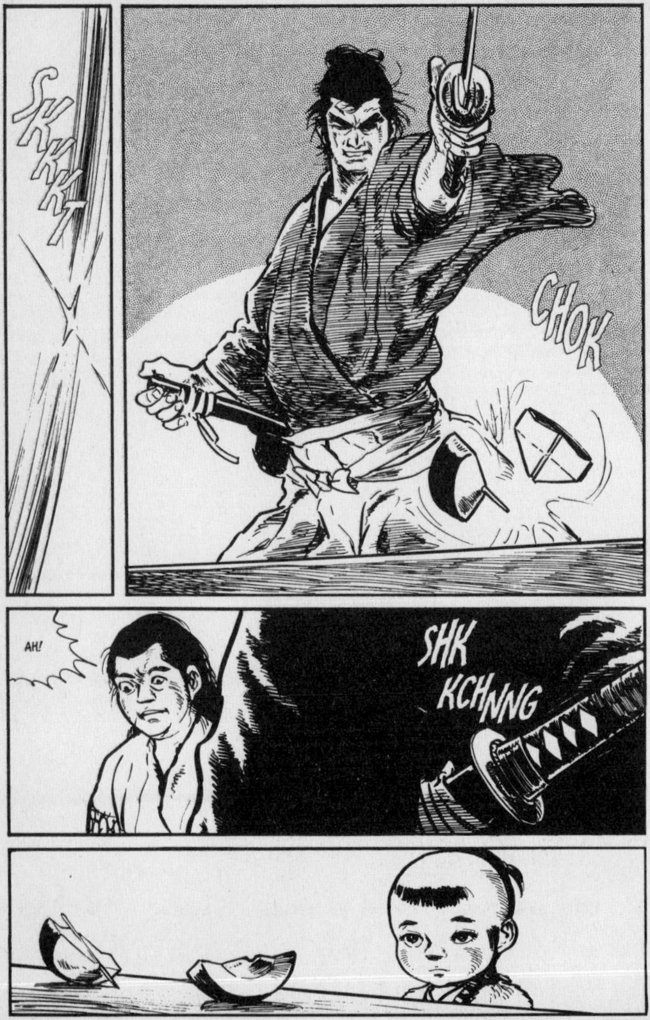
SKKKT
CHOK
AH!
SHK
KCHNNG

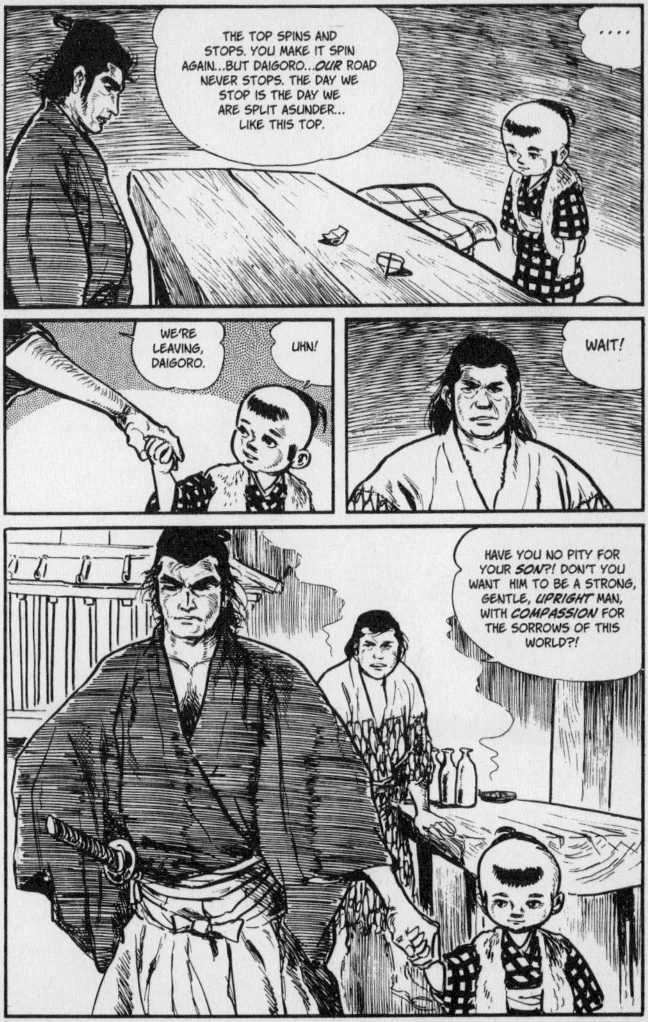
THE TOP SPINS AND STOPS. YOU MAKE IT SPIN AGAIN...BUT DAIGORO...OUR ROAD NEVER STOPS. THE DAY WE STOP IS THE DAY WE ARE SPLIT ASUNDER... LIKE THIS TOP.
....
WE'RE LEAVING, DAIGORO.
UHN!
WAIT!
HAVE YOU NO PITY FOR YOUR SON?! DON'T YOU WANT HIM TO BE A STRONG, GENTLE, UPRIGHT MAN, WITH COMPASSION FOR THE SORROWS OF THIS WORLD?!

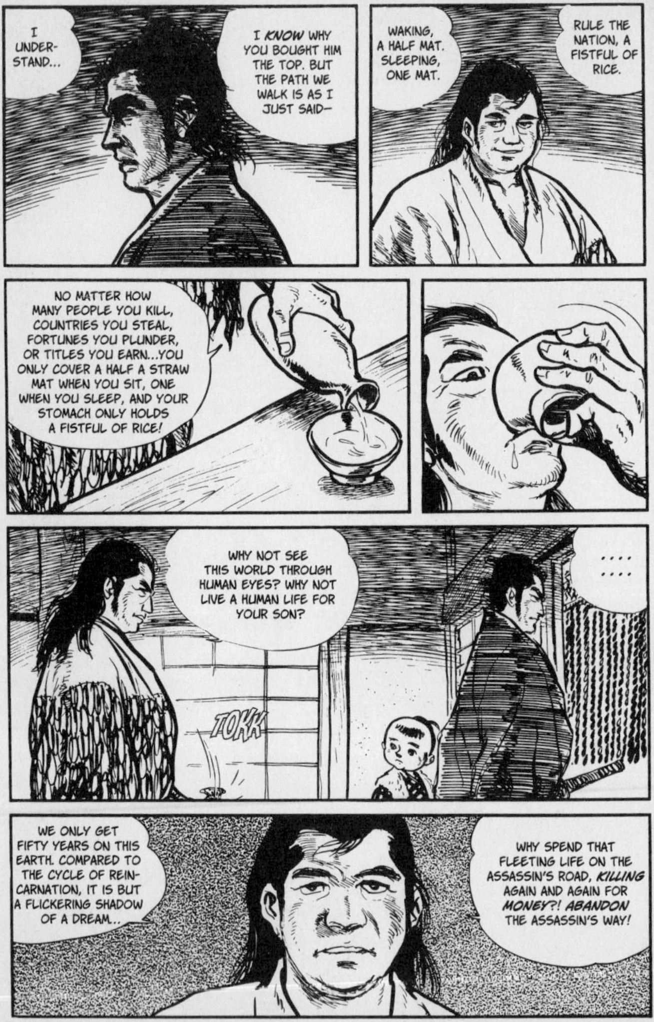
I UNDER-STAND...
I *KNOW* WHY YOU BOUGHT HIM THE TOP. BUT THE PATH WE WALK IS AS I JUST SAID—
WAKING, A HALF MAT. SLEEPING, ONE MAT.
RULE THE NATION, A FISTFUL OF RICE.
NO MATTER HOW MANY PEOPLE YOU KILL, COUNTRIES YOU STEAL, FORTUNES YOU PLUNDER, OR TITLES YOU EARN...YOU ONLY COVER A HALF A STRAW MAT WHEN YOU SIT, ONE WHEN YOU SLEEP, AND YOUR STOMACH ONLY HOLDS A FISTFUL OF RICE!
WHY NOT SEE THIS WORLD THROUGH HUMAN EYES? WHY NOT LIVE A HUMAN LIFE FOR YOUR SON?
TOKK
....
....
WE ONLY GET FIFTY YEARS ON THIS EARTH. COMPARED TO THE CYCLE OF REIN-CARNATION, IT IS BUT A FLICKERING SHADOW OF A DREAM...
WHY SPEND THAT FLEETING LIFE ON THE ASSASSIN'S ROAD, *KILLING* AGAIN AND AGAIN FOR *MONEY*?! *ABANDON* THE ASSASSIN'S WAY!

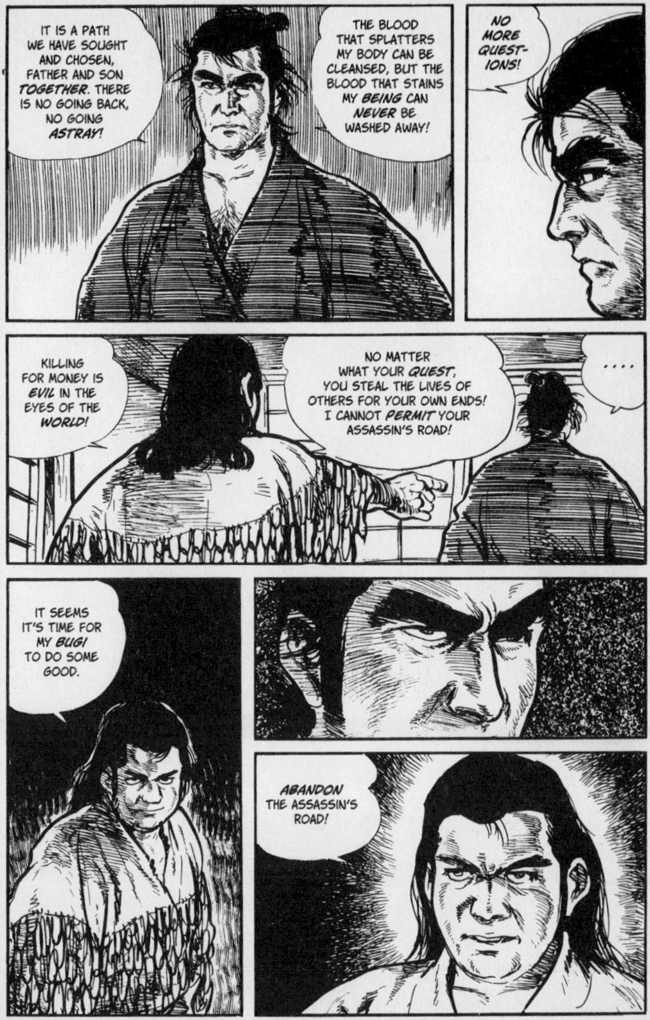
IT IS A PATH WE HAVE SOUGHT AND CHOSEN, FATHER AND SON TOGETHER. THERE IS NO GOING BACK, NO GOING ASTRAY!
THE BLOOD THAT SPLATTERS MY BODY CAN BE CLEANSED, BUT THE BLOOD THAT STAINS MY BEING CAN NEVER BE WASHED AWAY!
NO MORE QUEST-IONS!
KILLING FOR MONEY IS EVIL IN THE EYES OF THE WORLD!
NO MATTER WHAT YOUR QUEST, YOU STEAL THE LIVES OF OTHERS FOR YOUR OWN ENDS! I CANNOT PERMIT YOUR ASSASSIN'S ROAD!
....
IT SEEMS IT'S TIME FOR MY BUGI TO DO SOME GOOD.
ABANDON THE ASSASSIN'S ROAD!

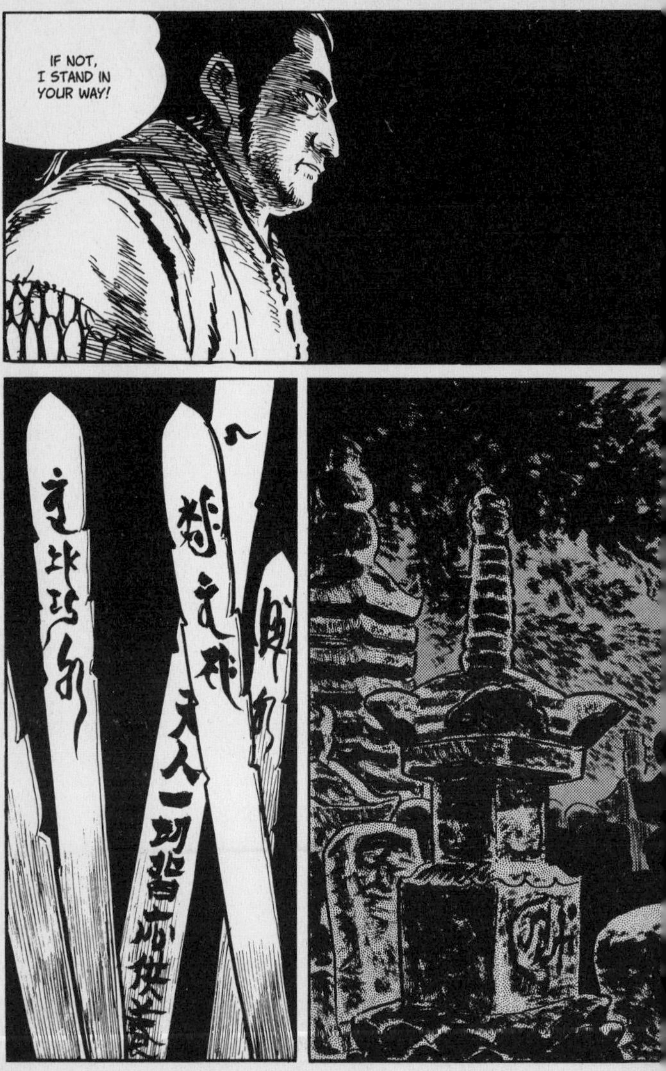
IF NOT, I STAND IN YOUR WAY!

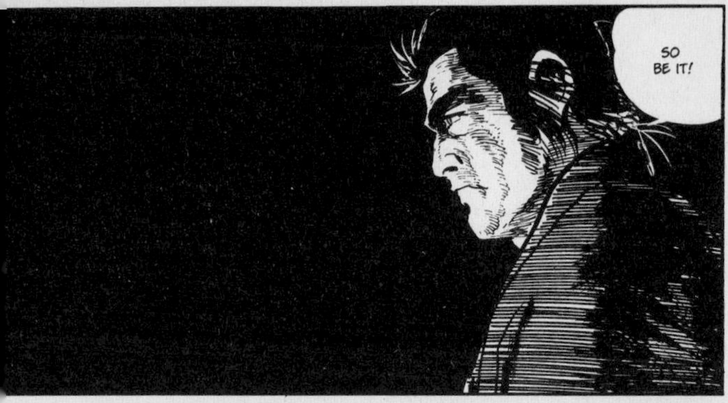
SO
BE IT!
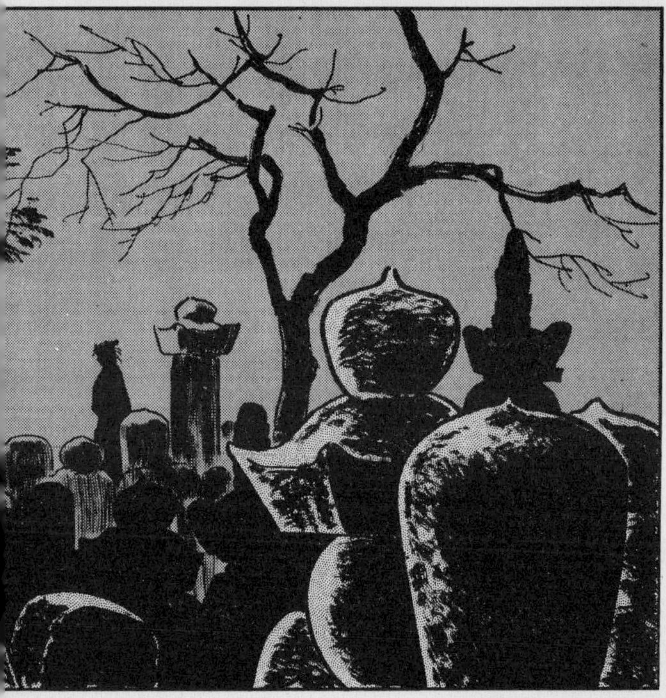

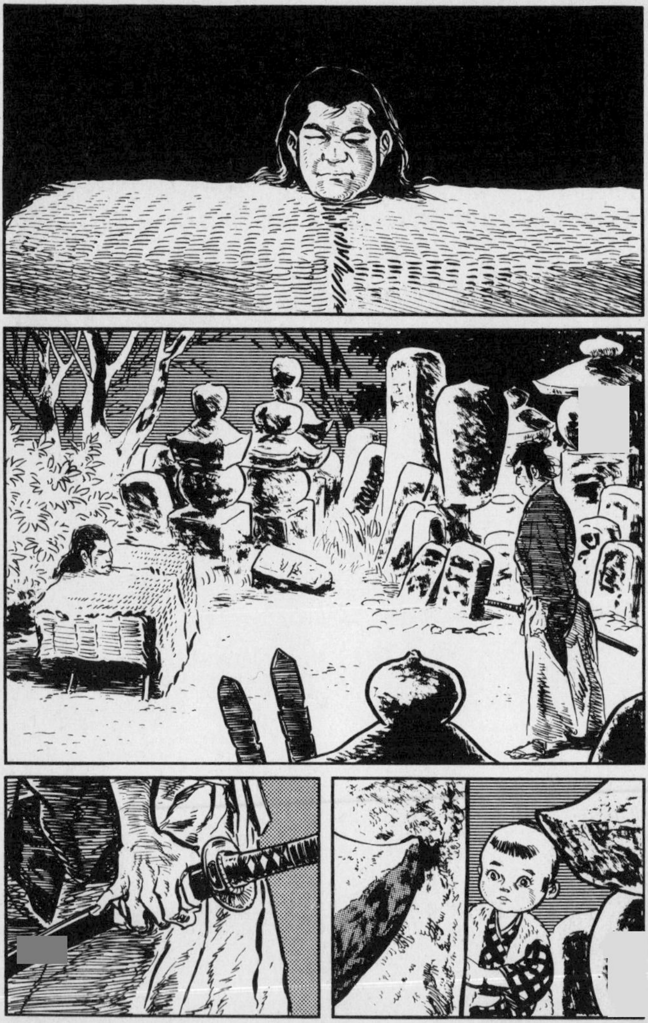

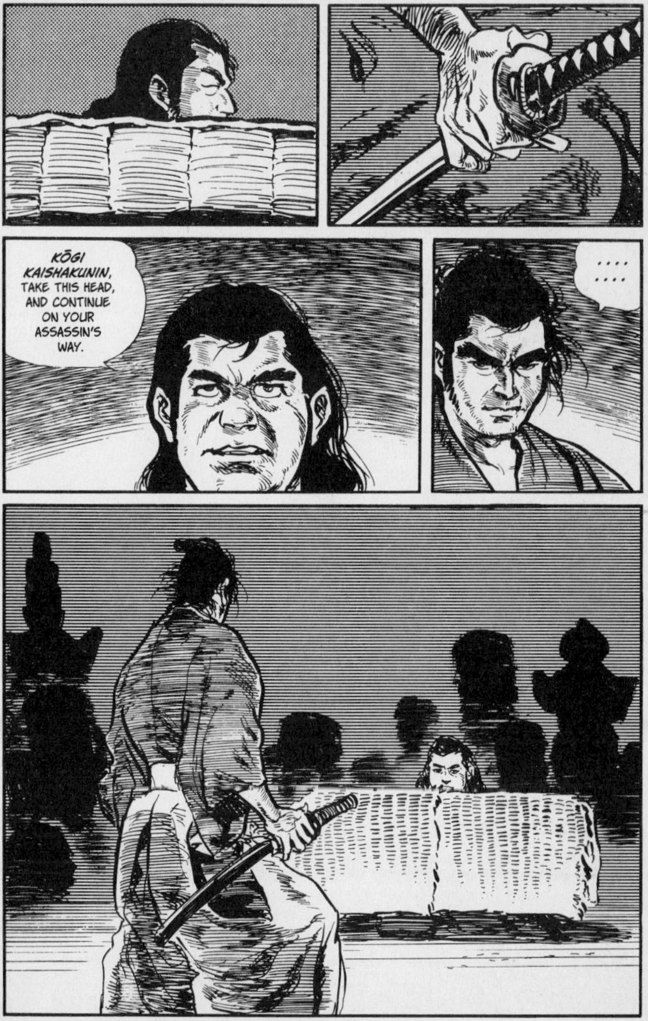
KŌGI KAISHAKUNIN, TAKE THIS HEAD, AND CONTINUE ON YOUR ASSASSIN'S WAY.
....
....

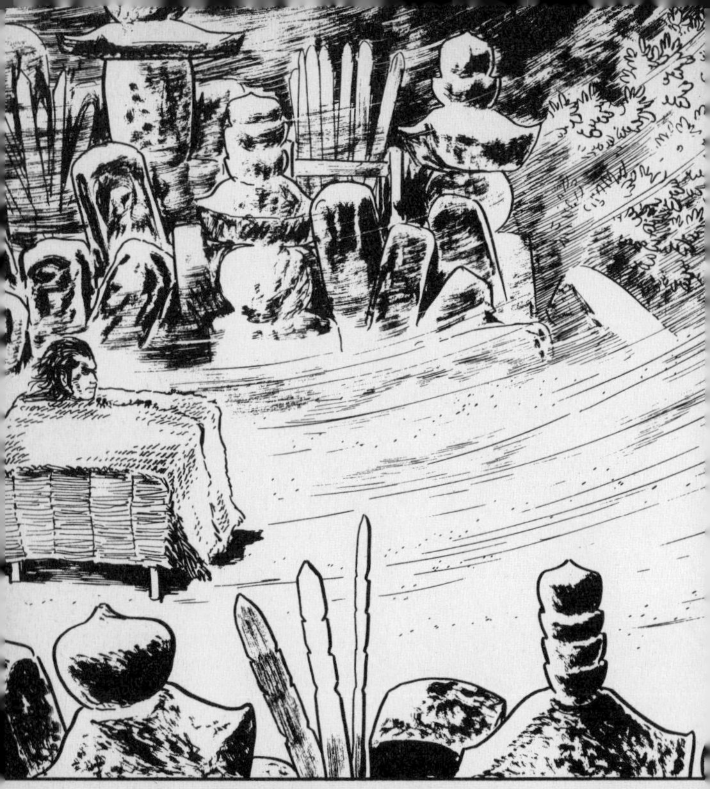
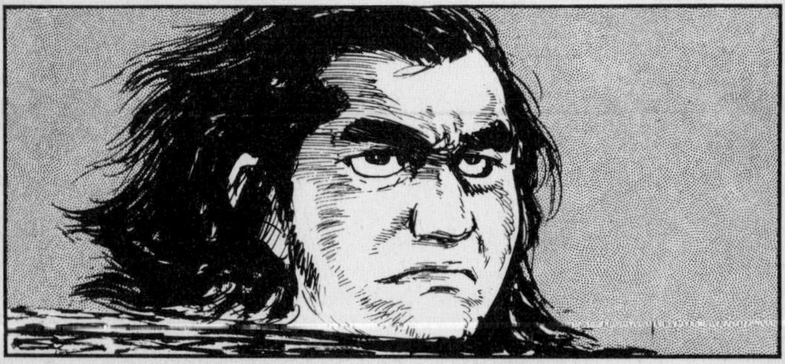

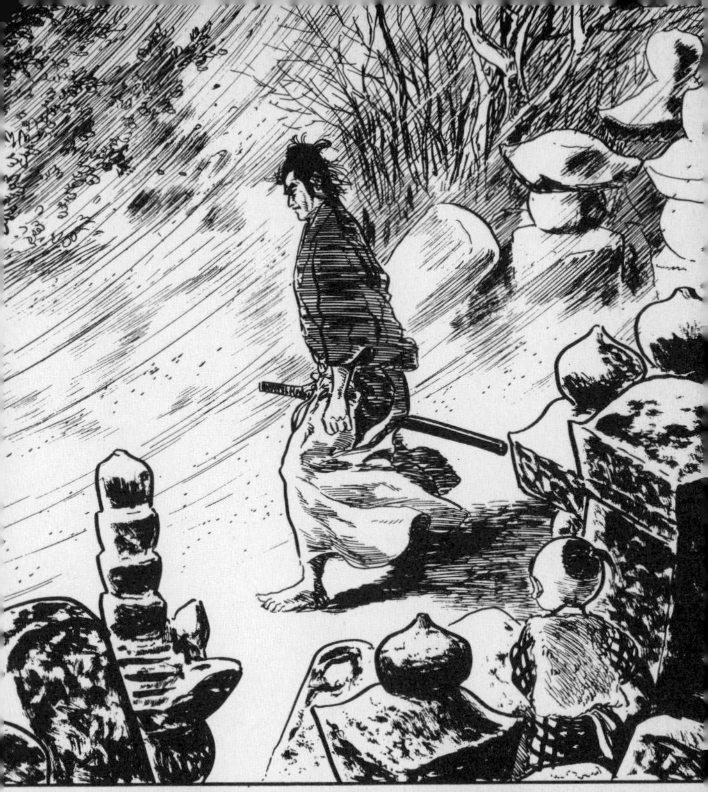
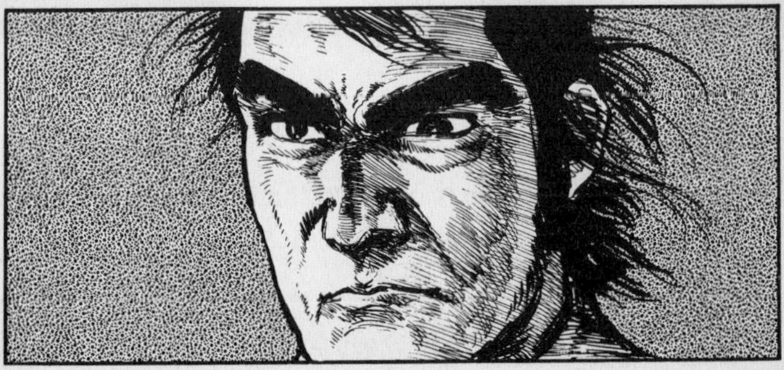

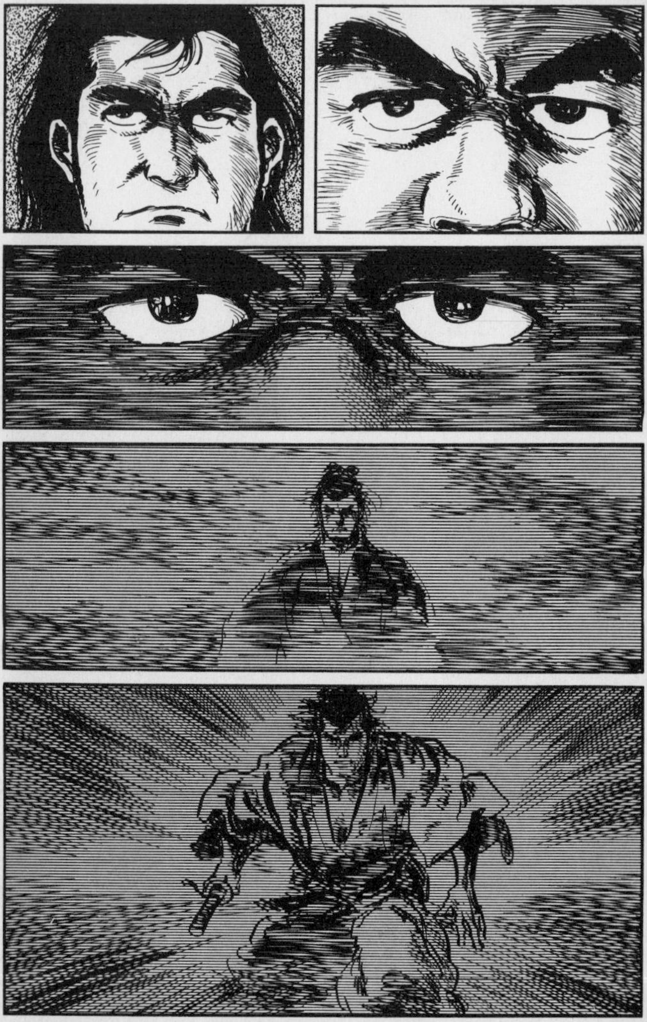

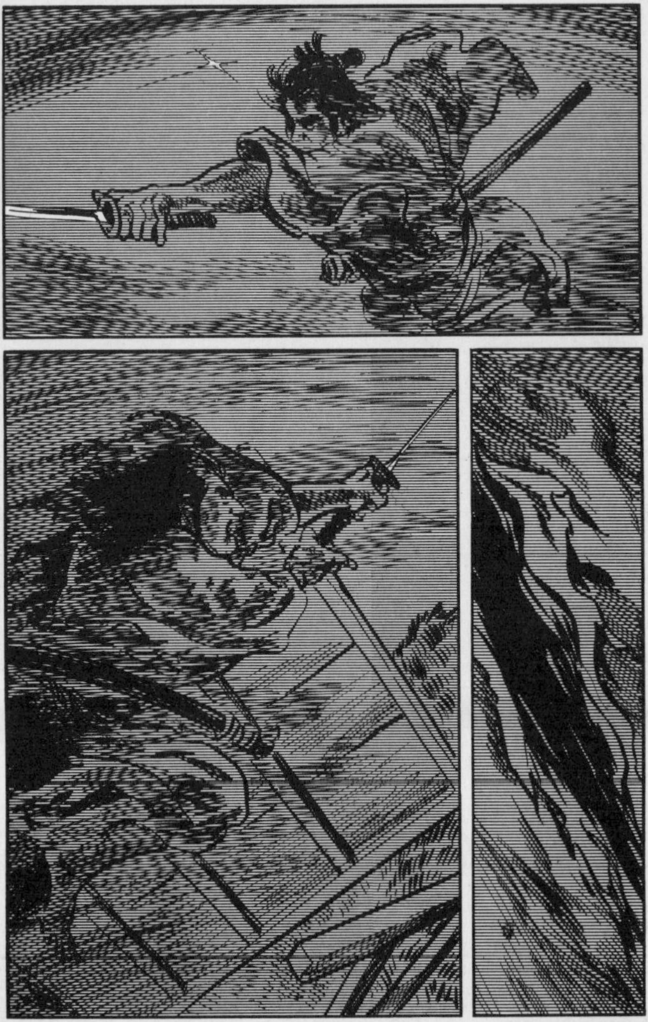

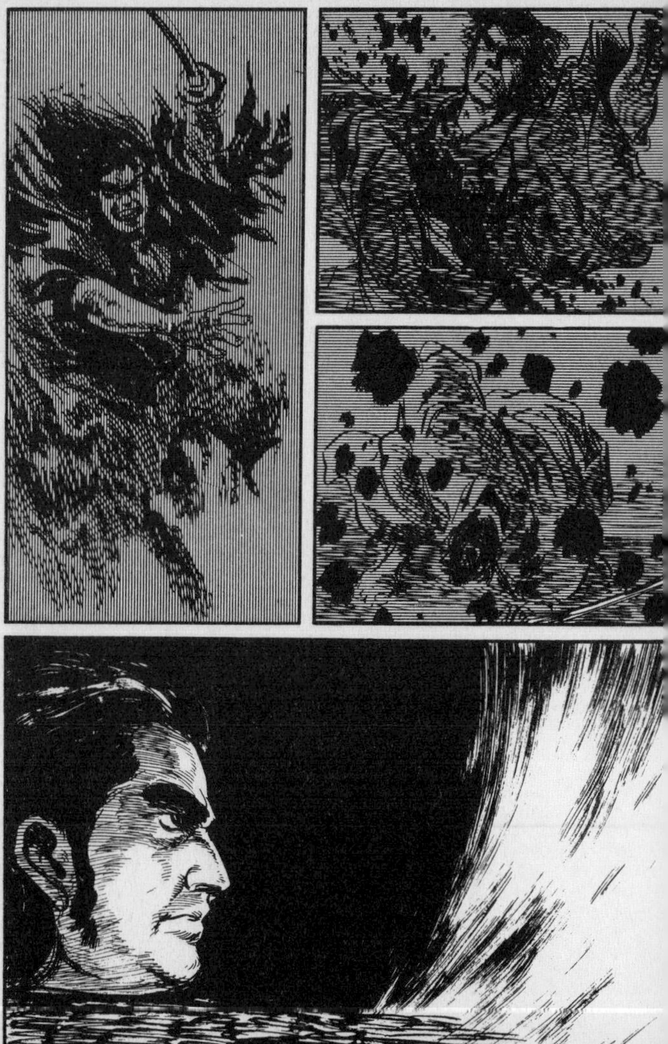

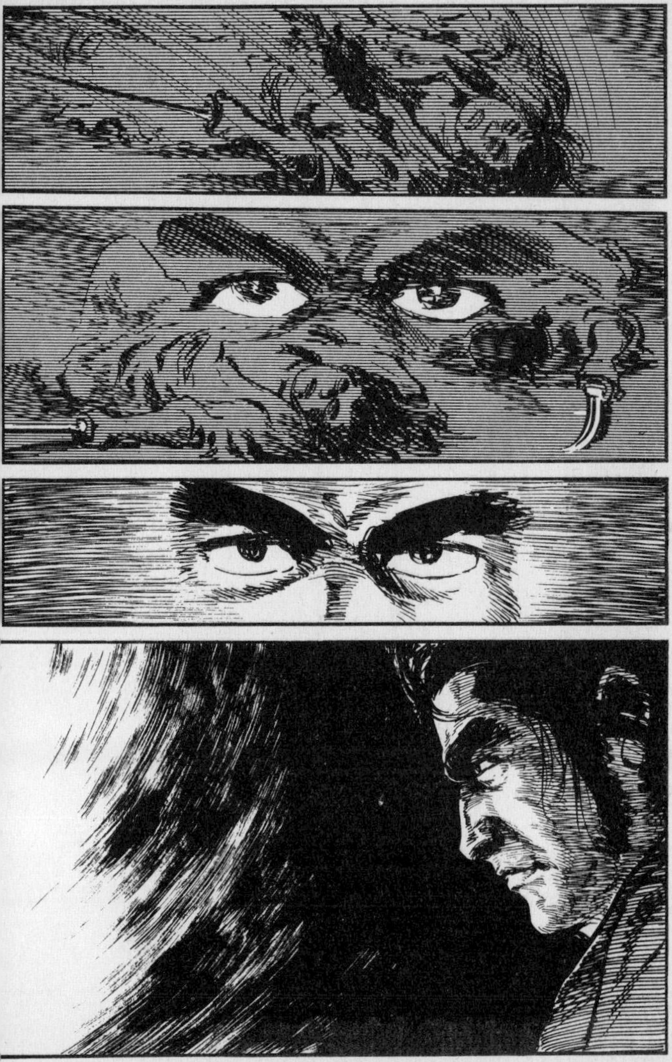

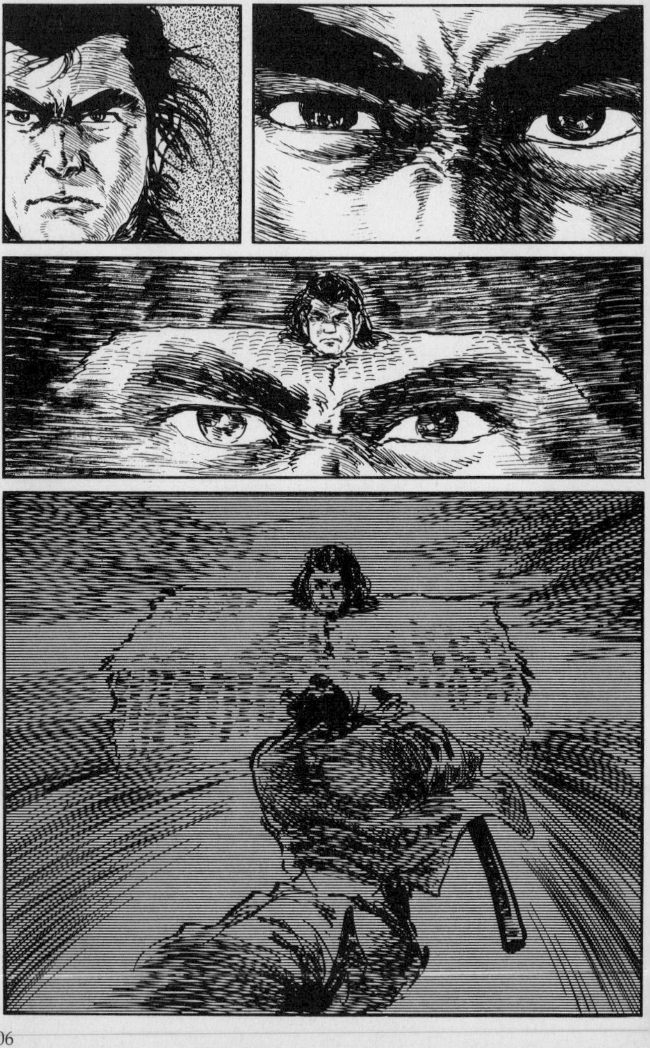

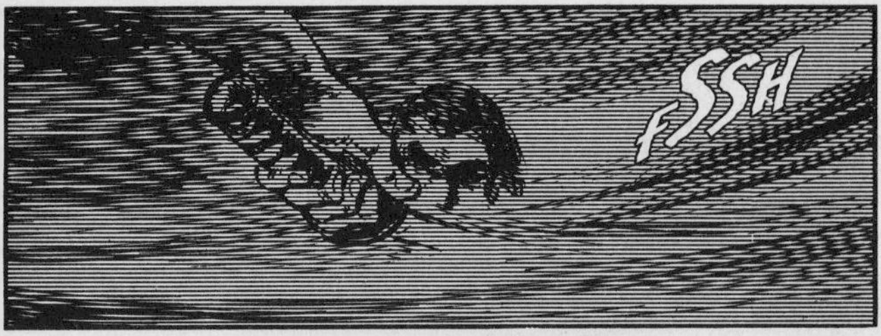
FSSH
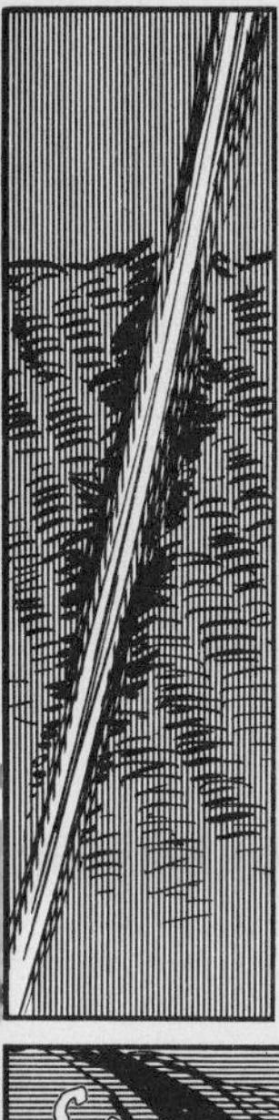
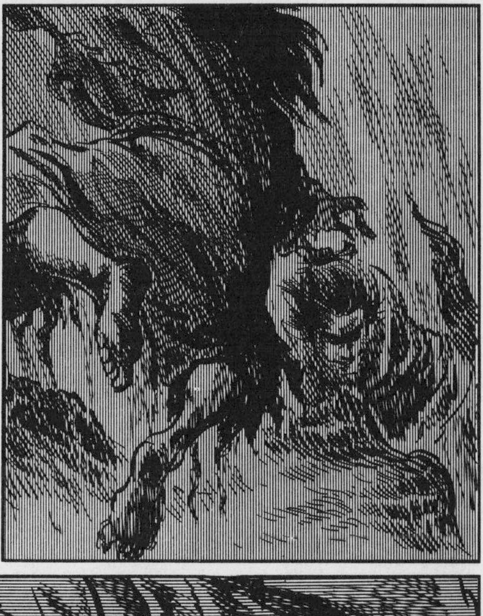
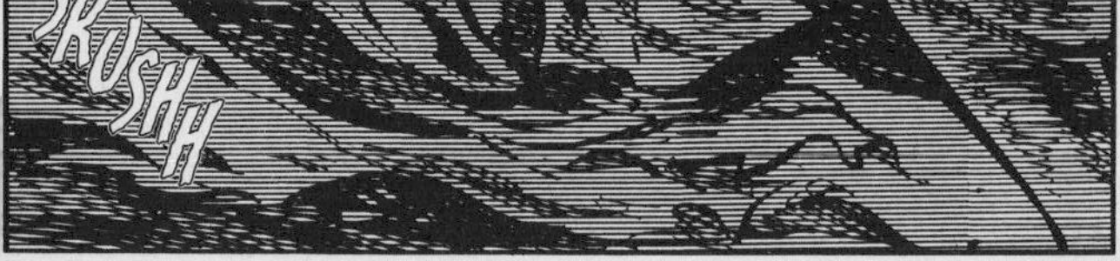
SKUSHH

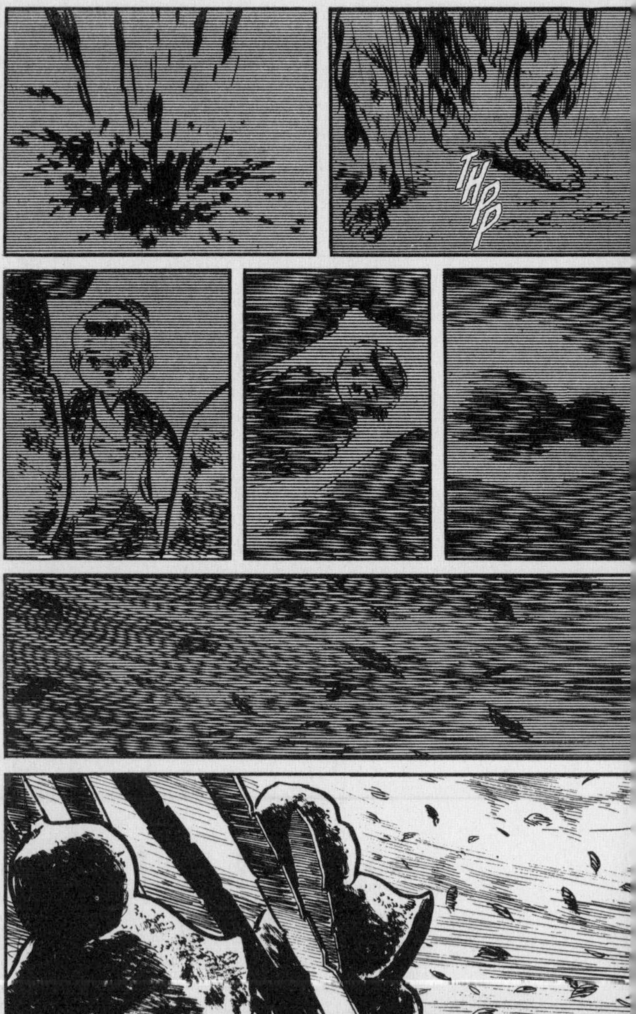
THPP

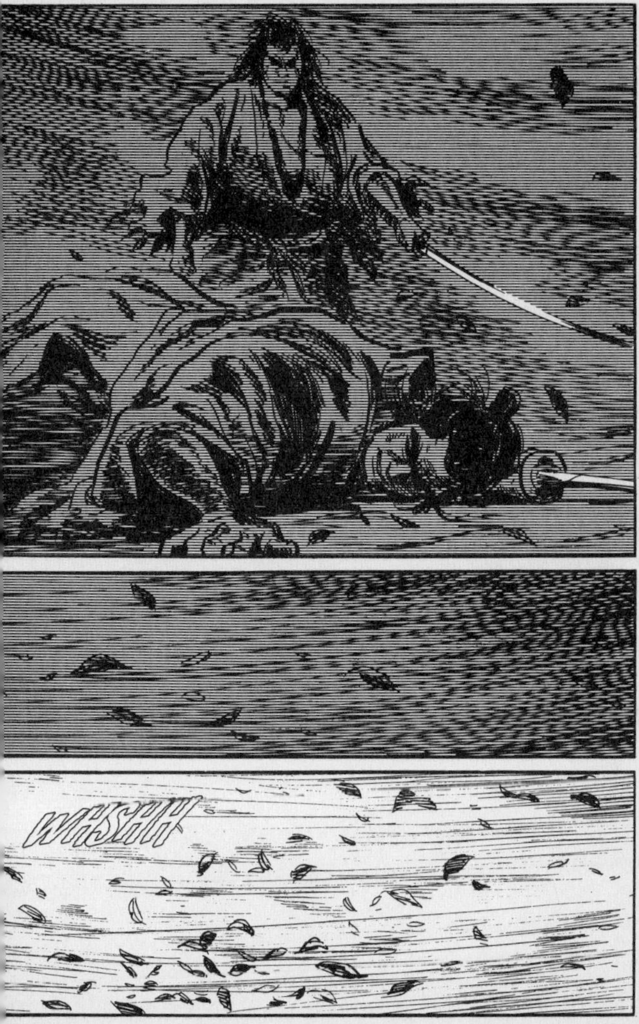
WHSHH

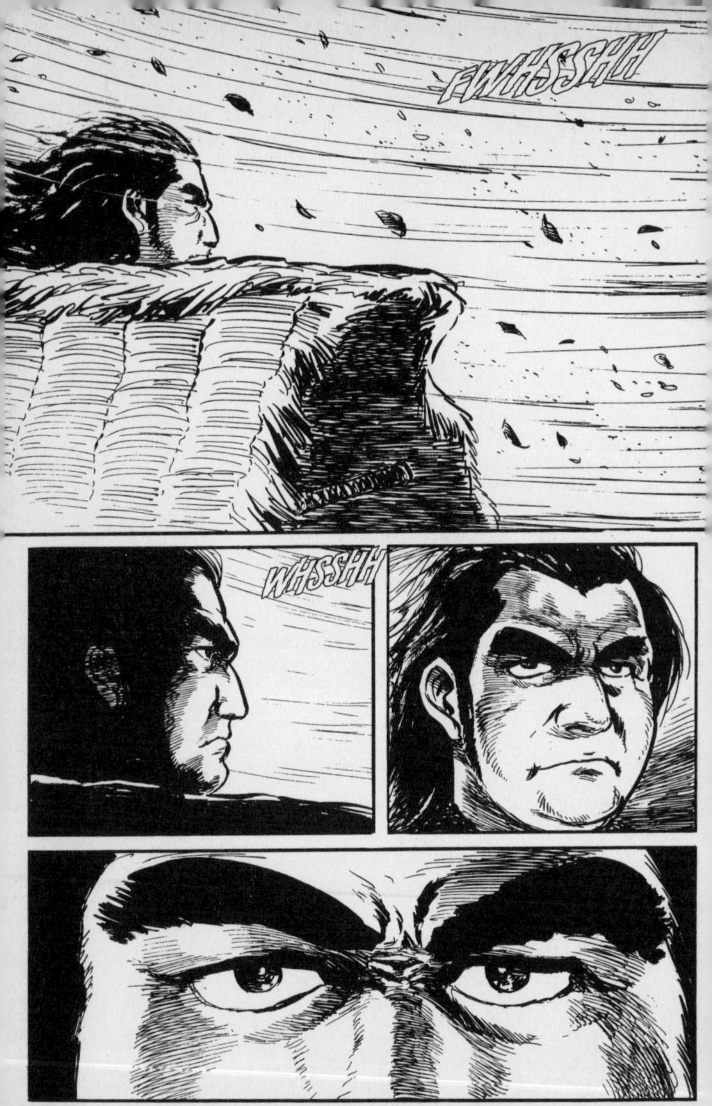
FWHSSHH
WHSSHH

WHSSSHH

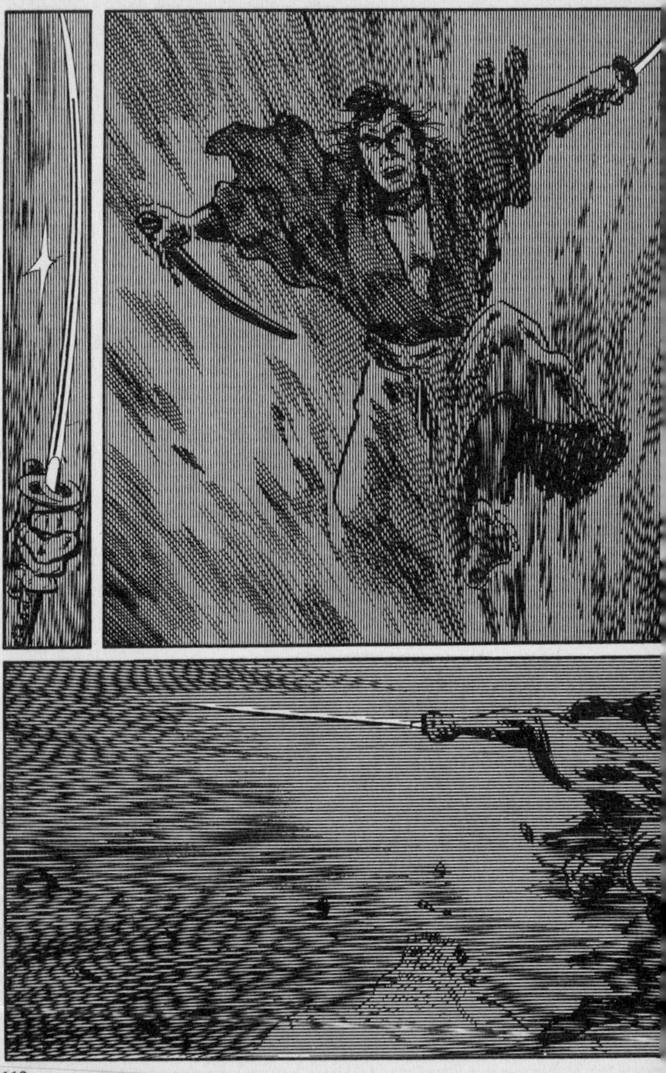

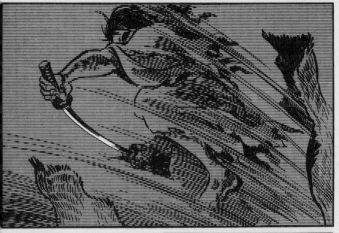

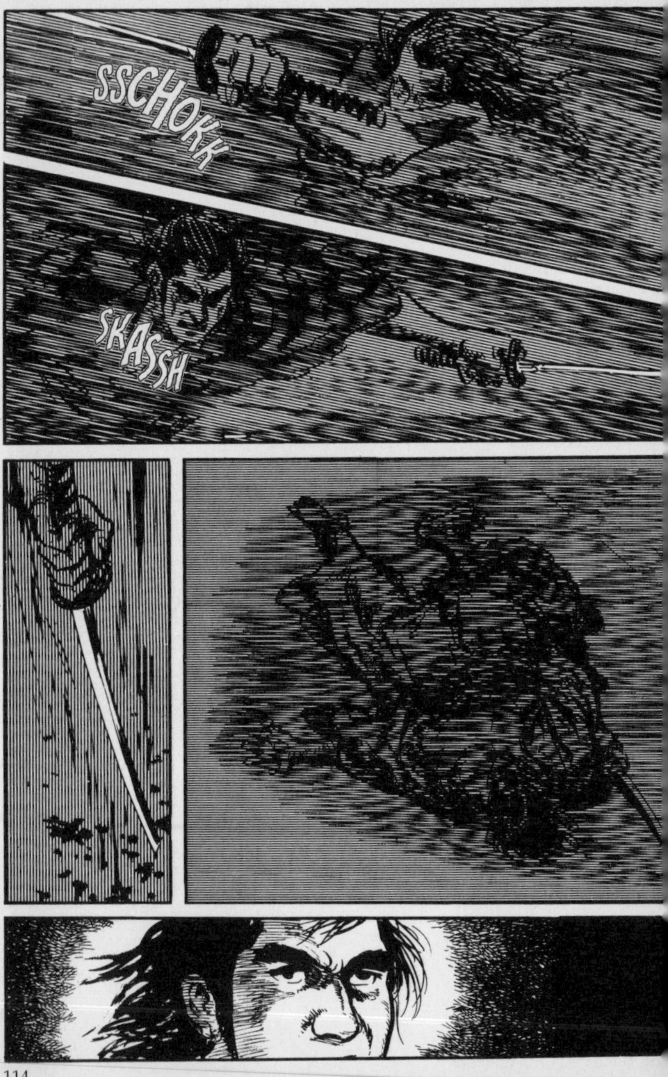
SSCHOKK
SKASSH

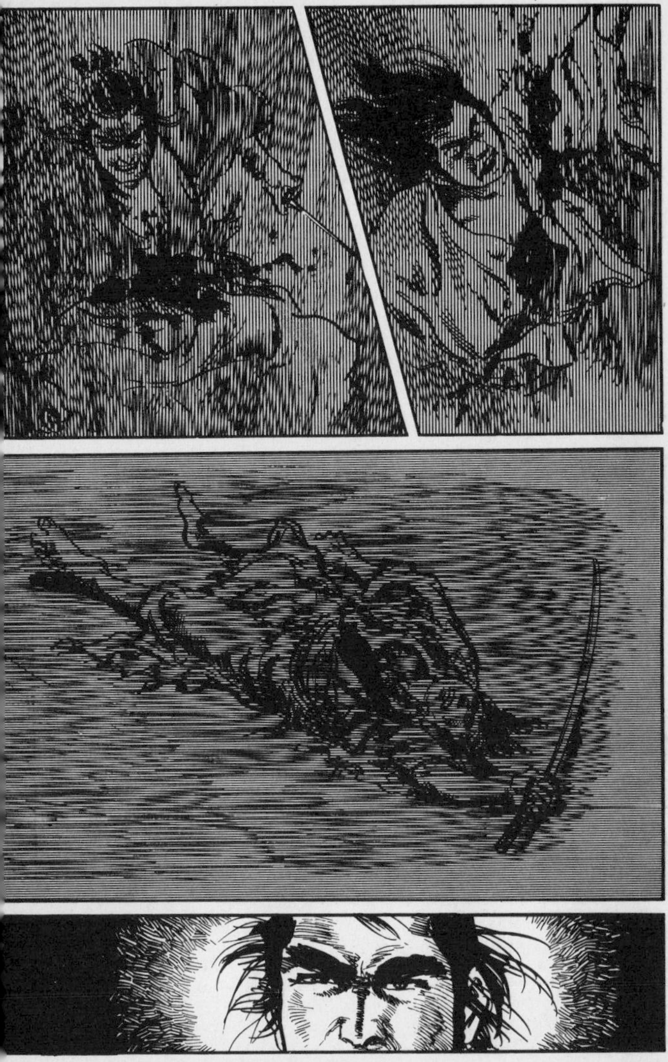

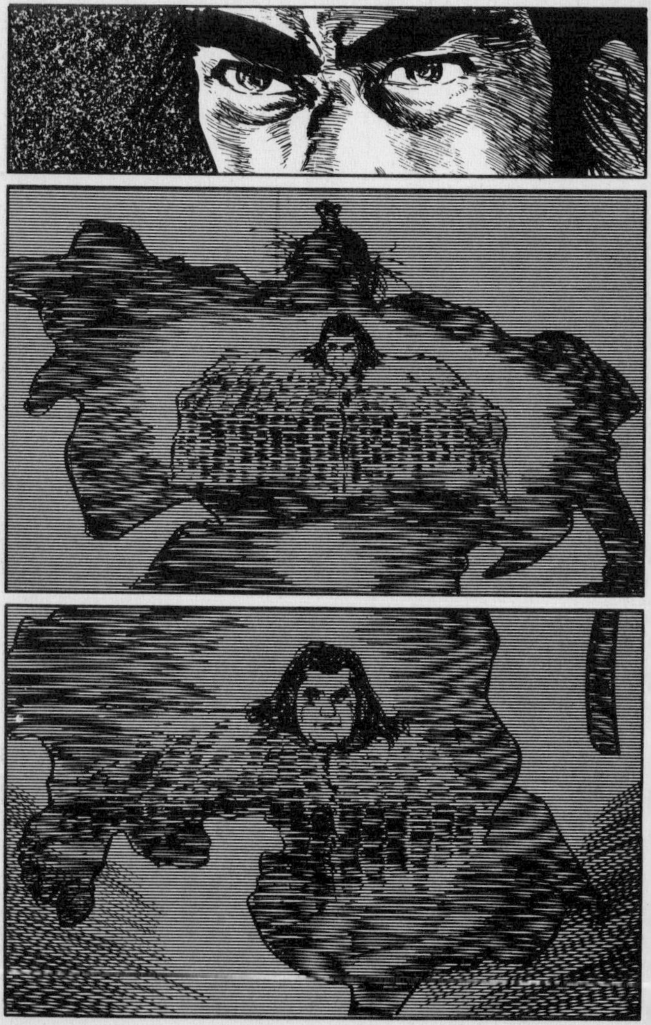

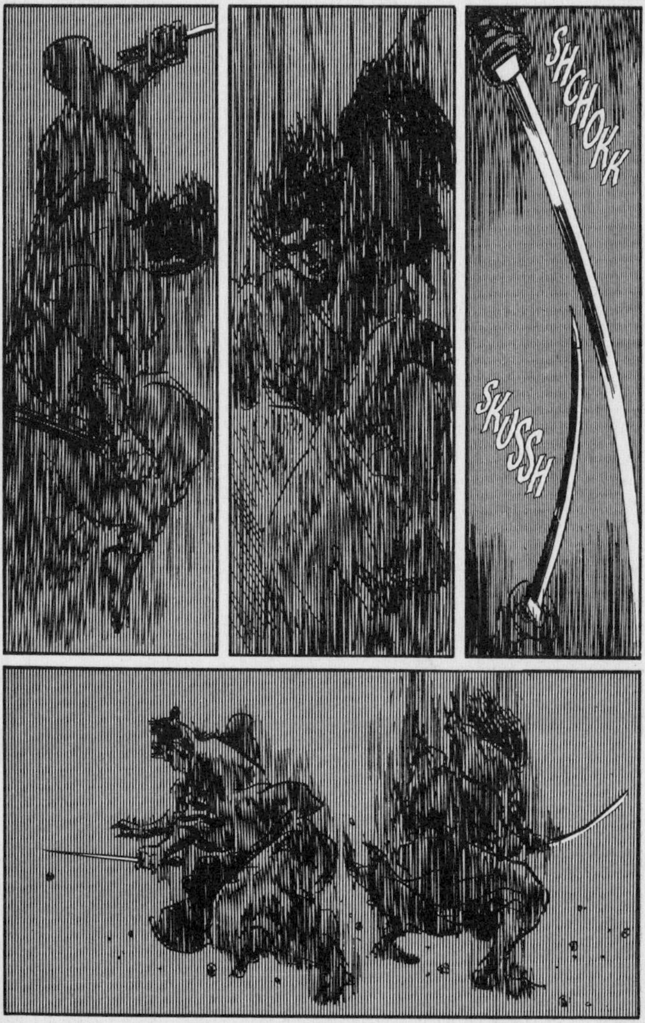
SHCHOKK
SKUSSH

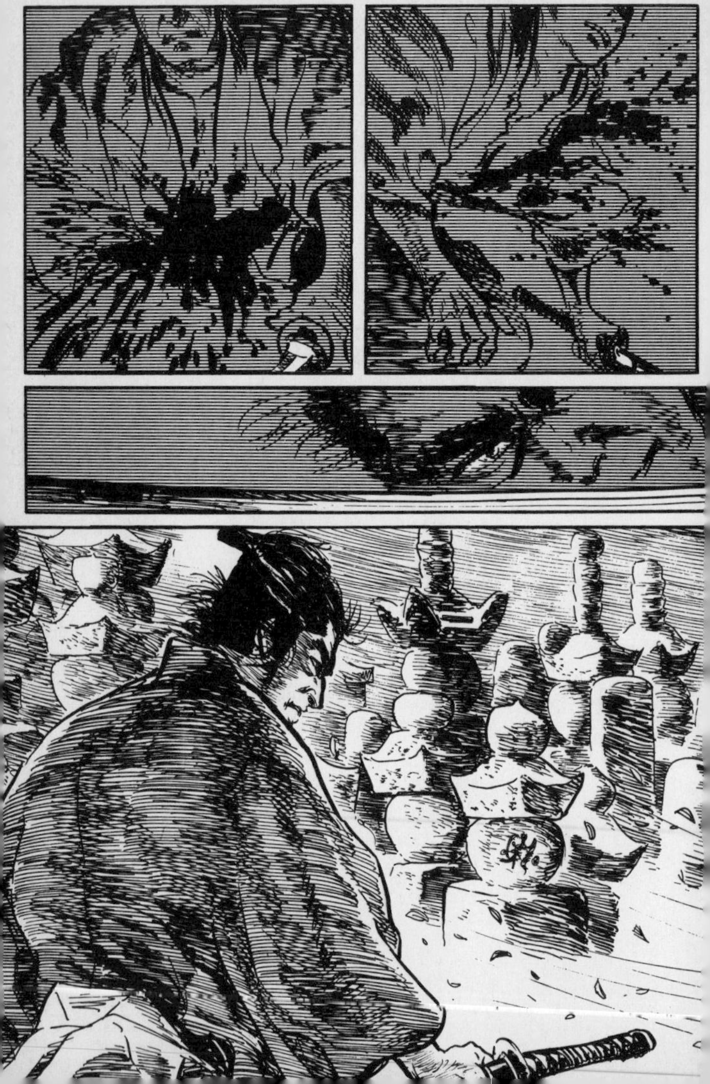

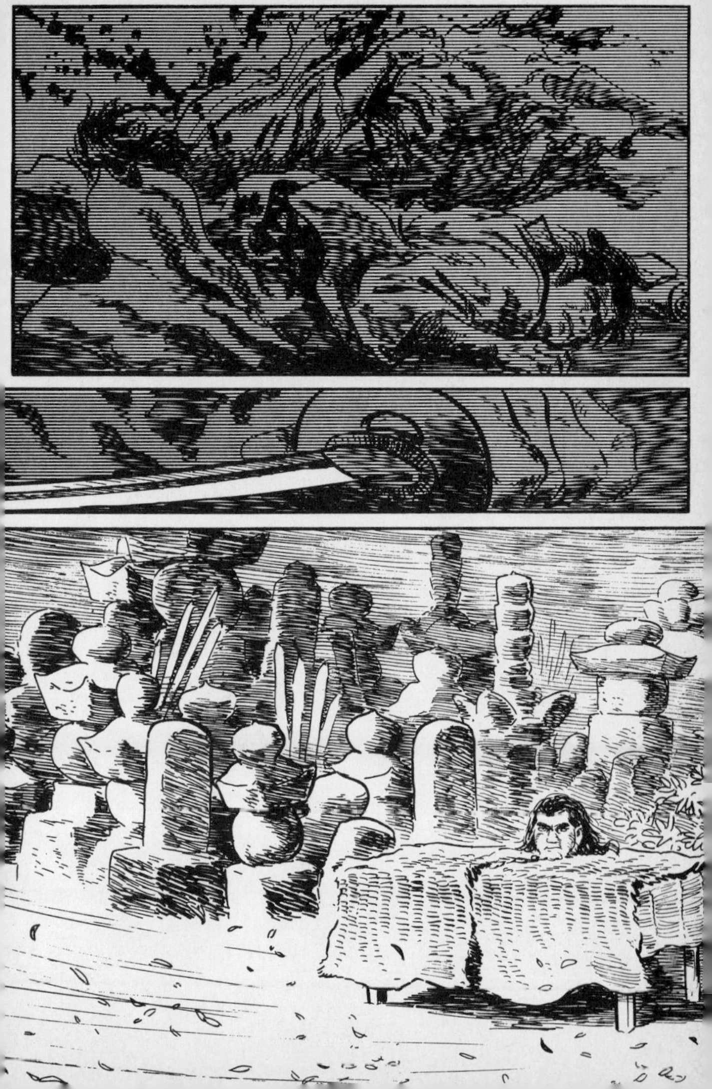

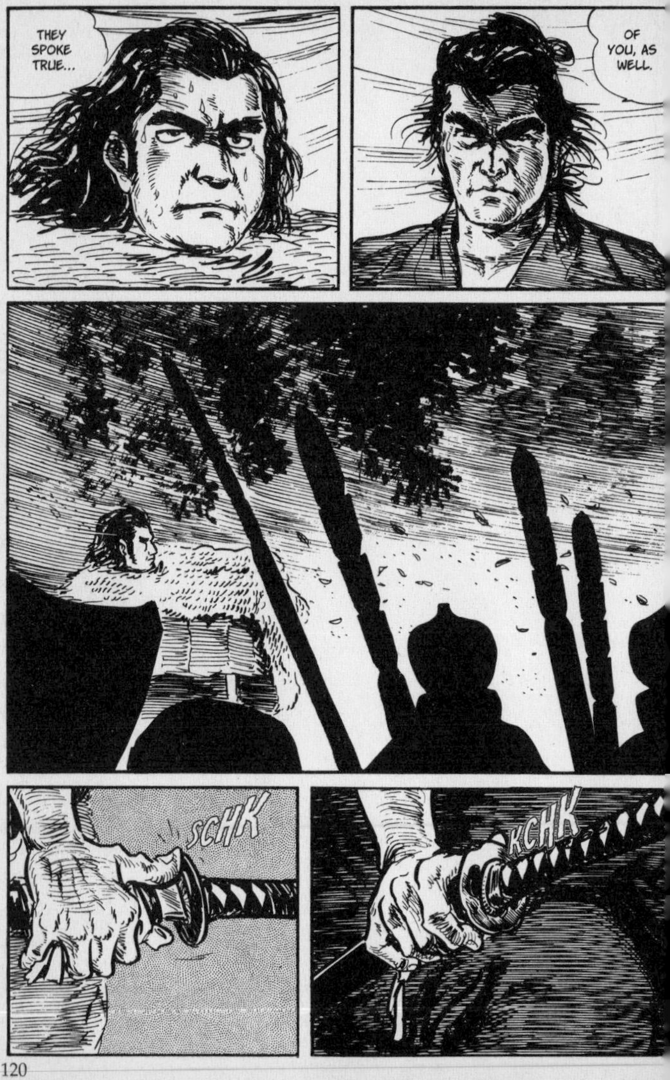
THEY SPOKE TRUE...
OF YOU, AS WELL.
SCHK
KCHK

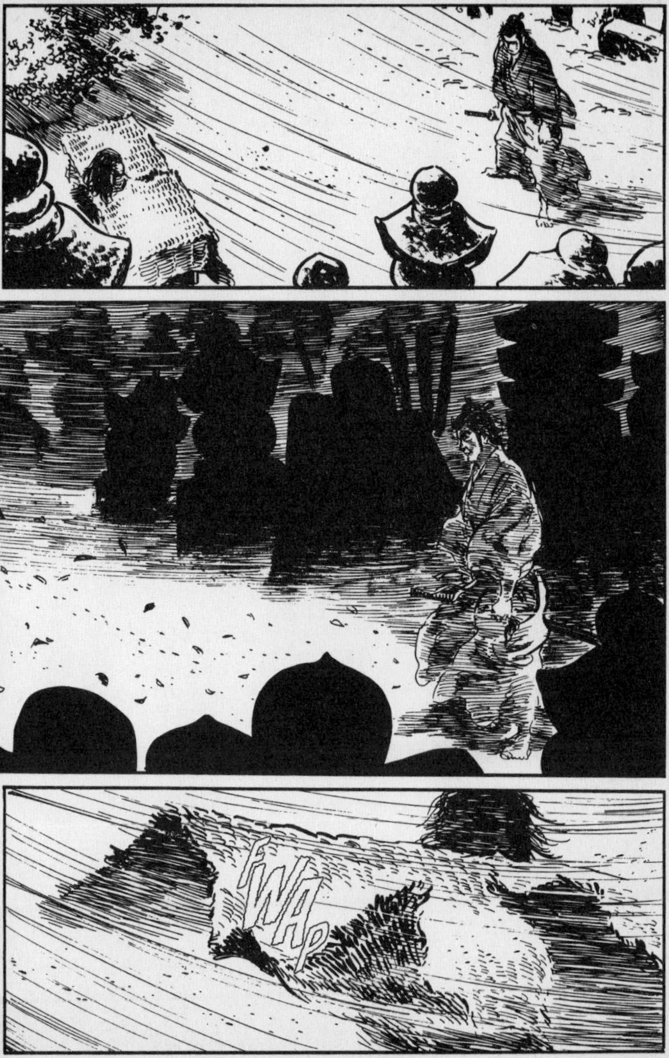
FWAP

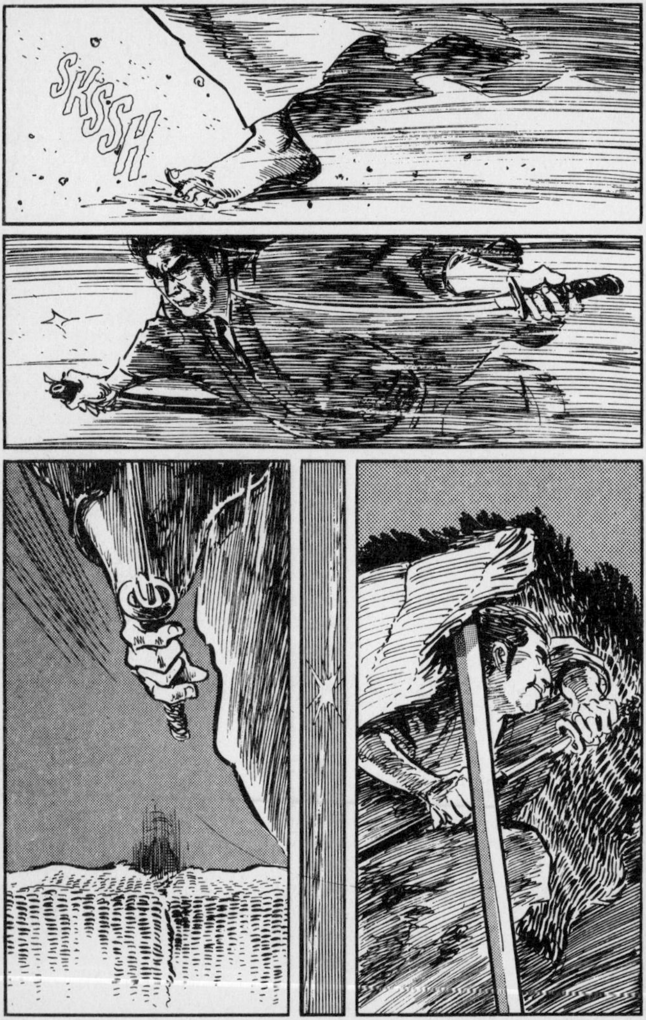
SKSSH

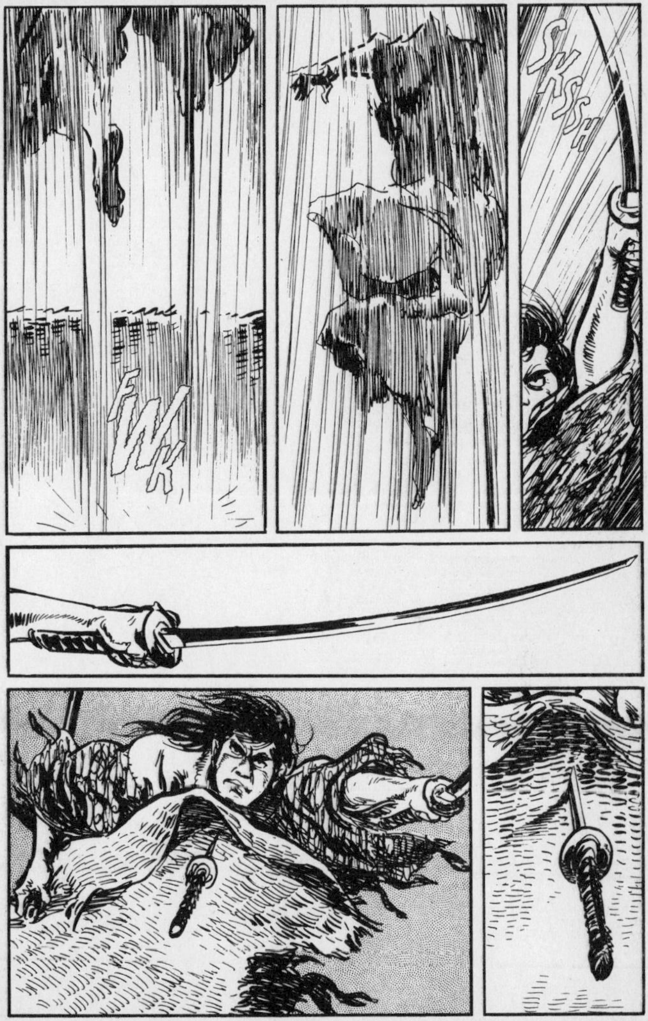
FWK
SKSSH

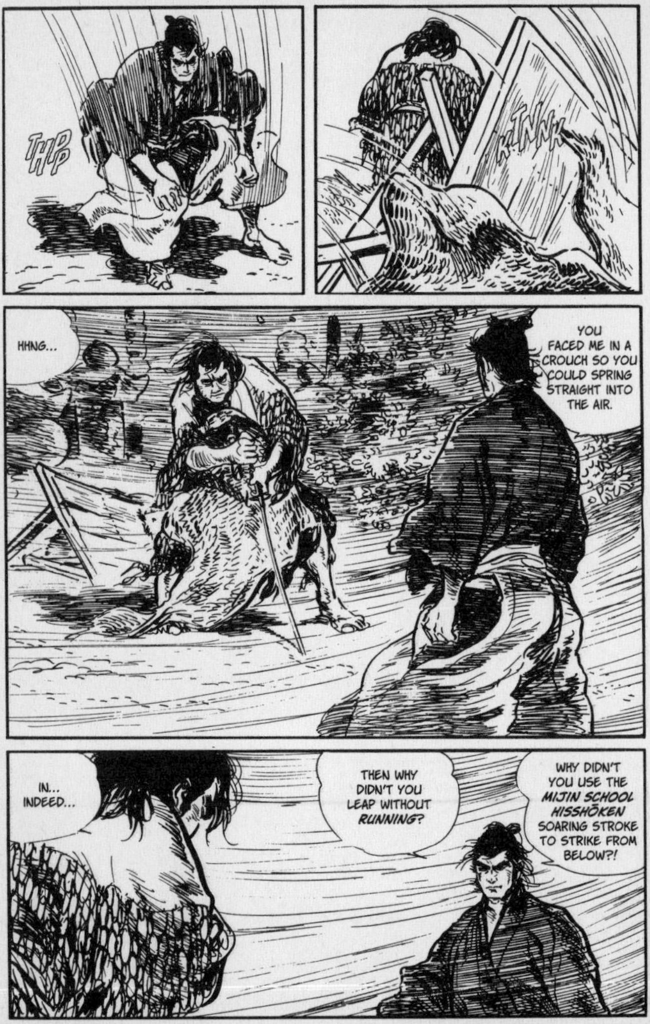
THPP
K-INNK
HHNG...
YOU FACED ME IN A CROUCH SO YOU COULD SPRING STRAIGHT INTO THE AIR.
IN... INDEED...
THEN WHY DIDN'T YOU LEAP WITHOUT *RUNNING*?
WHY DIDN'T YOU USE THE *MIJIN SCHOOL HISSHŌKEN* SOARING STROKE TO STRIKE FROM BELOW?!

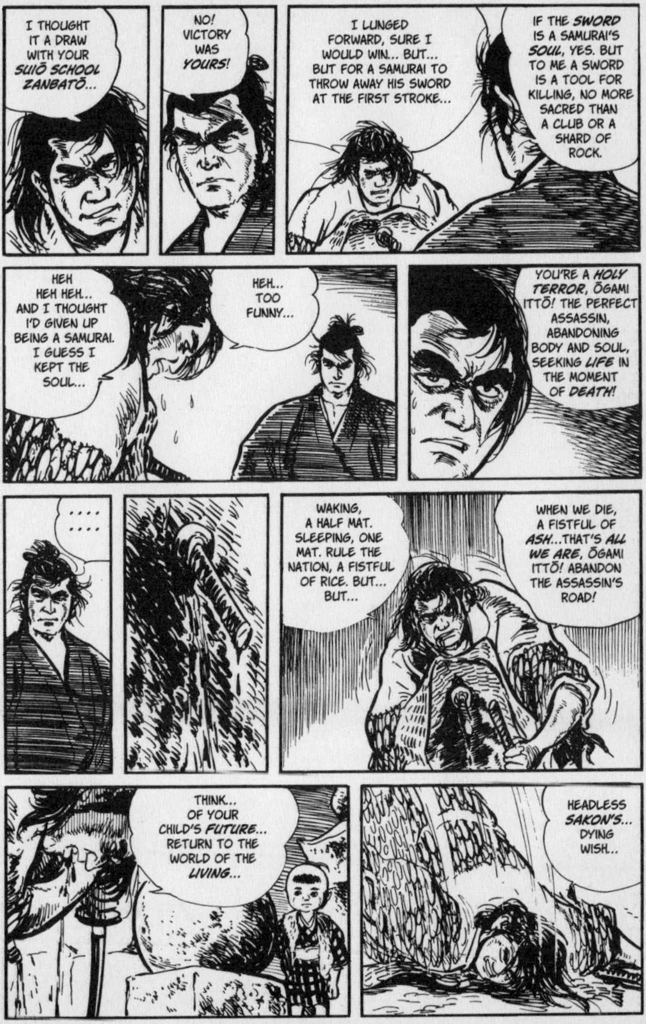

I THOUGHT IT A DRAW WITH YOUR SUIŌ SCHOOL ZANBATŌ...
NO! VICTORY WAS YOURS!
I LUNGED FORWARD, SURE I WOULD WIN... BUT... BUT FOR A SAMURAI TO THROW AWAY HIS SWORD AT THE FIRST STROKE...
IF THE SWORD IS A SAMURAI'S SOUL, YES. BUT TO ME A SWORD IS A TOOL FOR KILLING, NO MORE SACRED THAN A CLUB OR A SHARD OF ROCK.
HEH HEH HEH... AND I THOUGHT I'D GIVEN UP BEING A SAMURAI. I GUESS I KEPT THE SOUL...
HEH... TOO FUNNY...
YOU'RE A HOLY TERROR, ŌGAMI ITTŌ! THE PERFECT ASSASSIN, ABANDONING BODY AND SOUL, SEEKING LIFE IN THE MOMENT OF DEATH!
....
WAKING, A HALF MAT. SLEEPING, ONE MAT. RULE THE NATION, A FISTFUL OF RICE. BUT... BUT...
WHEN WE DIE, A FISTFUL OF ASH...THAT'S ALL WE ARE, ŌGAMI ITTŌ! ABANDON THE ASSASSIN'S ROAD!
THINK... OF YOUR CHILD'S FUTURE... RETURN TO THE WORLD OF THE LIVING...
HEADLESS SAKON'S... DYING WISH...

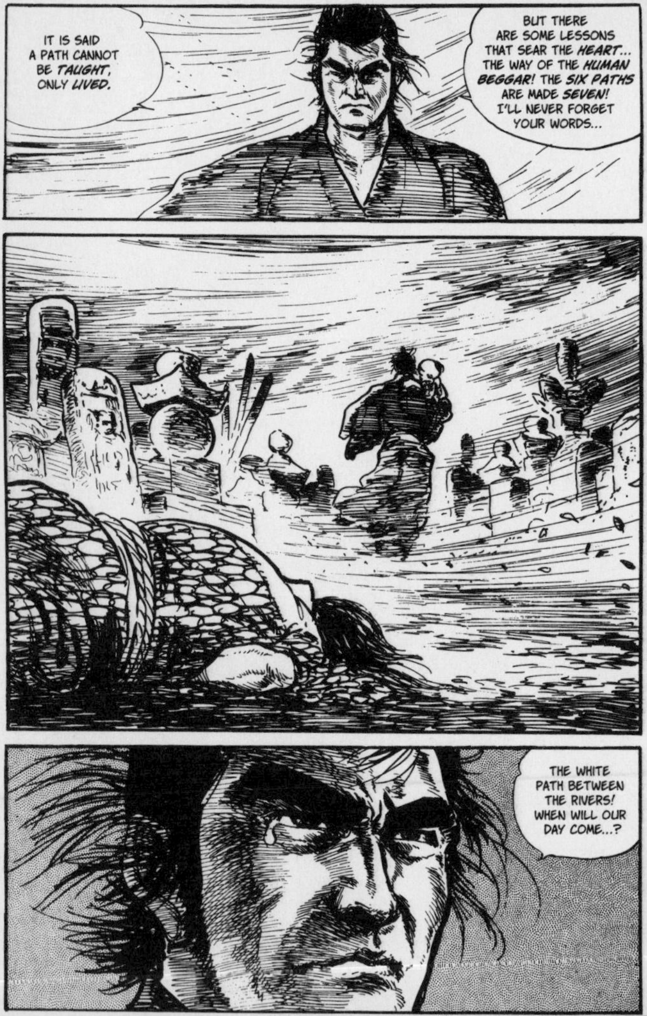
IT IS SAID A PATH CANNOT BE *TAUGHT*, ONLY *LIVED*.
BUT THERE ARE SOME LESSONS THAT SEAR THE *HEART*... THE WAY OF THE *HUMAN BEGGAR*! THE *SIX PATHS* ARE MADE *SEVEN*! I'LL NEVER FORGET YOUR WORDS...
THE WHITE PATH BETWEEN THE RIVERS! WHEN WILL OUR DAY COME...?

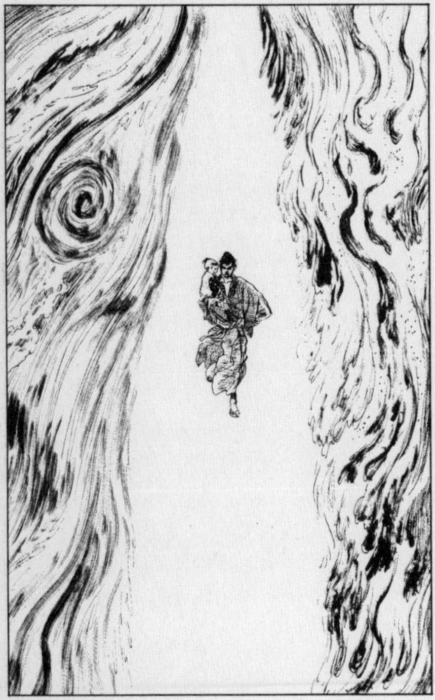

the seventeenth

The White Path Between the Rivers

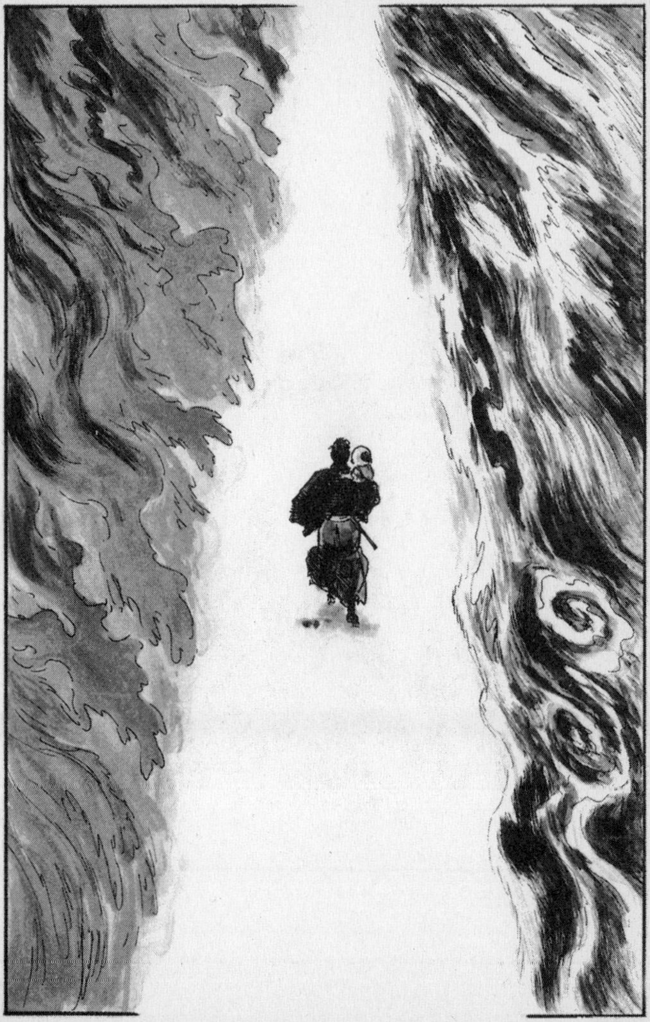

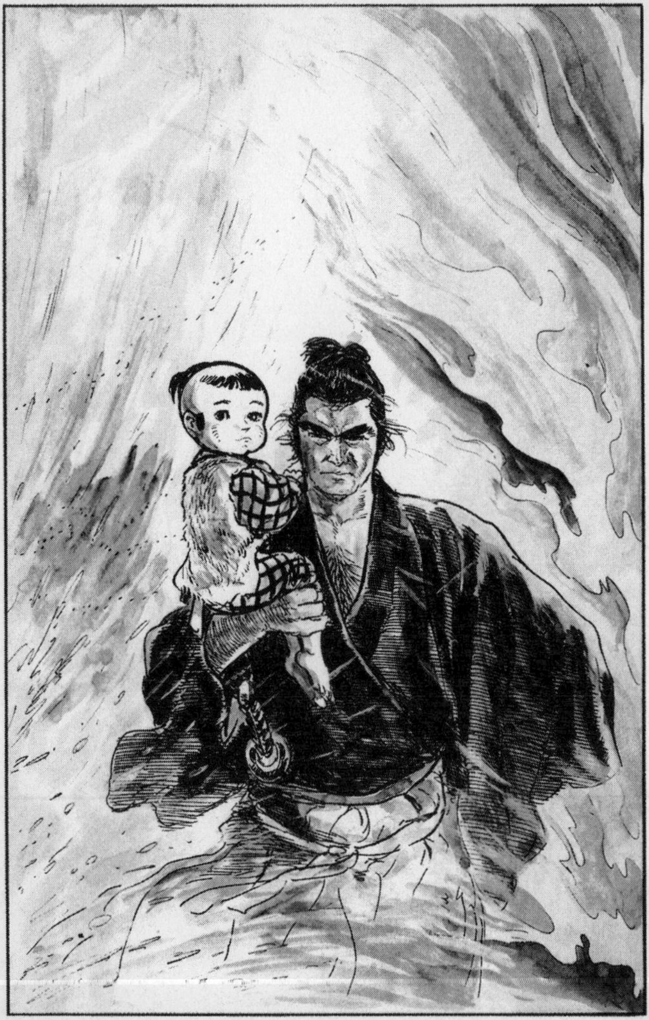

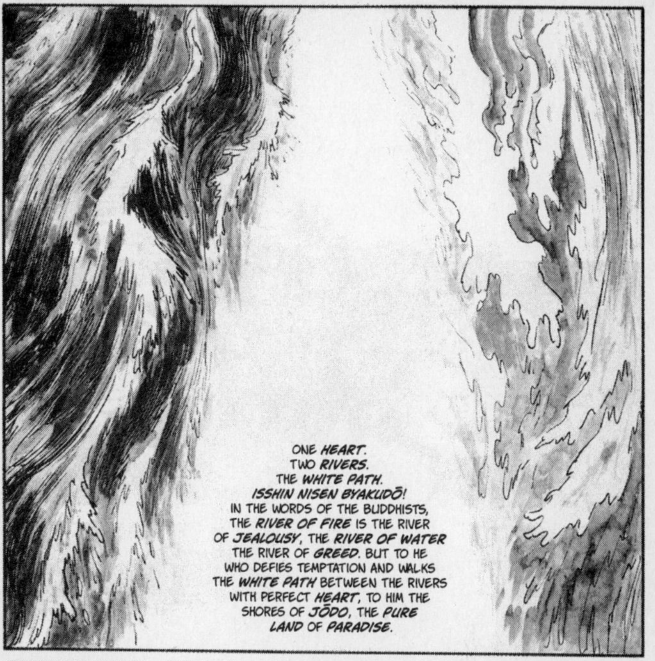
ONE HEART.
TWO RIVERS.
THE WHITE PATH.
ISSHIN NISEN BYAKUDŌ!
IN THE WORDS OF THE BUDDHISTS, THE RIVER OF FIRE IS THE RIVER OF JEALOUSY, THE RIVER OF WATER THE RIVER OF GREED. BUT TO HE WHO DEFIES TEMPTATION AND WALKS THE WHITE PATH BETWEEN THE RIVERS WITH PERFECT HEART, TO HIM THE SHORES OF JŌDO, THE PURE LAND OF PARADISE.
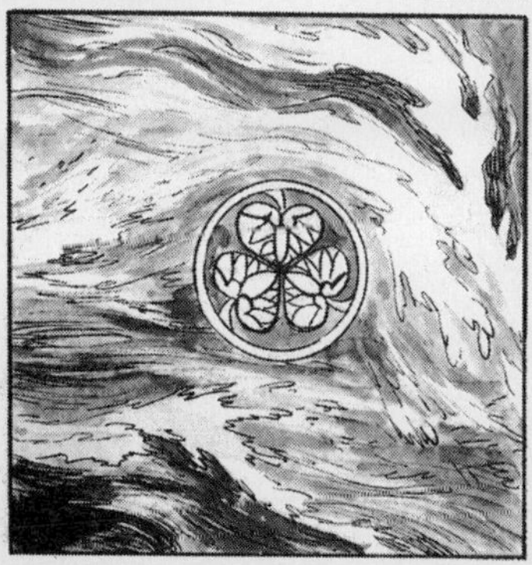
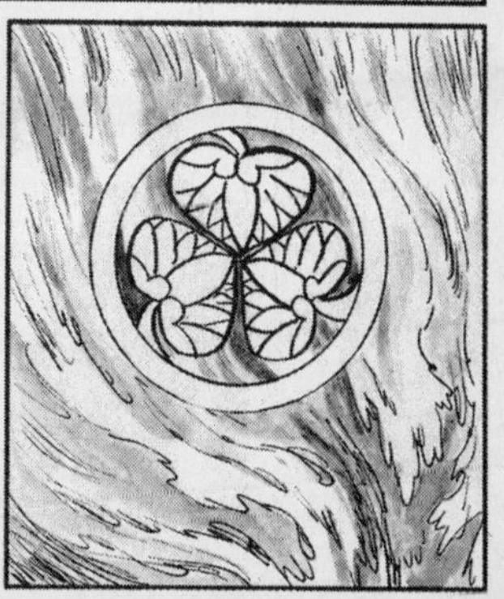

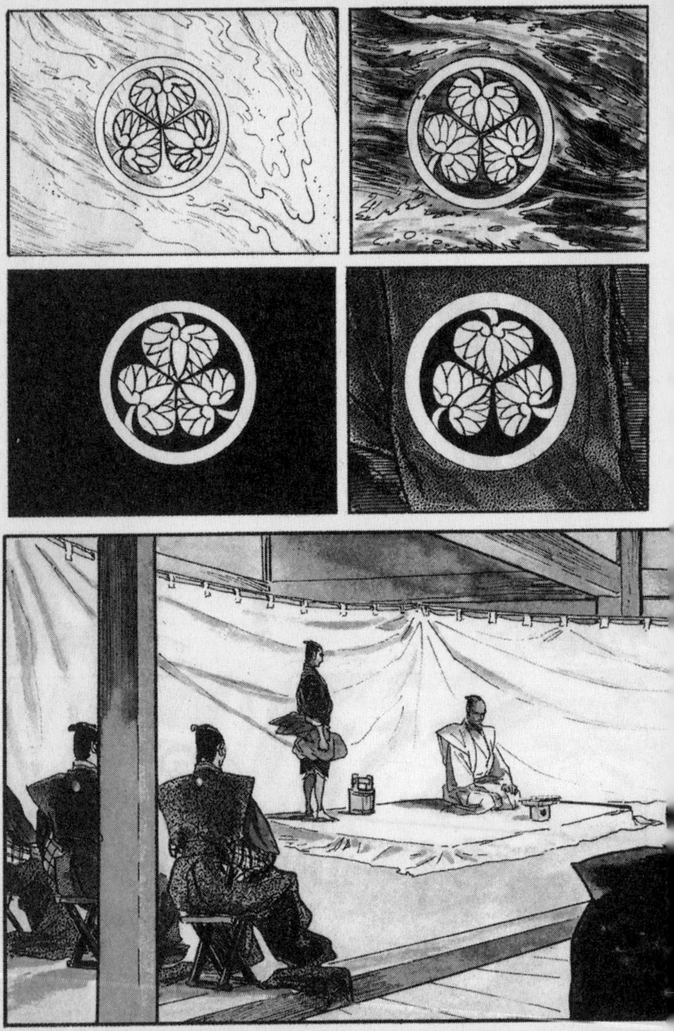

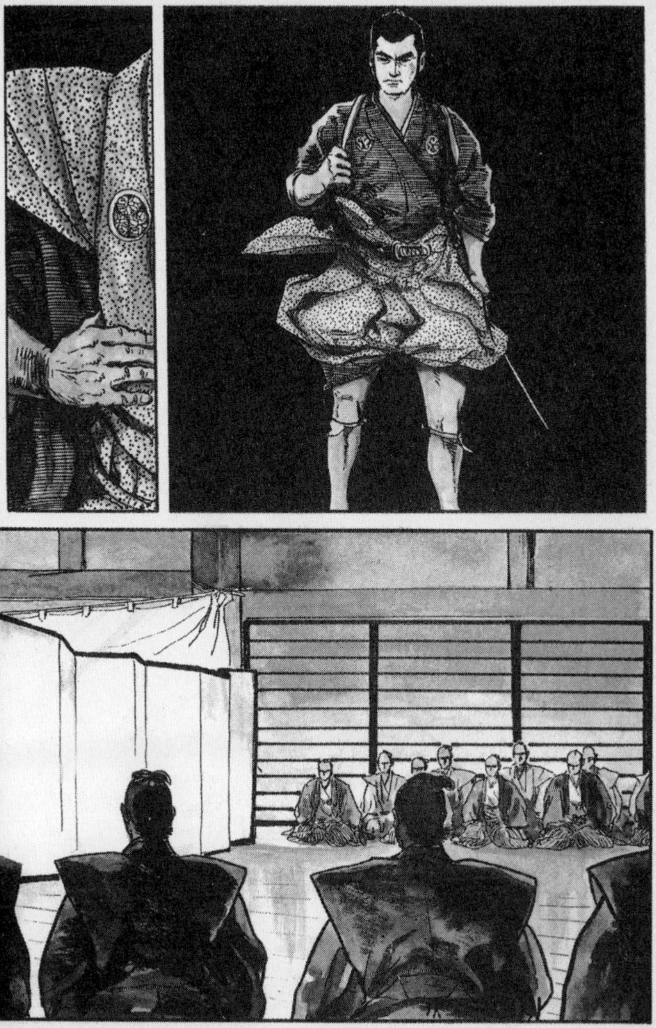

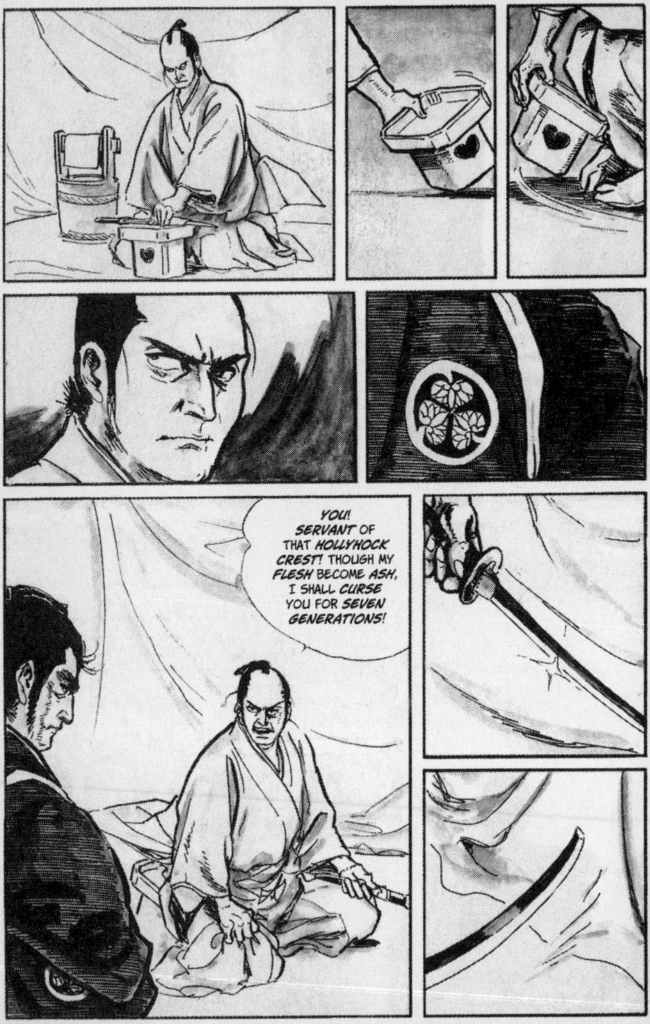
YOU! SERVANT OF THAT HOLLYHOCK CREST! THOUGH MY FLESH BECOME ASH, I SHALL CURSE YOU FOR SEVEN GENERATIONS!

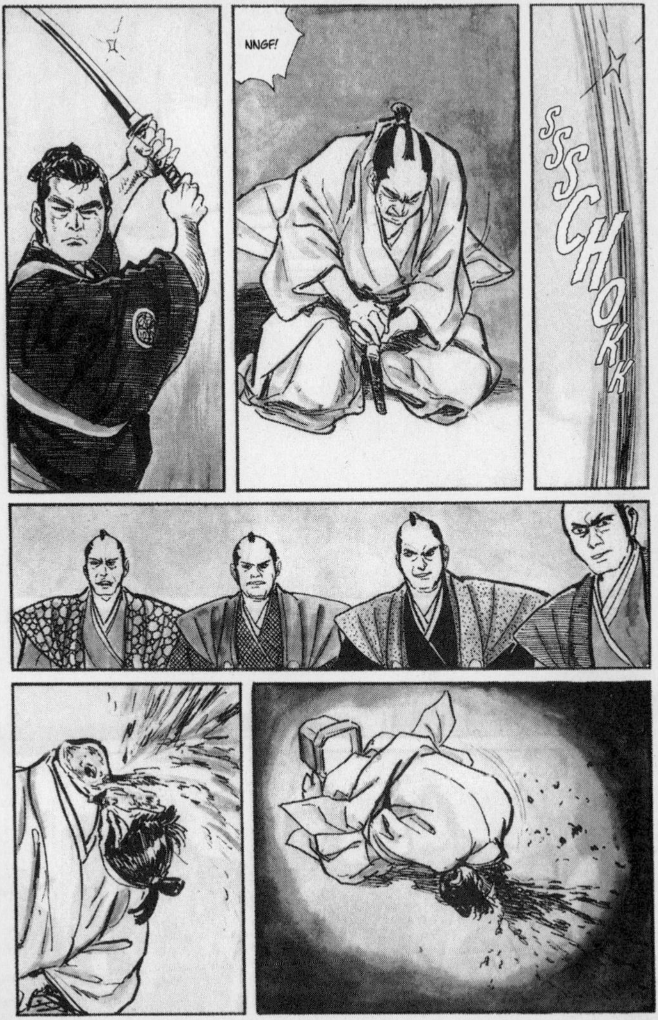
NNGF!
SSSCHOKK

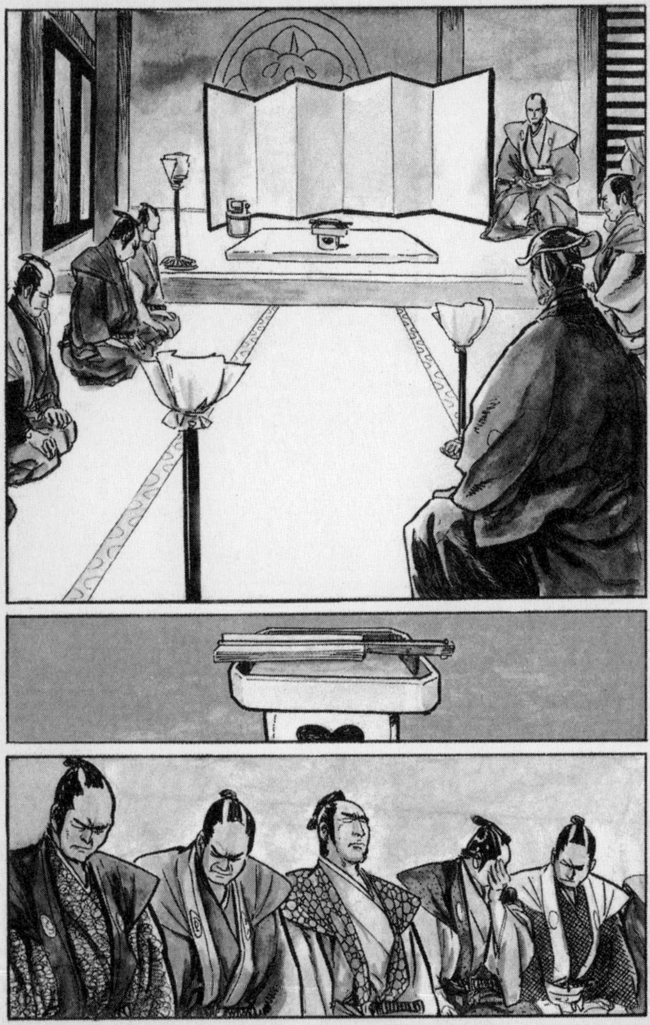

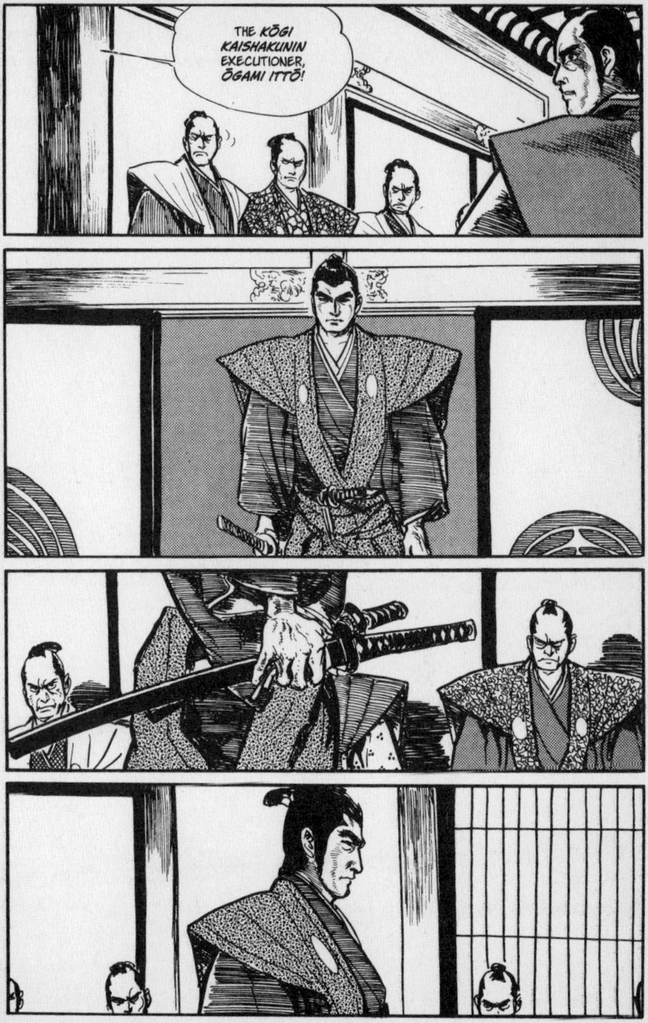
THE *KŌGI KAISHAKUNIN* EXECUTIONER, *ŌGAMI ITTŌ!*

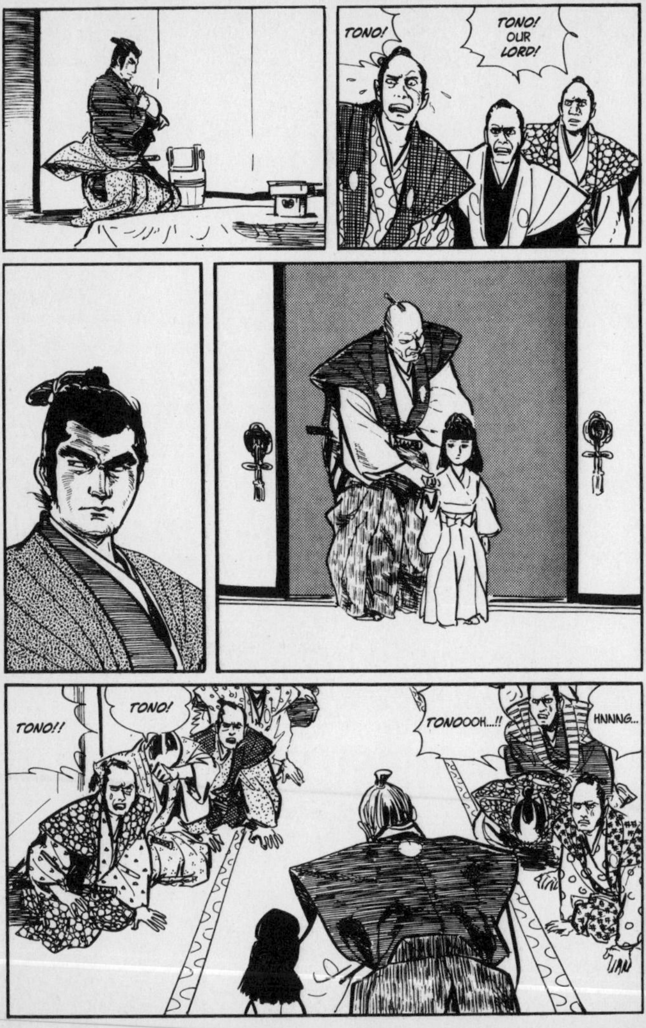
TONO!
TONO! OUR LORD!
TONO!!
TONO!
TONOOOH...!!
HNNNG...

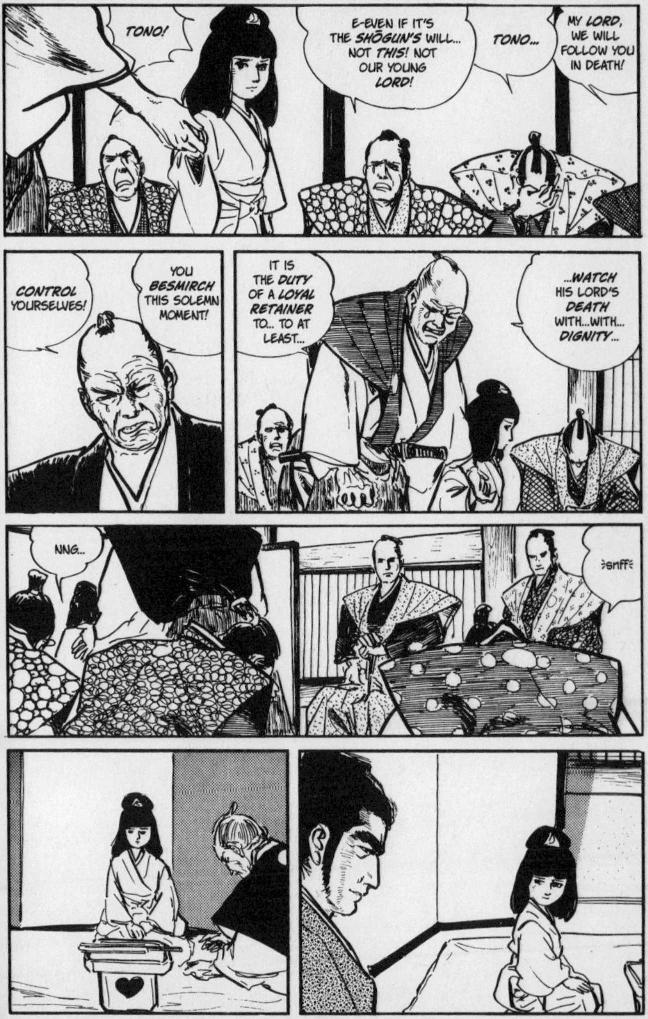
TONO!
E-EVEN IF IT'S THE SHŌGUN'S WILL... NOT THIS! NOT OUR YOUNG LORD!
TONO...
MY LORD, WE WILL FOLLOW YOU IN DEATH!
CONTROL YOURSELVES!
YOU BESMIRCH THIS SOLEMN MOMENT!
IT IS THE DUTY OF A LOYAL RETAINER TO... TO AT LEAST...
...WATCH HIS LORD'S DEATH WITH...WITH... DIGNITY...
NNG...
snff

YOU NEED ONLY TOUCH YOUR FAN TO YOUR STOMACH, MY LORD.

READY? CALM YOUR HEART...

SUCH IS A *LORD* OF COUNTRY AND CASTLE... A *SAMURAI* AMONG *SAMURAI*.

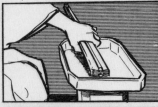

140

FSSST
SKSSH
MY LORD!
AHHHG!
TONO...!!

FOR CENTURIES, THE *TOKUGAWA SHŌGUNATE* CONTROLLED THE *DAIMYŌ* LORDS OF JAPAN'S UNRULY *HAN* WITH AN IRON FIST. THE SLIGHTEST SIGN OF DEFIANCE COULD COST A *DAIMYŌ* HIS TITLE AND HIS LANDS; HIS FAMILY NAME COULD BE ABOLISHED, AND THE LORD HIMSELF BROUGHT TO *EDO CASTLE* FOR DEATH BY *SEPPUKU*. IN TIME, THREE SPECIAL AGENCIES AROSE TO ENFORCE THIS REIGN OF TERROR. FIRST, THE NINJA SPY NETWORK KNOWN AS THE ***O-NIWABAN***, OR GARDEN WARDENS, DEDICATED TO UNCOVERING EVIDENCE FOR BLACKMAILING AND DESTROYING TROUBLESOME *HAN*. SECOND, THE SHŌGUN'S SECRET ***ASSASSINS***, CHARGED WITH KILLING ANY *HAN* OFFICIAL WHO OBSTRUCTED THE SHŌGUNATE'S WILL. AND LAST, THE ***KŌGI KAISHAKUNIN***, THE DESIGNATED SECOND AND FINAL EXECUTIONER AT A *DAIMYŌ'S SEPPUKU* DEATH.

UNDER THE UNCOMPROMISING CODE OF ***BUSHIDŌ***, THE WAY OF THE WARRIOR, IT WAS UNTHINKABLE FOR A *DAIMYŌ'S* RETAINER TO TURN HIS SWORD UPON HIS MASTER, EVEN TO END THE AGONY OF *SEPPUKU*. AND THUS THE SHŌGUN APPOINTED HIS OWN CHOSEN ***KŌGI KAISHAKUNIN*** TO PERFORM THE FINAL CUT FOR A DISHONORED LORD. THIS EXECUTIONER WAS ALLOWED TO BEAR THE HOLLYHOCK CREST OF THE ***TOKUGAWA CLAN*** ITSELF ON HIS ROBES OF OFFICE. SYMBOLICALLY, IT WAS THE SHŌGUN HIMSELF, AND NO OTHER, WHO CUT OFF THE HEADS OF THE *DAIMYŌ*.

ŌGAMI ITTŌ WAS THIS CHOSEN MAN, THE ***KŌGI KAISHAKUNIN***, SELECTED BY THE SHŌGUN HIMSELF TO SERVE AS HIS EXECUTIONER IN THE HOLLYHOCK ROBES OF THE TOKUGAWA CLAN.

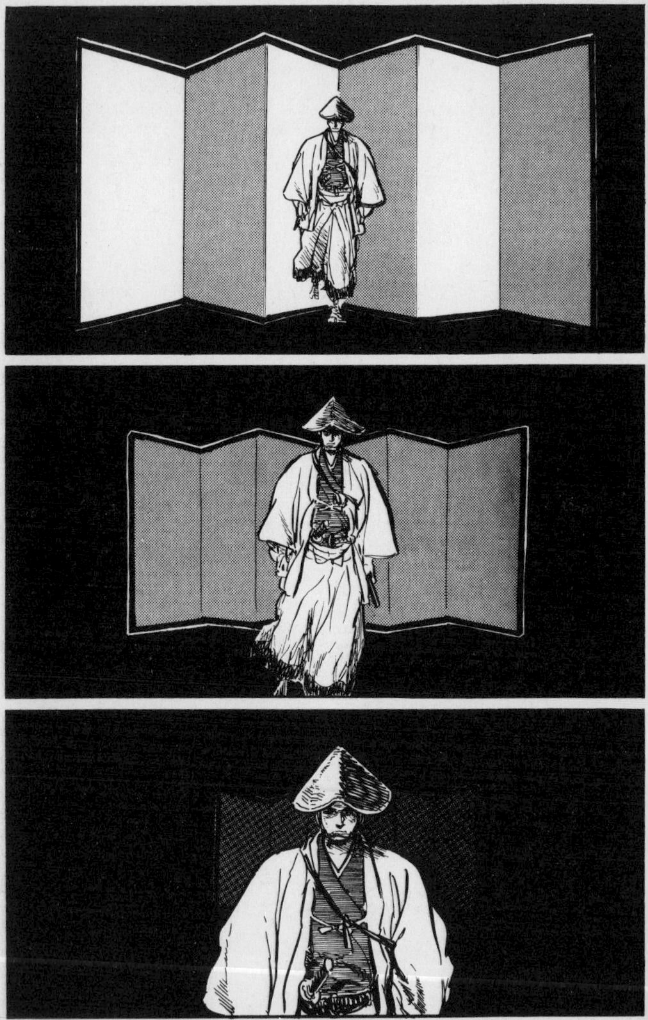

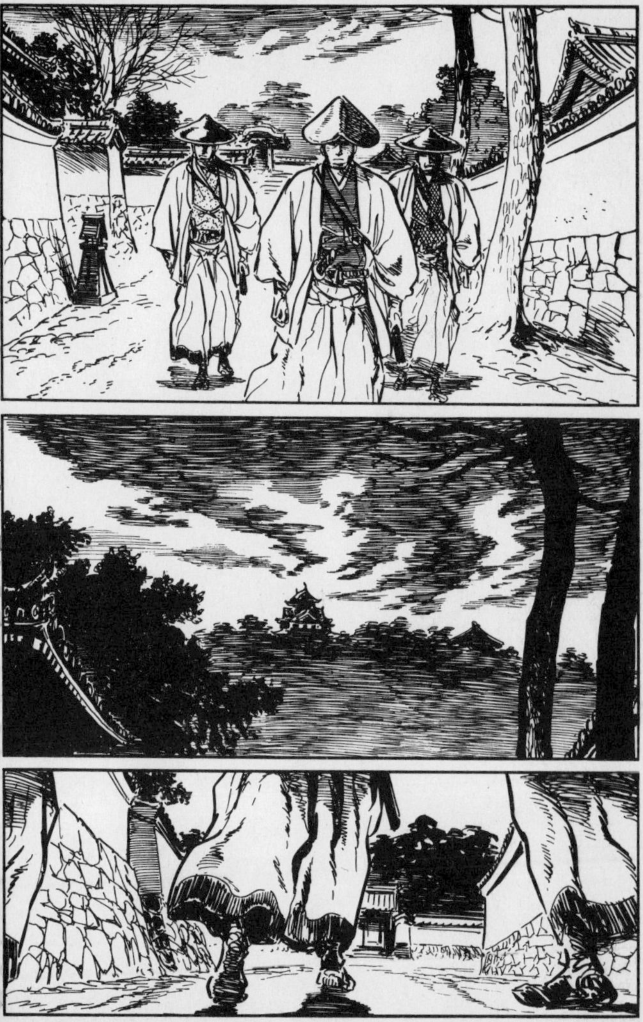

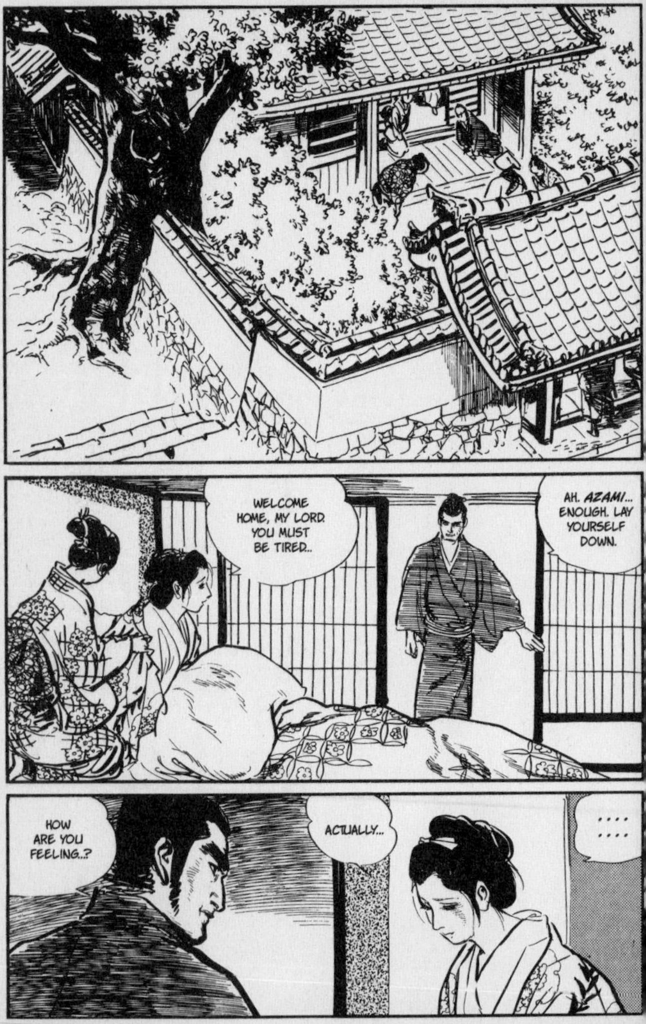
WELCOME HOME, MY LORD. YOU MUST BE TIRED...
AH. AZAMI... ENOUGH. LAY YOURSELF DOWN.
HOW ARE YOU FEELING..?
ACTUALLY...
....
....

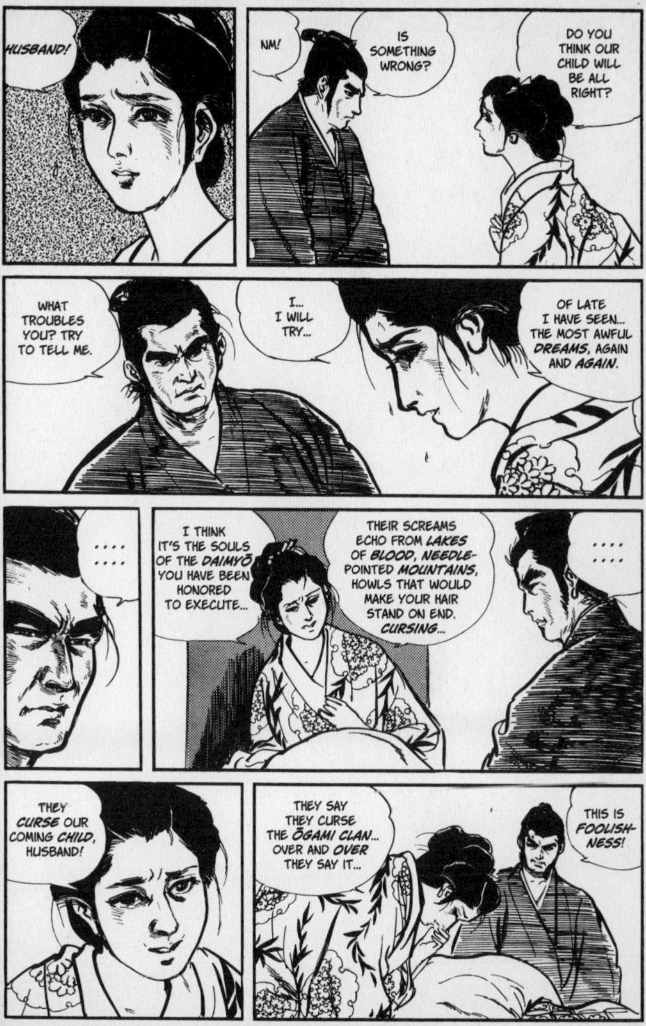
HUSBAND!
NM!
IS SOMETHING WRONG?
DO YOU THINK OUR CHILD WILL BE ALL RIGHT?
WHAT TROUBLES YOU? TRY TO TELL ME.
I... I WILL TRY...
OF LATE I HAVE SEEN... THE MOST AWFUL DREAMS, AGAIN AND AGAIN.
....
I THINK IT'S THE SOULS OF THE DAIMYŌ YOU HAVE BEEN HONORED TO EXECUTE...
THEIR SCREAMS ECHO FROM LAKES OF BLOOD, NEEDLE-POINTED MOUNTAINS, HOWLS THAT WOULD MAKE YOUR HAIR STAND ON END. CURSING...
....
THEY CURSE OUR COMING CHILD, HUSBAND!
THEY SAY THEY CURSE THE ŌGAMI CLAN... OVER AND OVER THEY SAY IT...
THIS IS FOOLISHNESS!

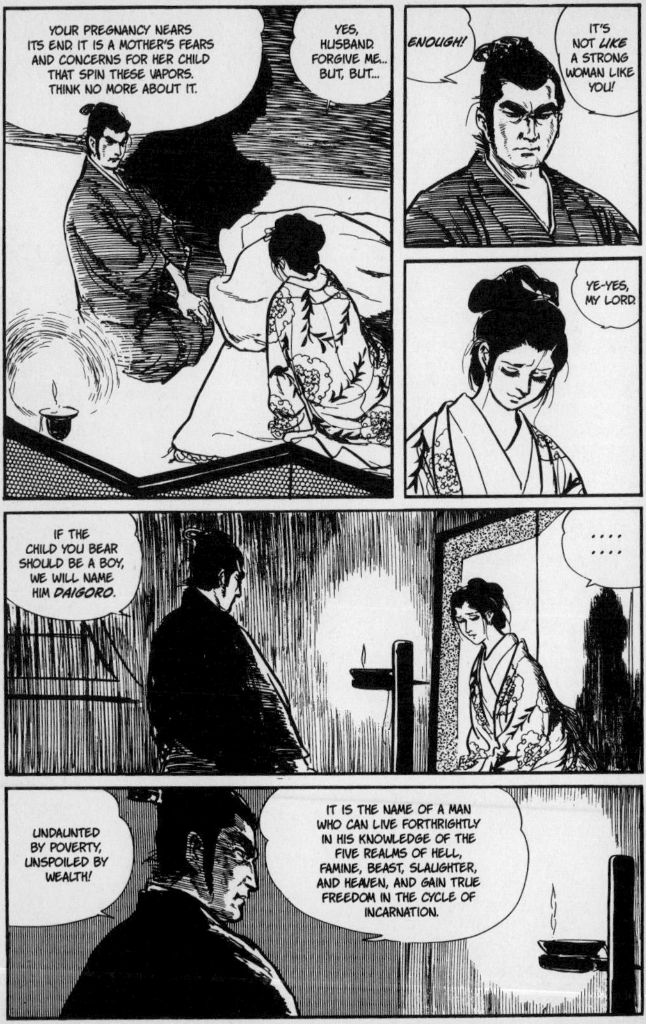
YOUR PREGNANCY NEARS ITS END. IT IS A MOTHER'S FEARS AND CONCERNS FOR HER CHILD THAT SPIN THESE VAPORS. THINK NO MORE ABOUT IT.
YES, HUSBAND. FORGIVE ME... BUT, BUT...
IT'S NOT *LIKE* A STRONG WOMAN LIKE YOU!
ENOUGH!
YE-YES, MY LORD.
IF THE CHILD YOU BEAR SHOULD BE A BOY, WE WILL NAME HIM *DAIGORO*.
....
....
UNDAUNTED BY POVERTY, UNSPOILED BY WEALTH!
IT IS THE NAME OF A MAN WHO CAN LIVE FORTHRIGHTLY IN HIS KNOWLEDGE OF THE FIVE REALMS OF HELL, FAMINE, BEAST, SLAUGHTER, AND HEAVEN, AND GAIN TRUE FREEDOM IN THE CYCLE OF INCARNATION.

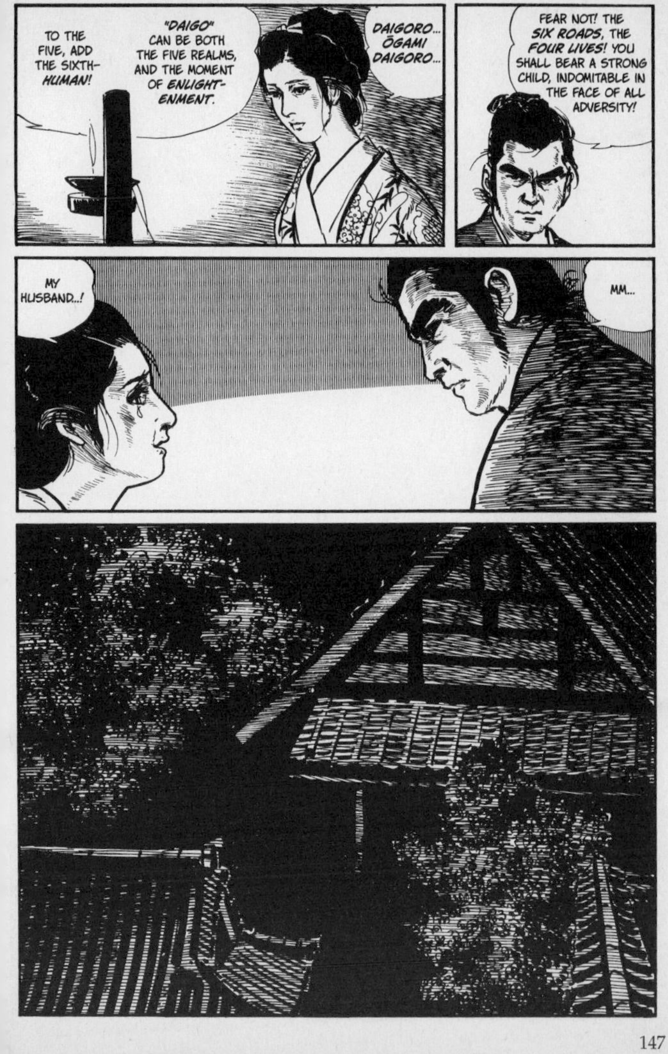
TO THE FIVE, ADD THE SIXTH—*HUMAN!*
"*DAIGO*" CAN BE BOTH THE FIVE REALMS, AND THE MOMENT OF *ENLIGHTENMENT*.
DAIGORO... ŌGAMI DAIGORO...
FEAR NOT! THE *SIX ROADS*, THE *FOUR LIVES!* YOU SHALL BEAR A STRONG CHILD, INDOMITABLE IN THE FACE OF ALL ADVERSITY!
MY HUSBAND...!
MM...

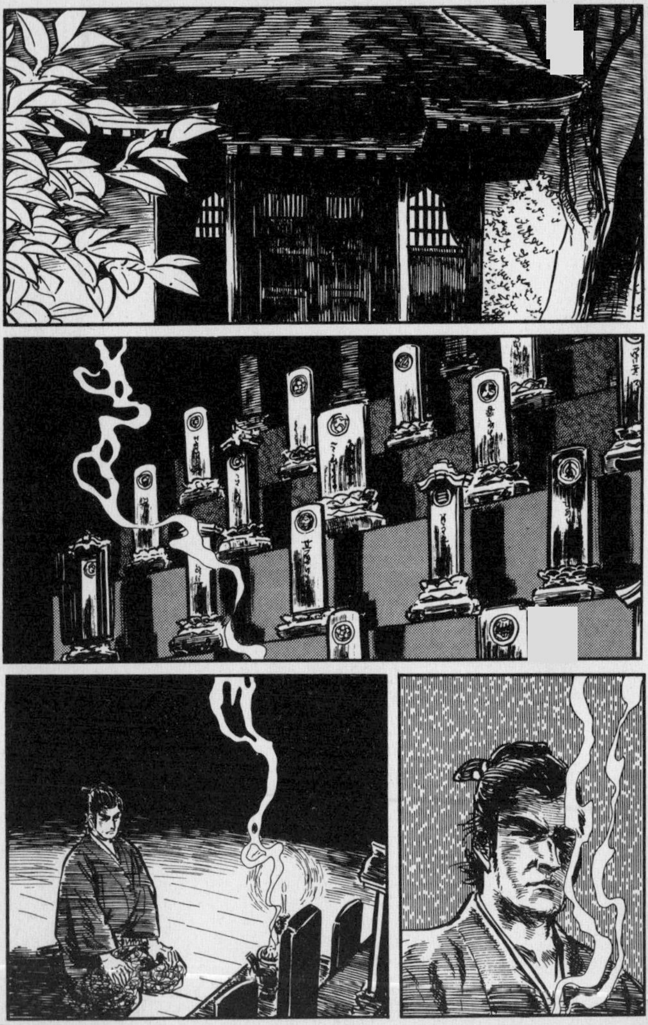

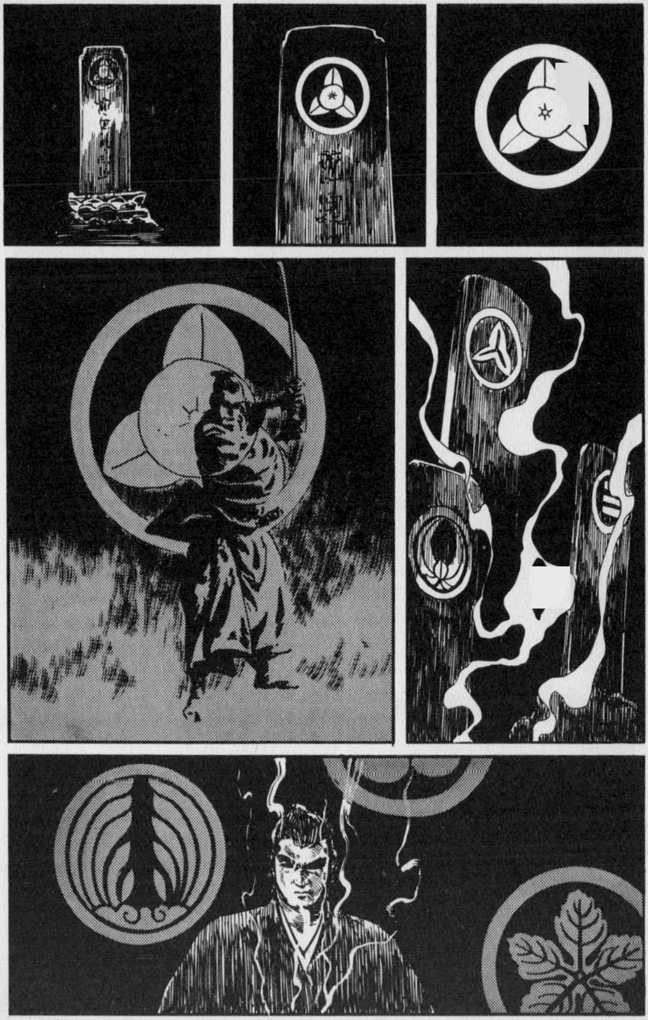

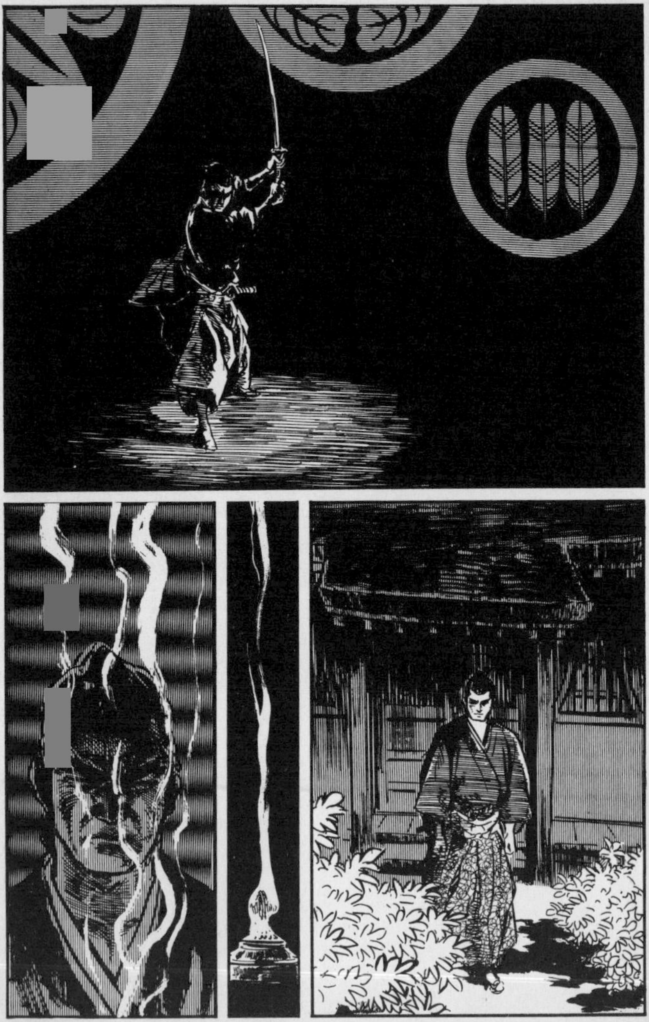

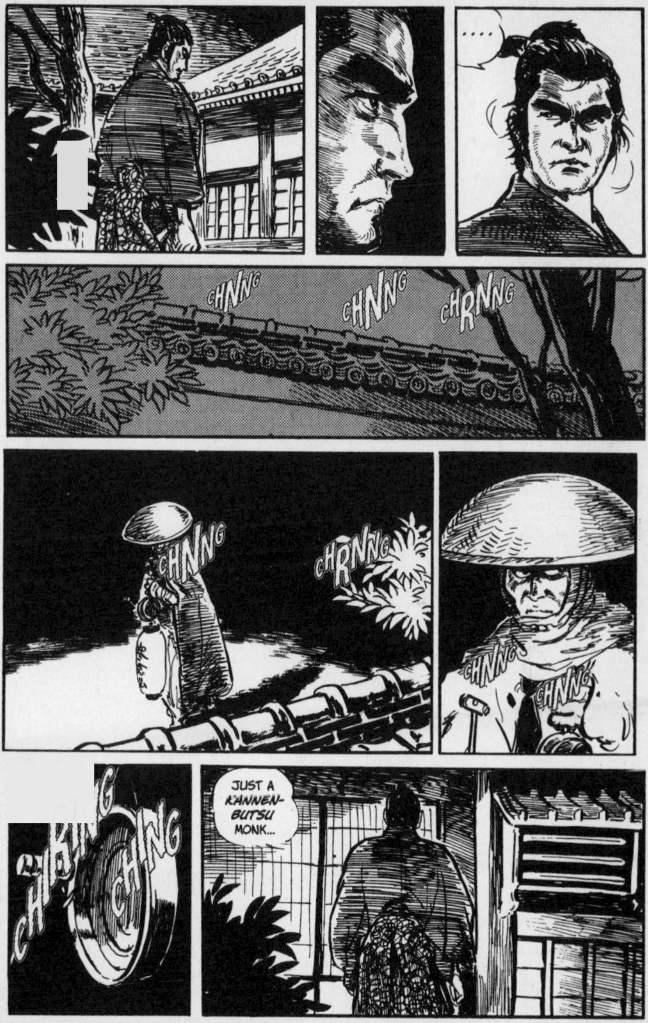
....
CHNNG
CHNNG
CHRNNG
CHNNG
CHRNNG
CHNNG
CHNNG
CHING
JUST A KANNEN-BUTSU MONK...

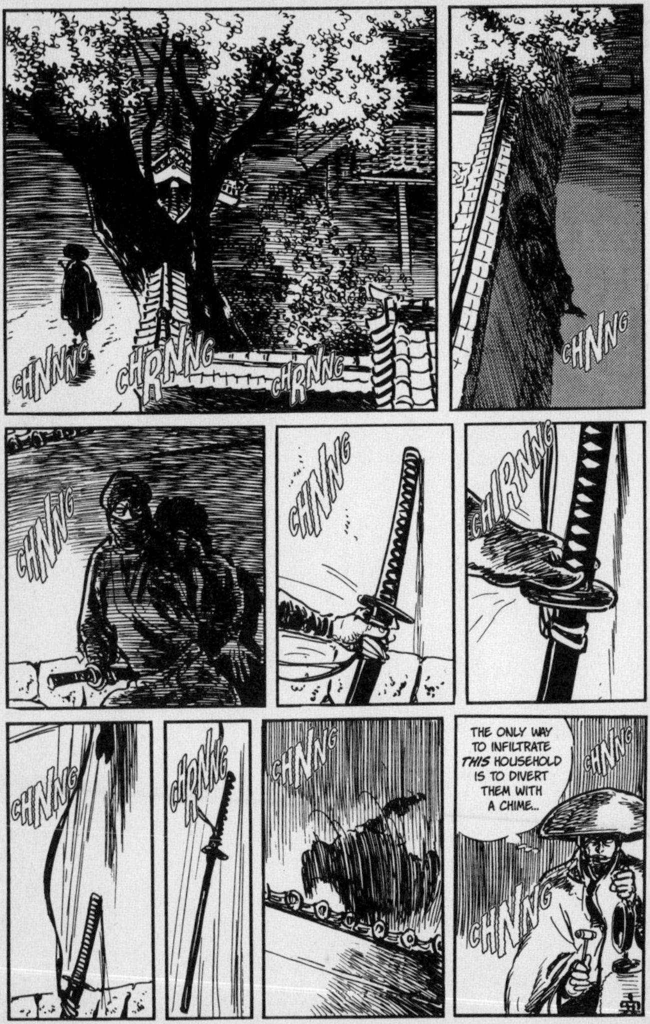
CHNNNG
CHRNNG
CHRNNG
CHNNG
CHNNG
CHNNG
CHIRNNG
CHNNG
CHRNNG
CHNNG
THE ONLY WAY TO INFILTRATE *THIS* HOUSEHOLD IS TO DIVERT THEM WITH A CHIME...
CHNNG
CHNNG

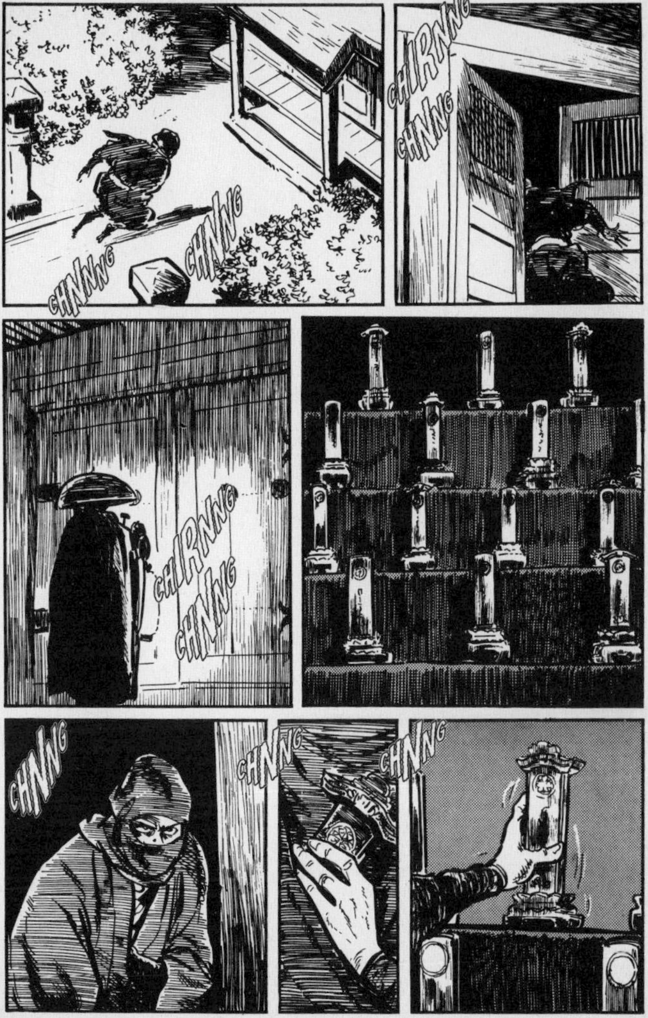
CHNNNG
CHNNG
CHIRNNG
CHNNG
CHIRNNG
CHNNG
CHNNG
CHNNG
CHNNG

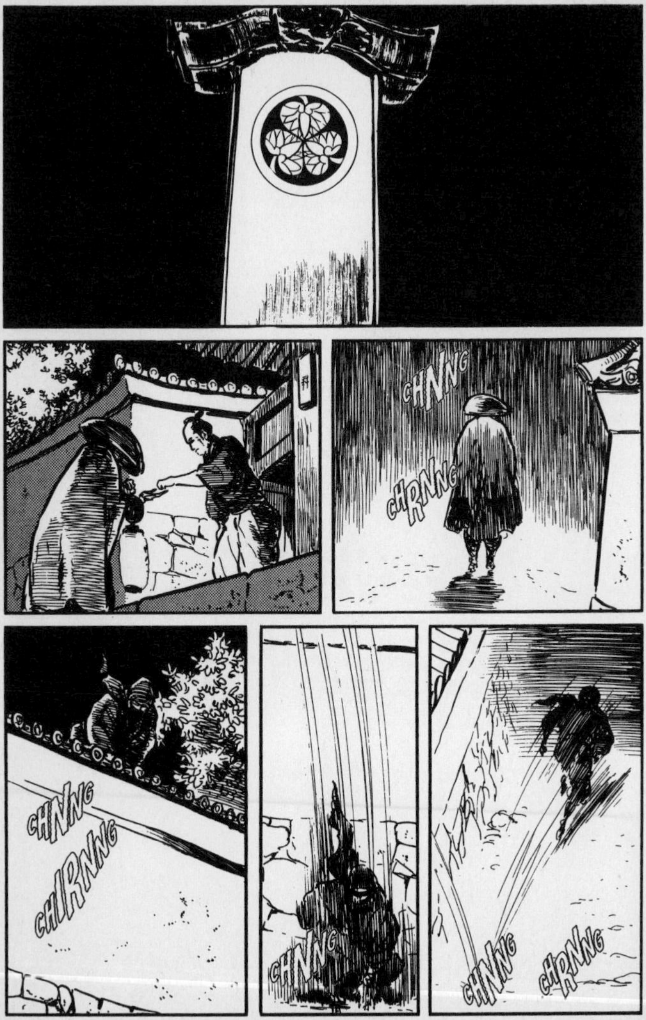

CHNNG
CHRNNG
CHNNG
CHIRNNG
CHNNG
CHNNG
CHRNNG

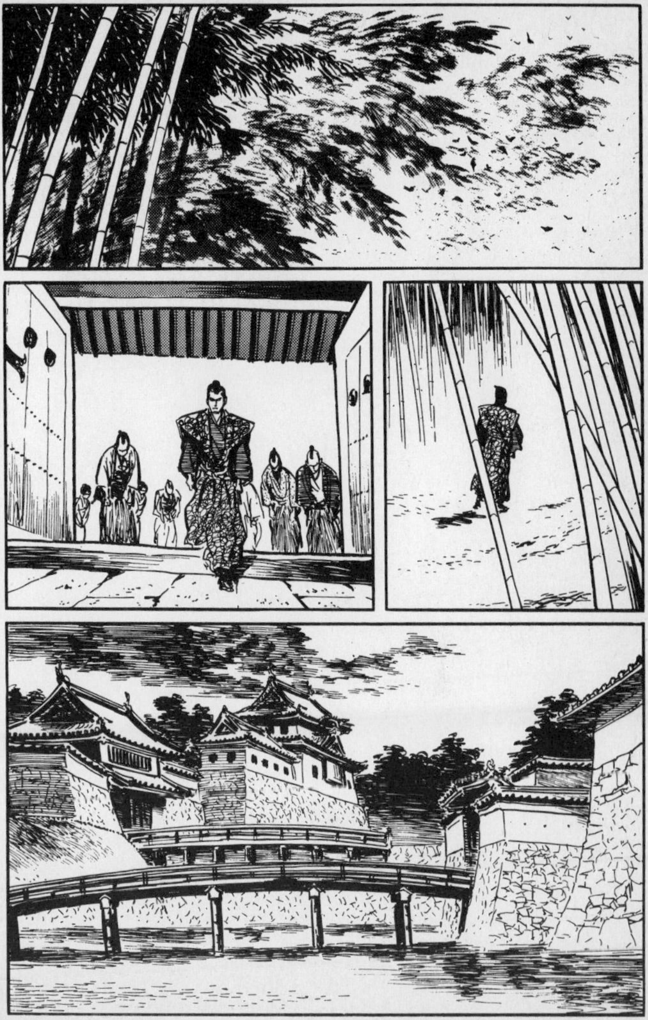

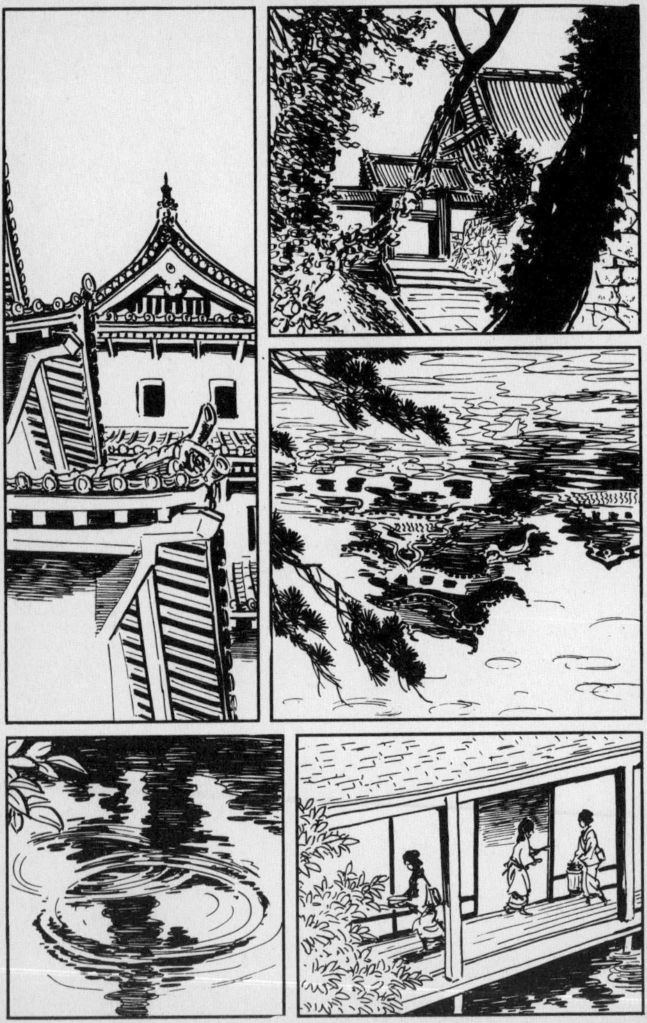

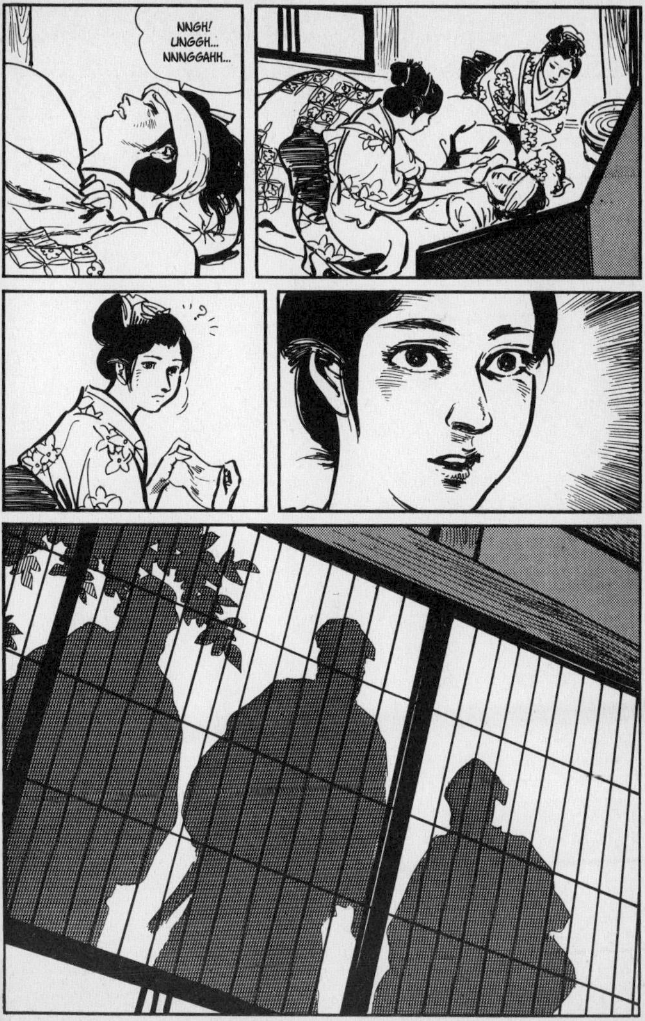
NNGH!
UNGGH...
NNNGGAHH...
?

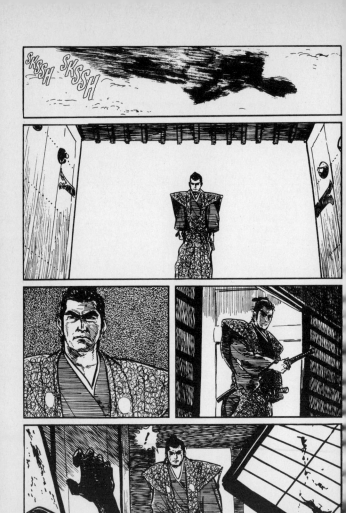

SKSSH SKSSH

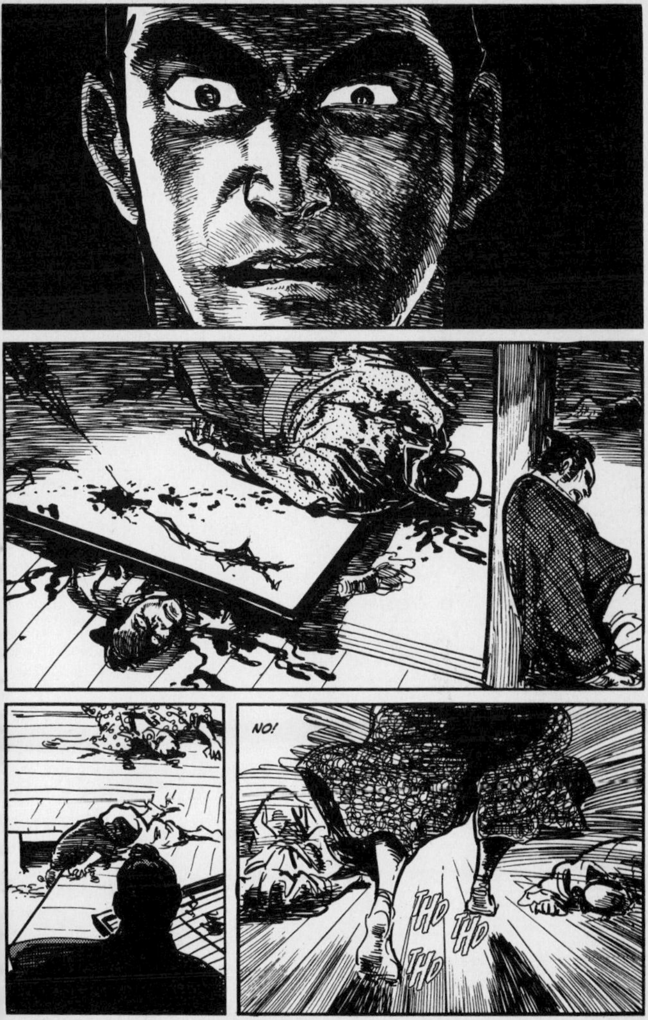
NO!
THD
THD
THD

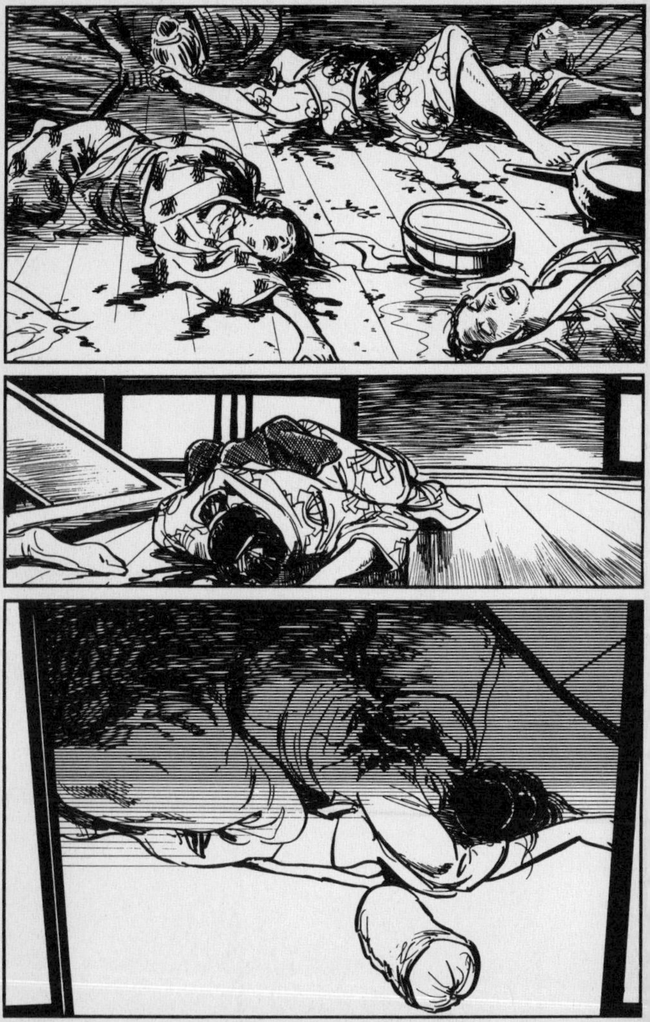

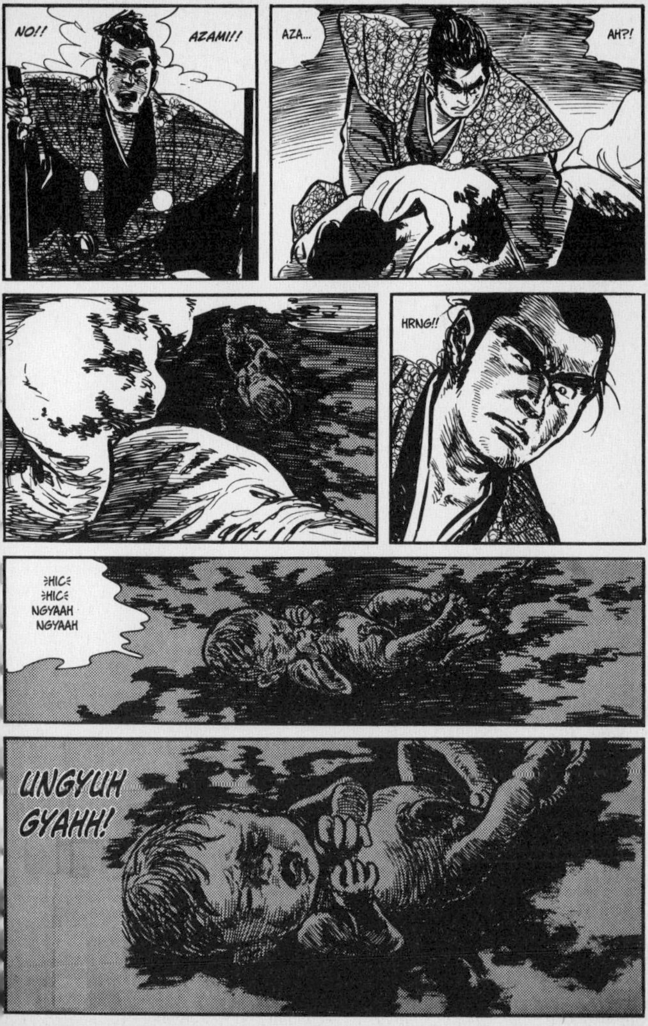
NO!!
AZAMI!!
AZA...
AH?!
HRNG!!
HIC
HIC
NGYAAH
NGYAAH
UNGYUH
GYAHH!

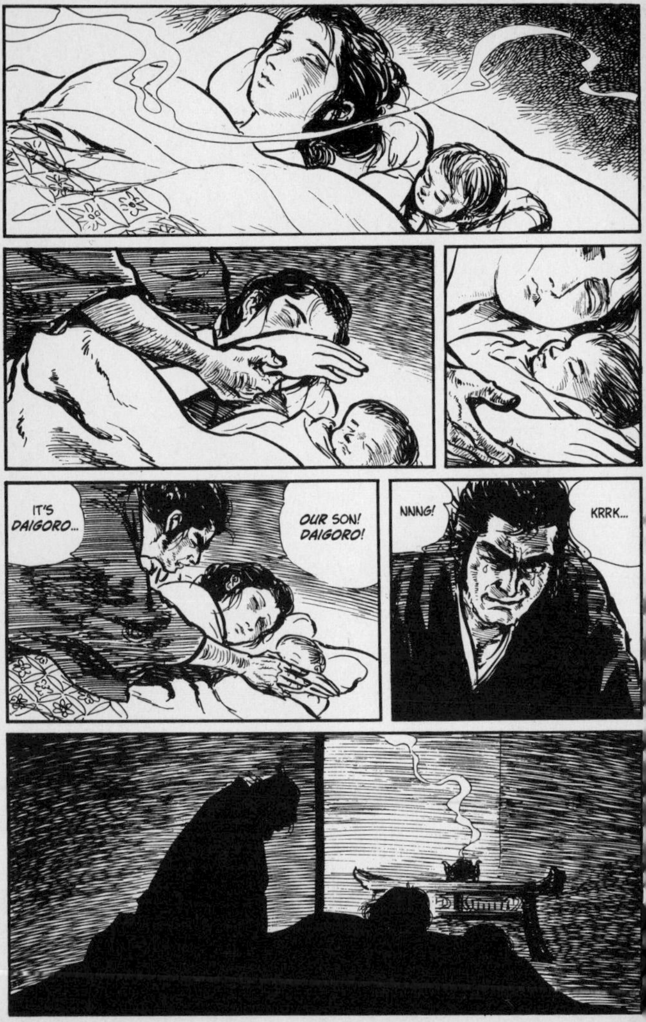
IT'S DAIGORO...
OUR SON! DAIGORO!
NNNG!
KRRK...

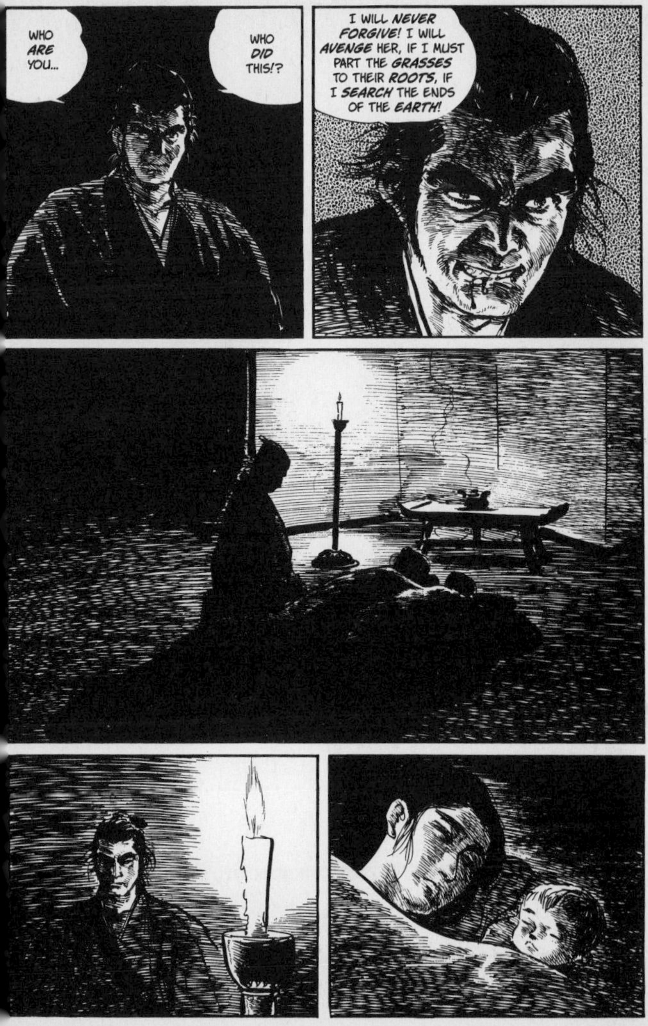
WHO *ARE* YOU...
WHO *DID* THIS!?
I WILL *NEVER FORGIVE*! I WILL *AVENGE* HER, IF I MUST PART THE *GRASSES* TO THEIR *ROOTS*, IF I *SEARCH* THE ENDS OF THE *EARTH*!

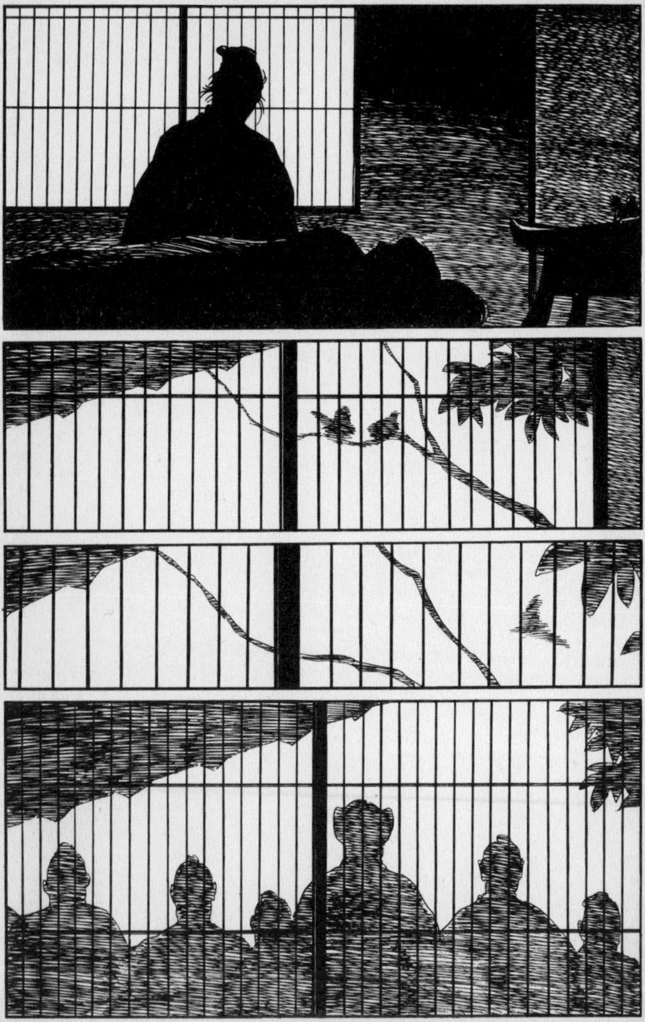

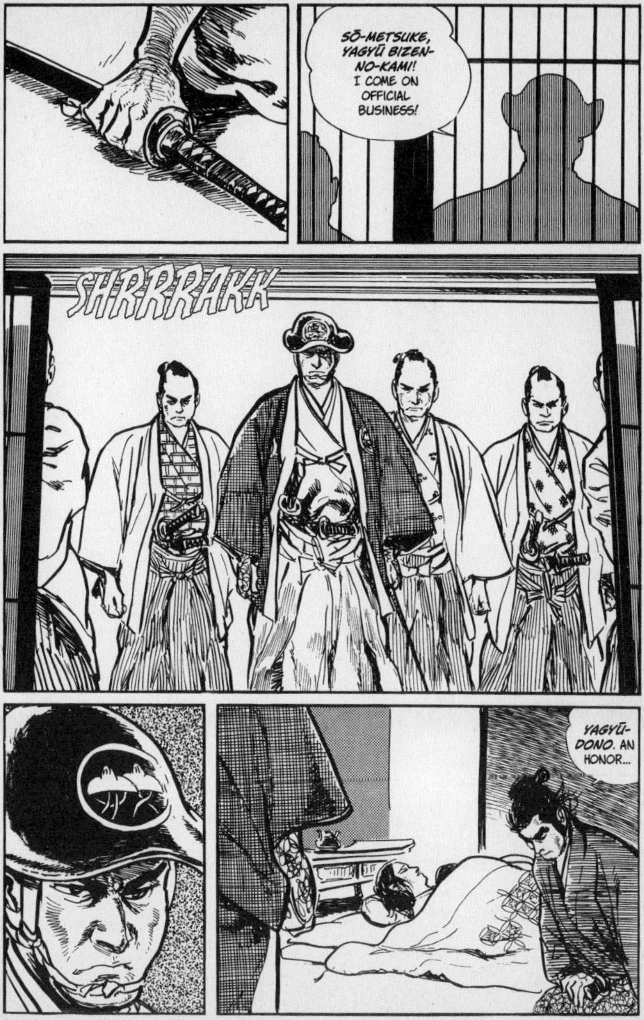
SŌ-METSUKE, YAGYŪ BIZEN-NO-KAMI! I COME ON OFFICIAL BUSINESS!
SHRRRAKK
YAGYŪ-DONO. AN HONOR...

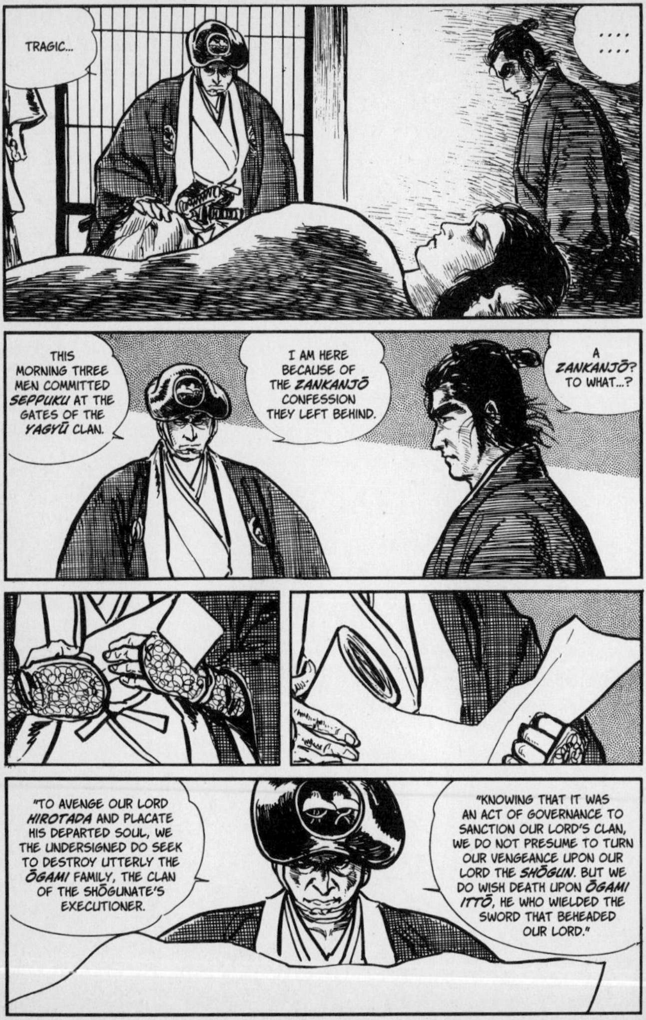
TRAGIC...
....
....
THIS MORNING THREE MEN COMMITTED *SEPPUKU* AT THE GATES OF THE *YAGYŪ* CLAN.
I AM HERE BECAUSE OF THE *ZANKANJŌ* CONFESSION THEY LEFT BEHIND.
A *ZANKANJŌ*? TO WHAT...?
"TO AVENGE OUR LORD *HIROTADA* AND PLACATE HIS DEPARTED SOUL, WE THE UNDERSIGNED DO SEEK TO DESTROY UTTERLY THE *ŌGAMI* FAMILY, THE CLAN OF THE SHŌGUNATE'S EXECUTIONER.
"KNOWING THAT IT WAS AN ACT OF GOVERNANCE TO SANCTION OUR LORD'S CLAN, WE DO NOT PRESUME TO TURN OUR VENGEANCE UPON OUR LORD THE *SHŌGUN*. BUT WE DO WISH DEATH UPON *ŌGAMI ITTŌ*, HE WHO WIELDED THE SWORD THAT BEHEADED OUR LORD."

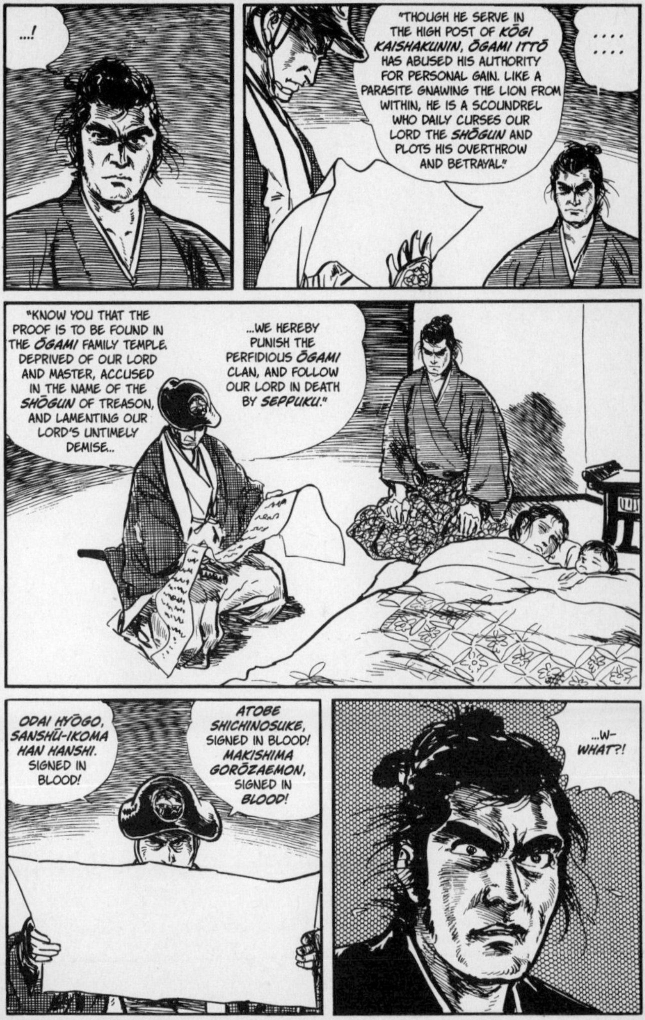
...!
"THOUGH HE SERVE IN THE HIGH POST OF *KŌGI KAISHAKUNIN, ŌGAMI ITTŌ* HAS ABUSED HIS AUTHORITY FOR PERSONAL GAIN. LIKE A PARASITE GNAWING THE LION FROM WITHIN, HE IS A SCOUNDREL WHO DAILY CURSES OUR LORD THE *SHŌGUN* AND PLOTS HIS OVERTHROW AND BETRAYAL."
....
"KNOW YOU THAT THE PROOF IS TO BE FOUND IN THE *ŌGAMI* FAMILY TEMPLE. DEPRIVED OF OUR LORD AND MASTER, ACCUSED IN THE NAME OF THE *SHŌGUN* OF TREASON, AND LAMENTING OUR LORD'S UNTIMELY DEMISE...
...WE HEREBY PUNISH THE PERFIDIOUS *ŌGAMI* CLAN, AND FOLLOW OUR LORD IN DEATH BY *SEPPUKU*."
ODAI HYŌGO, SANSHŪ-IKOMA HAN HANSHI. SIGNED IN BLOOD!
ATOBE SHICHINOSUKE, SIGNED IN BLOOD! *MAKISHIMA GORŌZAEMON,* SIGNED IN *BLOOD!*
...W-*WHAT?!*

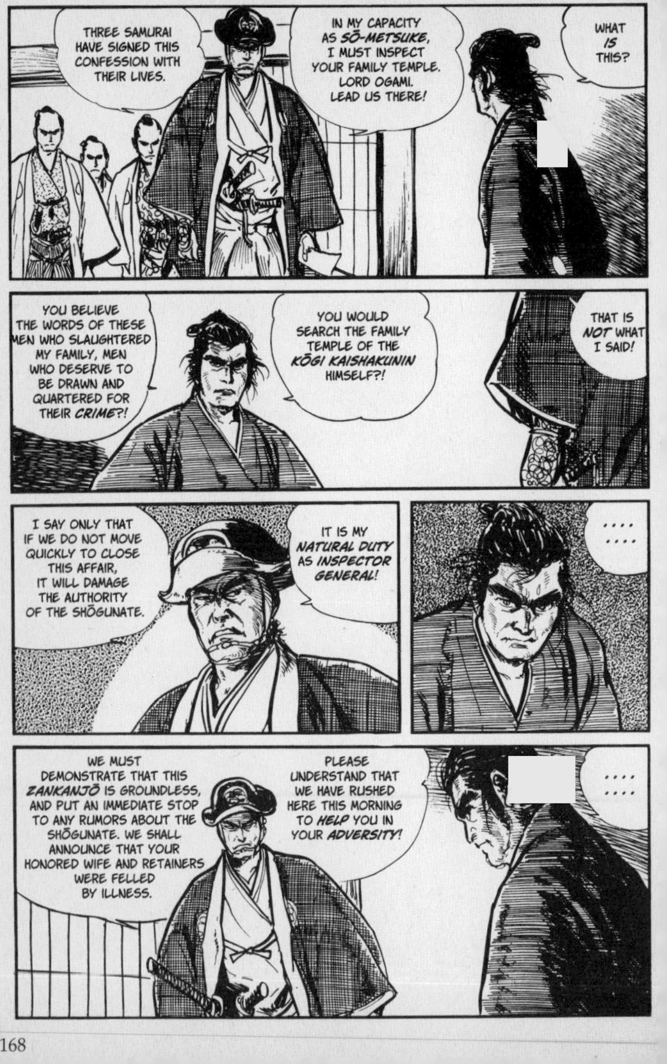
THREE SAMURAI HAVE SIGNED THIS CONFESSION WITH THEIR LIVES.
IN MY CAPACITY AS *SŌ-METSUKE*, I MUST INSPECT YOUR FAMILY TEMPLE. LORD OGAMI. LEAD US THERE!
WHAT *IS* THIS?
YOU BELIEVE THE WORDS OF THESE MEN WHO SLAUGHTERED MY FAMILY, MEN WHO DESERVE TO BE DRAWN AND QUARTERED FOR THEIR *CRIME*?!
YOU WOULD SEARCH THE FAMILY TEMPLE OF THE *KŌGI KAISHAKUNIN* HIMSELF?!
THAT IS *NOT* WHAT I SAID!
I SAY ONLY THAT IF WE DO NOT MOVE QUICKLY TO CLOSE THIS AFFAIR, IT WILL DAMAGE THE AUTHORITY OF THE SHŌGUNATE.
IT IS MY *NATURAL DUTY* AS *INSPECTOR GENERAL*!
....
WE MUST DEMONSTRATE THAT THIS *ZANKANJŌ* IS GROUNDLESS, AND PUT AN IMMEDIATE STOP TO ANY RUMORS ABOUT THE SHŌGUNATE. WE SHALL ANNOUNCE THAT YOUR HONORED WIFE AND RETAINERS WERE FELLED BY ILLNESS.
PLEASE UNDERSTAND THAT WE HAVE RUSHED HERE THIS MORNING TO *HELP* YOU IN YOUR *ADVERSITY*!
....

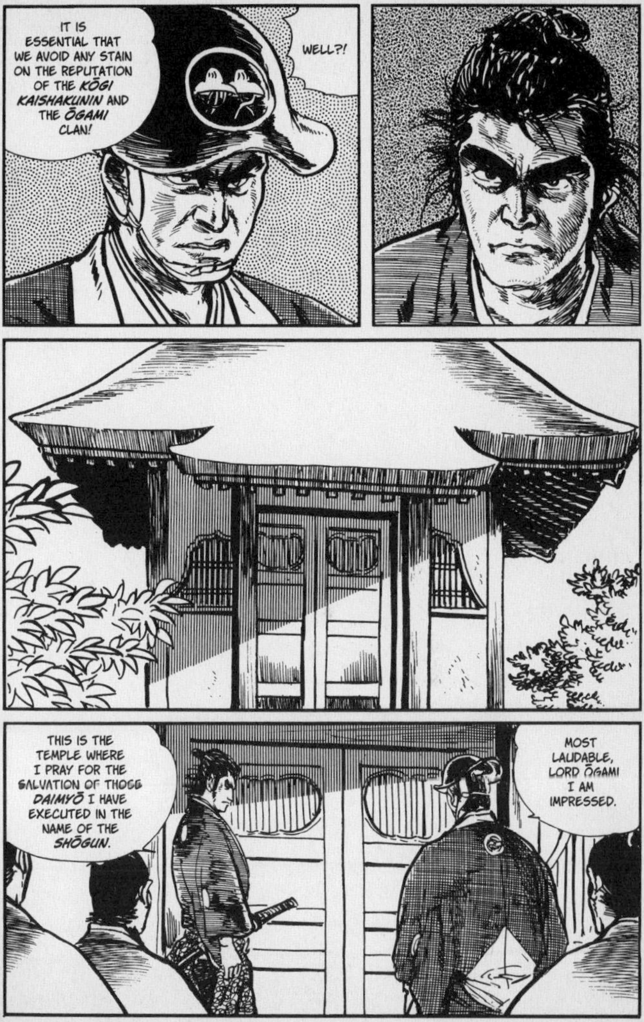
IT IS ESSENTIAL THAT WE AVOID ANY STAIN ON THE REPUTATION OF THE *KŌGI KAISHAKUNIN* AND THE *ŌGAMI* CLAN!
WELL?!
THIS IS THE TEMPLE WHERE I PRAY FOR THE SALVATION OF THOSE *DAIMYŌ* I HAVE EXECUTED IN THE NAME OF THE *SHŌGUN*.
MOST LAUDABLE, LORD ŌGAMI I AM IMPRESSED.

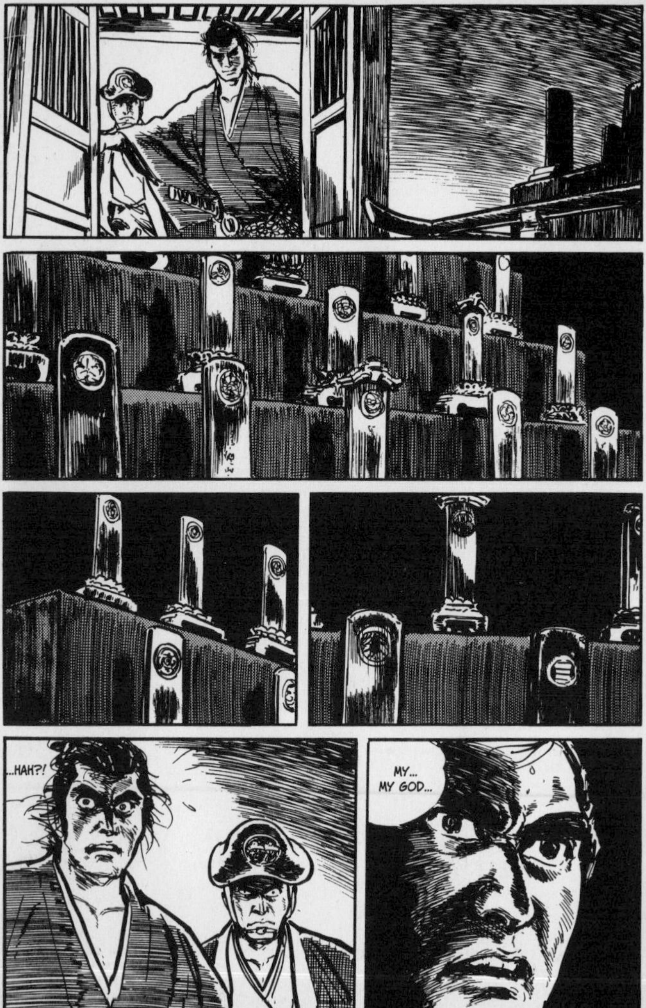
...HAH?!
MY...
MY GOD...

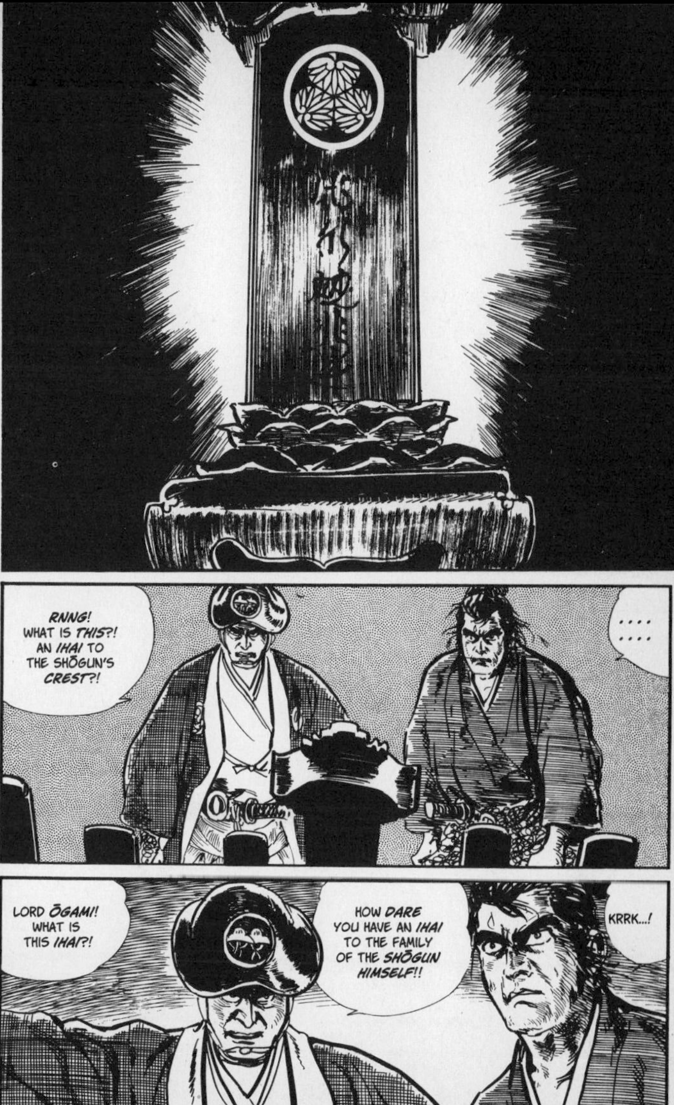
RNNG! WHAT IS THIS?! AN IHAI TO THE SHŌGUN'S CREST?!
....
LORD ŌGAMI! WHAT IS THIS IHAI?!
HOW DARE YOU HAVE AN IHAI TO THE FAMILY OF THE SHŌGUN HIMSELF!!
KRRK...!

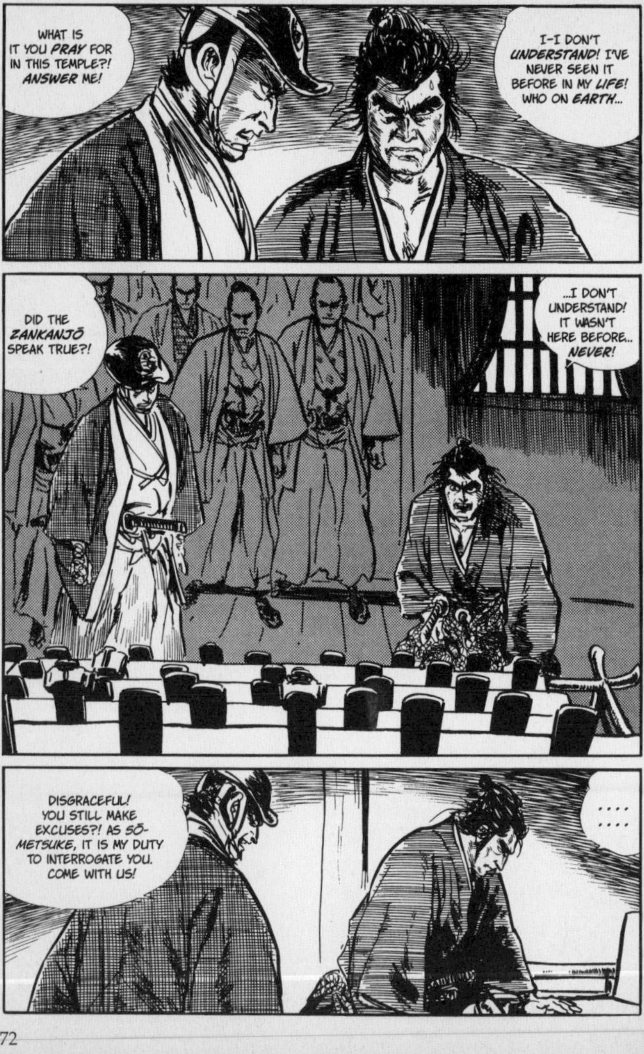
WHAT IS IT YOU PRAY FOR IN THIS TEMPLE?! ANSWER ME!
I-I DON'T UNDERSTAND! I'VE NEVER SEEN IT BEFORE IN MY LIFE! WHO ON EARTH...
DID THE ZANKANJŌ SPEAK TRUE?!
...I DON'T UNDERSTAND! IT WASN'T HERE BEFORE... NEVER!
DISGRACEFUL! YOU STILL MAKE EXCUSES?! AS SŌ-METSUKE, IT IS MY DUTY TO INTERROGATE YOU. COME WITH US!
....
....

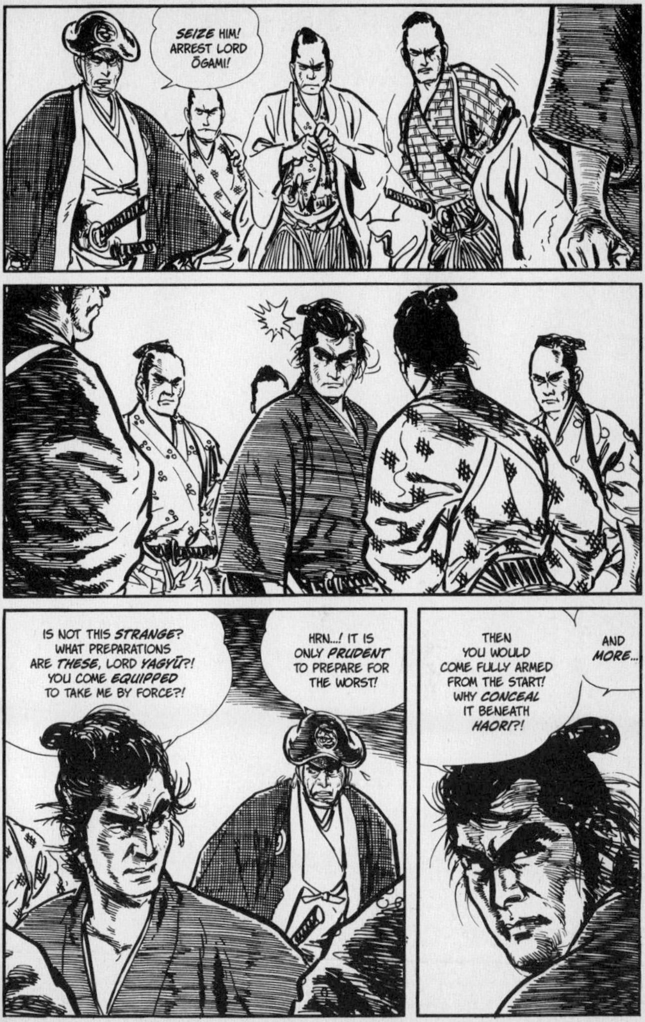
SEIZE HIM! ARREST LORD ŌGAMI!
IS NOT THIS STRANGE? WHAT PREPARATIONS ARE THESE, LORD YAGYŪ?! YOU COME EQUIPPED TO TAKE ME BY FORCE?!
HRN...! IT IS ONLY PRUDENT TO PREPARE FOR THE WORST!
THEN YOU WOULD COME FULLY ARMED FROM THE START! WHY CONCEAL IT BENEATH HAORI?!
AND MORE...

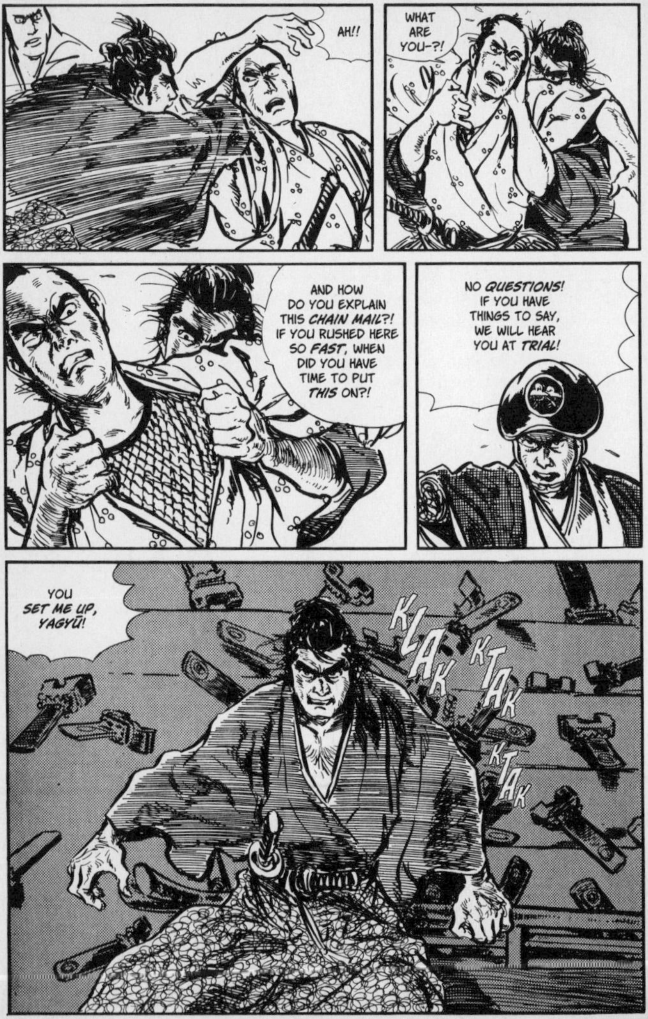
AH!!
WHAT ARE YOU-?!
AND HOW DO YOU EXPLAIN THIS *CHAIN MAIL*?! IF YOU RUSHED HERE SO *FAST*, WHEN DID YOU HAVE TIME TO PUT *THIS* ON?!
NO *QUESTIONS*! IF YOU HAVE THINGS TO SAY, WE WILL HEAR YOU AT *TRIAL*!
YOU *SET ME UP, YAGYŪ*!
KLAK
KTAK
KTAK

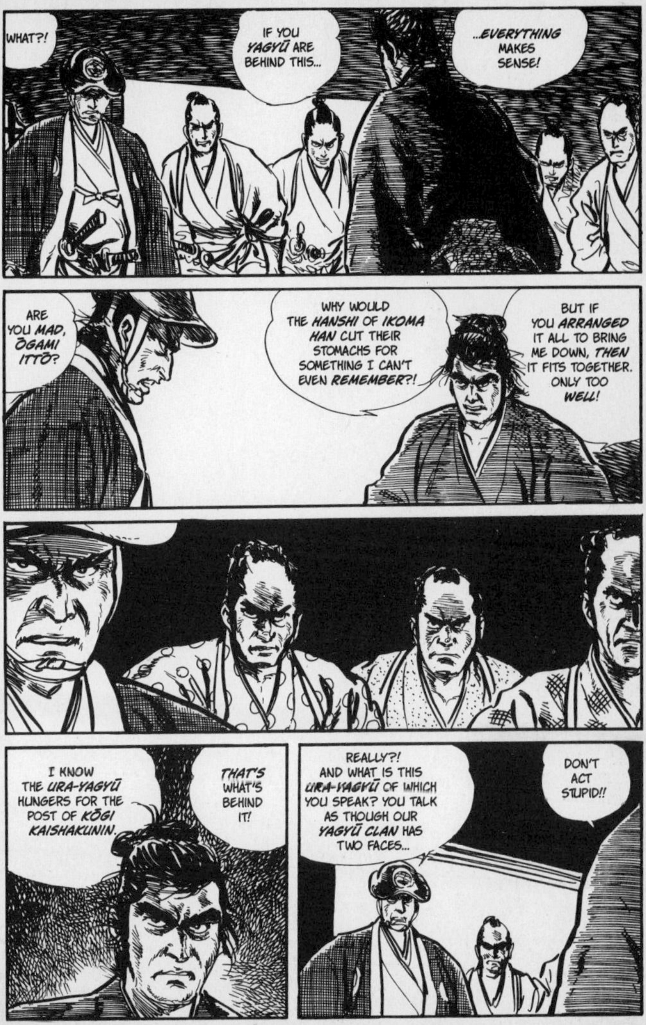
WHAT?!
IF YOU YAGYŪ ARE BEHIND THIS...
...EVERYTHING MAKES SENSE!
ARE YOU MAD, ŌGAMI ITTŌ?
WHY WOULD THE HANSHI OF IKOMA HAN CUT THEIR STOMACHS FOR SOMETHING I CAN'T EVEN REMEMBER?!
BUT IF YOU ARRANGED IT ALL TO BRING ME DOWN, THEN IT FITS TOGETHER. ONLY TOO WELL!
I KNOW THE URA-YAGYŪ HUNGERS FOR THE POST OF KŌGI KAISHAKUNIN.
THAT'S WHAT'S BEHIND IT!
REALLY?! AND WHAT IS THIS URA-YAGYŪ OF WHICH YOU SPEAK? YOU TALK AS THOUGH OUR YAGYŪ CLAN HAS TWO FACES...
DON'T ACT STUPID!!

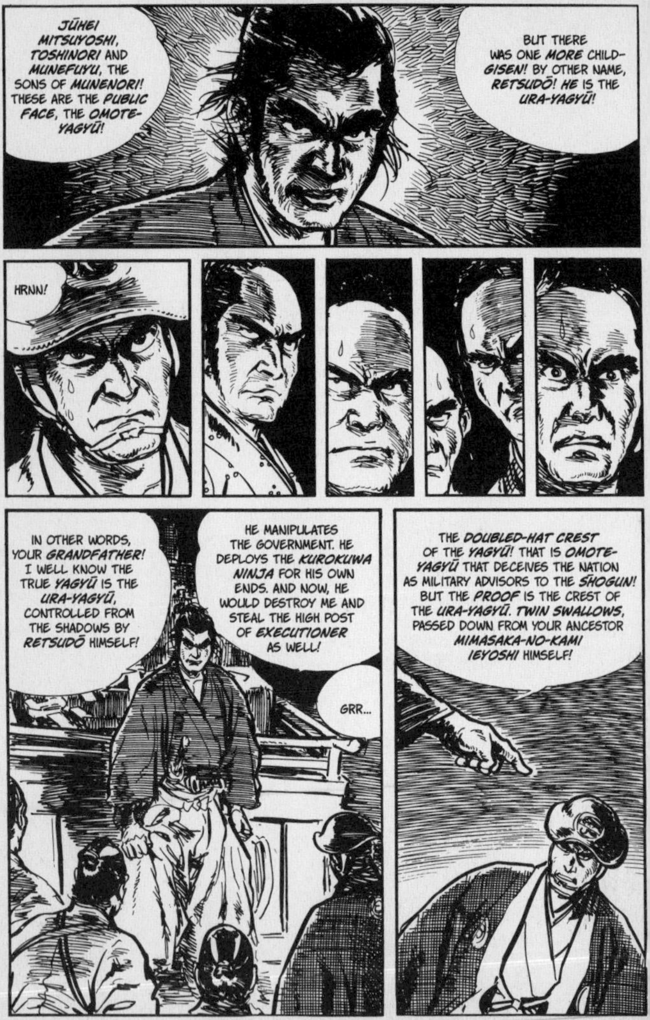
JŪHEI MITSUYOSHI, TOSHINORI AND MUNEFUYU, THE SONS OF MUNENORI! THESE ARE THE PUBLIC FACE, THE OMOTE-YAGYŪ!
BUT THERE WAS ONE MORE CHILD- GISEN! BY OTHER NAME, RETSUDŌ! HE IS THE URA-YAGYŪ!
HRNN!
IN OTHER WORDS, YOUR GRANDFATHER! I WELL KNOW THE TRUE YAGYŪ IS THE URA-YAGYŪ, CONTROLLED FROM THE SHADOWS BY RETSUDŌ HIMSELF!
HE MANIPULATES THE GOVERNMENT. HE DEPLOYS THE KUROKUWA NINJA FOR HIS OWN ENDS. AND NOW, HE WOULD DESTROY ME AND STEAL THE HIGH POST OF EXECUTIONER AS WELL!
GRR...
THE DOUBLED-HAT CREST OF THE YAGYŪ! THAT IS OMOTE-YAGYŪ THAT DECEIVES THE NATION AS MILITARY ADVISORS TO THE SHOGUN! BUT THE PROOF IS THE CREST OF THE URA-YAGYŪ. TWIN SWALLOWS, PASSED DOWN FROM YOUR ANCESTOR MIMASAKA-NO-KAMI IEYOSHI HIMSELF!

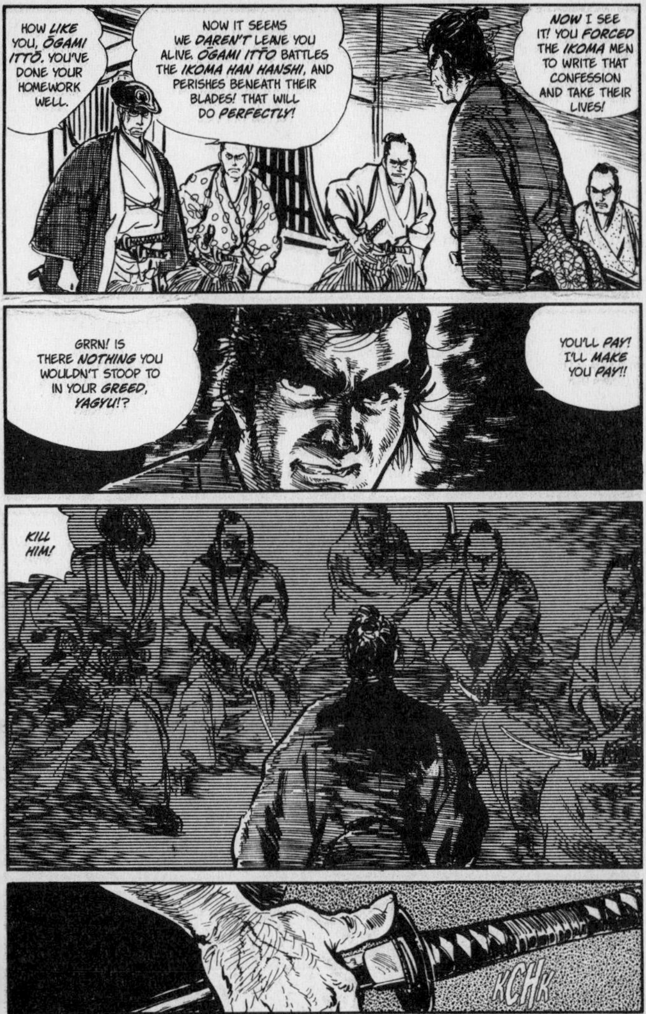
HOW LIKE YOU, ŌGAMI ITTŌ. YOU'VE DONE YOUR HOMEWORK WELL.
NOW IT SEEMS WE DAREN'T LEAVE YOU ALIVE. ŌGAMI ITTŌ BATTLES THE IKOMA HAN HANSHI, AND PERISHES BENEATH THEIR BLADES! THAT WILL DO PERFECTLY!
NOW I SEE IT! YOU FORCED THE IKOMA MEN TO WRITE THAT CONFESSION AND TAKE THEIR LIVES!
GRRN! IS THERE NOTHING YOU WOULDN'T STOOP TO IN YOUR GREED, YAGYU!?
YOU'LL PAY! I'LL MAKE YOU PAY!!
KILL HIM!
KCHK

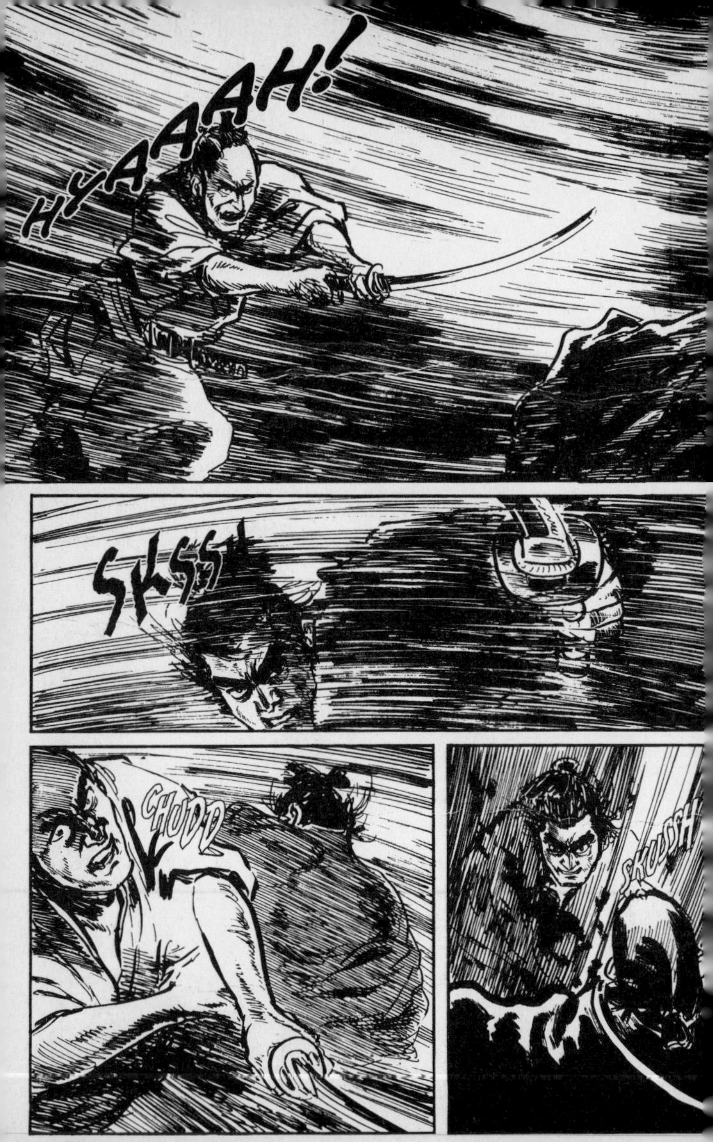
HYAAAAH!
SKSST
CHUDD
SKUSSH

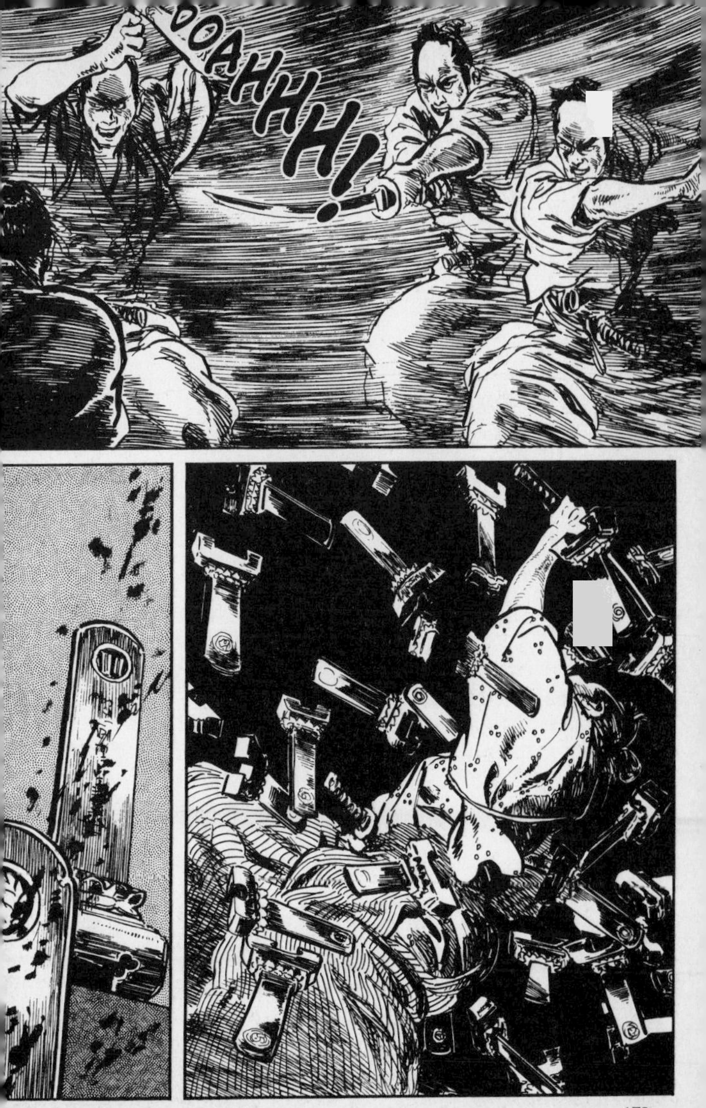
DOAHHH!

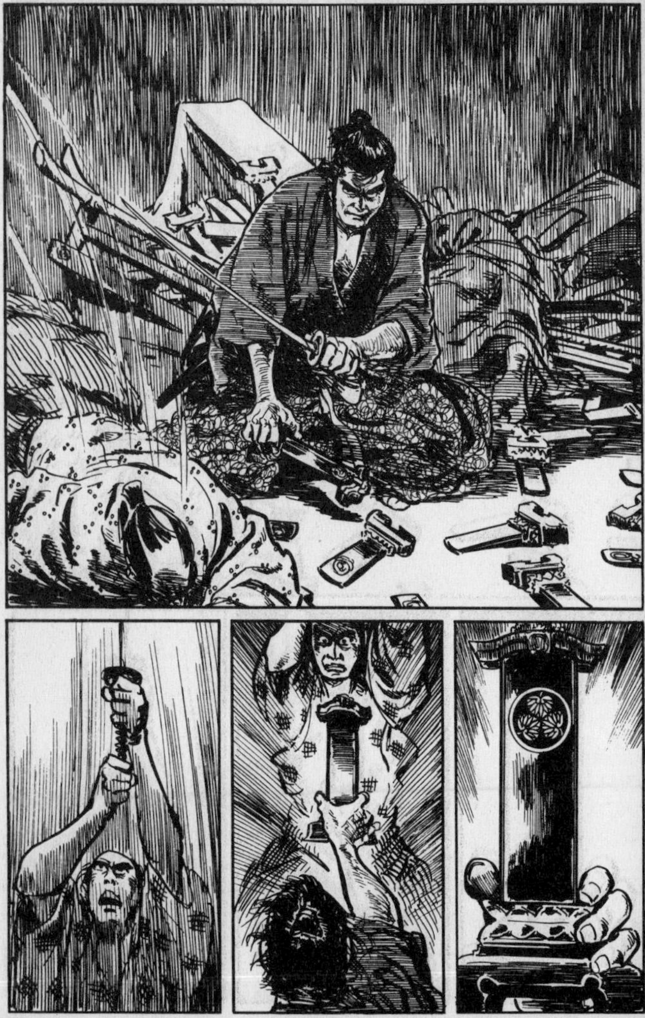

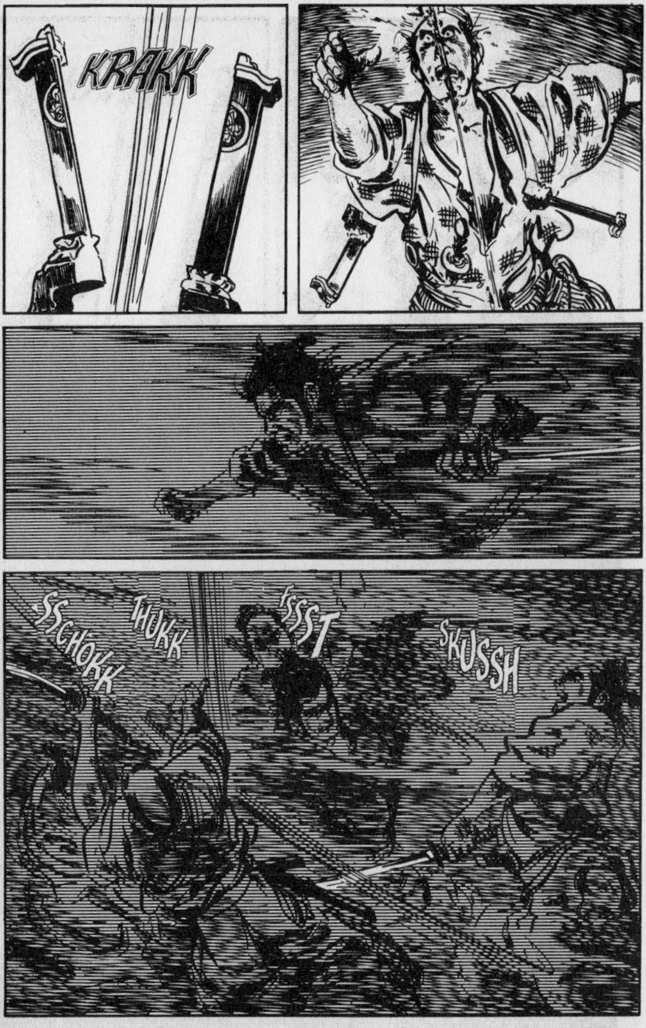
KRAKK
SSCHOKK
THUKK
FSSST
SKUSSH

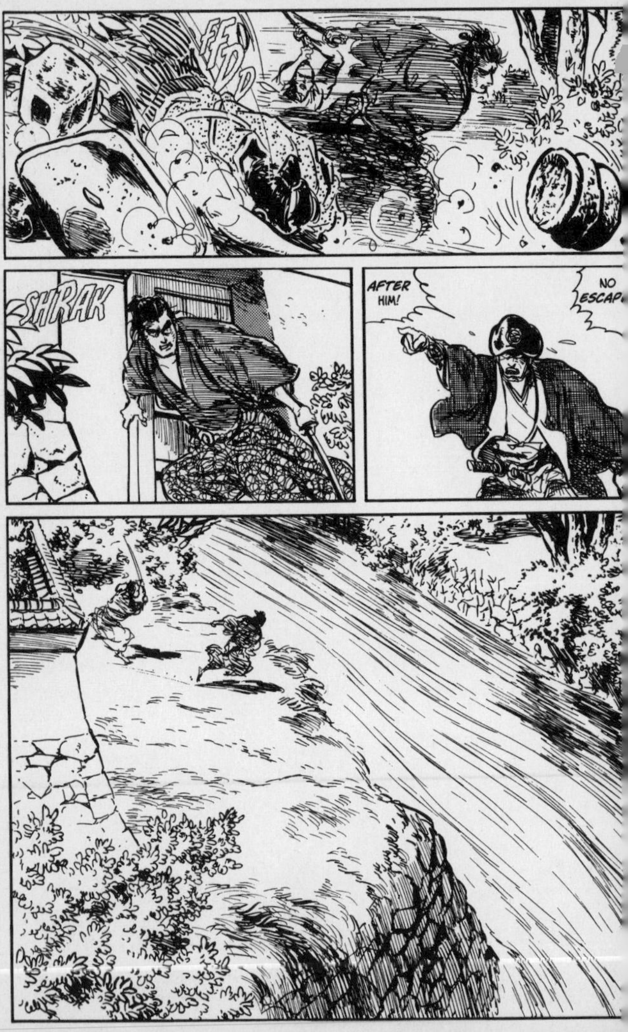
SHRAK
AFTER HIM!
NO ESCAP

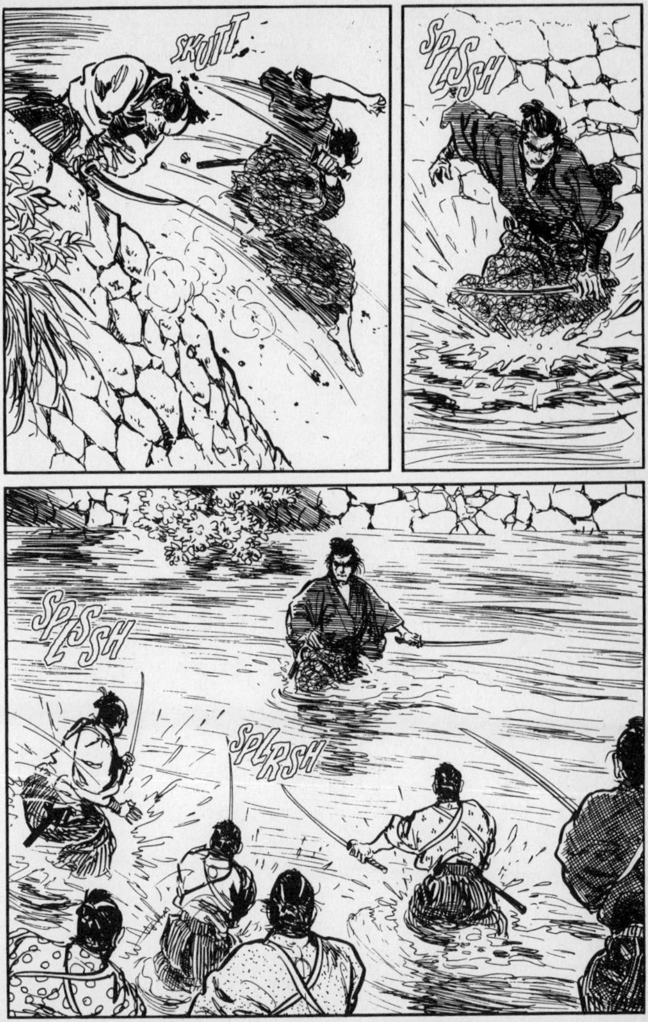
SKUTT
SPLSSH
SPLSSH
SPLRSH

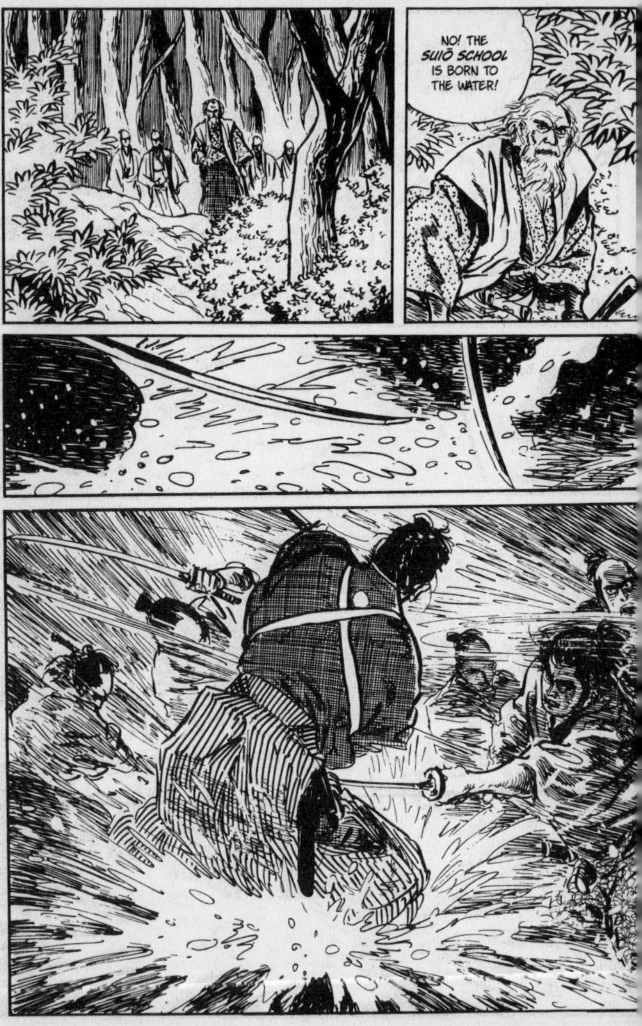
NO! THE SUIŌ SCHOOL IS BORN TO THE WATER!

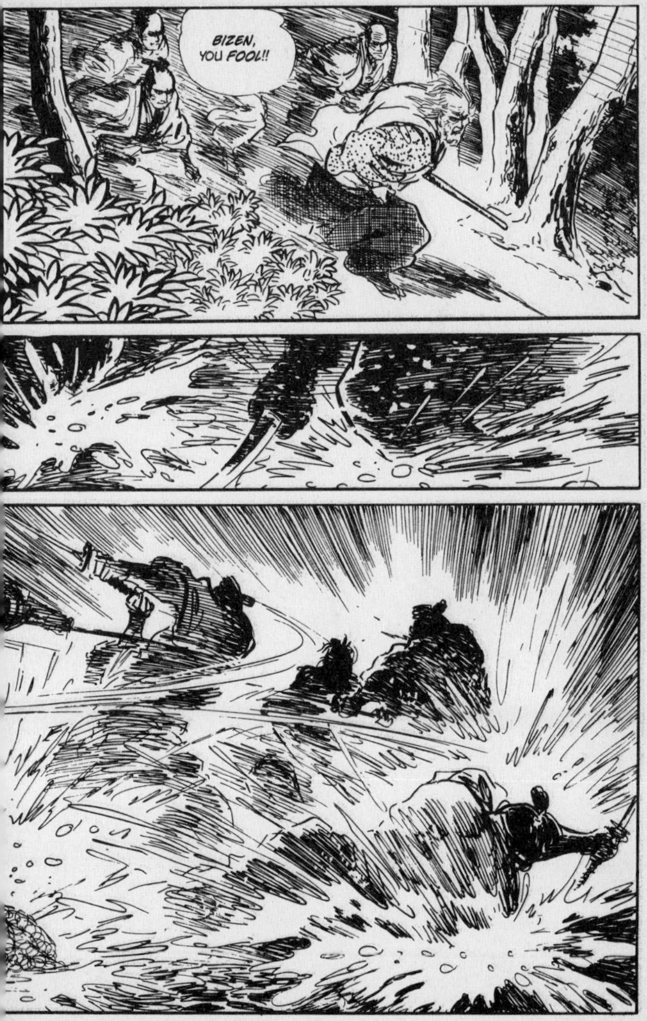
BIZEN, YOU FOOL!!

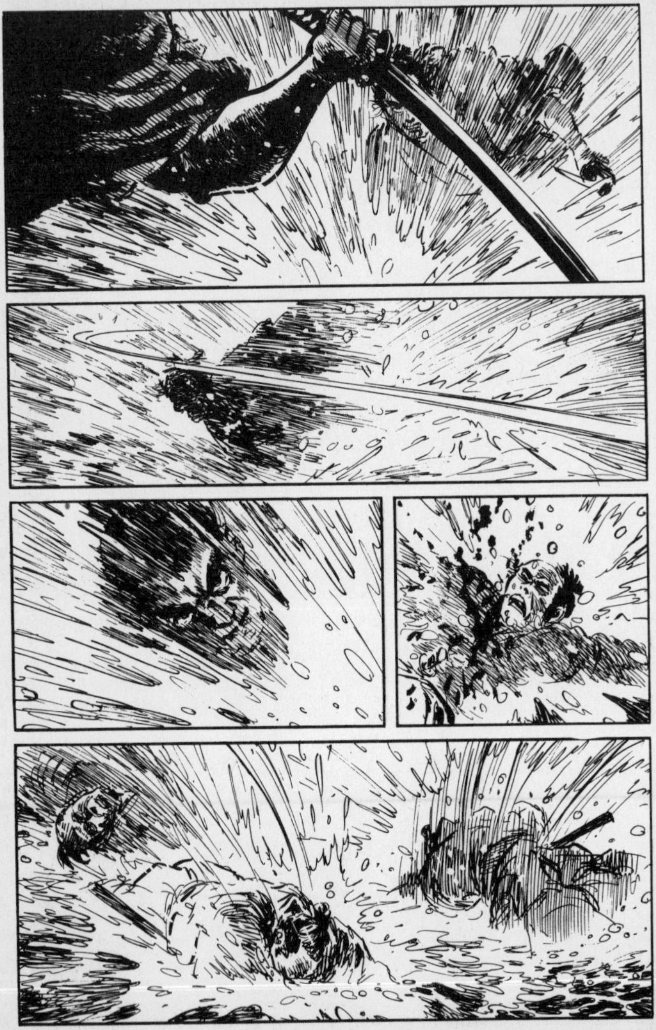

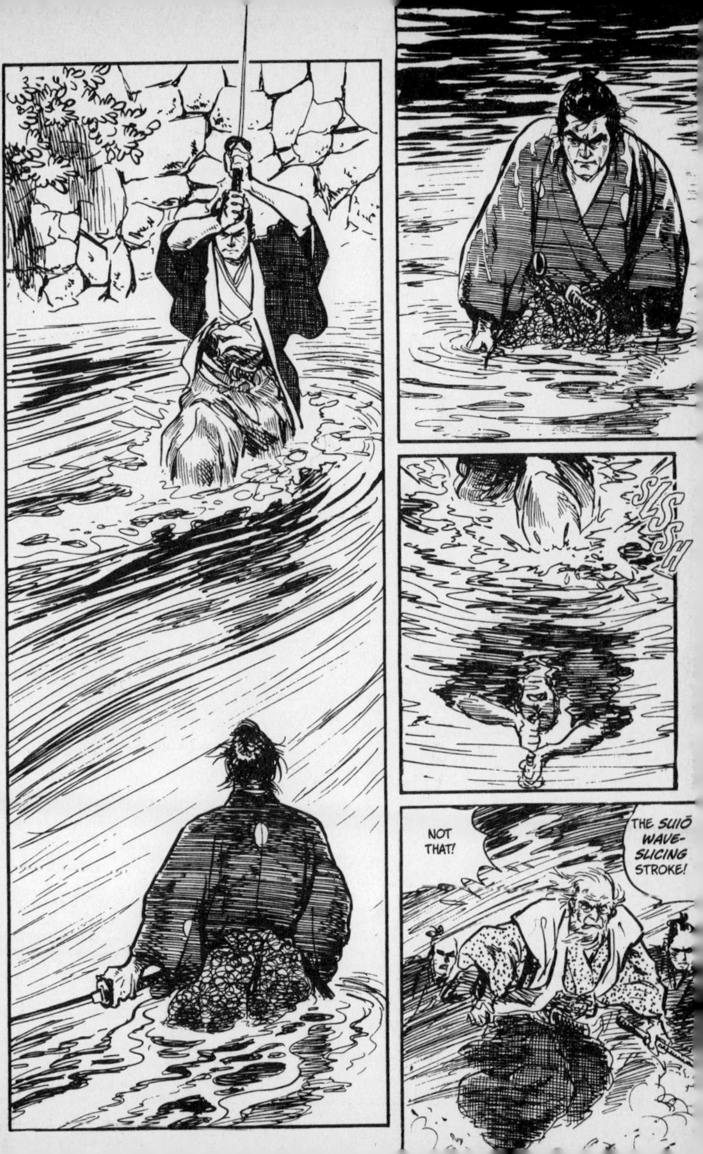
SLSSH
NOT THAT!
THE SUIŌ WAVE-SLICING STROKE!

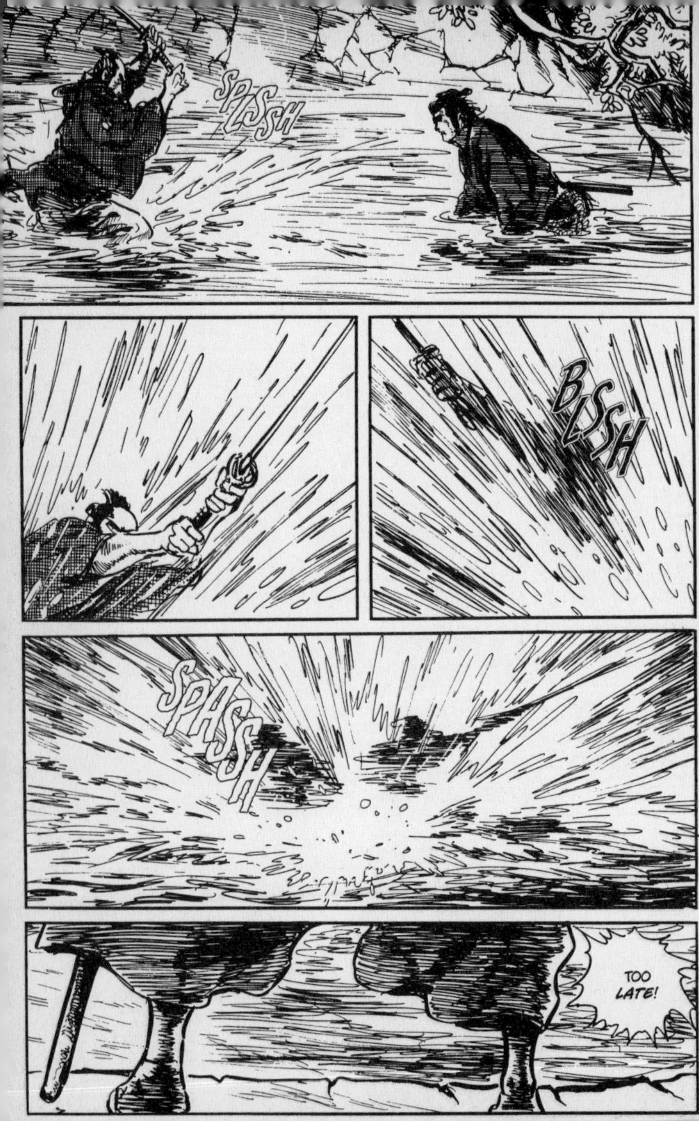
SPLSSH
BLSSH
SPASSH
TOO LATE!

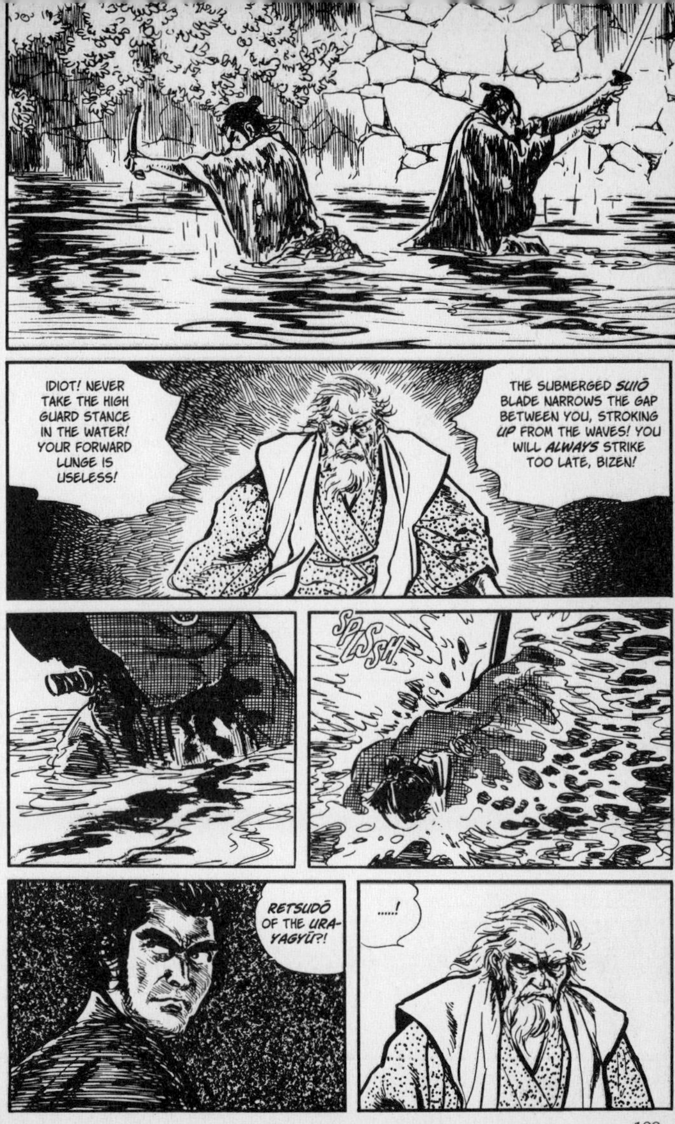
IDIOT! NEVER TAKE THE HIGH GUARD STANCE IN THE WATER! YOUR FORWARD LUNGE IS USELESS!
THE SUBMERGED *SUIŌ* BLADE NARROWS THE GAP BETWEEN YOU, STROKING *UP* FROM THE WAVES! YOU WILL *ALWAYS* STRIKE TOO LATE, BIZEN!
SPLSSH
RETSUDŌ OF THE *URA-YAGYŪ*?!
......!

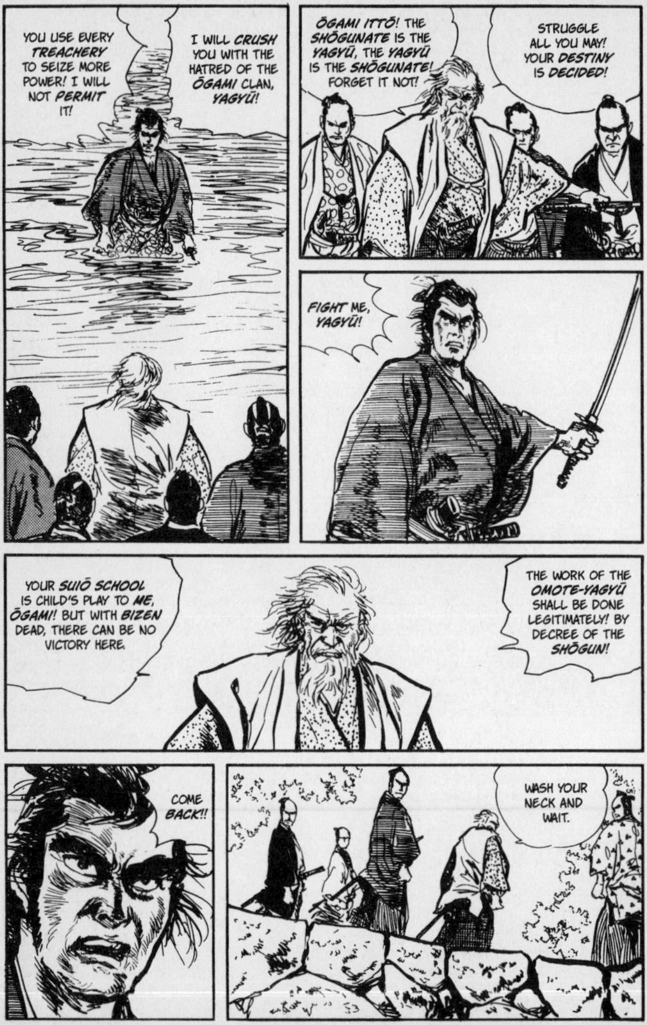
YOU USE EVERY *TREACHERY* TO SEIZE MORE POWER! I WILL NOT *PERMIT* IT!
I WILL *CRUSH* YOU WITH THE HATRED OF THE *ŌGAMI* CLAN, *YAGYŪ*!
ŌGAMI ITTŌ! THE *SHŌGUNATE* IS THE *YAGYŪ*, THE *YAGYŪ* IS THE *SHŌGUNATE*! FORGET IT NOT!
STRUGGLE ALL YOU MAY! YOUR *DESTINY* IS *DECIDED*!
FIGHT ME, *YAGYŪ*!
YOUR *SUIŌ SCHOOL* IS CHILD'S PLAY TO *ME*, *ŌGAMI*! BUT WITH *BIZEN* DEAD, THERE CAN BE NO VICTORY HERE.
THE WORK OF THE *OMOTE-YAGYŪ* SHALL BE DONE LEGITIMATELY! BY DECREE OF THE *SHŌGUN*!
COME *BACK*!!
WASH YOUR NECK AND WAIT.

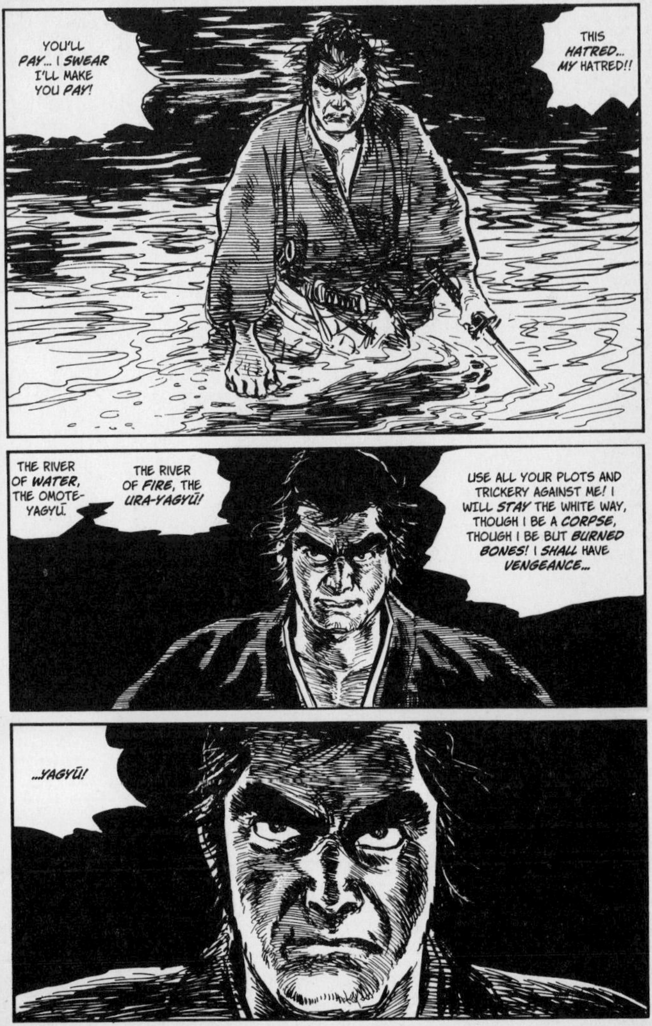
YOU'LL PAY... I SWEAR I'LL MAKE YOU PAY!
THIS HATRED... MY HATRED!!
THE RIVER OF WATER, THE OMOTE-YAGYŪ.
THE RIVER OF FIRE, THE URA-YAGYŪ!
USE ALL YOUR PLOTS AND TRICKERY AGAINST ME! I WILL STAY THE WHITE WAY, THOUGH I BE A CORPSE, THOUGH I BE BUT BURNED BONES! I SHALL HAVE VENGEANCE...
...YAGYŪ!

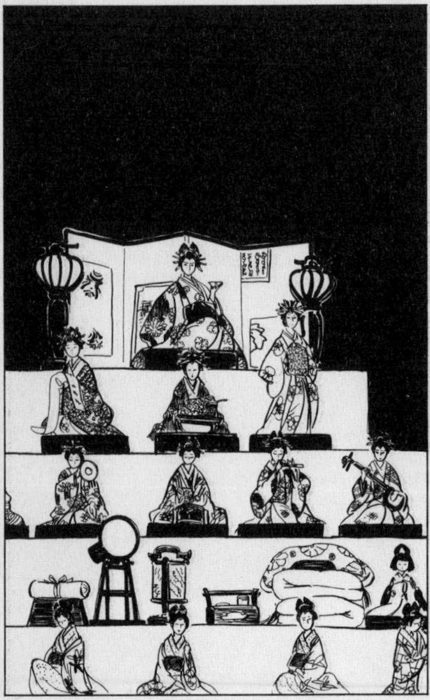

the eighteenth

The Virgin and the Whore

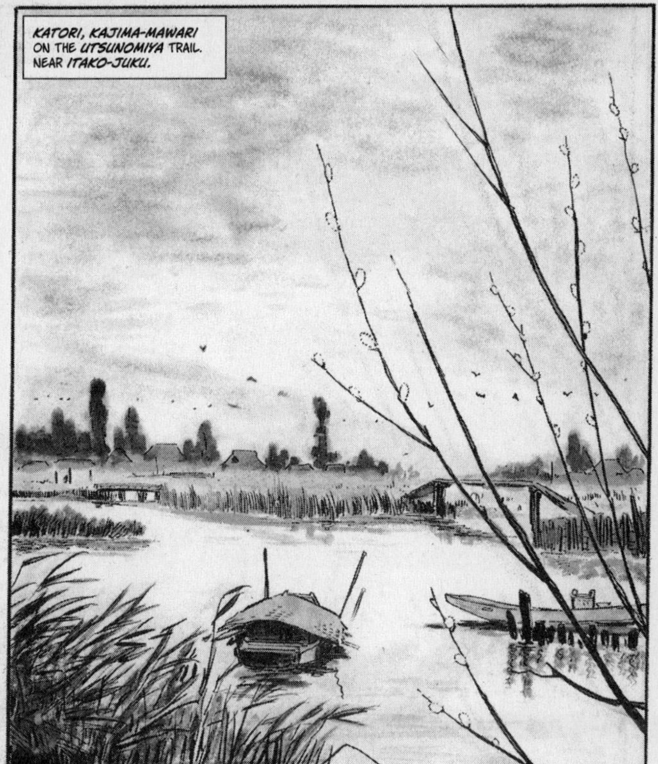
KATORI, KAJIMA-MAWARI
ON THE UTSUNOMIYA TRAIL.
NEAR ITAKO-JUKU.

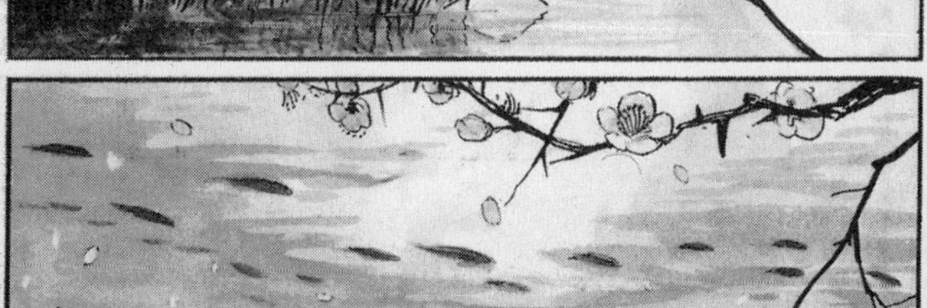

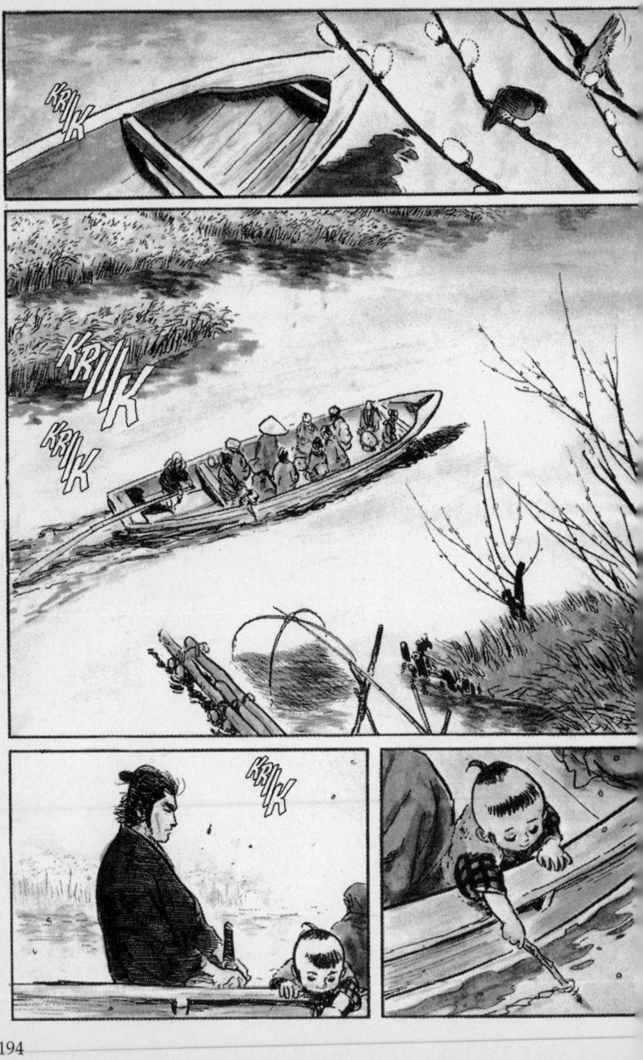
KRIK
KRIK
KRIK
KRIK

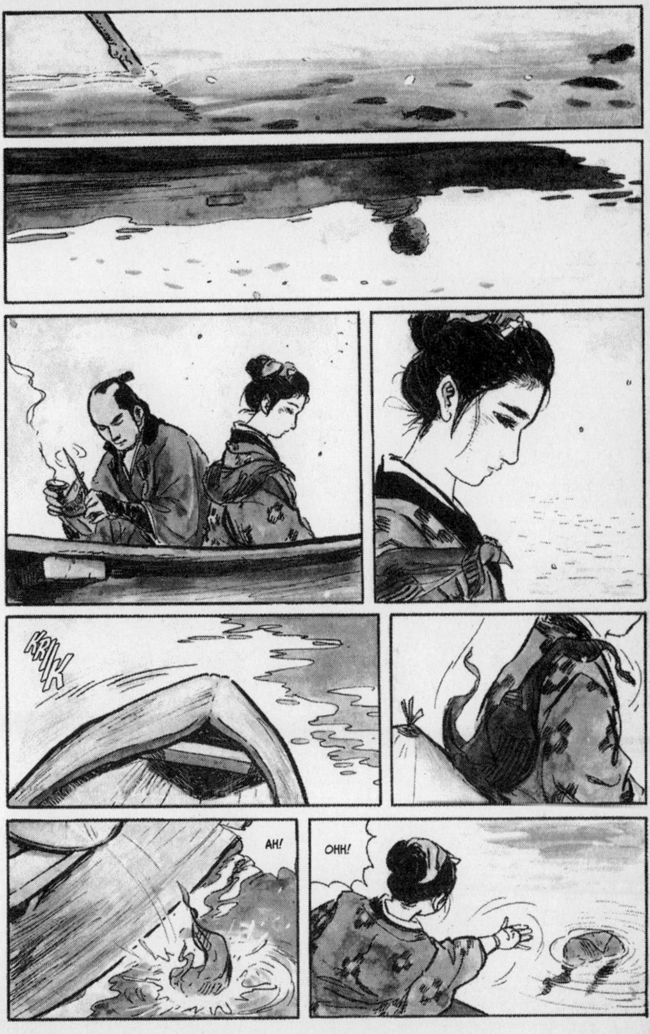
KRIIK
AH!
OHH!

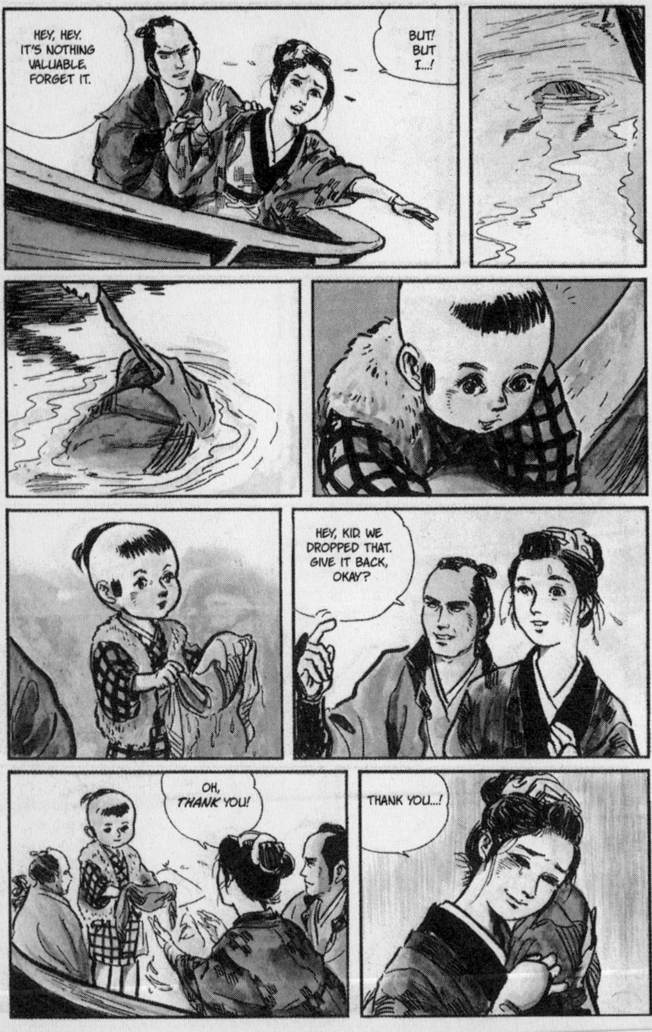
HEY, HEY. IT'S NOTHING VALUABLE. FORGET IT.
BUT! BUT I...!
HEY, KID. WE DROPPED THAT. GIVE IT BACK, OKAY?
OH, *THANK* YOU!
THANK YOU...!

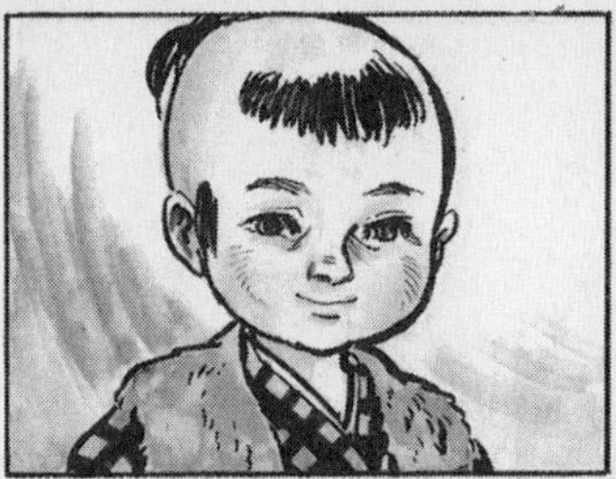
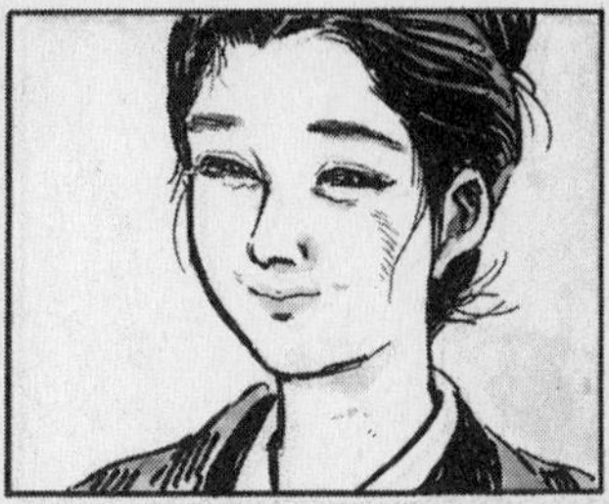
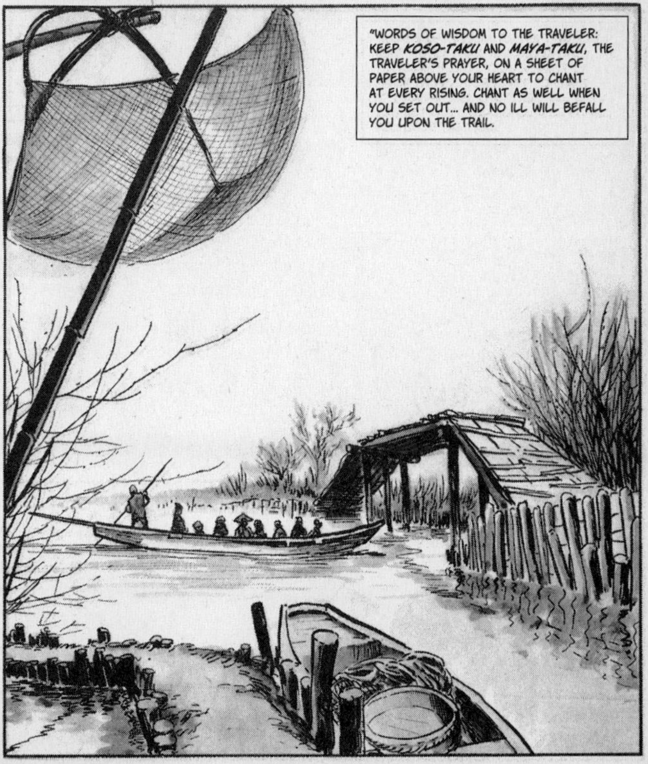
"WORDS OF WISDOM TO THE TRAVELER: KEEP *KOSO-TAKU* AND *MAYA-TAKU*, THE TRAVELER'S PRAYER, ON A SHEET OF PAPER ABOVE YOUR HEART TO CHANT AT EVERY RISING. CHANT AS WELL WHEN YOU SET OUT... AND NO ILL WILL BEFALL YOU UPON THE TRAIL.

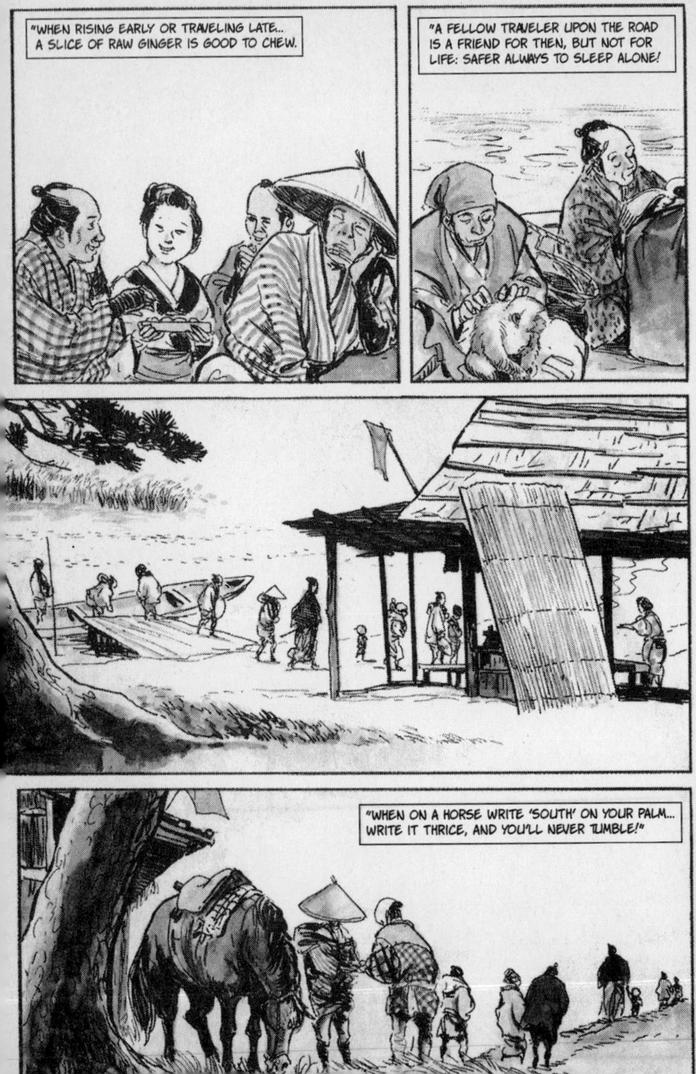
"WHEN RISING EARLY OR TRAVELING LATE... A SLICE OF RAW GINGER IS GOOD TO CHEW.
"A FELLOW TRAVELER UPON THE ROAD IS A FRIEND FOR THEN, BUT NOT FOR LIFE: SAFER ALWAYS TO SLEEP ALONE!
"WHEN ON A HORSE WRITE 'SOUTH' ON YOUR PALM... WRITE IT THRICE, AND YOU'LL NEVER TUMBLE!"

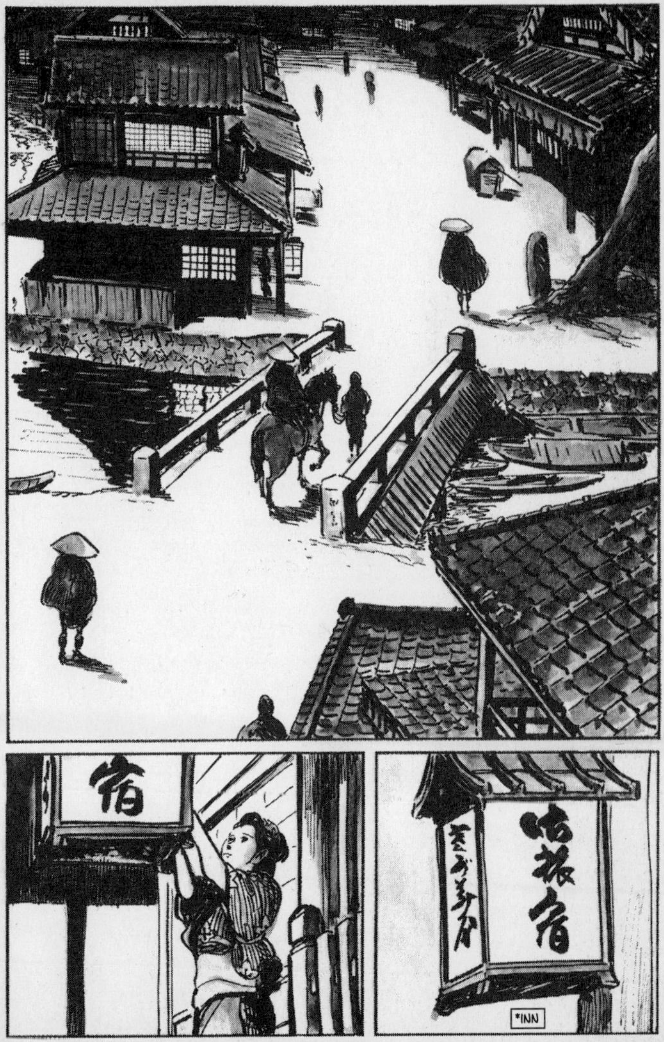
宿
*INN

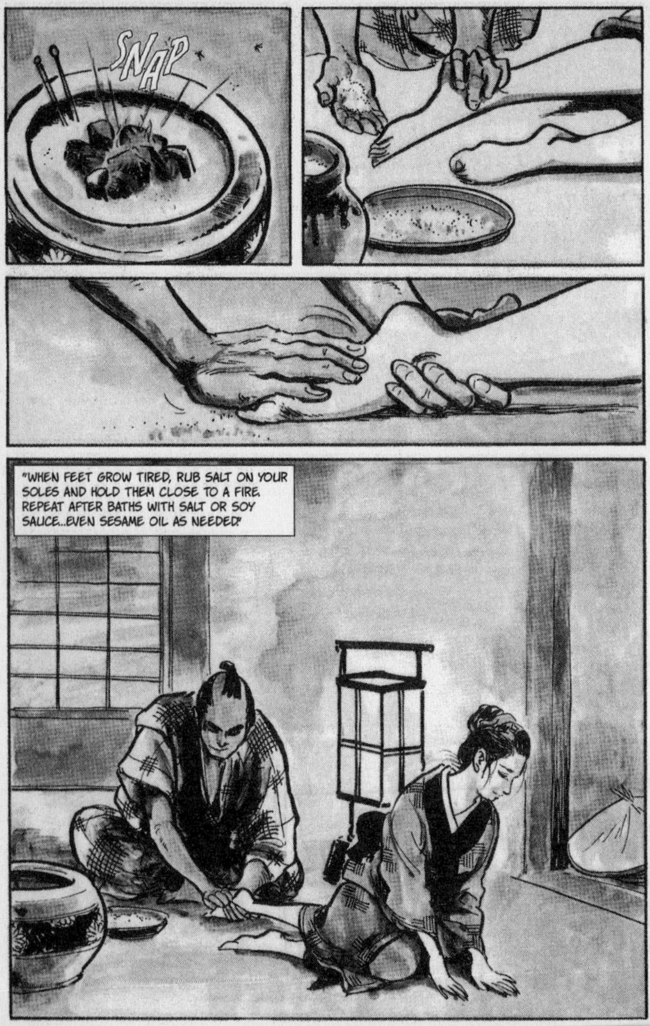
SNAP
"WHEN FEET GROW TIRED, RUB SALT ON YOUR SOLES AND HOLD THEM CLOSE TO A FIRE. REPEAT AFTER BATHS WITH SALT OR SOY SAUCE...EVEN SESAME OIL AS NEEDED."

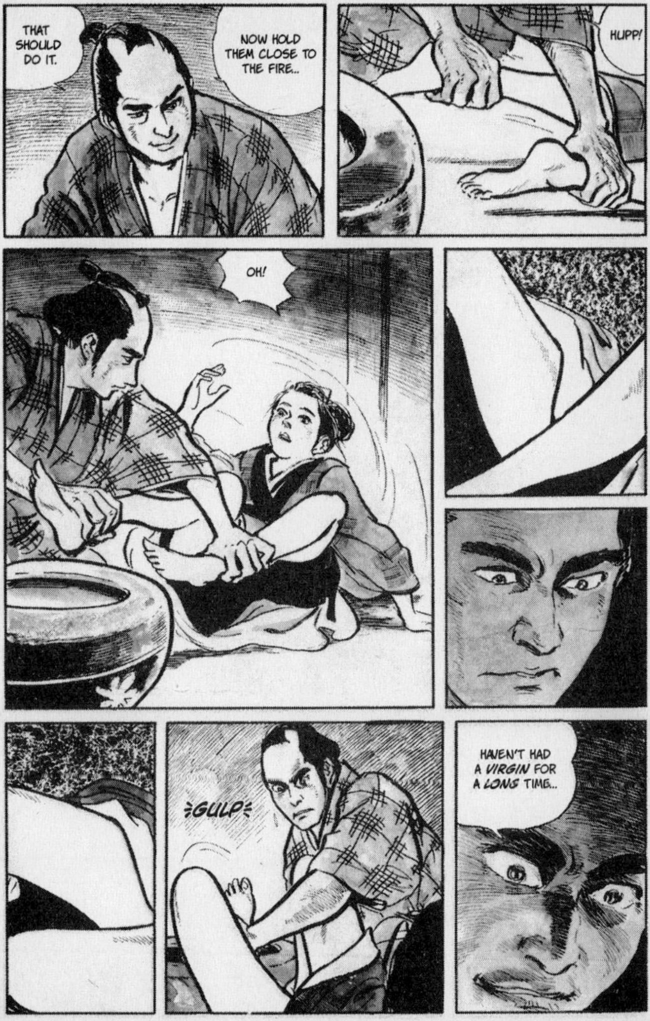
THAT SHOULD DO IT.
NOW HOLD THEM CLOSE TO THE FIRE..
HUPP!
OH!
GULP
HAVEN'T HAD A VIRGIN FOR A LONG TIME..

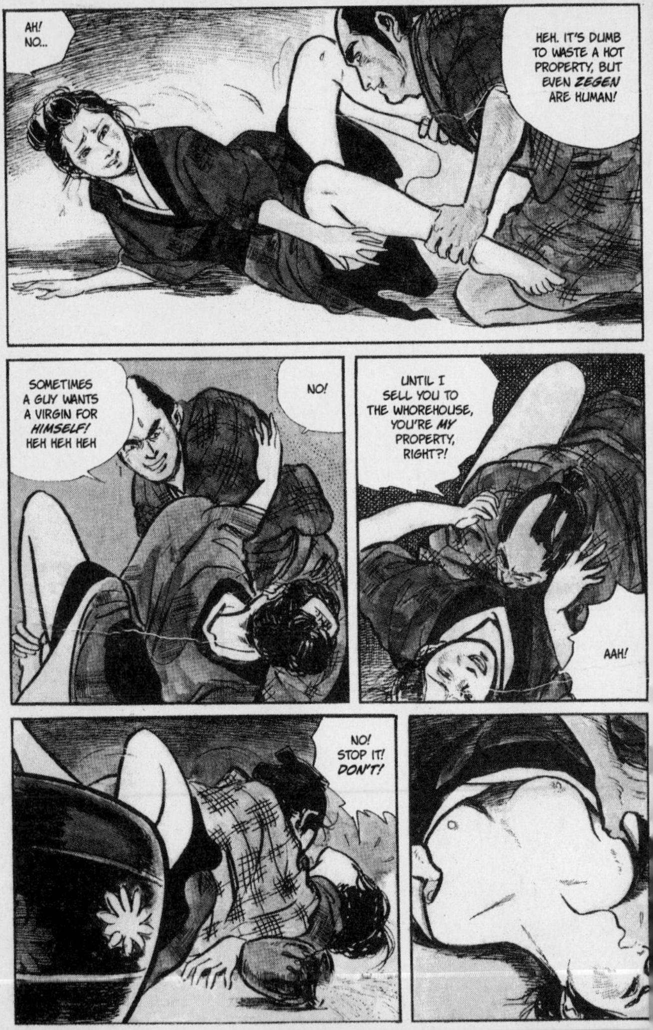
AH! NO...
HEH. IT'S DUMB TO WASTE A HOT PROPERTY, BUT EVEN *ZEGEN* ARE HUMAN!
SOMETIMES A GUY WANTS A VIRGIN FOR *HIMSELF!* HEH HEH HEH
NO!
UNTIL I SELL YOU TO THE WHOREHOUSE, YOU'RE *MY* PROPERTY, RIGHT?!
AAH!
NO! STOP IT! ***DON'T!***

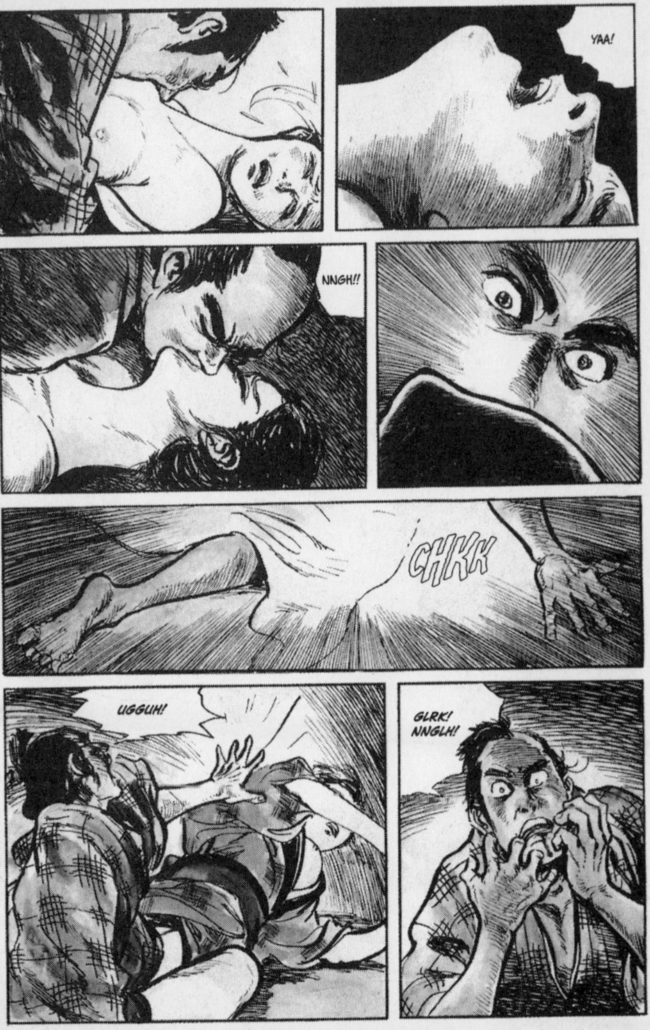
YAA!
NNGH!!
CHKK
UGGUH!
GLRK!
NNGLH!

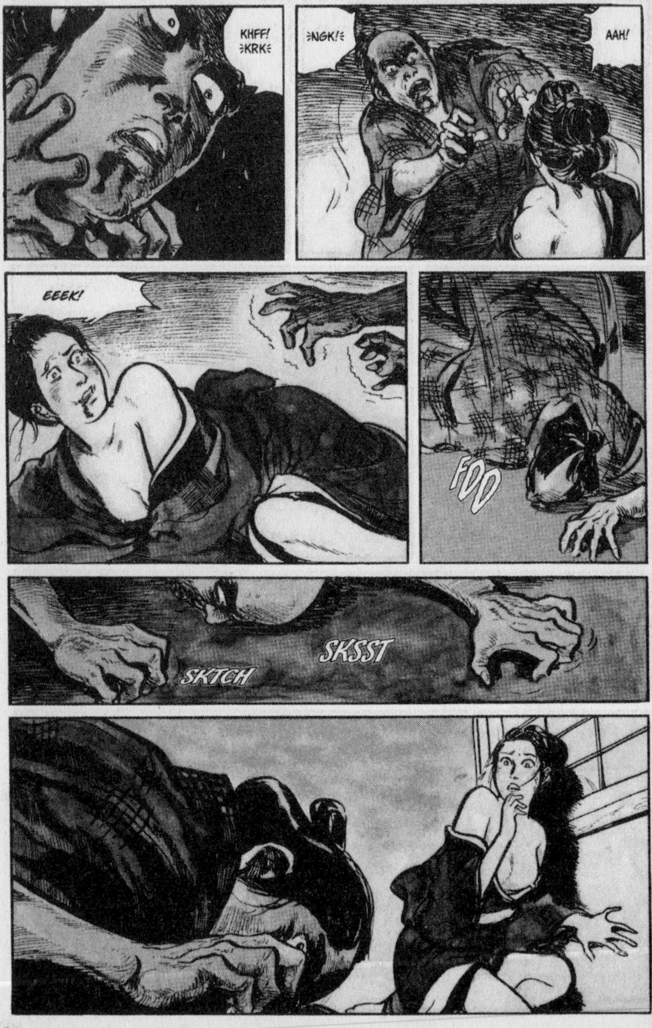
KHFF!
KRK
NGK!
AAH!
EEEK!
FDD
SKTCH
SKSST

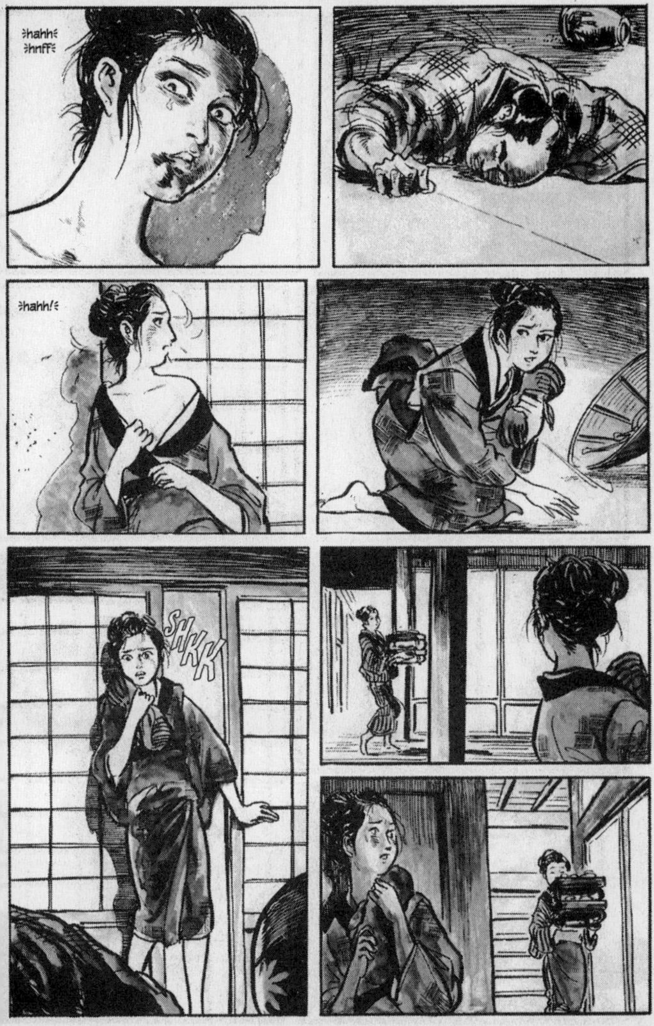

hahh
hnff
hahh!
SHKK

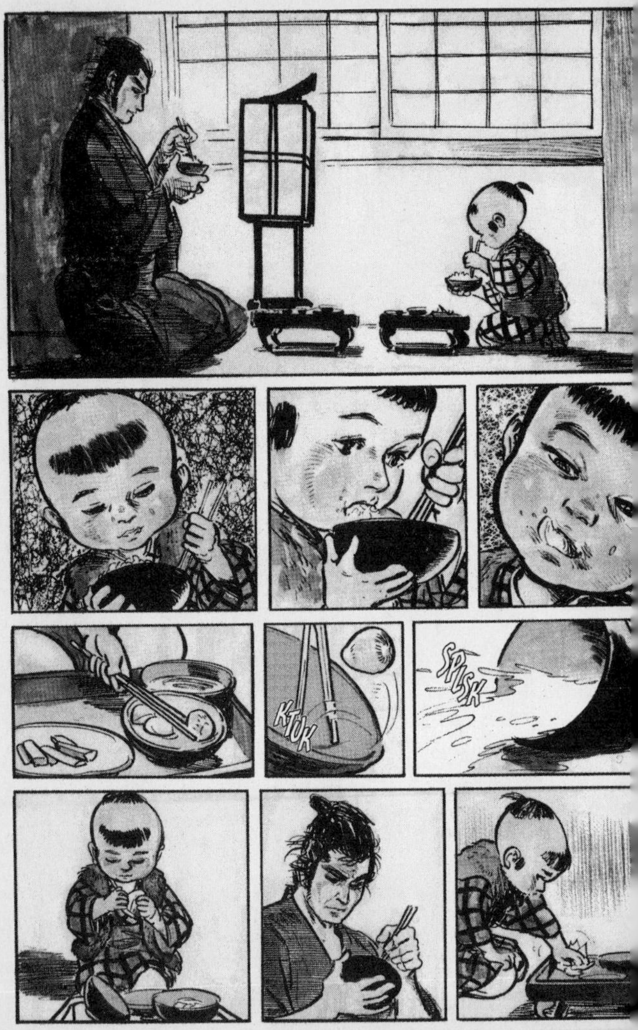
KTUK
SPLSK

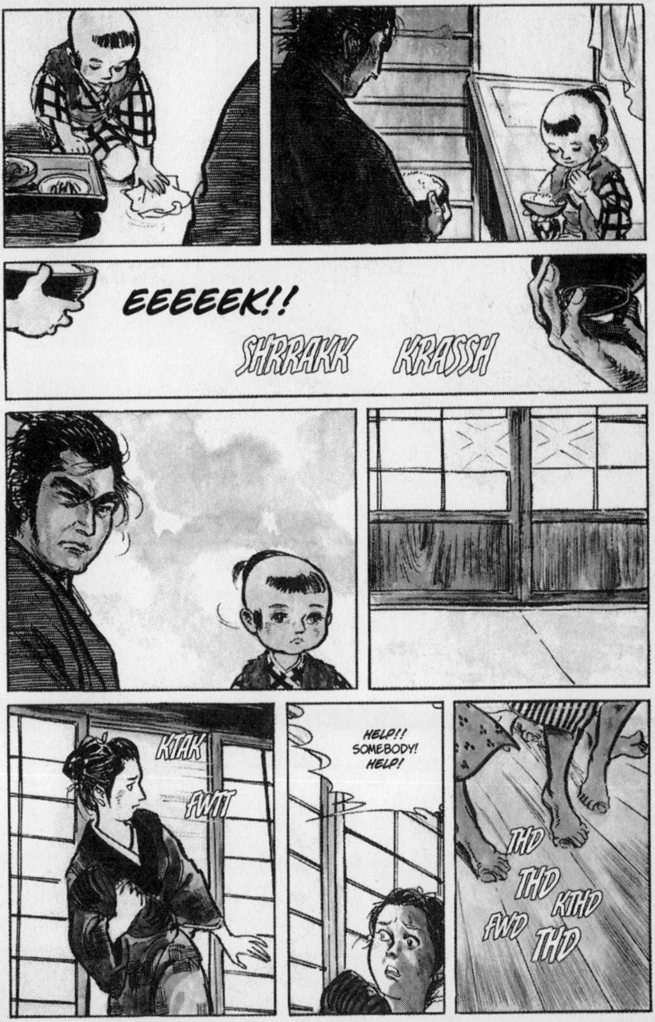
EEEEEK!!
SHRRAKK
KRASSH
KTAK
FWIT
HELP!! SOMEBODY! HELP!
THD
THD
KTHD
FWD
THD

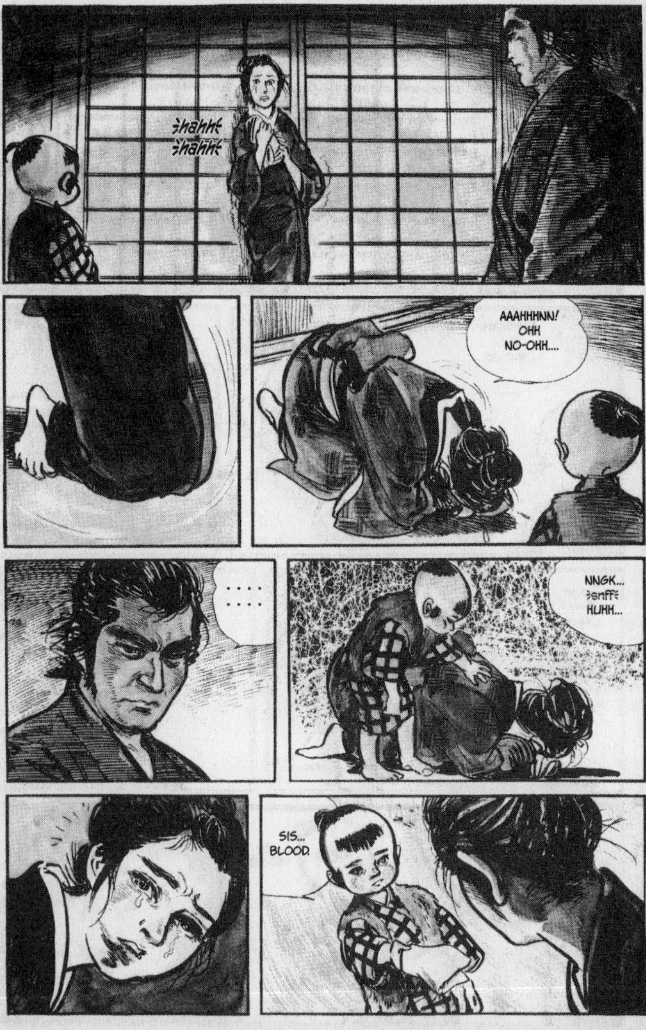

hahh hahh
AAAHHHNN! OHH NO-OHH....
. . . .
. . . .
NNGK... snff HUHH...
SIS... BLOOD.

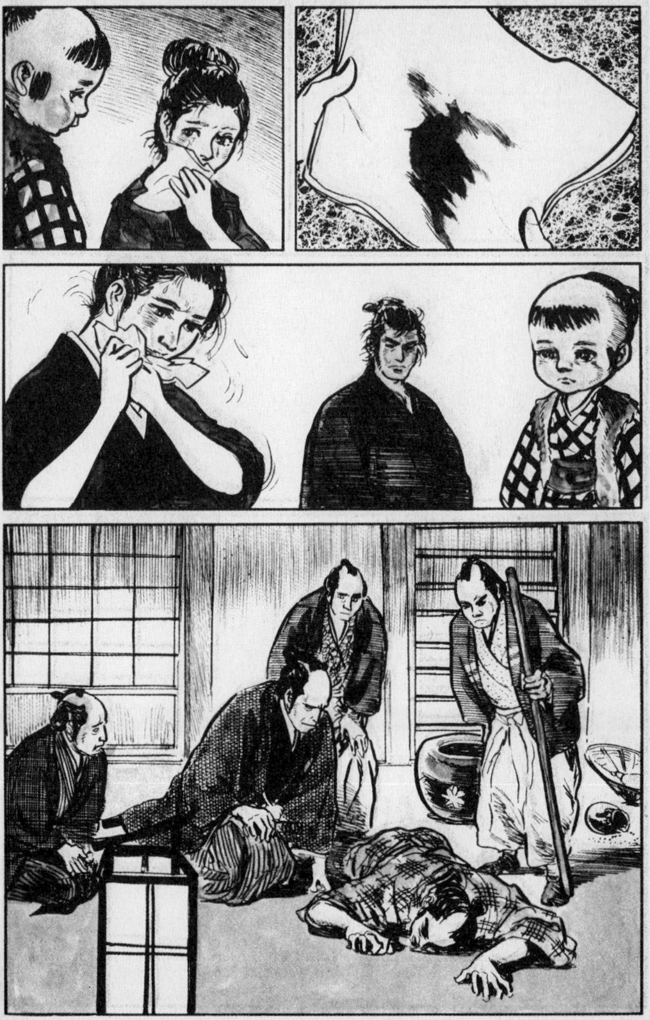

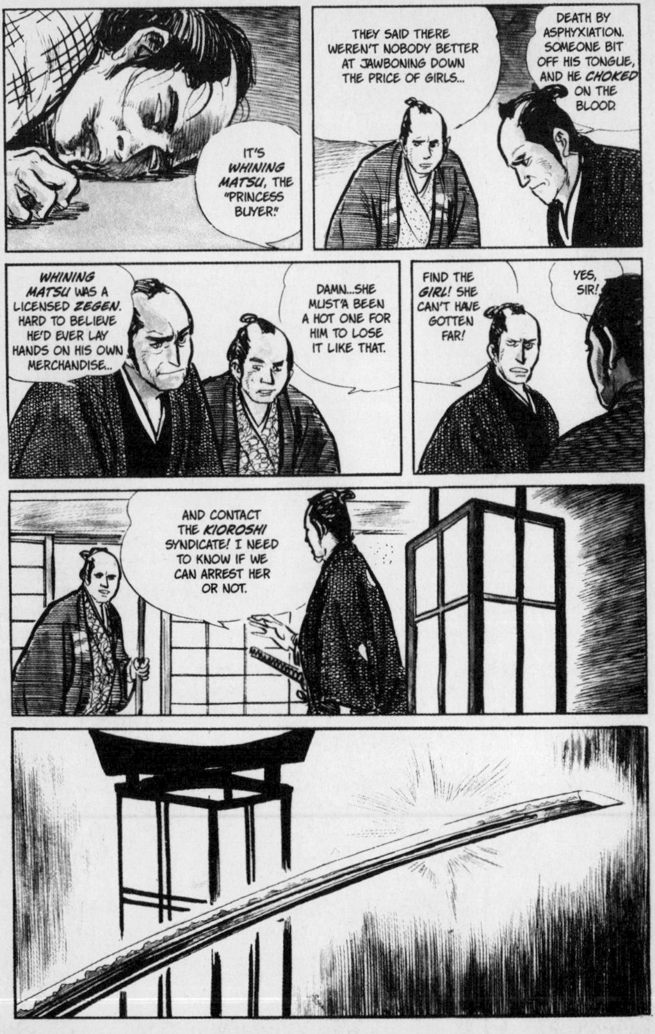
IT'S WHINING MATSU, THE "PRINCESS BUYER."
THEY SAID THERE WEREN'T NOBODY BETTER AT JAWBONING DOWN THE PRICE OF GIRLS...
DEATH BY ASPHYXIATION. SOMEONE BIT OFF HIS TONGUE, AND HE CHOKED ON THE BLOOD.
WHINING MATSU WAS A LICENSED ZEGEN. HARD TO BELIEVE HE'D EVER LAY HANDS ON HIS OWN MERCHANDISE...
DAMN...SHE MUST'A BEEN A HOT ONE FOR HIM TO LOSE IT LIKE THAT.
FIND THE GIRL! SHE CAN'T HAVE GOTTEN FAR!
YES, SIR!
AND CONTACT THE KIOROSHI SYNDICATE! I NEED TO KNOW IF WE CAN ARREST HER OR NOT.

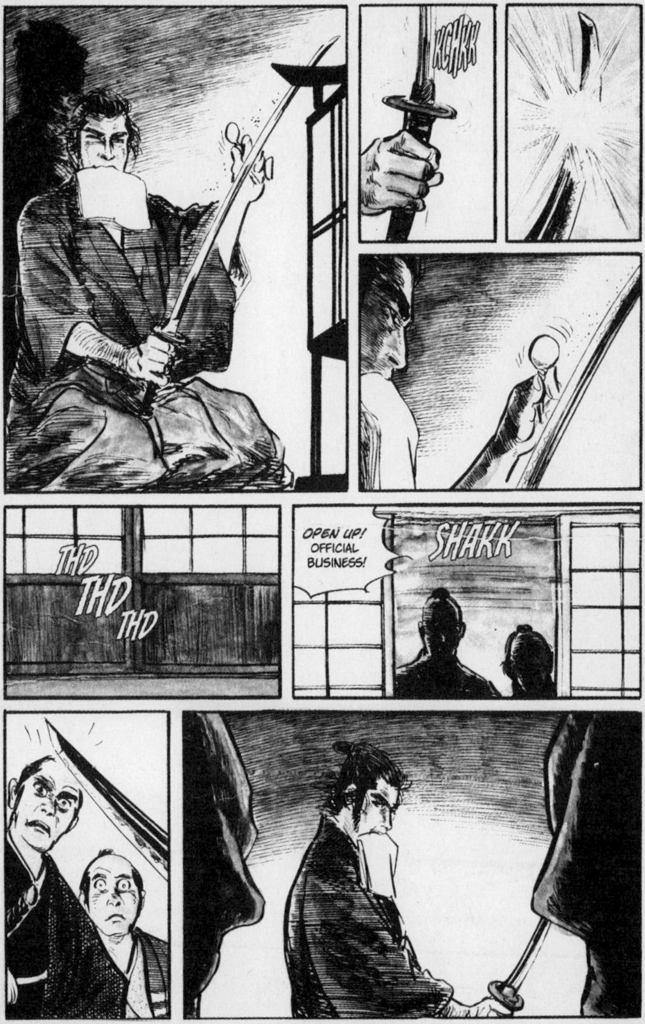
KCHKK
THD
THD
THD
OPEN UP! OFFICIAL BUSINESS!
SHAKK

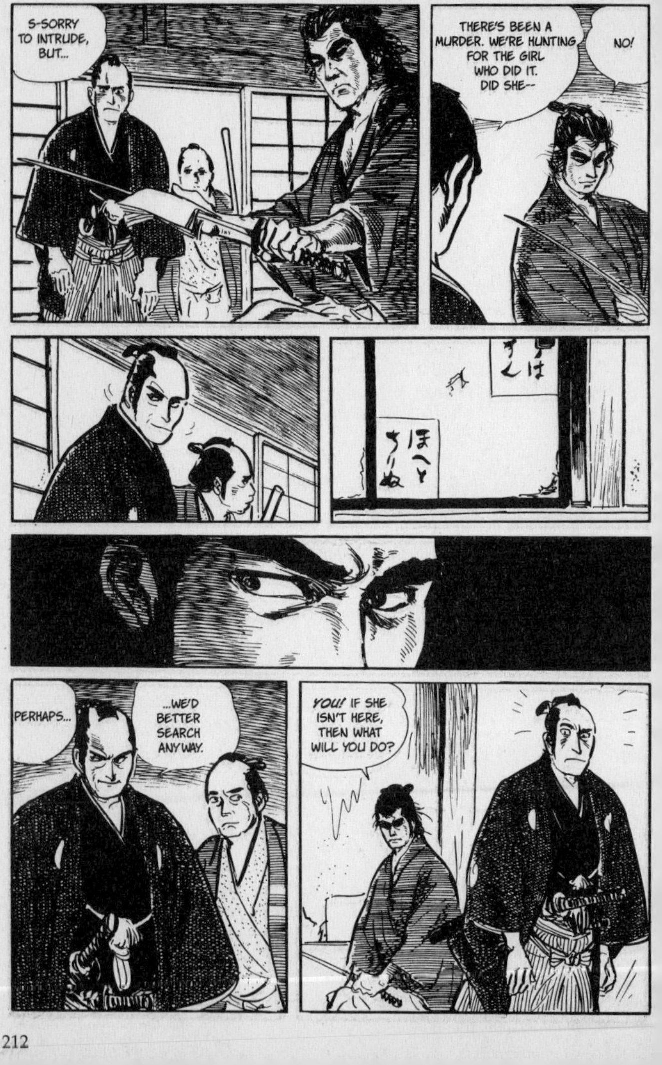
S-SORRY TO INTRUDE, BUT...
THERE'S BEEN A MURDER. WE'RE HUNTING FOR THE GIRL WHO DID IT. DID SHE--
NO!
ほへと
ちりぬ
PERHAPS...
...WE'D BETTER SEARCH ANYWAY.
YOU! IF SHE ISN'T HERE, THEN WHAT WILL YOU DO?

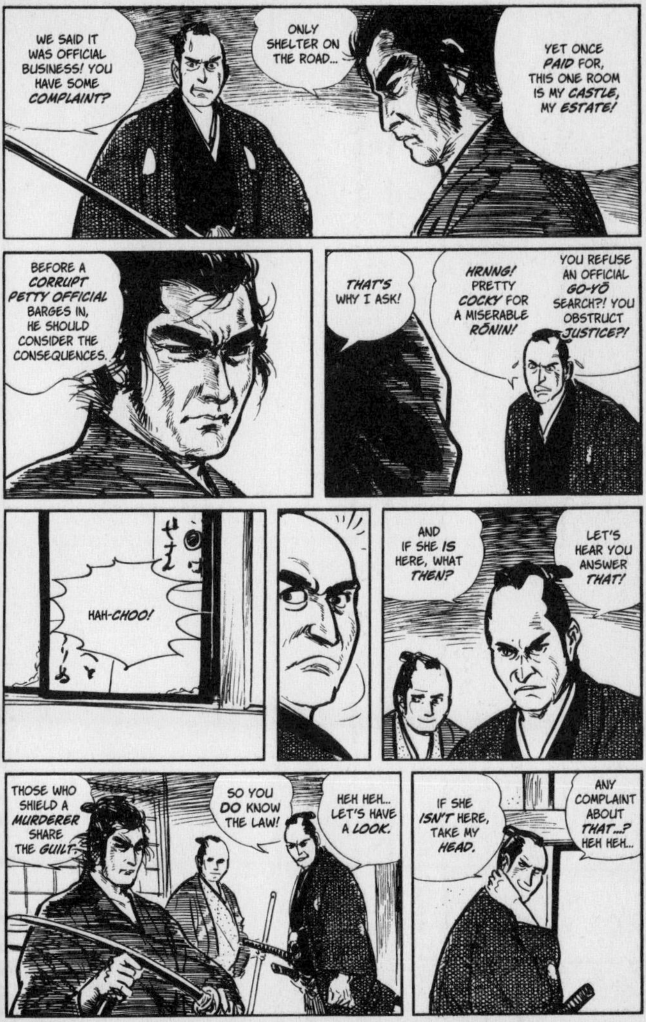

WE SAID IT WAS OFFICIAL BUSINESS! YOU HAVE SOME COMPLAINT?
ONLY SHELTER ON THE ROAD...
YET ONCE PAID FOR, THIS ONE ROOM IS MY CASTLE, MY ESTATE!
BEFORE A CORRUPT PETTY OFFICIAL BARGES IN, HE SHOULD CONSIDER THE CONSEQUENCES.
THAT'S WHY I ASK!
HRNNG! PRETTY COCKY FOR A MISERABLE RŌNIN!
YOU REFUSE AN OFFICIAL GO-YŌ SEARCH?! YOU OBSTRUCT JUSTICE?!
HAH-CHOO!
AND IF SHE IS HERE, WHAT THEN?
LET'S HEAR YOU ANSWER THAT!
THOSE WHO SHIELD A MURDERER SHARE THE GUILT.
SO YOU DO KNOW THE LAW!
HEH HEH... LET'S HAVE A LOOK.
IF SHE ISN'T HERE, TAKE MY HEAD.
ANY COMPLAINT ABOUT THAT...? HEH HEH...

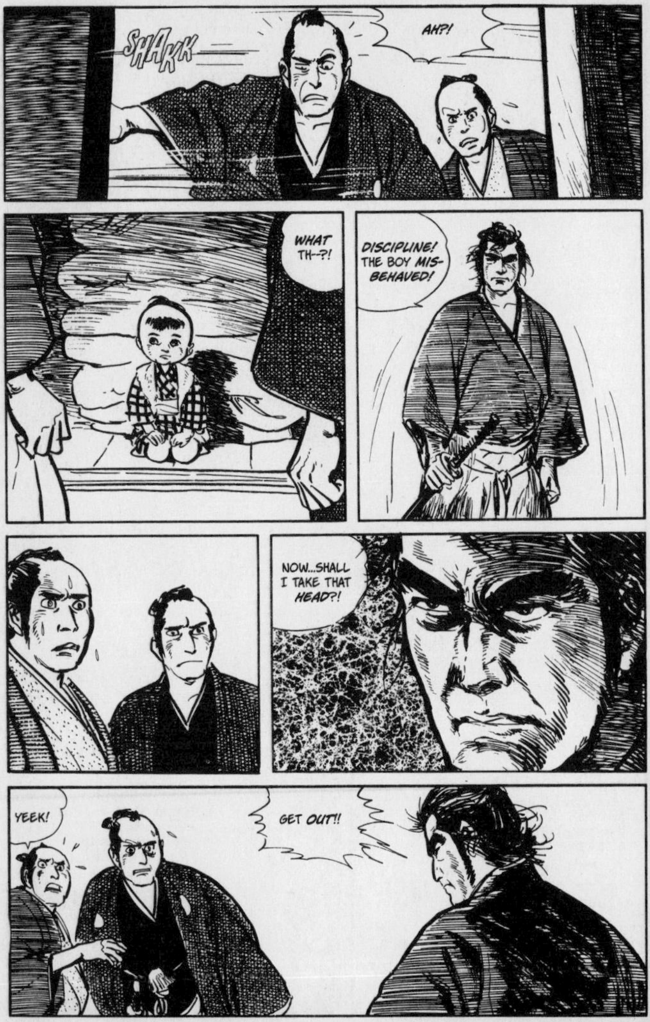
SHAKK
AH?!
WHAT TH--?!
DISCIPLINE! THE BOY MIS-BEHAVED!
NOW...SHALL I TAKE THAT HEAD?!
YEEK!
GET OUT!!

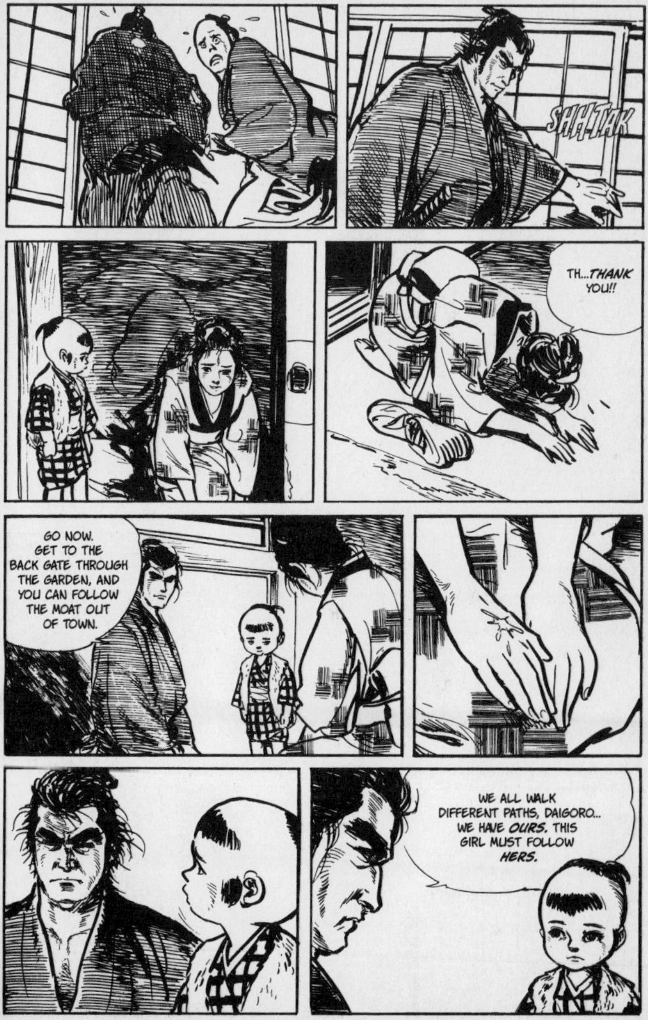
SHHTAK
TH...THANK YOU!!
GO NOW. GET TO THE BACK GATE THROUGH THE GARDEN, AND YOU CAN FOLLOW THE MOAT OUT OF TOWN.
WE ALL WALK DIFFERENT PATHS, DAIGORO... WE HAVE OURS. THIS GIRL MUST FOLLOW HERS.

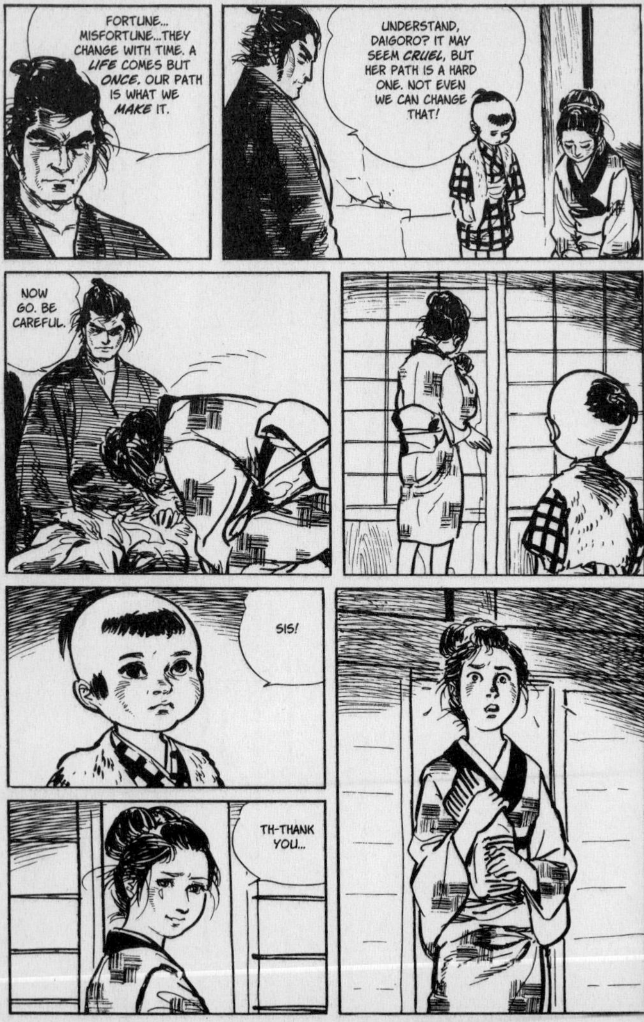
FORTUNE... MISFORTUNE...THEY CHANGE WITH TIME. A *LIFE* COMES BUT *ONCE.* OUR PATH IS WHAT WE *MAKE* IT.
UNDERSTAND, DAIGORO? IT MAY SEEM *CRUEL*, BUT HER PATH IS A HARD ONE. NOT EVEN WE CAN CHANGE THAT!
NOW GO. BE CAREFUL.
SIS!
TH-THANK YOU...

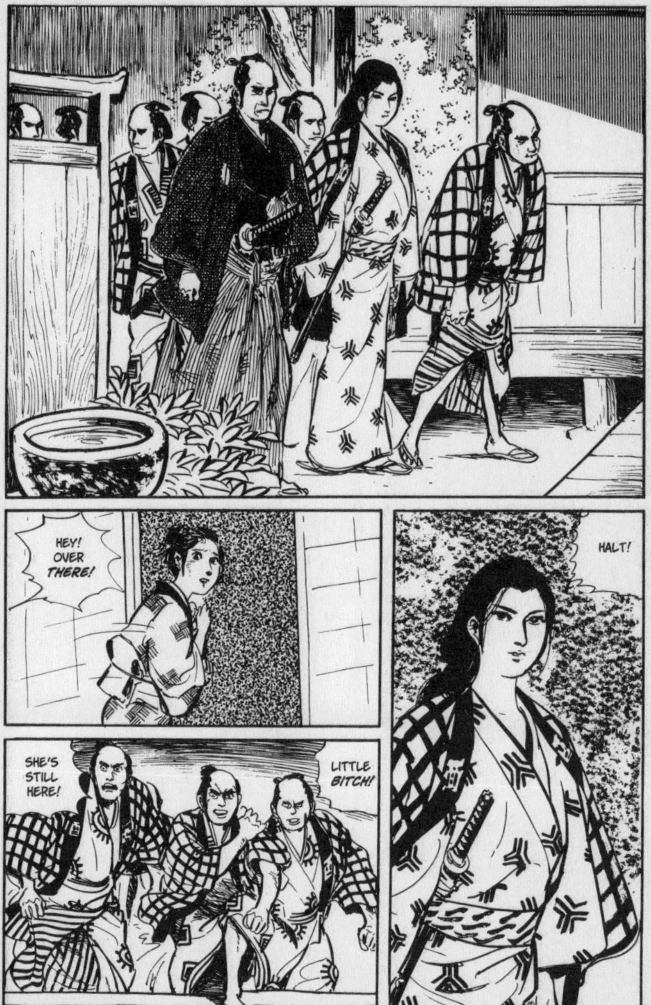
HEY! OVER THERE!
SHE'S STILL HERE!
LITTLE BITCH!
HALT!

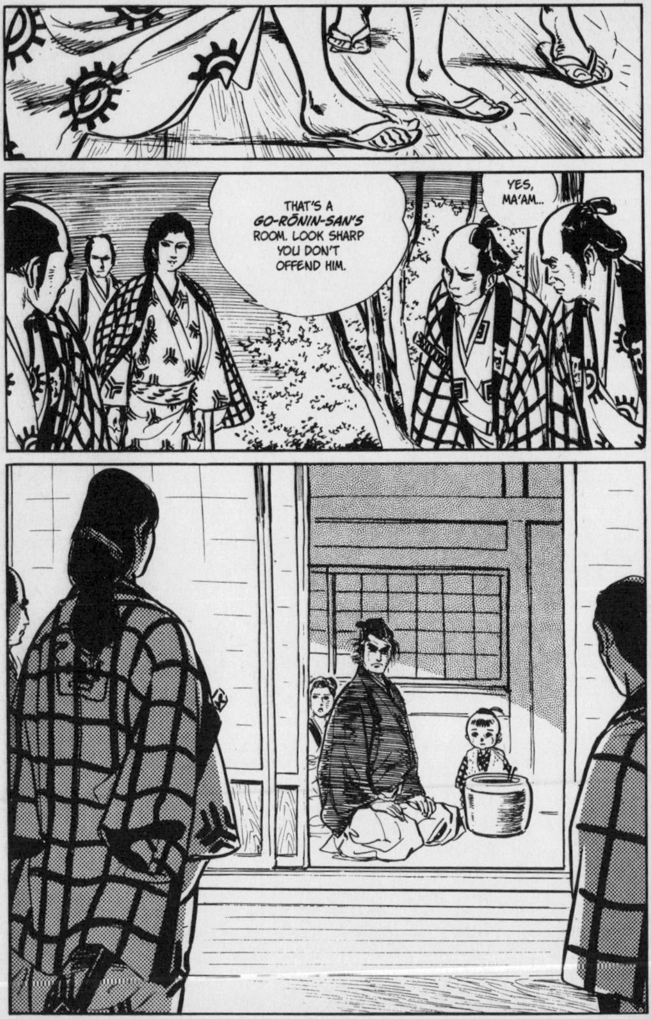
THAT'S A *GO-RŌNIN-SAN'S* ROOM. LOOK SHARP YOU DON'T OFFEND HIM.
YES, MA'AM...

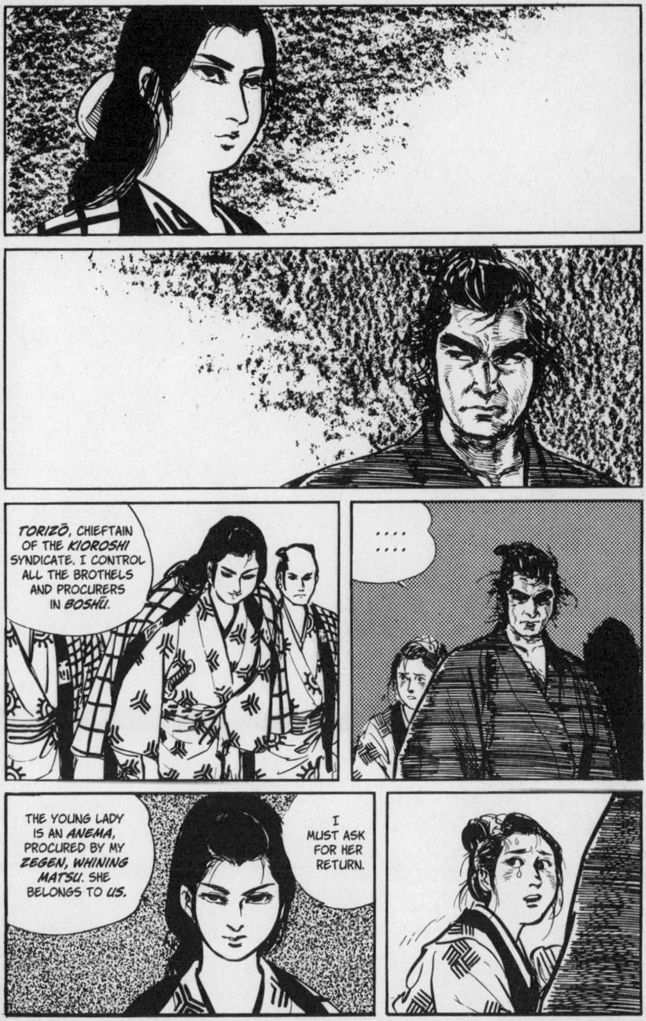
TORIZŌ, CHIEFTAIN OF THE KIOROSHI SYNDICATE. I CONTROL ALL THE BROTHELS AND PROCURERS IN BOSHŪ.
....
....
THE YOUNG LADY IS AN ANEMA, PROCURED BY MY ZEGEN, WHINING MATSU. SHE BELONGS TO US.
I MUST ASK FOR HER RETURN.

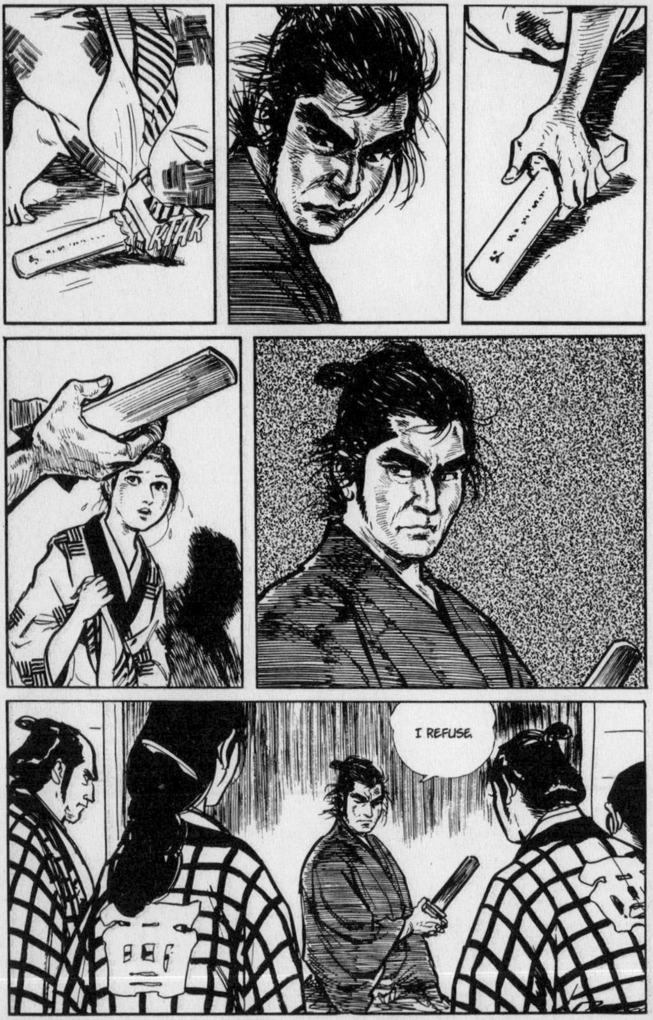
KTAK
I REFUSE.

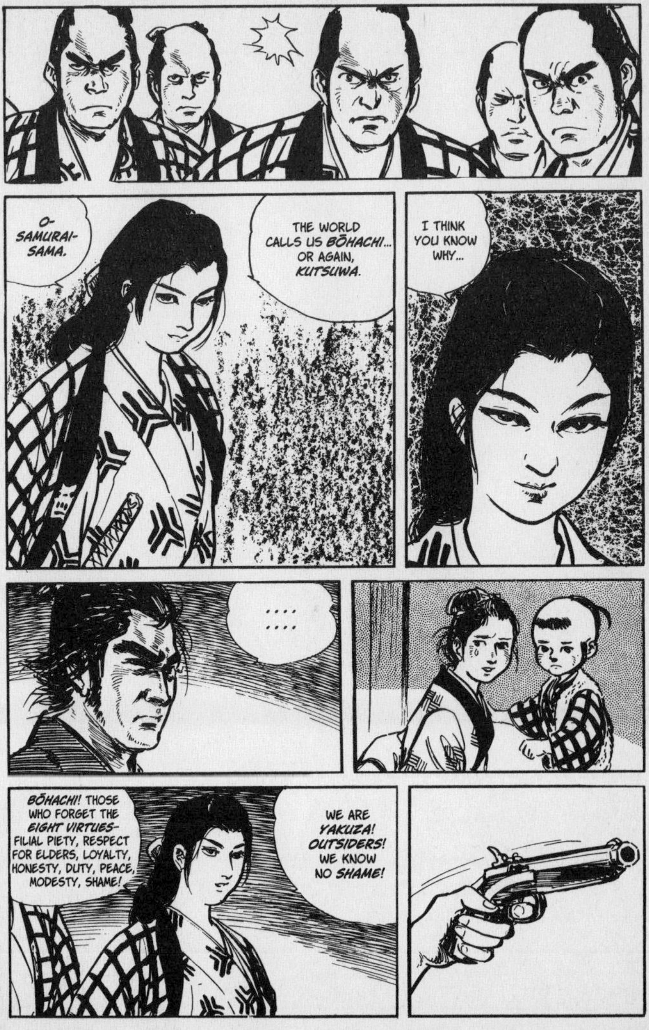
O-SAMURAI-SAMA.
THE WORLD CALLS US BŌHACHI... OR AGAIN, KUTSUWA.
I THINK YOU KNOW WHY...
....
....
BŌHACHI! THOSE WHO FORGET THE EIGHT VIRTUES- FILIAL PIETY, RESPECT FOR ELDERS, LOYALTY, HONESTY, DUTY, PEACE, MODESTY, SHAME!
WE ARE YAKUZA! OUTSIDERS! WE KNOW NO SHAME!

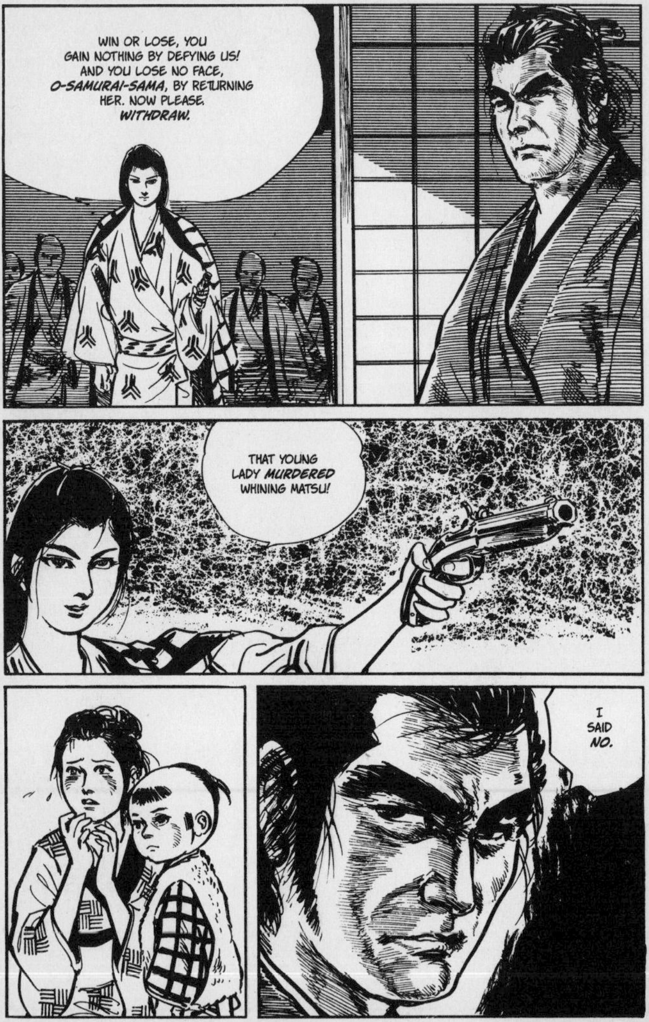
WIN OR LOSE, YOU GAIN NOTHING BY DEFYING US! AND YOU LOSE NO FACE, O-SAMURAI-SAMA, BY RETURNING HER. NOW PLEASE. WITHDRAW.
THAT YOUNG LADY MURDERED WHINING MATSU!
I SAID NO.

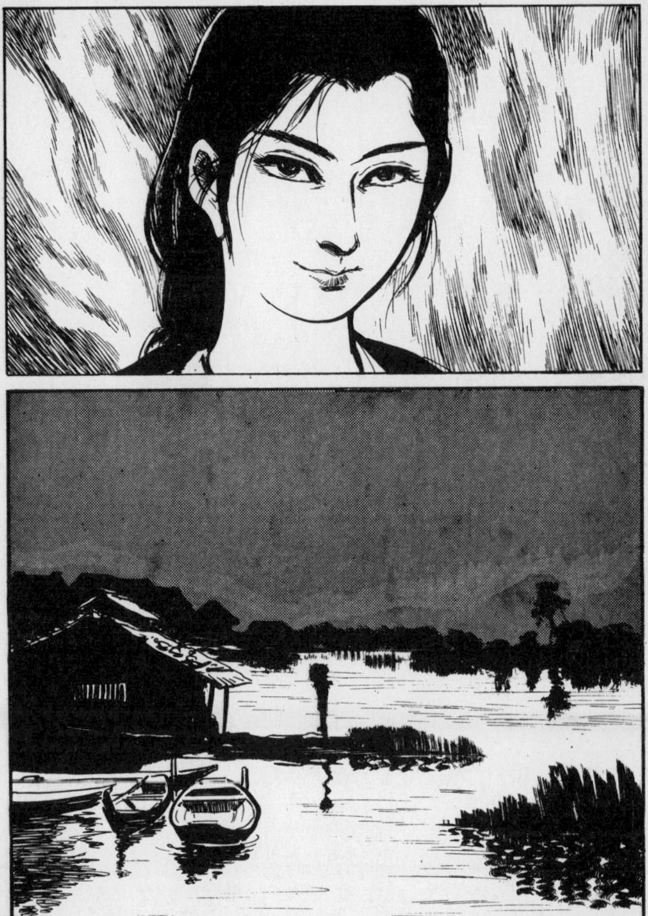

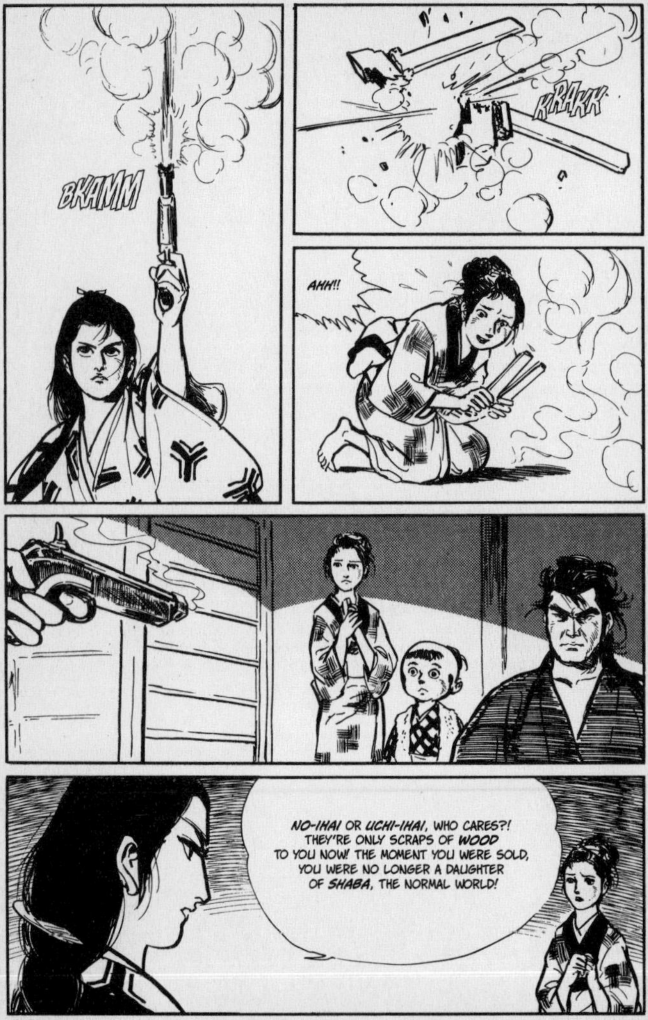
BKAMM
KRAKK
AHH!!
NO-IHAI OR UCHI-IHAI, WHO CARES?! THEY'RE ONLY SCRAPS OF WOOD TO YOU NOW! THE MOMENT YOU WERE SOLD, YOU WERE NO LONGER A DAUGHTER OF SHABA, THE NORMAL WORLD!

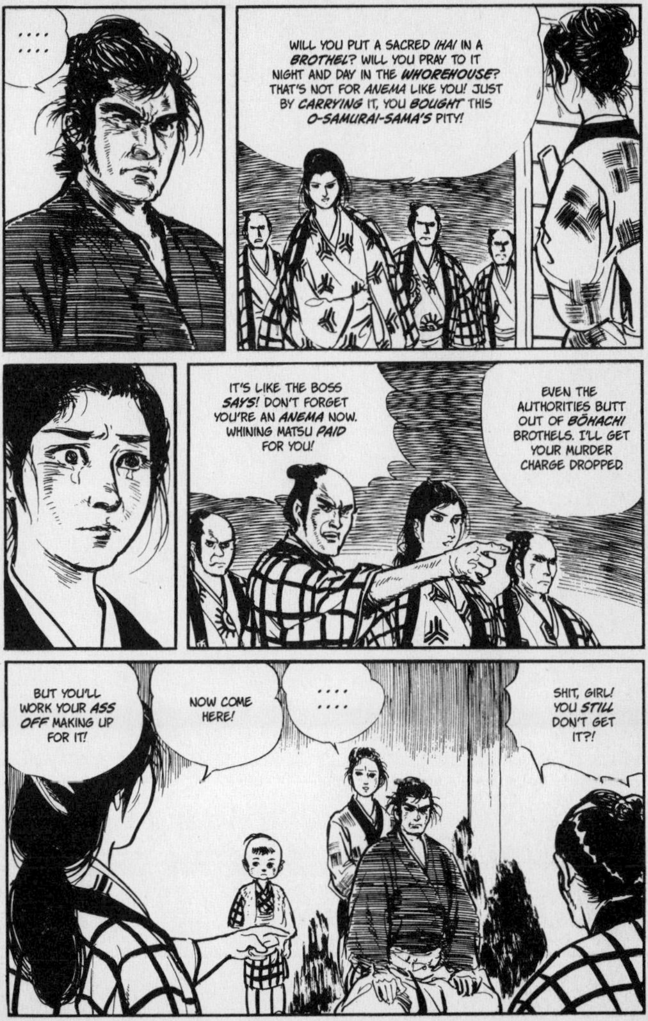
....
....
WILL YOU PUT A SACRED IHAI IN A BROTHEL? WILL YOU PRAY TO IT NIGHT AND DAY IN THE WHOREHOUSE? THAT'S NOT FOR ANEMA LIKE YOU! JUST BY CARRYING IT, YOU BOUGHT THIS O-SAMURAI-SAMA'S PITY!
IT'S LIKE THE BOSS SAYS! DON'T FORGET YOU'RE AN ANEMA NOW. WHINING MATSU PAID FOR YOU!
EVEN THE AUTHORITIES BUTT OUT OF BŌHACHI BROTHELS. I'LL GET YOUR MURDER CHARGE DROPPED.
BUT YOU'LL WORK YOUR ASS OFF MAKING UP FOR IT!
NOW COME HERE!
....
....
SHIT, GIRL! YOU STILL DON'T GET IT?!

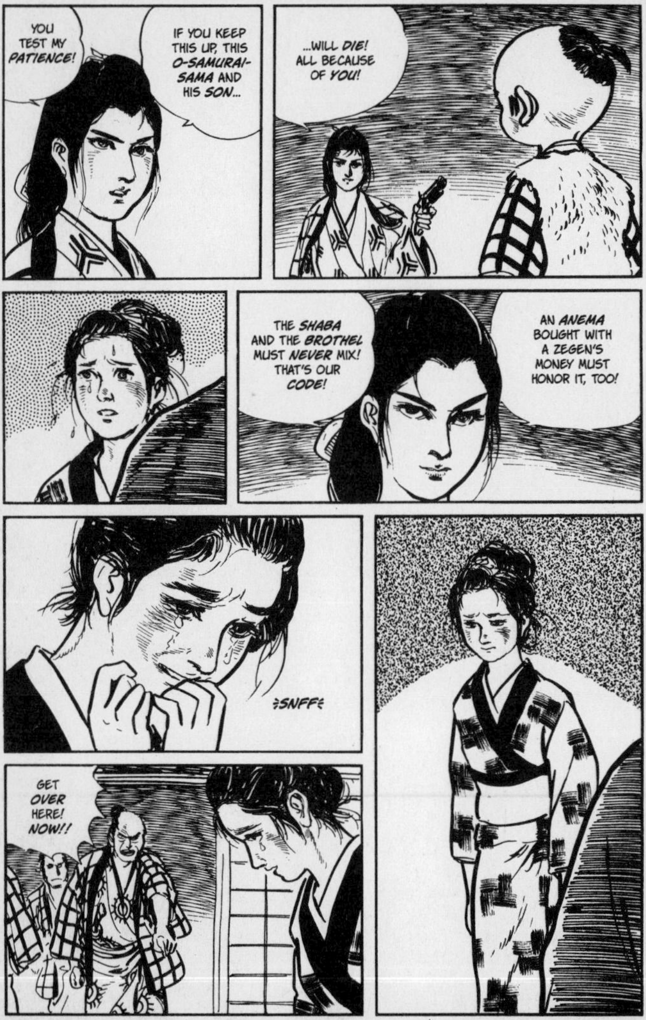
YOU TEST MY PATIENCE!
IF YOU KEEP THIS UP, THIS O-SAMURAI-SAMA AND HIS SON...
...WILL DIE! ALL BECAUSE OF YOU!
THE SHABA AND THE BROTHEL MUST NEVER MIX! THAT'S OUR CODE!
AN ANEMA BOUGHT WITH A ZEGEN'S MONEY MUST HONOR IT, TOO!
SNFF
GET OVER HERE! NOW!!

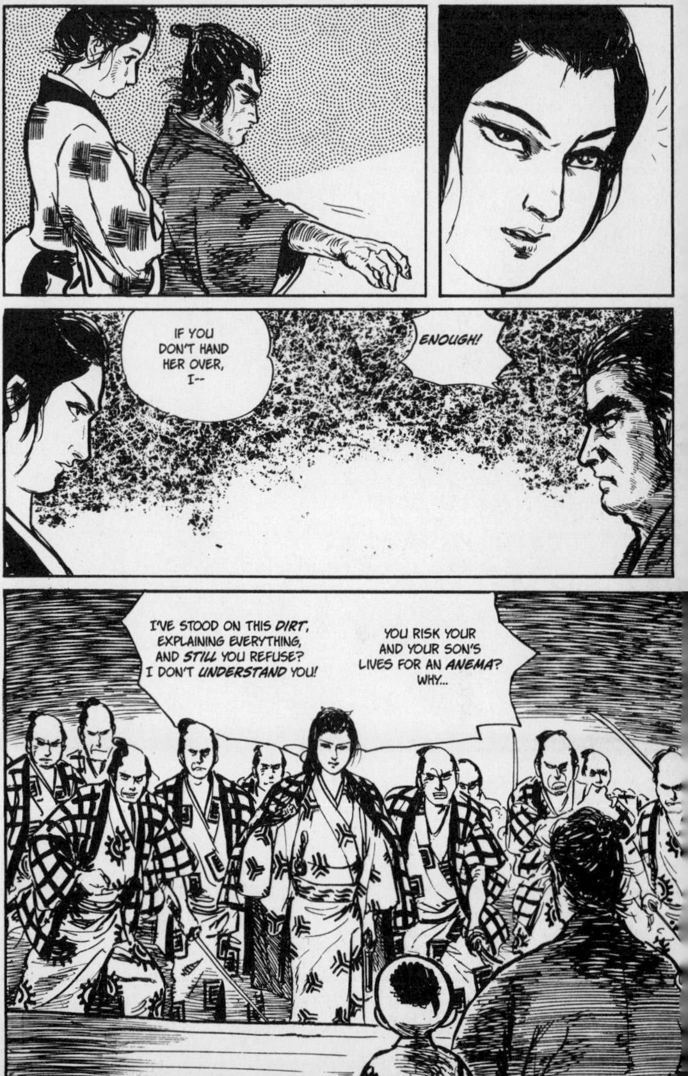
IF YOU DON'T HAND HER OVER, I--
ENOUGH!
I'VE STOOD ON THIS DIRT, EXPLAINING EVERYTHING, AND STILL YOU REFUSE? I DON'T UNDERSTAND YOU!
YOU RISK YOUR AND YOUR SON'S LIVES FOR AN ANEMA? WHY...

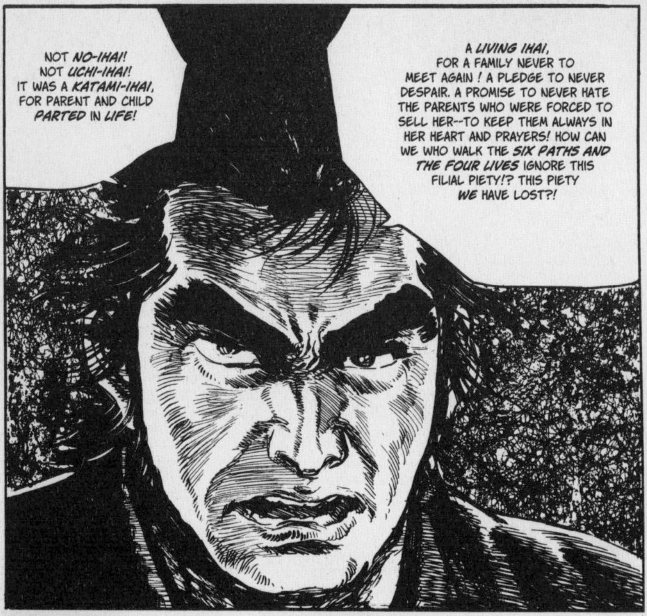
NOT NO-IHAI! NOT UCHI-IHAI! IT WAS A KATAMI-IHAI, FOR PARENT AND CHILD PARTED IN LIFE!
A LIVING IHAI, FOR A FAMILY NEVER TO MEET AGAIN ! A PLEDGE TO NEVER DESPAIR. A PROMISE TO NEVER HATE THE PARENTS WHO WERE FORCED TO SELL HER--TO KEEP THEM ALWAYS IN HER HEART AND PRAYERS! HOW CAN WE WHO WALK THE SIX PATHS AND THE FOUR LIVES IGNORE THIS FILIAL PIETY!? THIS PIETY WE HAVE LOST?!
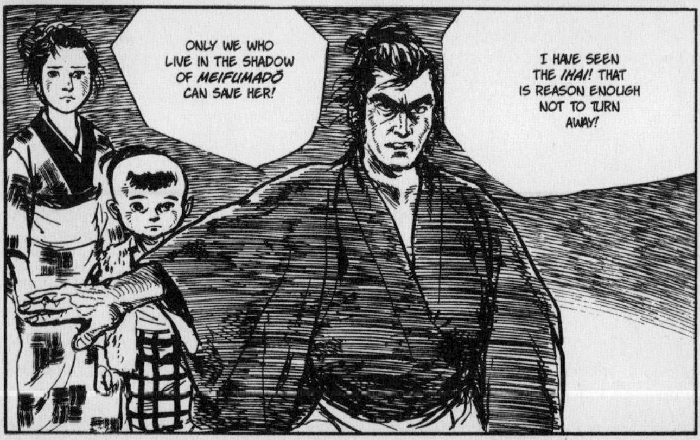
ONLY WE WHO LIVE IN THE SHADOW OF MEIFUMADŌ CAN SAVE HER!
I HAVE SEEN THE IHAI! THAT IS REASON ENOUGH NOT TO TURN AWAY!

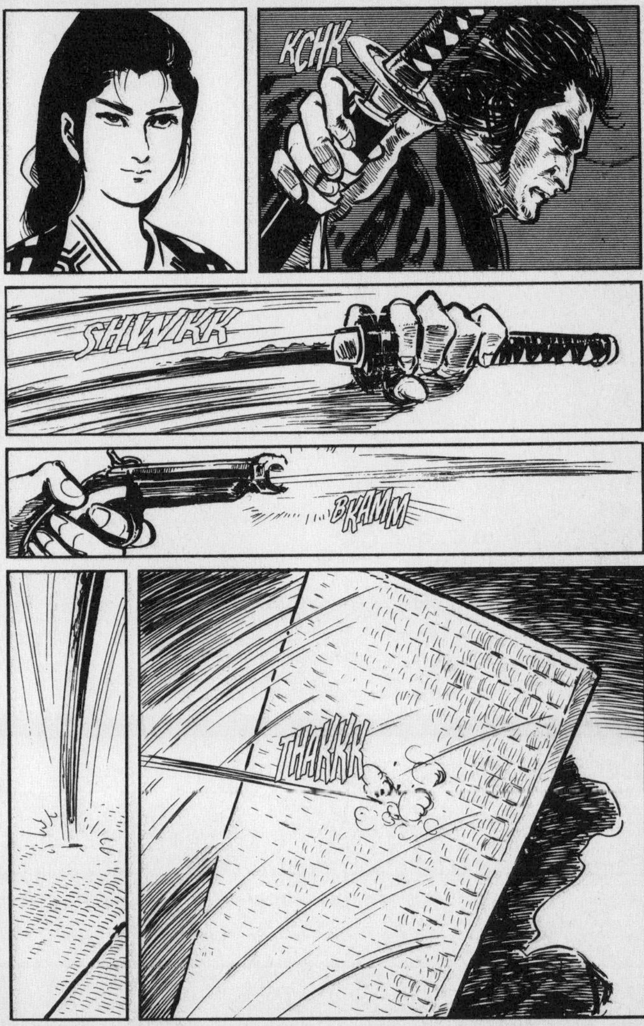
KCHK
SHWKK
BKAMM
THAKKK

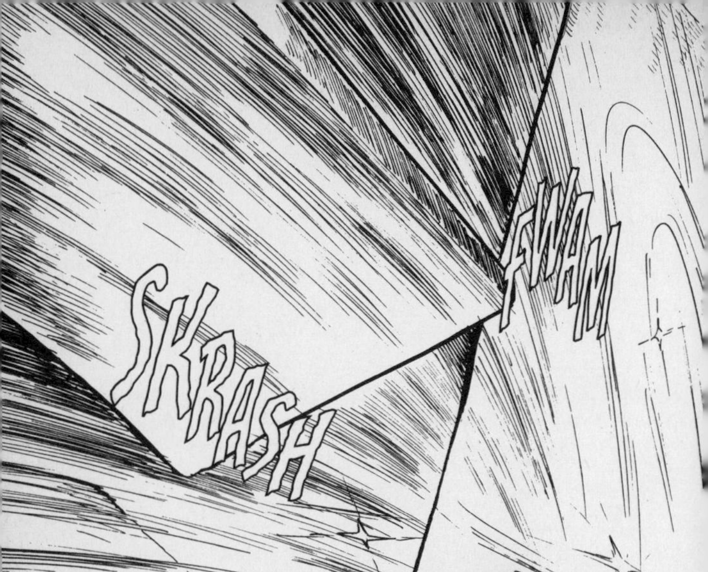
SKRASH
FWAM
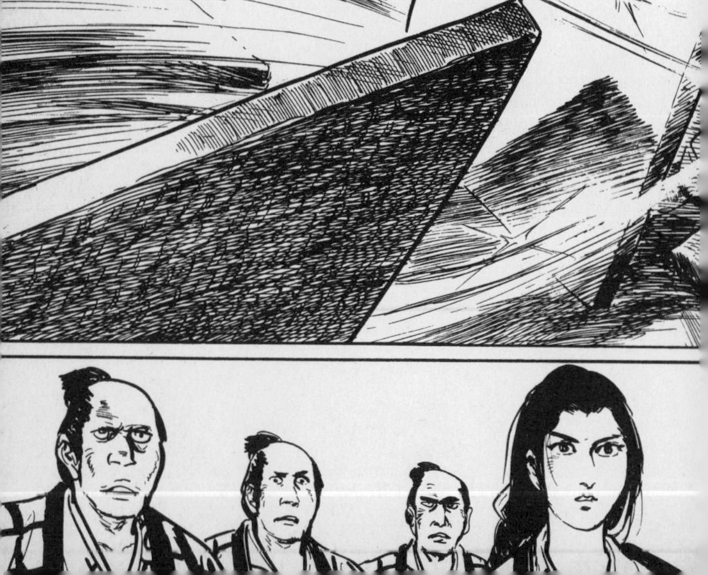

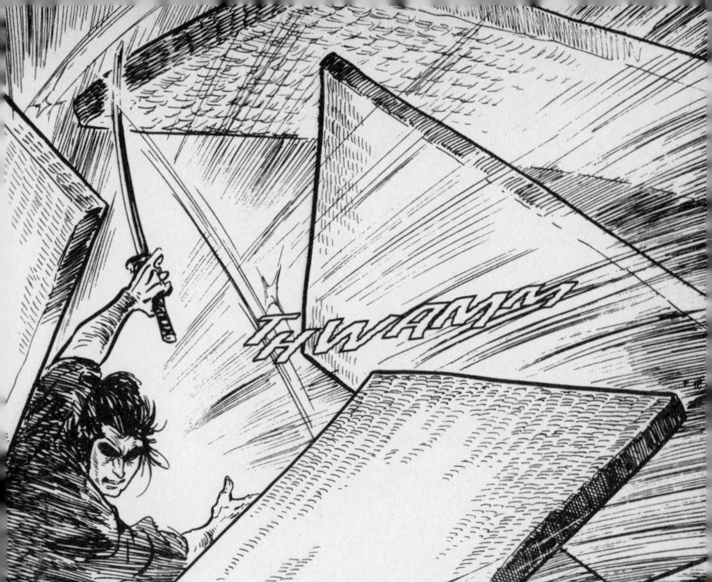
THWAMM
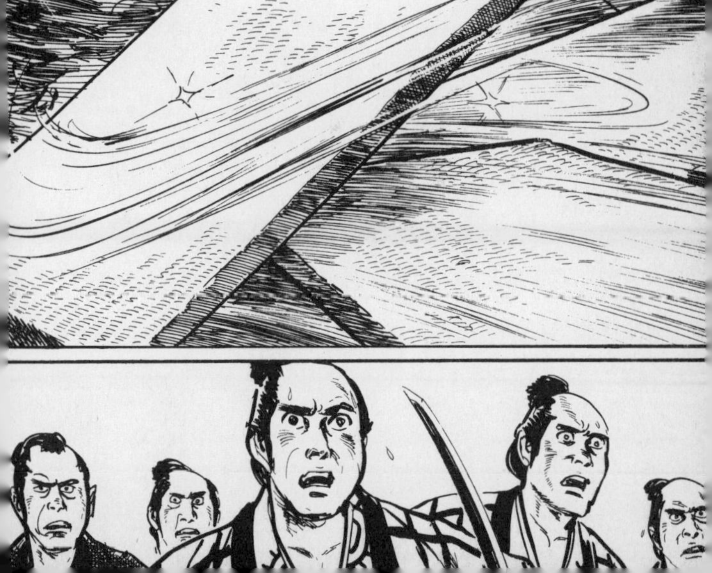

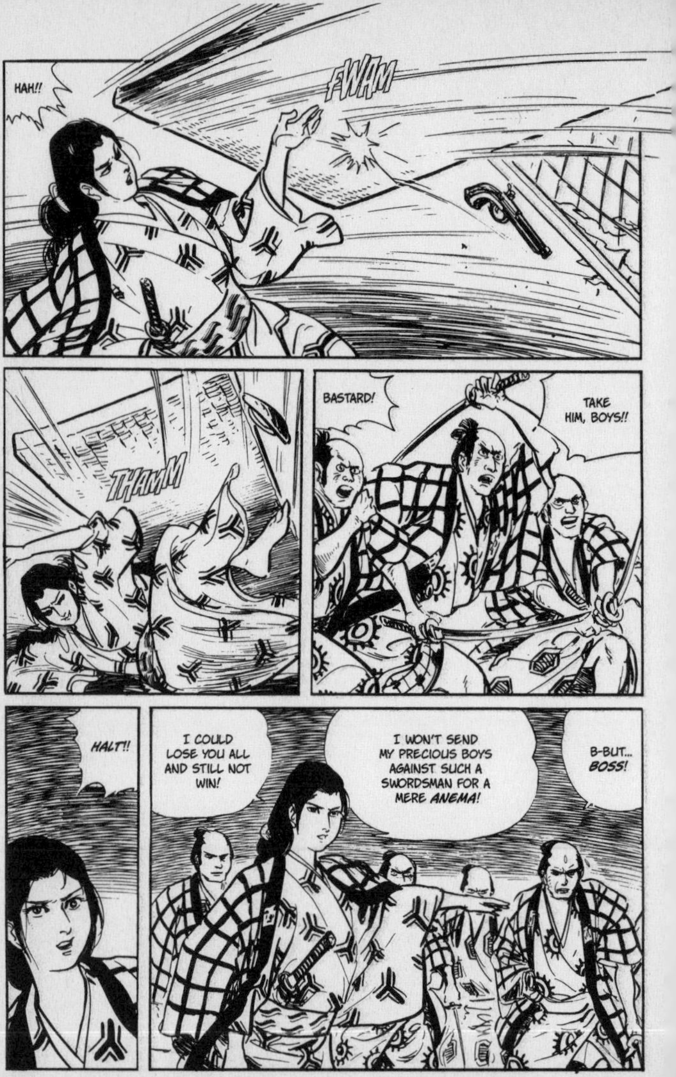
HAH!!
FWAM
THAMM
BASTARD!
TAKE HIM, BOYS!!
HALT!!
I COULD LOSE YOU ALL AND STILL NOT WIN!
I WON'T SEND MY PRECIOUS BOYS AGAINST SUCH A SWORDSMAN FOR A MERE *ANEMA*!
B-BUT... *BOSS*!

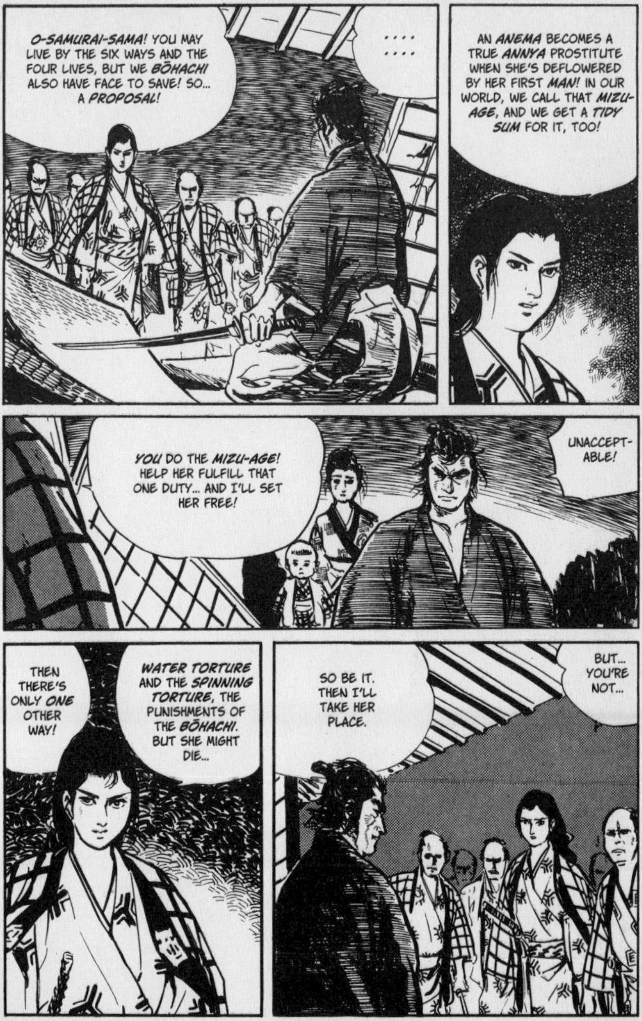
O-SAMURAI-SAMA! YOU MAY LIVE BY THE SIX WAYS AND THE FOUR LIVES, BUT WE BŌHACHI ALSO HAVE FACE TO SAVE! SO... A PROPOSAL!
. . . .
. . . .
AN ANEMA BECOMES A TRUE ANNYA PROSTITUTE WHEN SHE'S DEFLOWERED BY HER FIRST MAN! IN OUR WORLD, WE CALL THAT MIZU-AGE, AND WE GET A TIDY SUM FOR IT, TOO!
YOU DO THE MIZU-AGE! HELP HER FULFILL THAT ONE DUTY... AND I'LL SET HER FREE!
UNACCEPT-ABLE!
THEN THERE'S ONLY ONE OTHER WAY!
WATER TORTURE AND THE SPINNING TORTURE, THE PUNISHMENTS OF THE BŌHACHI. BUT SHE MIGHT DIE...
SO BE IT. THEN I'LL TAKE HER PLACE.
BUT... YOU'RE NOT...

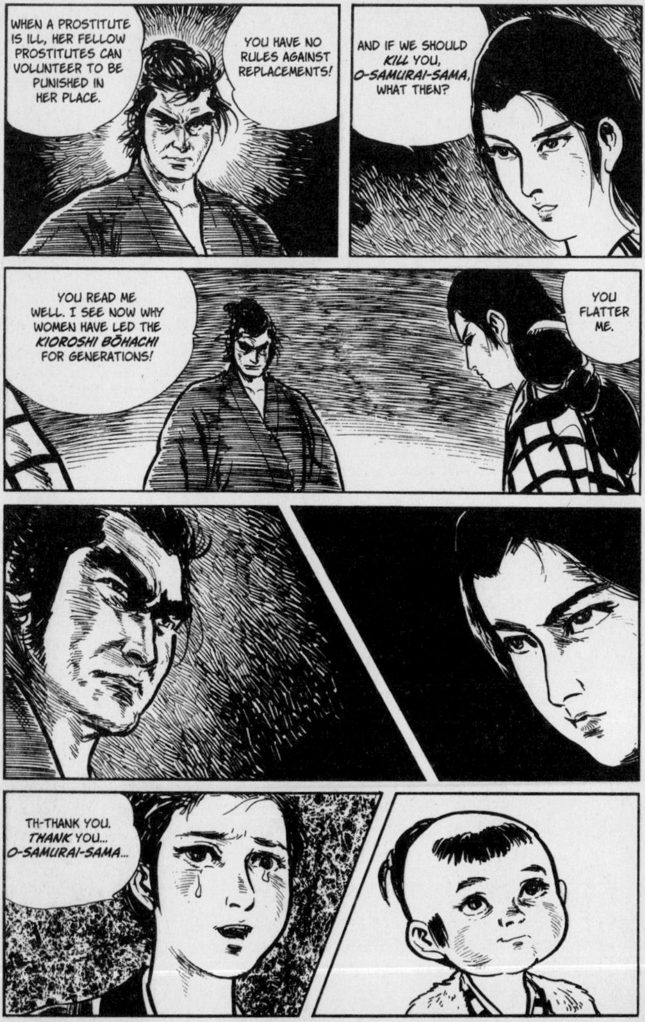
WHEN A PROSTITUTE IS ILL, HER FELLOW PROSTITUTES CAN VOLUNTEER TO BE PUNISHED IN HER PLACE.
YOU HAVE NO RULES AGAINST REPLACEMENTS!
AND IF WE SHOULD *KILL* YOU, *O-SAMURAI-SAMA*, WHAT THEN?
YOU READ ME WELL. I SEE NOW WHY WOMEN HAVE LED THE *KIOROSHI BŌHACHI* FOR GENERATIONS!
YOU FLATTER ME.
TH-THANK YOU. *THANK* YOU... *O-SAMURAI-SAMA*...

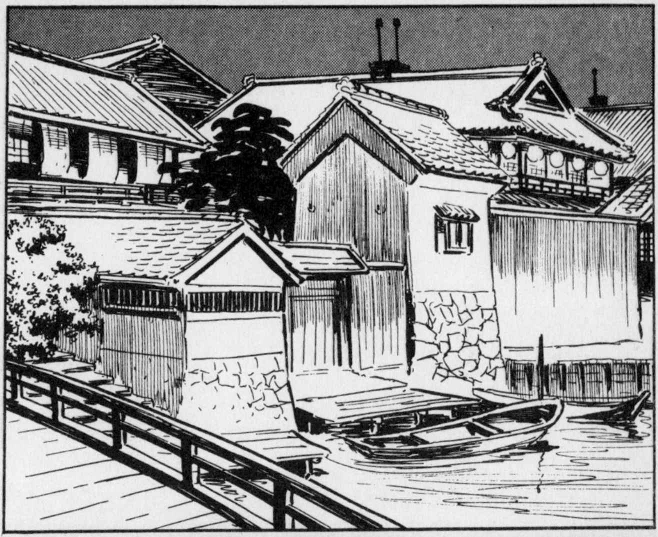

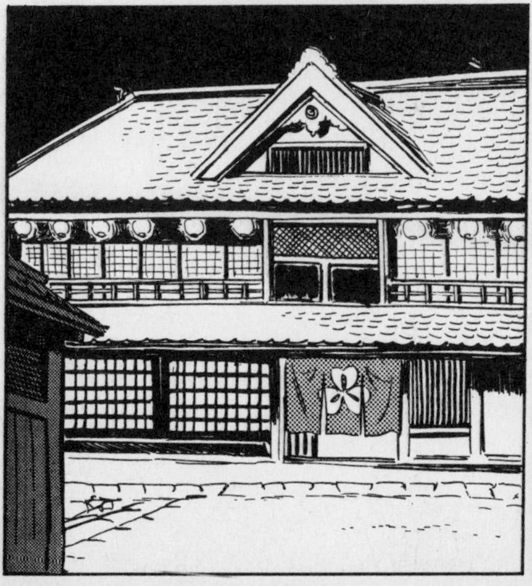

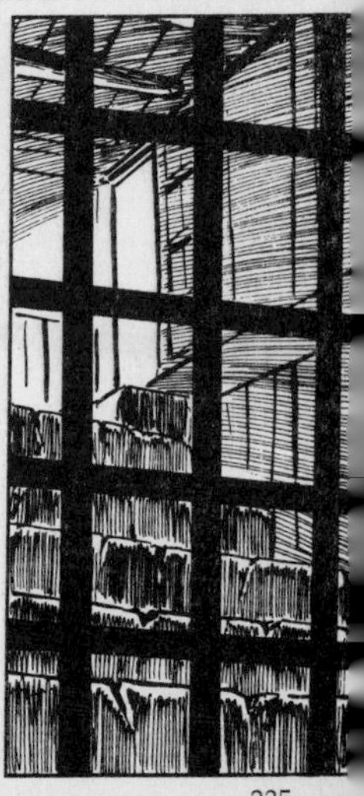

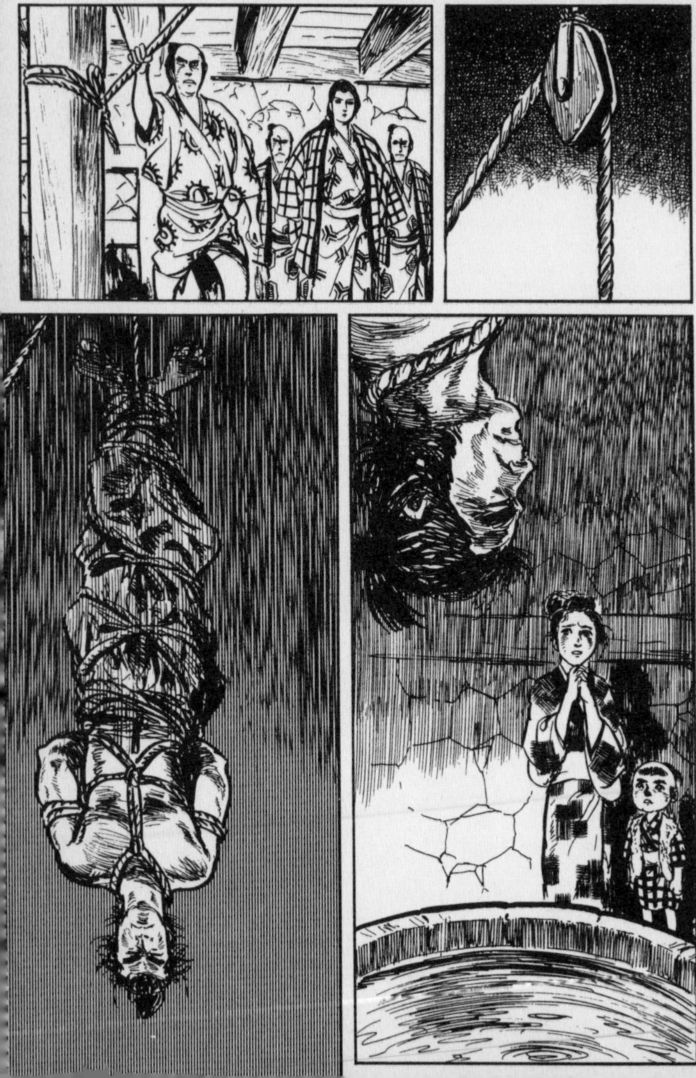

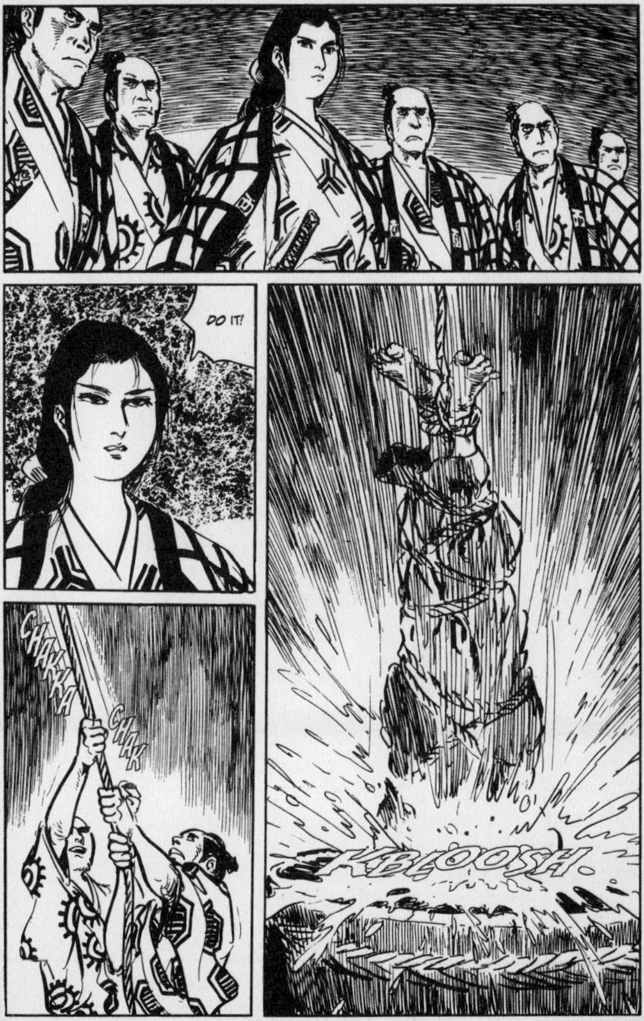
DO IT!
CHAKKA
CHAK
KBLOOSH

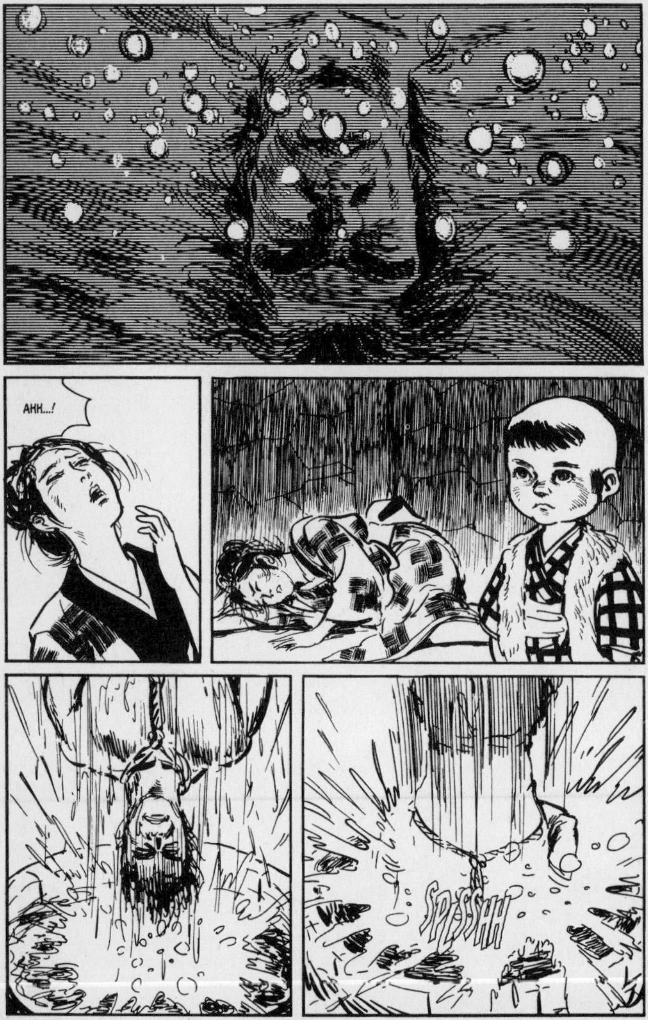
AHH...!
SPLSSHH

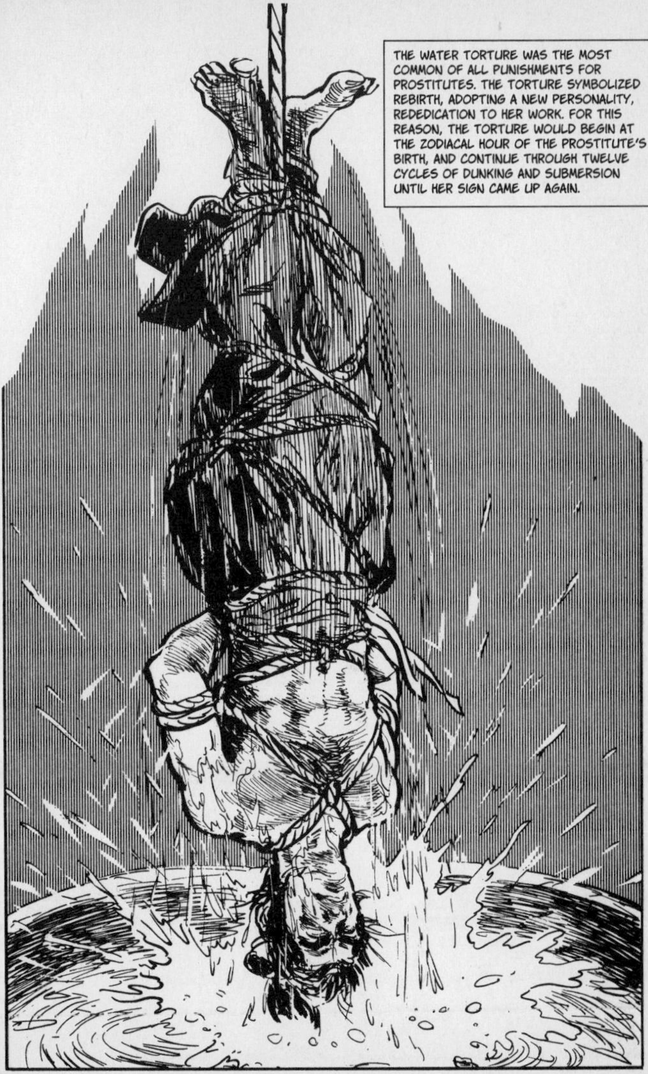
THE WATER TORTURE WAS THE MOST COMMON OF ALL PUNISHMENTS FOR PROSTITUTES. THE TORTURE SYMBOLIZED REBIRTH, ADOPTING A NEW PERSONALITY, REDEDICATION TO HER WORK. FOR THIS REASON, THE TORTURE WOULD BEGIN AT THE ZODIACAL HOUR OF THE PROSTITUTE'S BIRTH, AND CONTINUE THROUGH TWELVE CYCLES OF DUNKING AND SUBMERSION UNTIL HER SIGN CAME UP AGAIN.

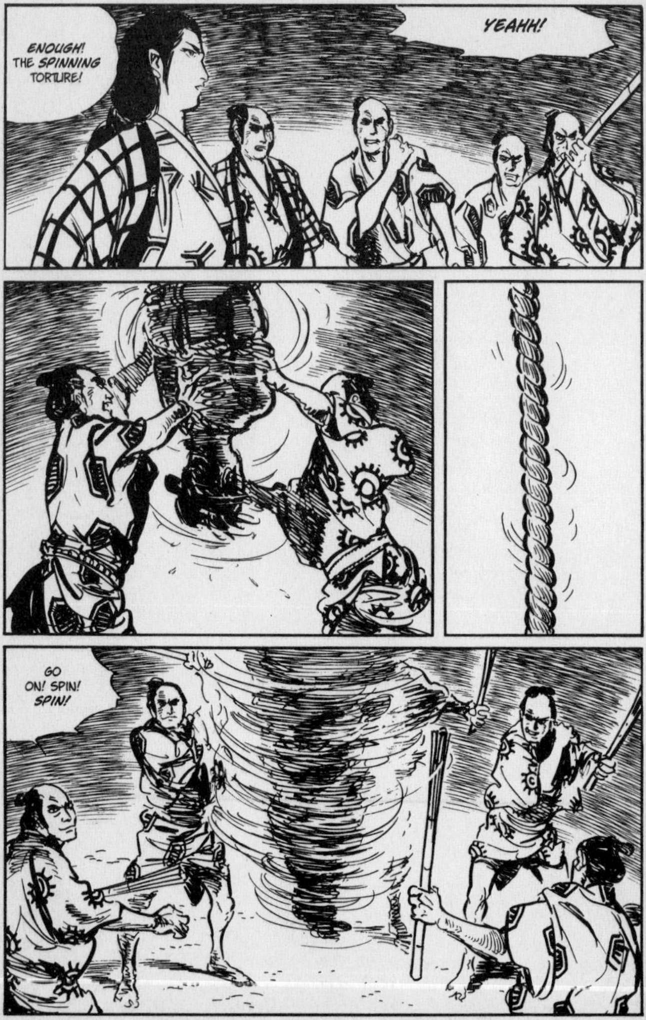
ENOUGH! THE SPINNING TORTURE!
YEAHH!
GO ON! SPIN! SPIN!

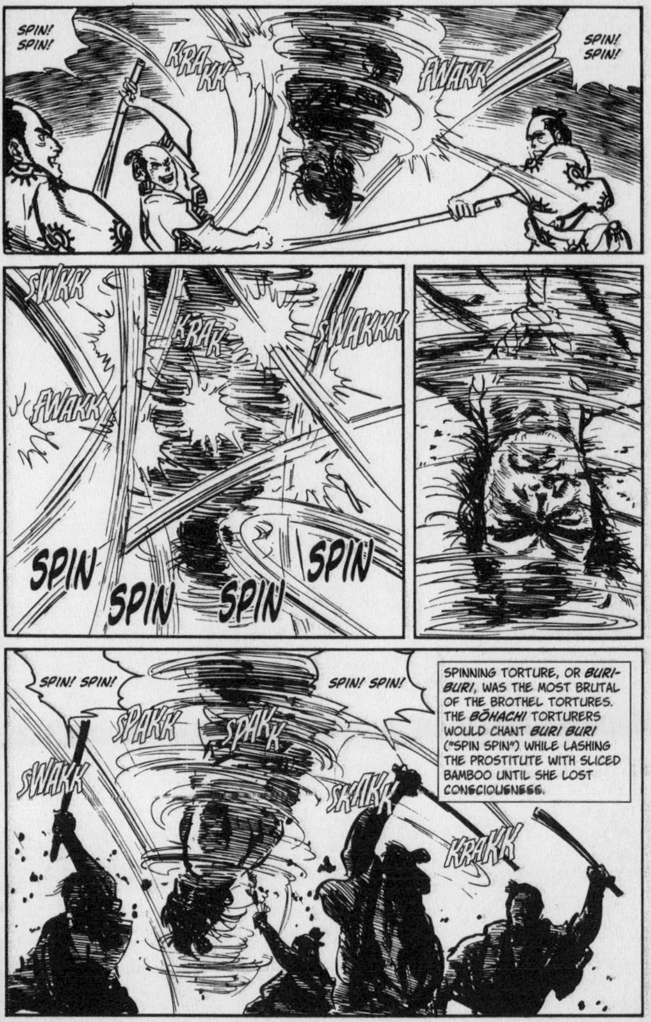
SPIN! SPIN!
KRAKK
FWAKK
SPIN! SPIN!
SWKK
KRAK
SWAKKK
FWAKK
SPIN
SPIN
SPIN
SPIN
SPIN! SPIN!
SPAKK
SPAKK
SPIN! SPIN!
SPINNING TORTURE, OR *BURI-BURI*, WAS THE MOST BRUTAL OF THE BROTHEL TORTURES. THE *BŌHACHI* TORTURERS WOULD CHANT *BURI BURI* ("SPIN SPIN"). WHILE LASHING THE PROSTITUTE WITH SLICED BAMBOO UNTIL SHE LOST CONSCIOUSNESS.
SWAKK
SWAKK
KRAKK

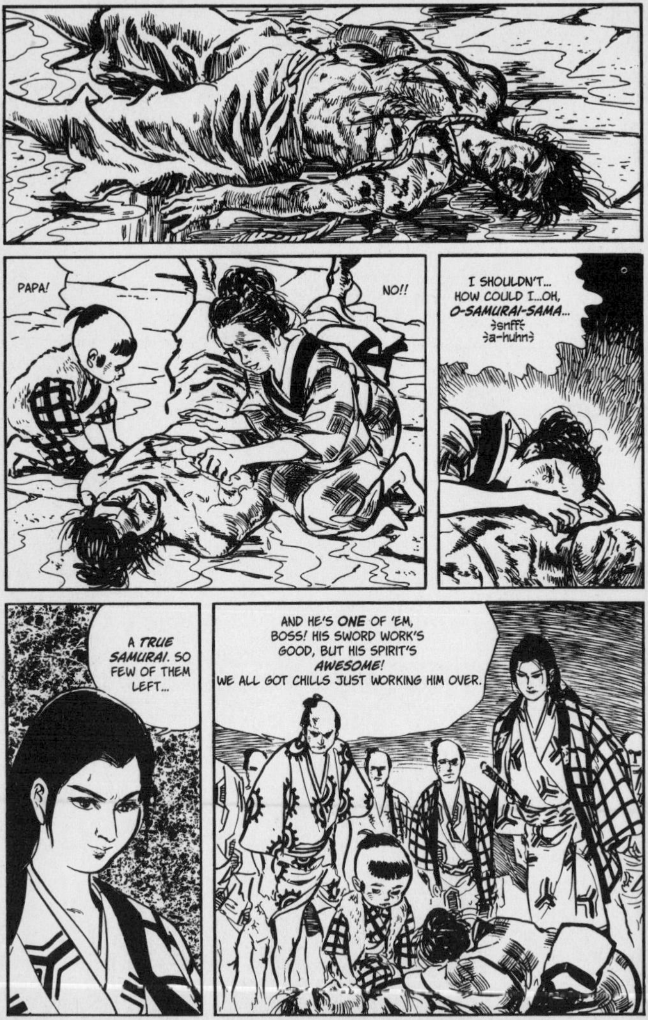
PAPA!
NO!!
I SHOULDN'T... HOW COULD I...OH, O-SAMURAI-SAMA...
snff
a-huhn
A TRUE SAMURAI. SO FEW OF THEM LEFT...
AND HE'S ONE OF 'EM, BOSS! HIS SWORD WORK'S GOOD, BUT HIS SPIRIT'S AWESOME! WE ALL GOT CHILLS JUST WORKING HIM OVER.

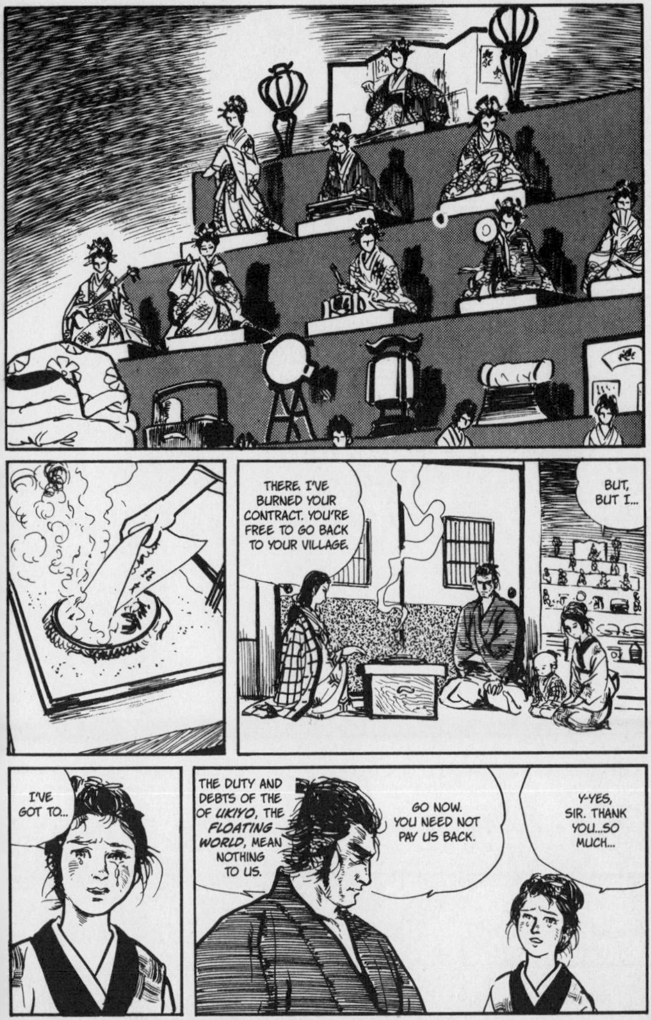
THERE. I'VE BURNED YOUR CONTRACT. YOU'RE FREE TO GO BACK TO YOUR VILLAGE.
BUT, BUT I...
I'VE GOT TO...
THE DUTY AND DEBTS OF THE OF *UKIYO*, THE *FLOATING WORLD*, MEAN NOTHING TO US.
GO NOW. YOU NEED NOT PAY US BACK.
Y-YES, SIR. THANK YOU...SO MUCH...

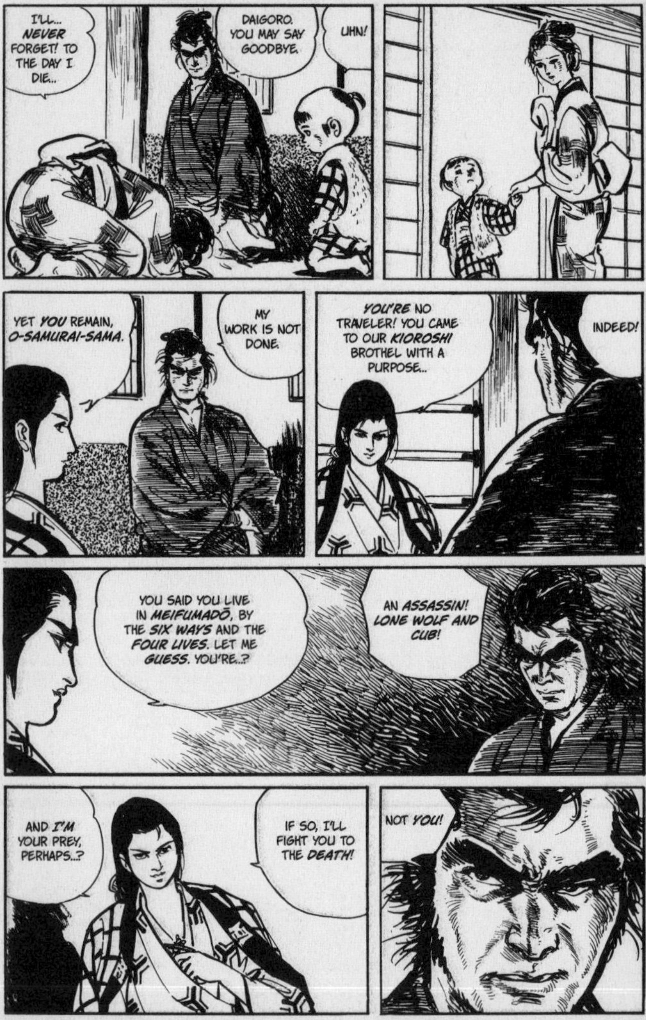
I'LL... NEVER FORGET! TO THE DAY I DIE...
DAIGORO. YOU MAY SAY GOODBYE.
UHN!
YET YOU REMAIN, O-SAMURAI-SAMA.
MY WORK IS NOT DONE.
YOU'RE NO TRAVELER! YOU CAME TO OUR KIOROSHI BROTHEL WITH A PURPOSE...
INDEED!
YOU SAID YOU LIVE IN MEIFUMADŌ, BY THE SIX WAYS AND THE FOUR LIVES. LET ME GUESS. YOU'RE...?
AN ASSASSIN! LONE WOLF AND CUB!
AND I'M YOUR PREY, PERHAPS...?
IF SO, I'LL FIGHT YOU TO THE DEATH!
NOT YOU!

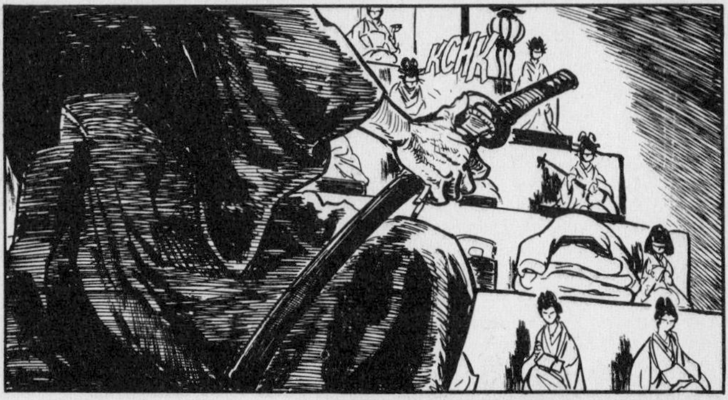
KCHK
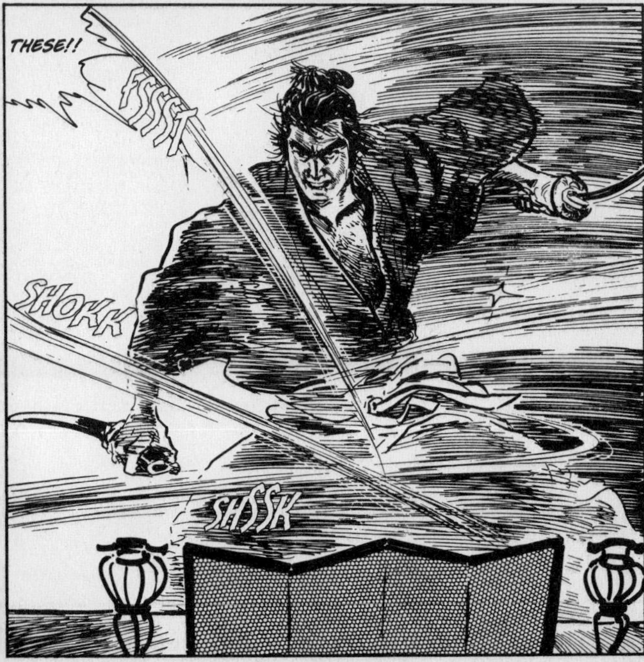
THESE!!
FSSST
SHOKK
SHSSK

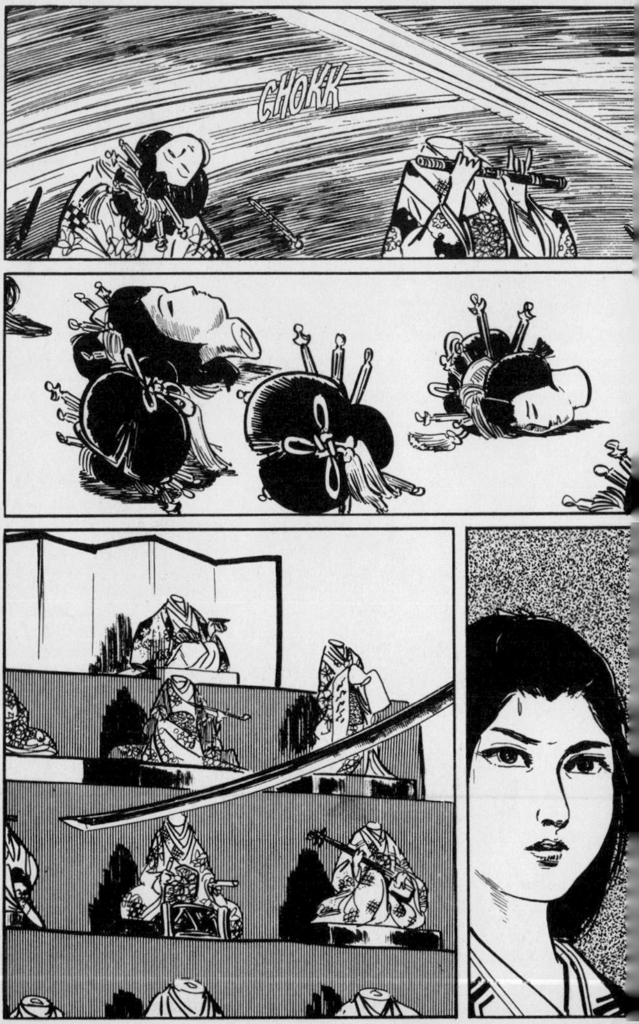
CHOKK

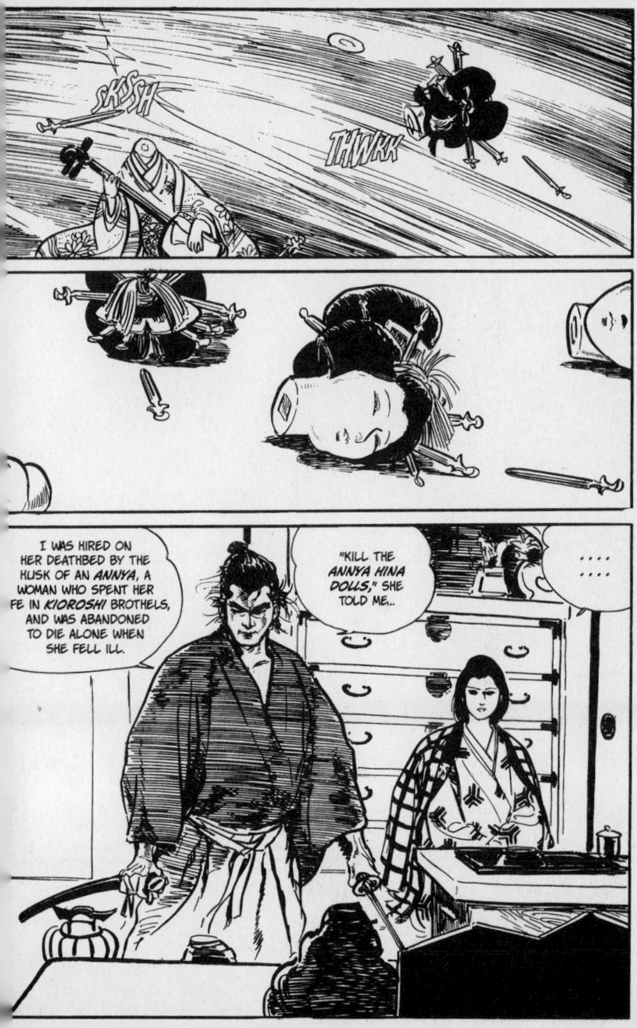
SKSSH
THWKK
I WAS HIRED ON HER DEATHBED BY THE HUSK OF AN *ANNYA*, A WOMAN WHO SPENT HER FE IN *KIOROSHI* BROTHELS, AND WAS ABANDONED TO DIE ALONE WHEN SHE FELL ILL.
"KILL THE *ANNYA HINA DOLLS,*" SHE TOLD ME..
....
....

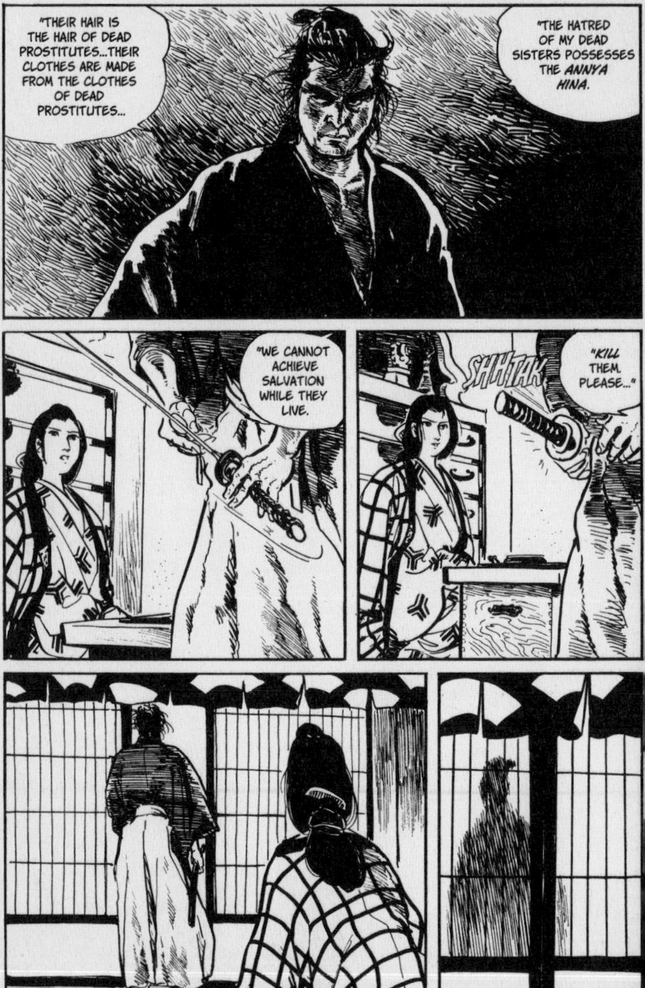
"THEIR HAIR IS THE HAIR OF DEAD PROSTITUTES...THEIR CLOTHES ARE MADE FROM THE CLOTHES OF DEAD PROSTITUTES...
"THE HATRED OF MY DEAD SISTERS POSSESSES THE *ANNYA HINA*.
"WE CANNOT ACHIEVE SALVATION WHILE THEY LIVE.
SHHTAK
"*KILL* THEM. PLEASE..."

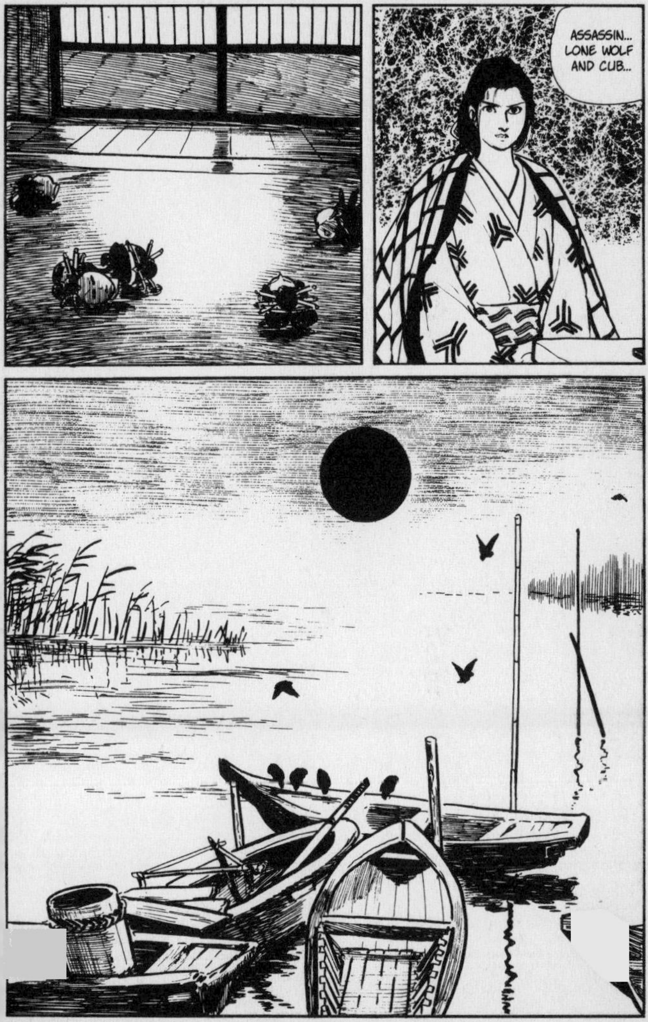
ASSASSIN... LONE WOLF AND CUB...

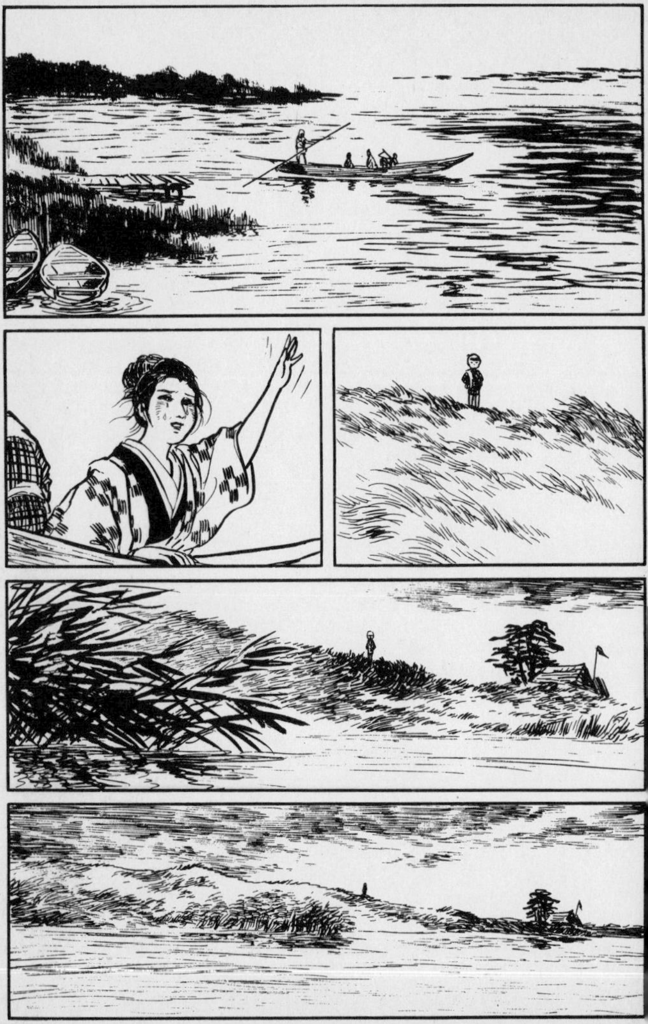

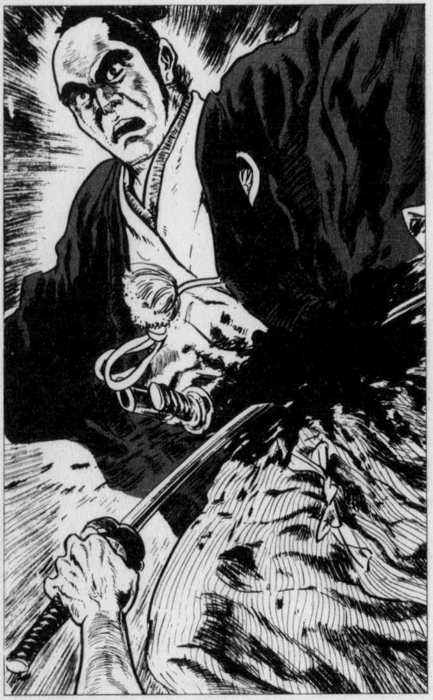

the nineteenth

Close Quarters

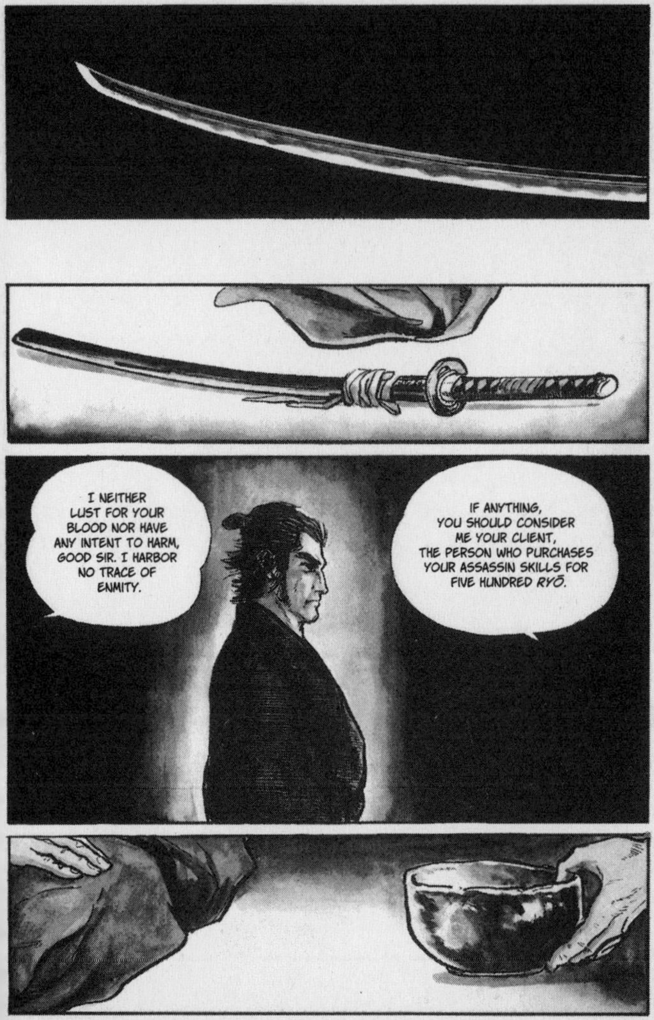
I NEITHER LUST FOR YOUR BLOOD NOR HAVE ANY INTENT TO HARM, GOOD SIR. I HARBOR NO TRACE OF ENMITY.
IF ANYTHING, YOU SHOULD CONSIDER ME YOUR CLIENT, THE PERSON WHO PURCHASES YOUR ASSASSIN SKILLS FOR FIVE HUNDRED *RYŌ*.

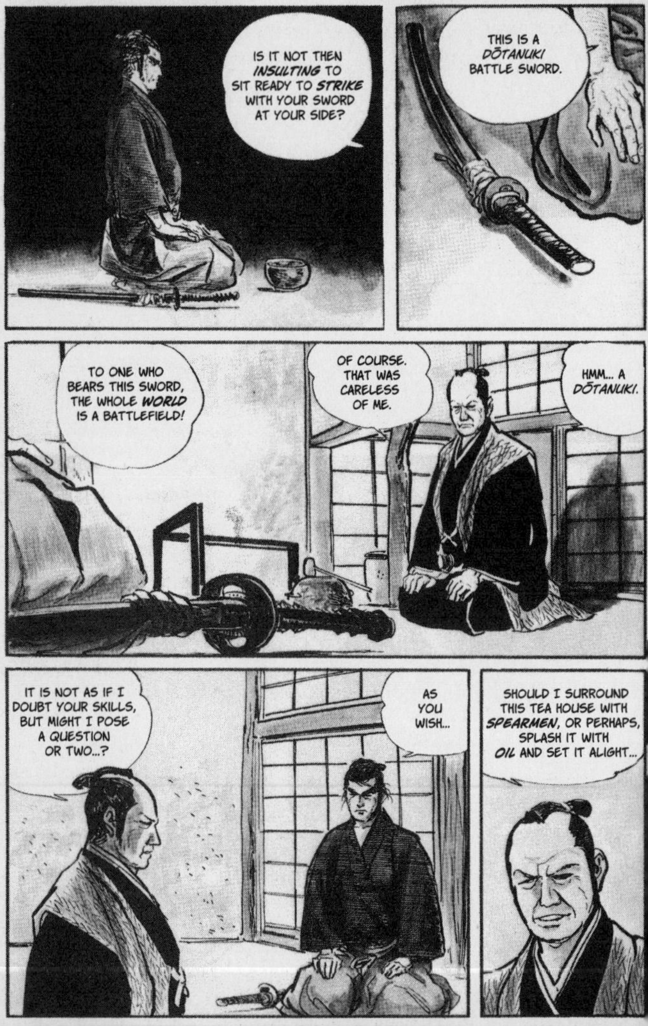
IS IT NOT THEN INSULTING TO SIT READY TO STRIKE WITH YOUR SWORD AT YOUR SIDE?
THIS IS A DŌTANUKI BATTLE SWORD.
TO ONE WHO BEARS THIS SWORD, THE WHOLE WORLD IS A BATTLEFIELD!
OF COURSE. THAT WAS CARELESS OF ME.
HMM... A DŌTANUKI.
IT IS NOT AS IF I DOUBT YOUR SKILLS, BUT MIGHT I POSE A QUESTION OR TWO...?
AS YOU WISH...
SHOULD I SURROUND THIS TEA HOUSE WITH SPEARMEN, OR PERHAPS, SPLASH IT WITH OIL AND SET IT ALIGHT...

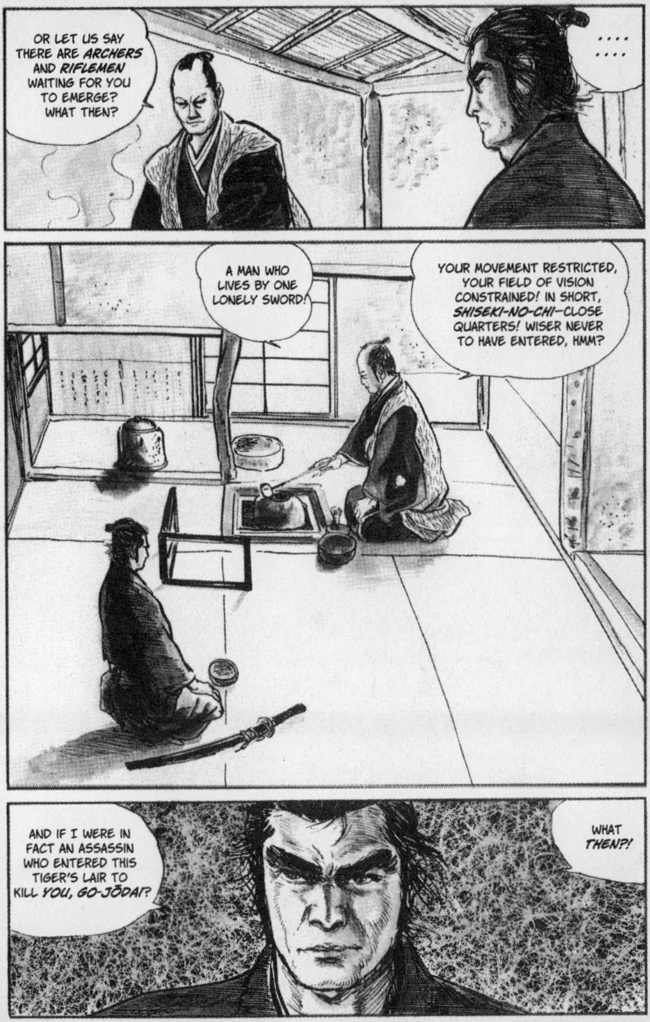
OR LET US SAY THERE ARE *ARCHERS* AND *RIFLEMEN* WAITING FOR YOU TO EMERGE? WHAT THEN?
....
....
A MAN WHO LIVES BY ONE LONELY SWORD!
YOUR MOVEMENT RESTRICTED, YOUR FIELD OF VISION CONSTRAINED! IN SHORT, *SHISEKI-NO-CHI*—CLOSE QUARTERS! WISER NEVER TO HAVE ENTERED, HMM?
AND IF I WERE IN FACT AN ASSASSIN WHO ENTERED THIS TIGER'S LAIR TO KILL *YOU, GO-JŌDAI*?
WHAT *THEN?!*

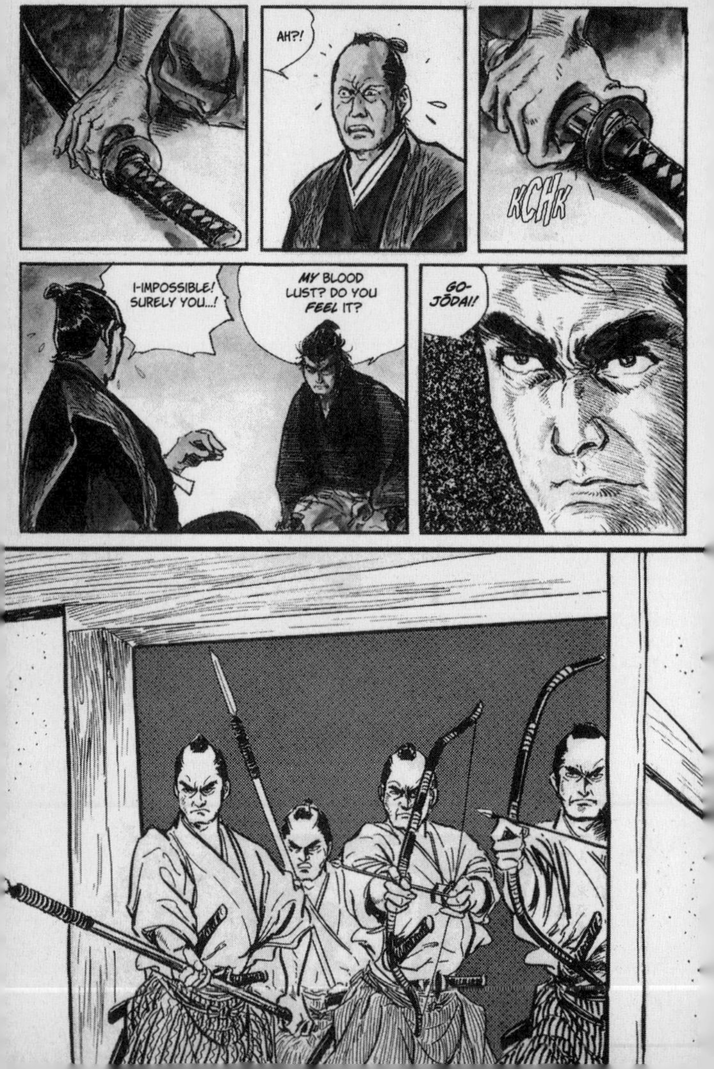
AH?!
KCHK
I-IMPOSSIBLE! SURELY YOU...!
MY BLOOD LUST? DO YOU FEEL IT?
GO-JŌDAI!

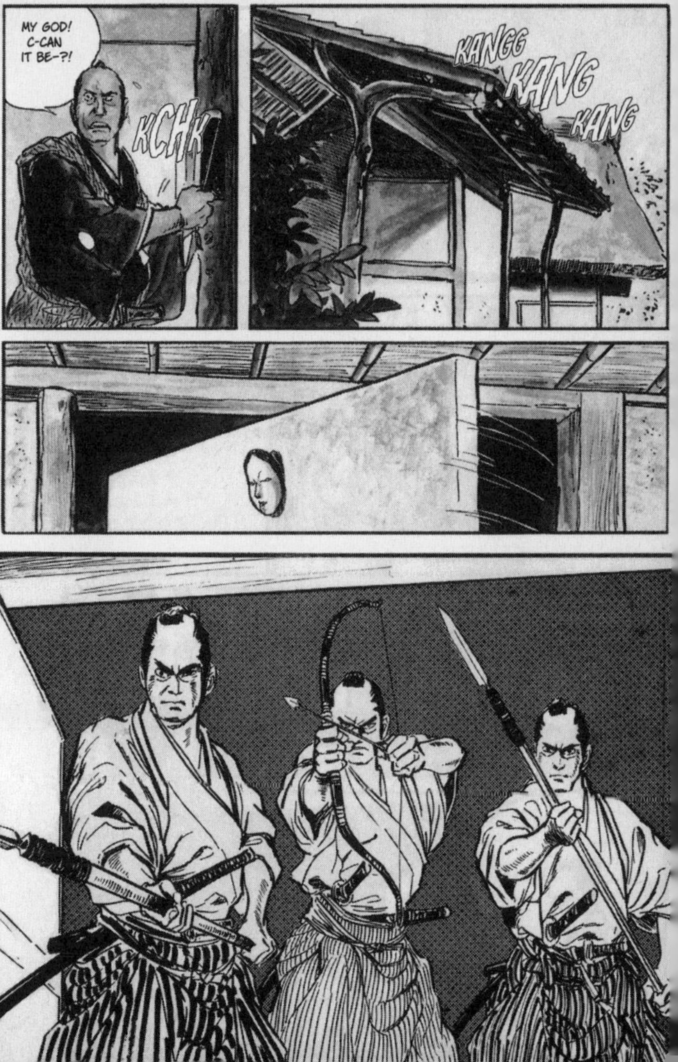
MY GOD! C-CAN IT BE-?!
KCHK
KANGG
KANG
KANG

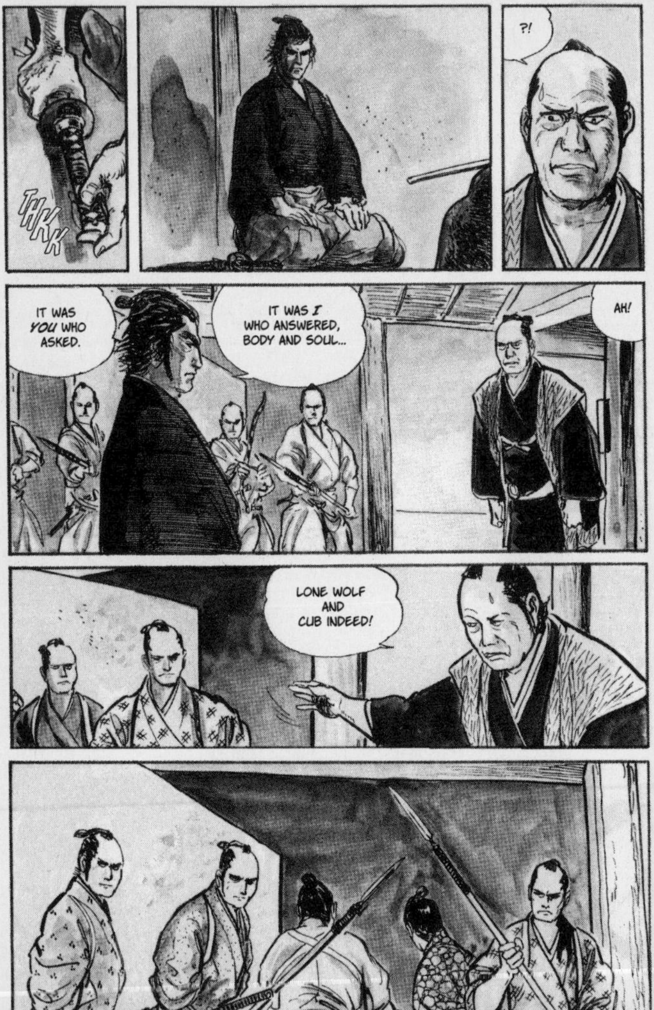
THKK
?!
IT WAS YOU WHO ASKED.
IT WAS I WHO ANSWERED, BODY AND SOUL...
AH!
LONE WOLF AND CUB INDEED!

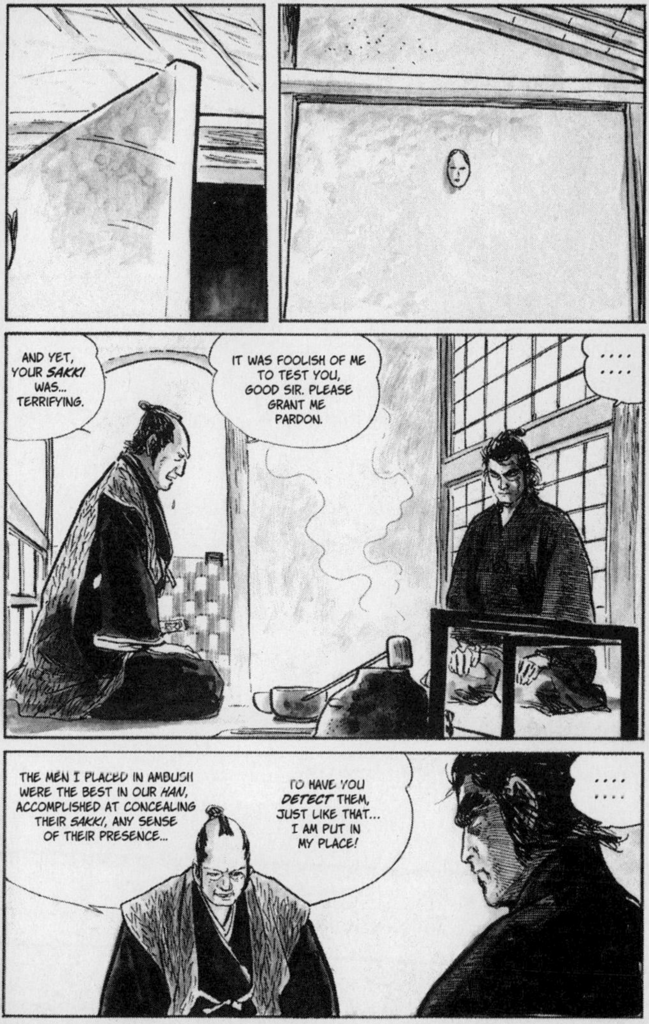

AND YET, YOUR *SAKKI* WAS... TERRIFYING.
IT WAS FOOLISH OF ME TO TEST YOU, GOOD SIR. PLEASE GRANT ME PARDON.
....
....
THE MEN I PLACED IN AMBUSH WERE THE BEST IN OUR *HAN*, ACCOMPLISHED AT CONCEALING THEIR *SAKKI*, ANY SENSE OF THEIR PRESENCE...
TO HAVE YOU *DETECT* THEM, JUST LIKE THAT... I AM PUT IN MY PLACE!
....
....

IN THAT CASE, YOUR *NEXT SHISEKI-NO-CHI...*

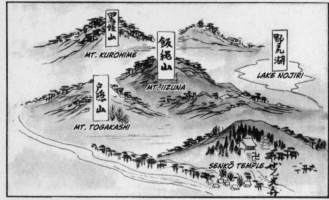

黒姫山
MT. KUROHIME

飯綱山
MT. IIZUNA

野尻湖
LAKE NOJIRI

戸隠山
MT. TOGAKASHI

善光寺
SENKŌ TEMPLE

260

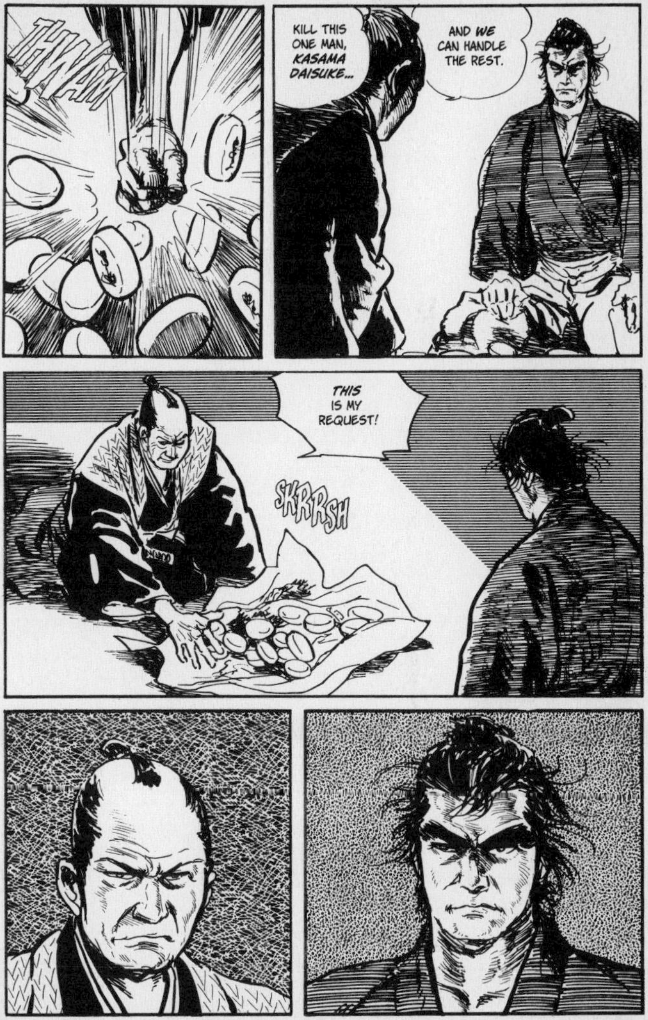
THWAM
KILL THIS ONE MAN, KASAMA DAISUKE...
AND WE CAN HANDLE THE REST.
THIS IS MY REQUEST!
SKRRSH

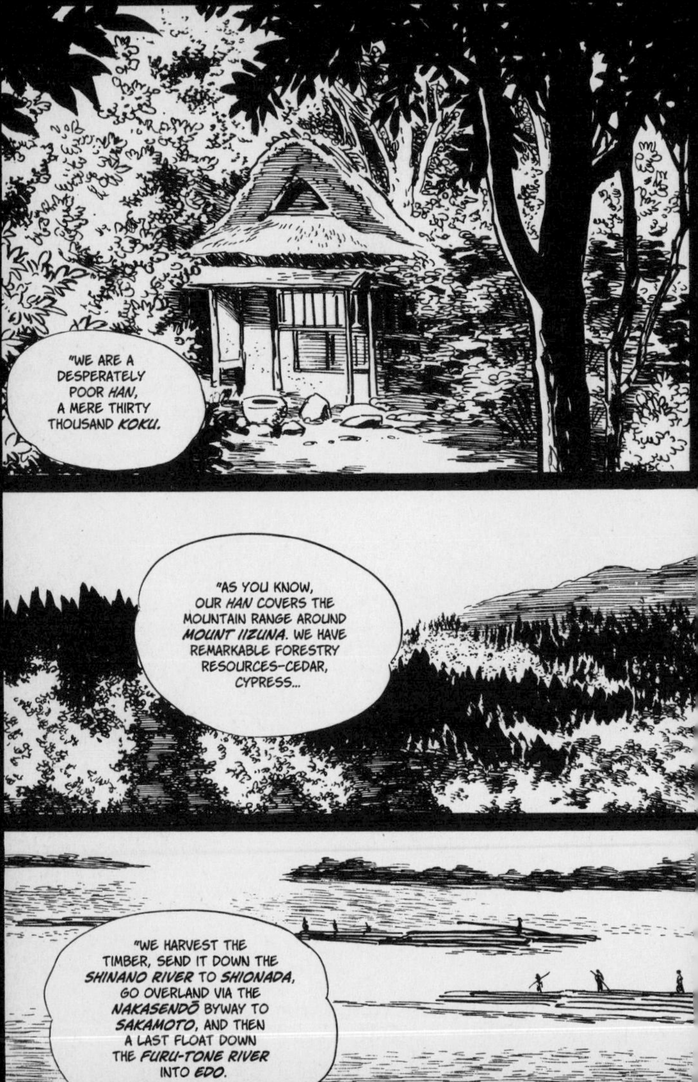
"WE ARE A DESPERATELY POOR *HAN*, A MERE THIRTY THOUSAND ***KOKU.***
"AS YOU KNOW, OUR *HAN* COVERS THE MOUNTAIN RANGE AROUND ***MOUNT IIZUNA***. WE HAVE REMARKABLE FORESTRY RESOURCES–CEDAR, CYPRESS...
"WE HARVEST THE TIMBER, SEND IT DOWN THE ***SHINANO RIVER*** TO ***SHIONADA***, GO OVERLAND VIA THE ***NAKASENDŌ*** BYWAY TO ***SAKAMOTO***, AND THEN A LAST FLOAT DOWN THE ***FURU-TONE RIVER*** INTO ***EDO***.

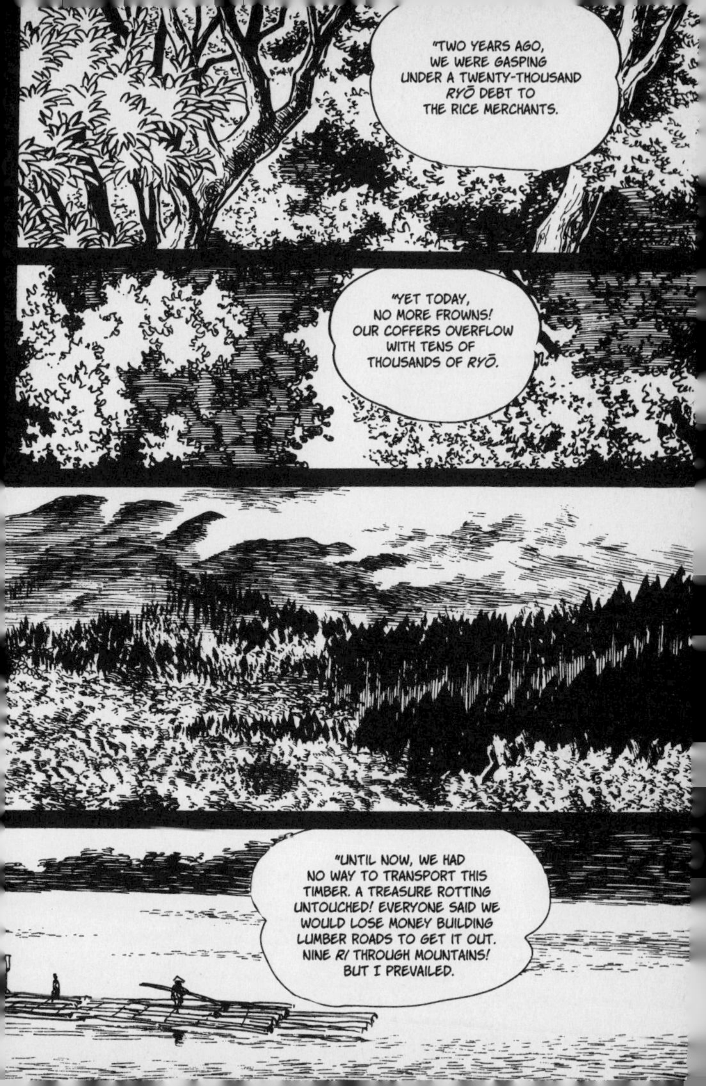
"TWO YEARS AGO, WE WERE GASPING UNDER A TWENTY-THOUSAND RYŌ DEBT TO THE RICE MERCHANTS.
"YET TODAY, NO MORE FROWNS! OUR COFFERS OVERFLOW WITH TENS OF THOUSANDS OF RYŌ.
"UNTIL NOW, WE HAD NO WAY TO TRANSPORT THIS TIMBER. A TREASURE ROTTING UNTOUCHED! EVERYONE SAID WE WOULD LOSE MONEY BUILDING LUMBER ROADS TO GET IT OUT. NINE RI THROUGH MOUNTAINS! BUT I PREVAILED.

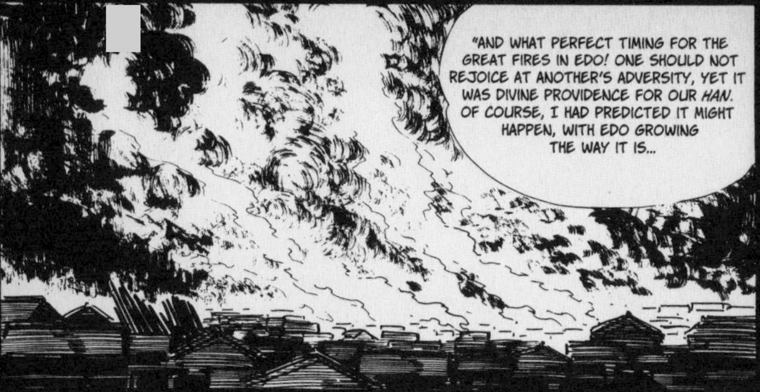
"AND WHAT PERFECT TIMING FOR THE GREAT FIRES IN EDO! ONE SHOULD NOT REJOICE AT ANOTHER'S ADVERSITY, YET IT WAS DIVINE PROVIDENCE FOR OUR HAN. OF COURSE, I HAD PREDICTED IT MIGHT HAPPEN, WITH EDO GROWING THE WAY IT IS...
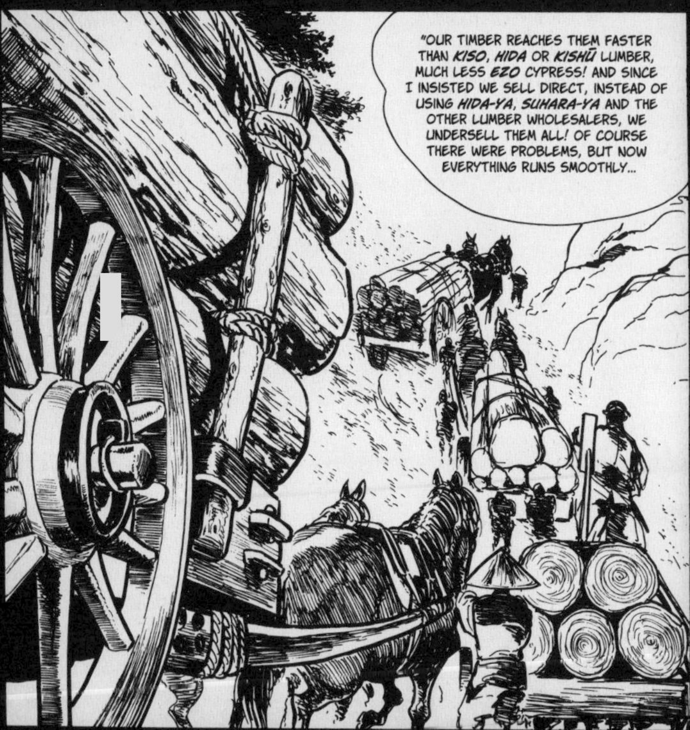
"OUR TIMBER REACHES THEM FASTER THAN KISO, HIDA OR KISHŪ LUMBER, MUCH LESS EZO CYPRESS! AND SINCE I INSISTED WE SELL DIRECT, INSTEAD OF USING HIDA-YA, SUHARA-YA AND THE OTHER LUMBER WHOLESALERS, WE UNDERSELL THEM ALL! OF COURSE THERE WERE PROBLEMS, BUT NOW EVERYTHING RUNS SMOOTHLY...

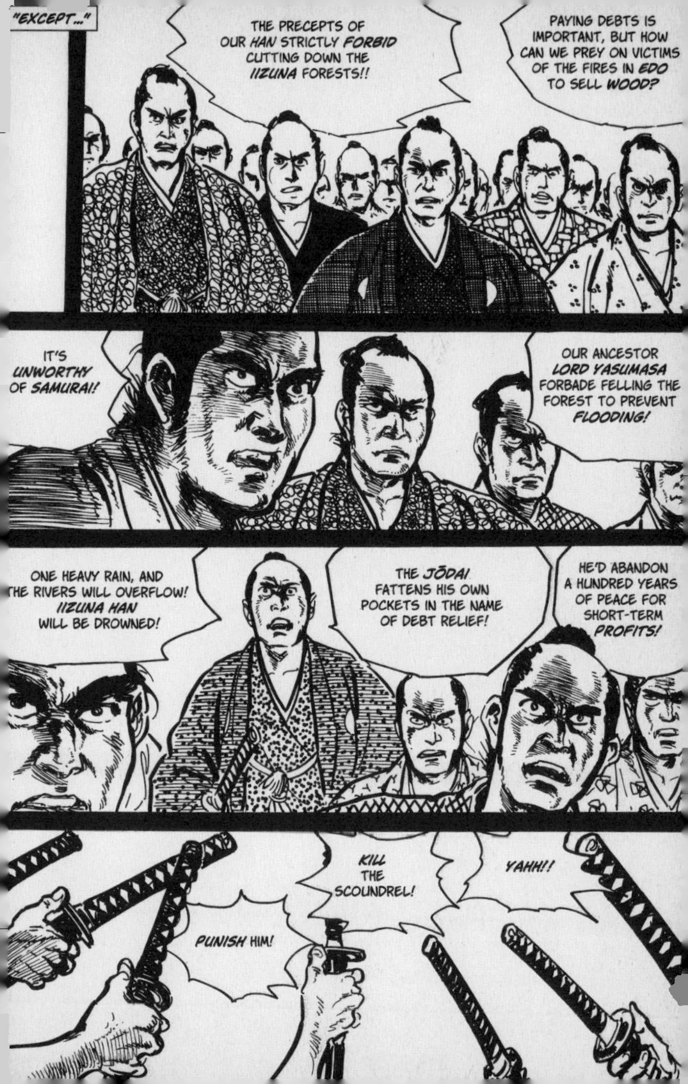
"EXCEPT..."
THE PRECEPTS OF OUR HAN STRICTLY FORBID CUTTING DOWN THE IIZUNA FORESTS!!
PAYING DEBTS IS IMPORTANT, BUT HOW CAN WE PREY ON VICTIMS OF THE FIRES IN EDO TO SELL WOOD?
IT'S UNWORTHY OF SAMURAI!
OUR ANCESTOR LORD YASUMASA FORBADE FELLING THE FOREST TO PREVENT FLOODING!
ONE HEAVY RAIN, AND THE RIVERS WILL OVERFLOW! IIZUNA HAN WILL BE DROWNED!
THE JŌDAI FATTENS HIS OWN POCKETS IN THE NAME OF DEBT RELIEF!
HE'D ABANDON A HUNDRED YEARS OF PEACE FOR SHORT-TERM PROFITS!
PUNISH HIM!
KILL THE SCOUNDREL!
YAHH!!

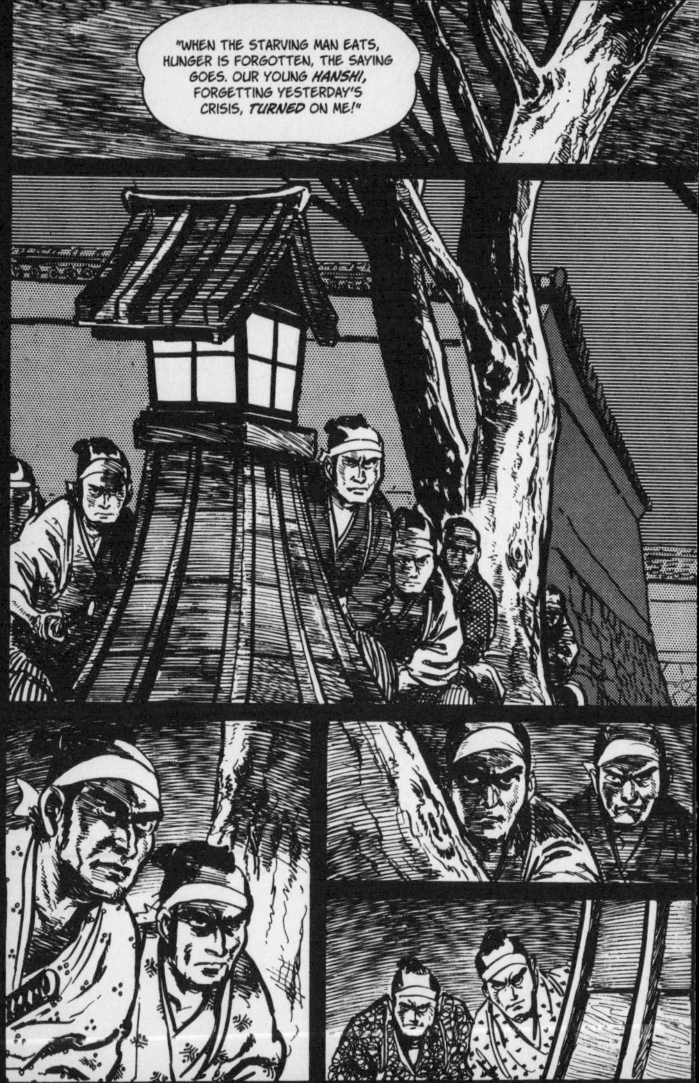
"WHEN THE STARVING MAN EATS, HUNGER IS FORGOTTEN, THE SAYING GOES. OUR YOUNG *HANSHI,* FORGETTING YESTERDAY'S CRISIS, *TURNED* ON ME!"

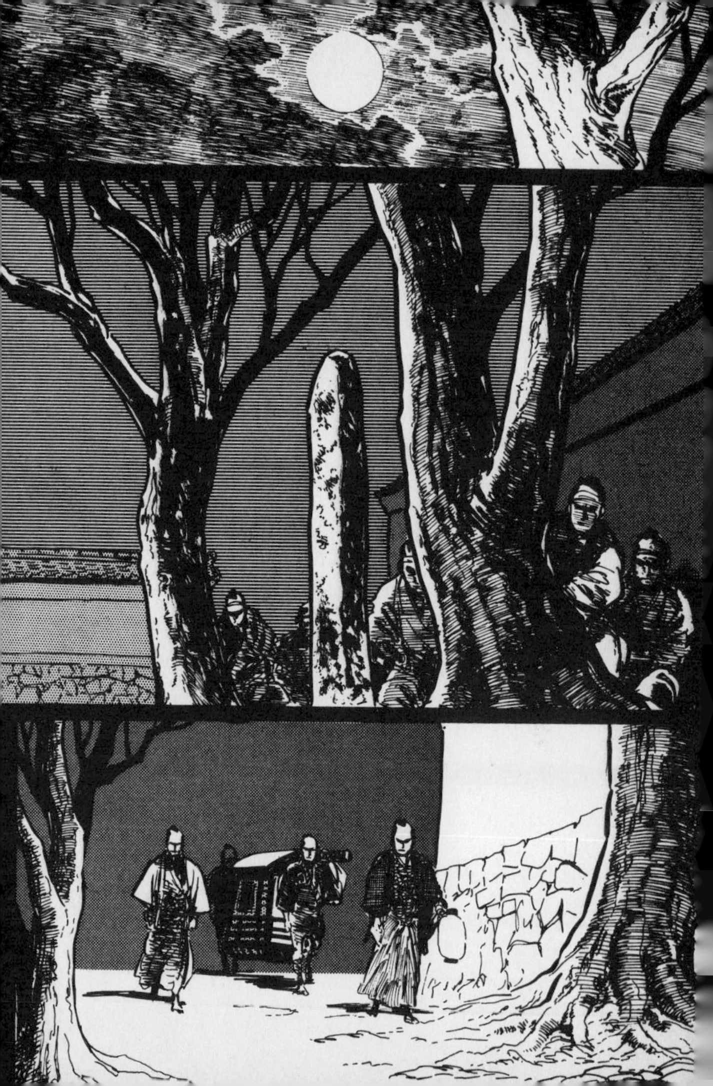

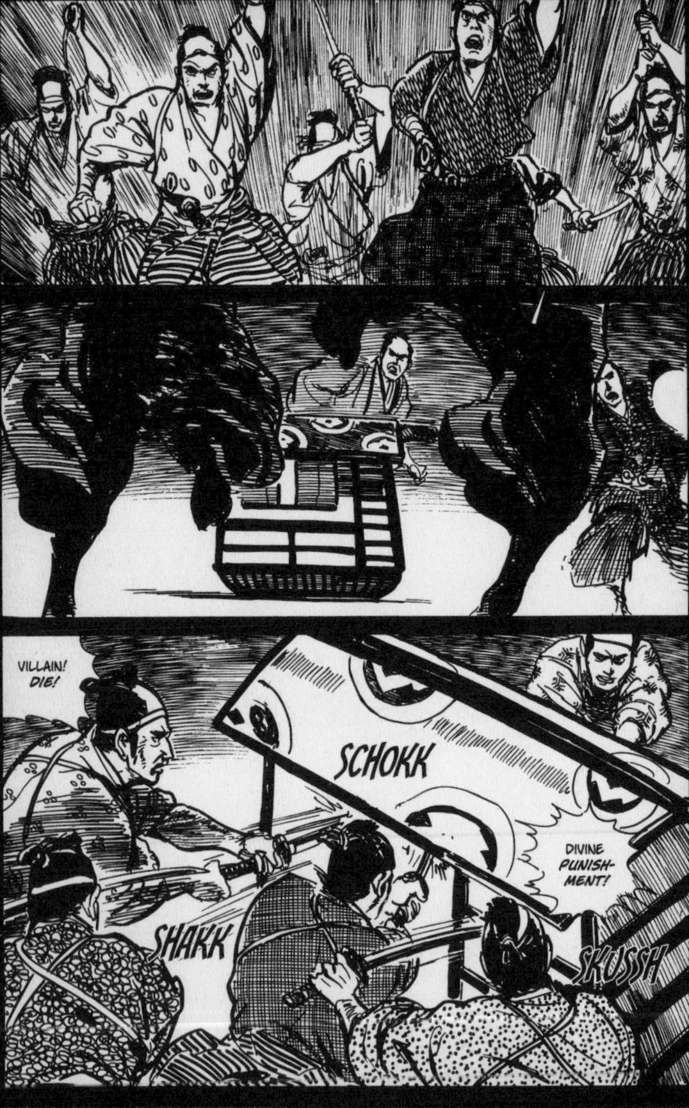
VILLAIN! DIE!
SCHOKK
DIVINE PUNISH-MENT!
SHAKK
SKUSSH

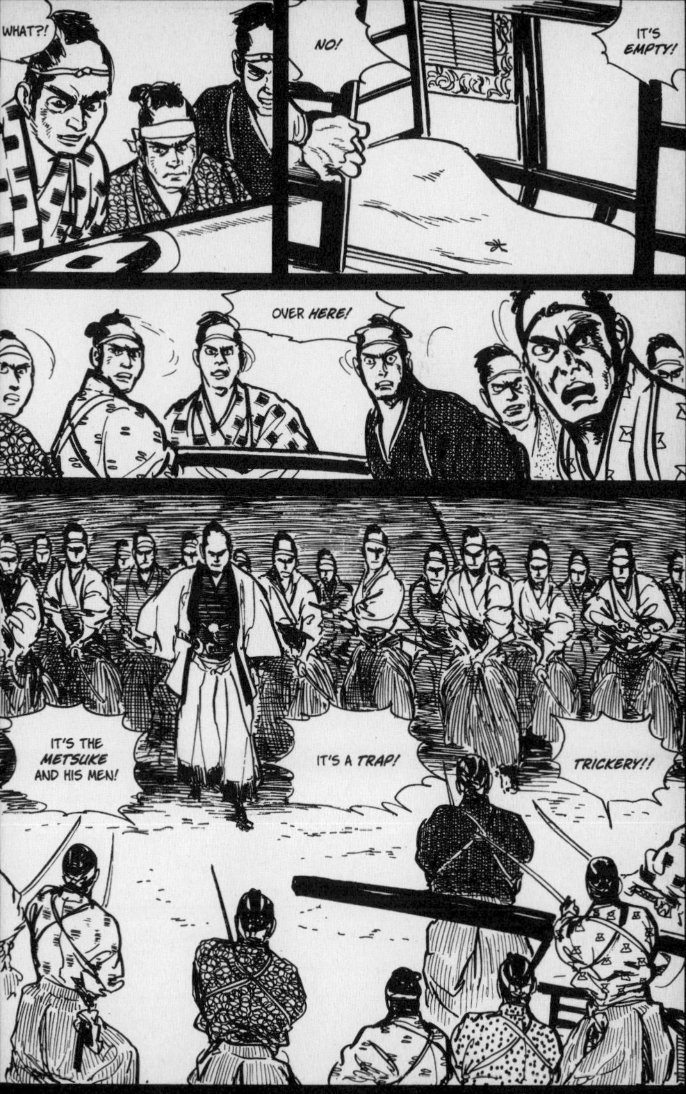
WHAT?!
NO!
IT'S EMPTY!
OVER HERE!
IT'S THE METSUKE AND HIS MEN!
IT'S A TRAP!
TRICKERY!!

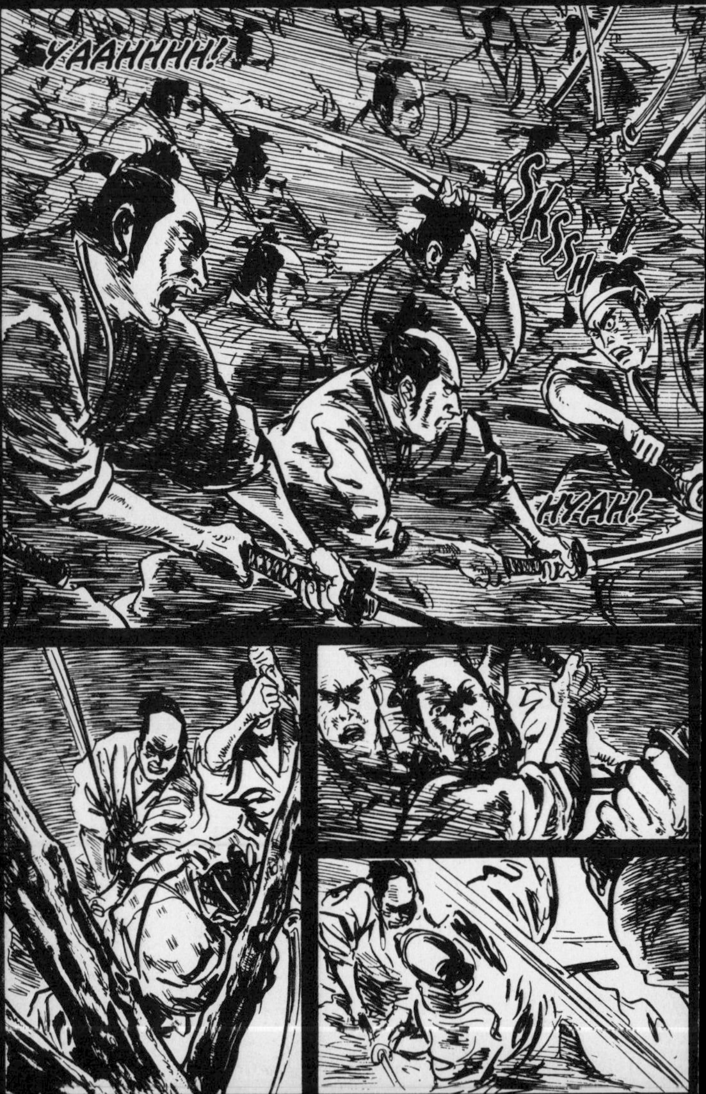
YAAHHHH!
SKSSH
HYAH!

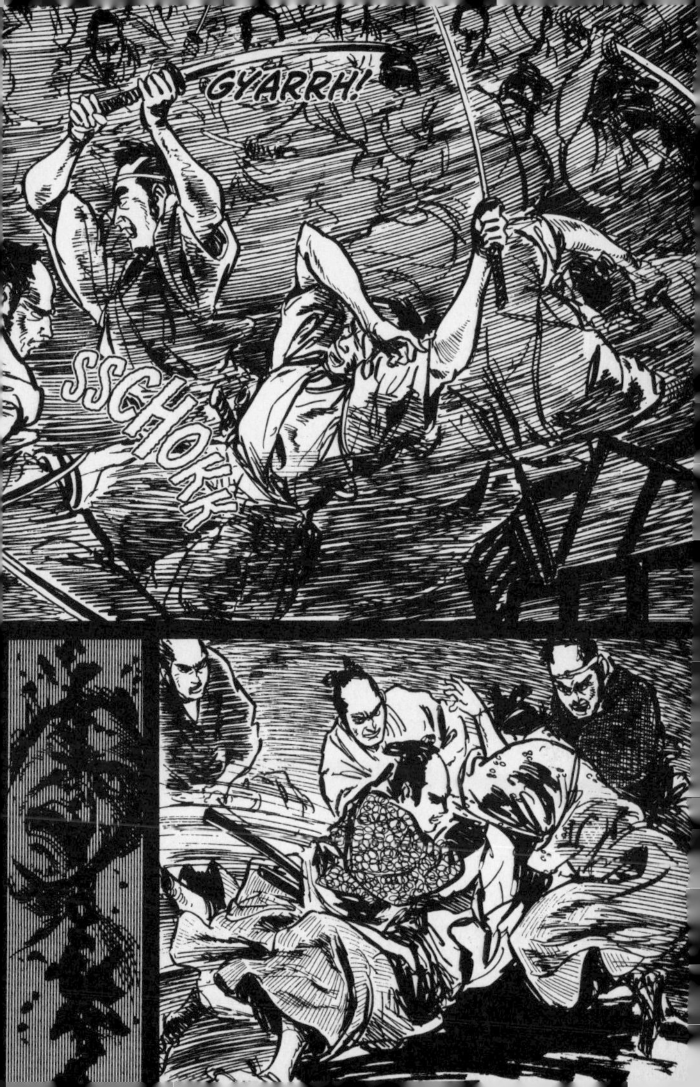
GYARRH!
SSCHOKK

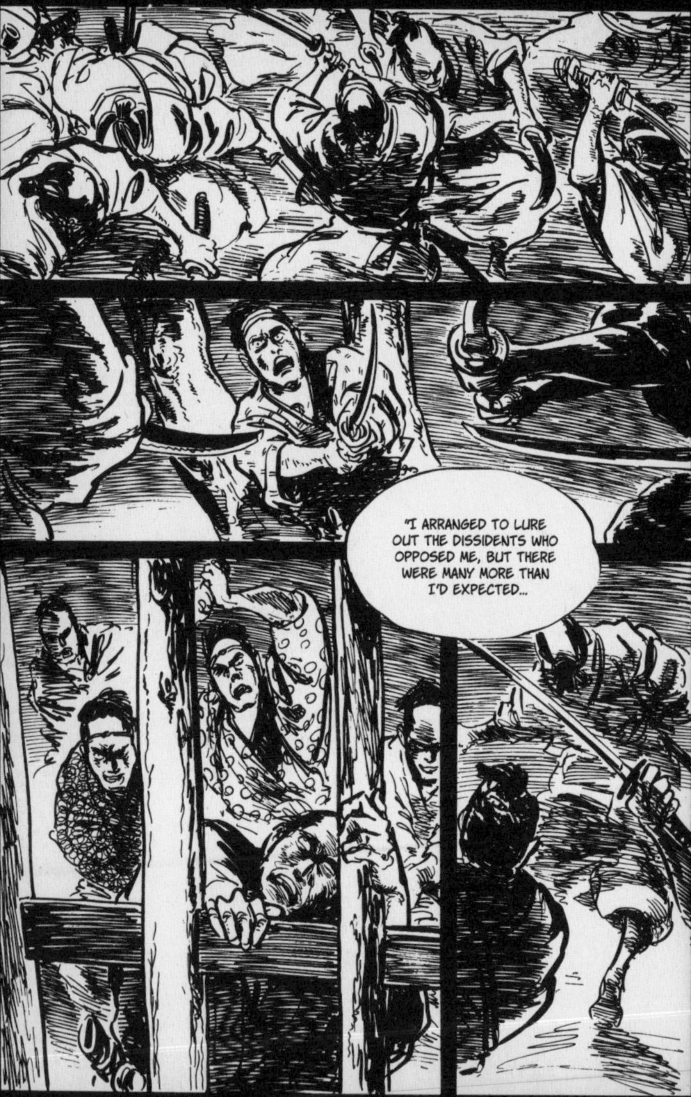
"I ARRANGED TO LURE OUT THE DISSIDENTS WHO OPPOSED ME, BUT THERE WERE MANY MORE THAN I'D EXPECTED...

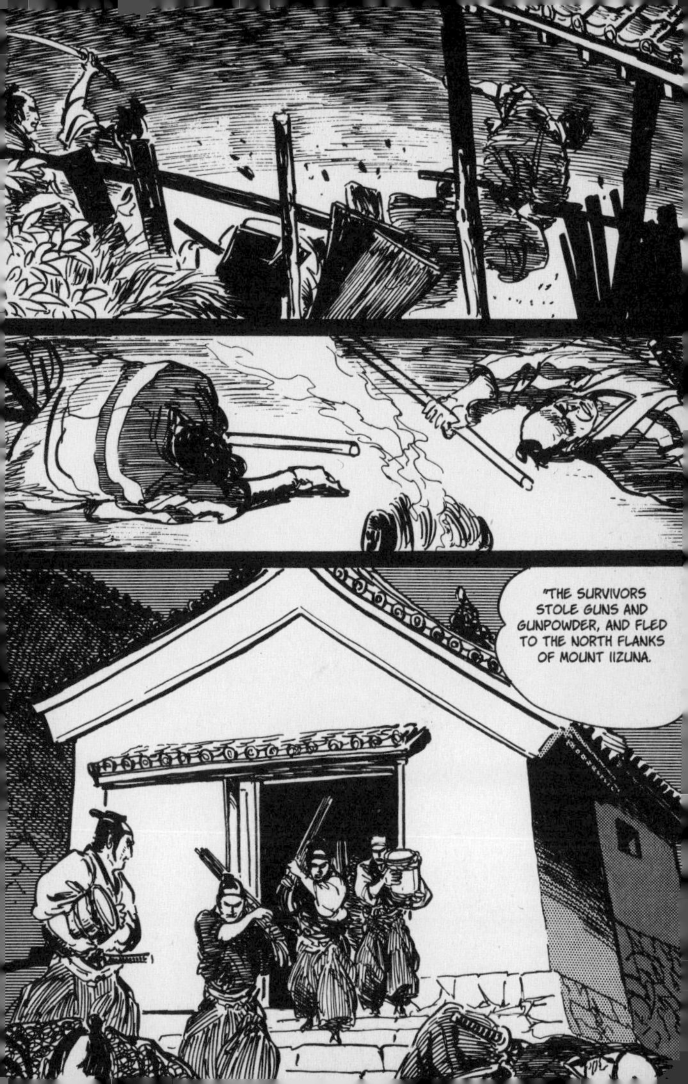
"THE SURVIVORS STOLE GUNS AND GUNPOWDER, AND FLED TO THE NORTH FLANKS OF MOUNT IIZUNA.

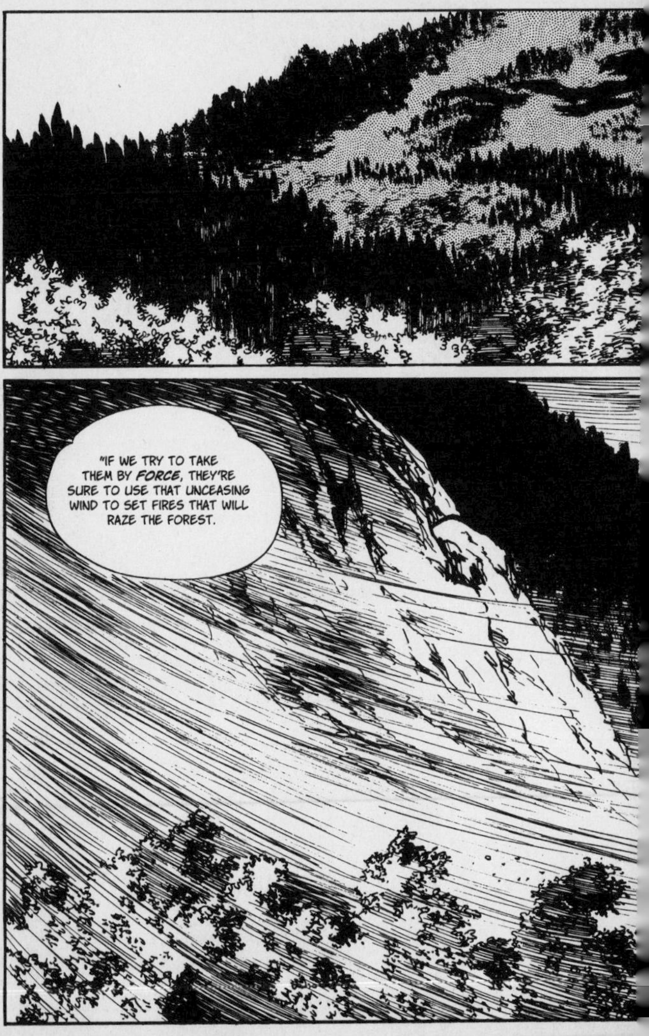
"IF WE TRY TO TAKE THEM BY *FORCE*, THEY'RE SURE TO USE THAT UNCEASING WIND TO SET FIRES THAT WILL RAZE THE FOREST.

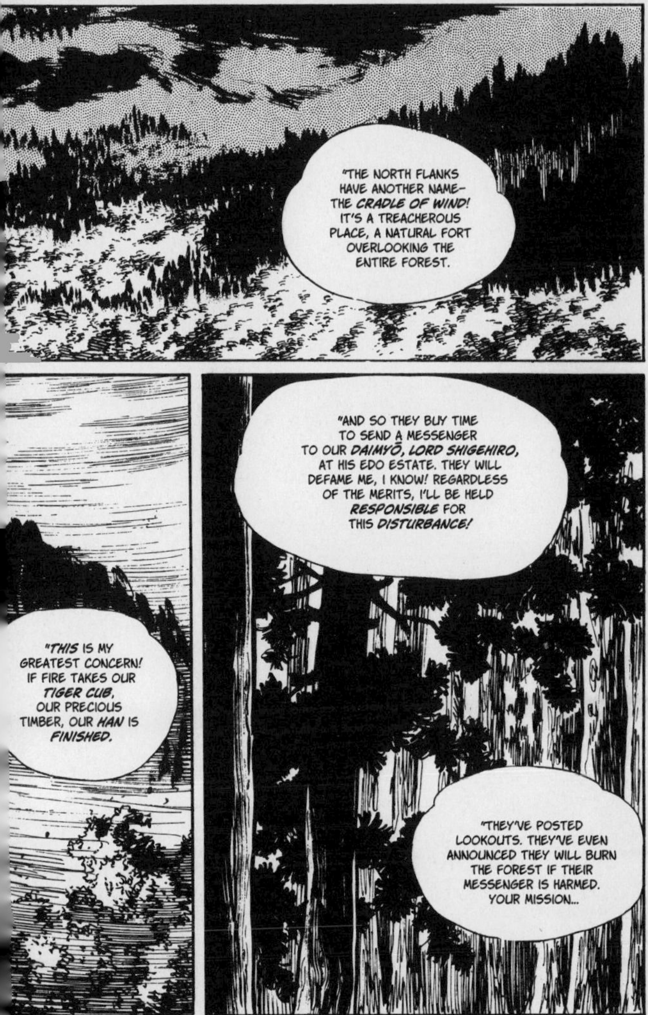
"THE NORTH FLANKS HAVE ANOTHER NAME– THE CRADLE OF WIND! IT'S A TREACHEROUS PLACE, A NATURAL FORT OVERLOOKING THE ENTIRE FOREST.
"THIS IS MY GREATEST CONCERN! IF FIRE TAKES OUR TIGER CUB, OUR PRECIOUS TIMBER, OUR HAN IS FINISHED.
"AND SO THEY BUY TIME TO SEND A MESSENGER TO OUR DAIMYŌ, LORD SHIGEHIRO, AT HIS EDO ESTATE. THEY WILL DEFAME ME, I KNOW! REGARDLESS OF THE MERITS, I'LL BE HELD RESPONSIBLE FOR THIS DISTURBANCE!
"THEY'VE POSTED LOOKOUTS. THEY'VE EVEN ANNOUNCED THEY WILL BURN THE FOREST IF THEIR MESSENGER IS HARMED. YOUR MISSION...

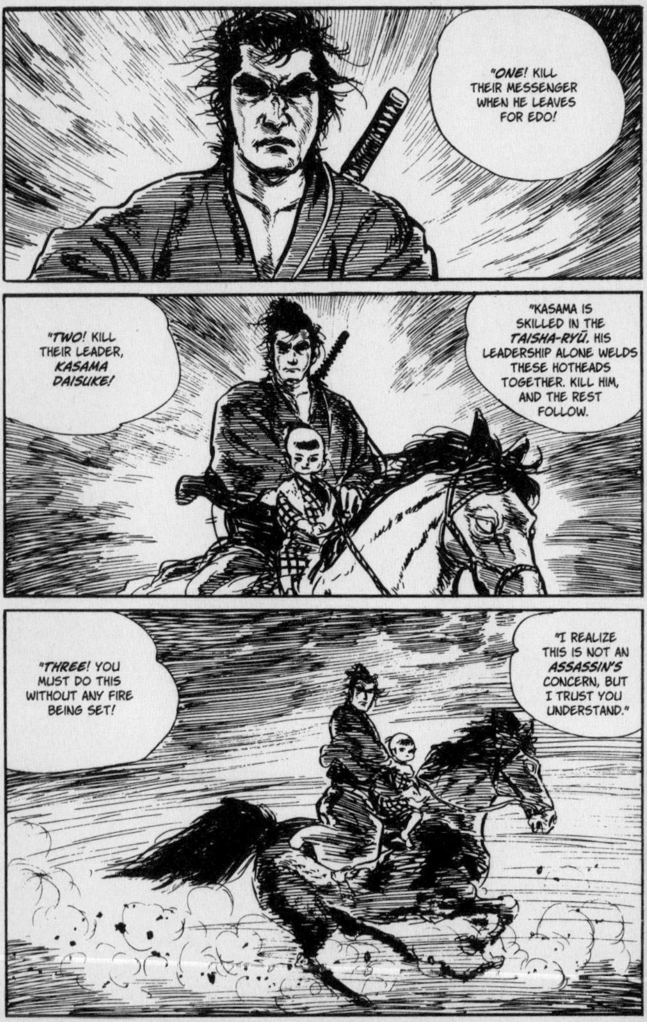
"ONE! KILL THEIR MESSENGER WHEN HE LEAVES FOR EDO!
"TWO! KILL THEIR LEADER, KASAMA DAISUKE!
"KASAMA IS SKILLED IN THE TAISHA-RYŪ. HIS LEADERSHIP ALONE WELDS THESE HOTHEADS TOGETHER. KILL HIM, AND THE REST FOLLOW.
"THREE! YOU MUST DO THIS WITHOUT ANY FIRE BEING SET!
"I REALIZE THIS IS NOT AN ASSASSIN'S CONCERN, BUT I TRUST YOU UNDERSTAND."

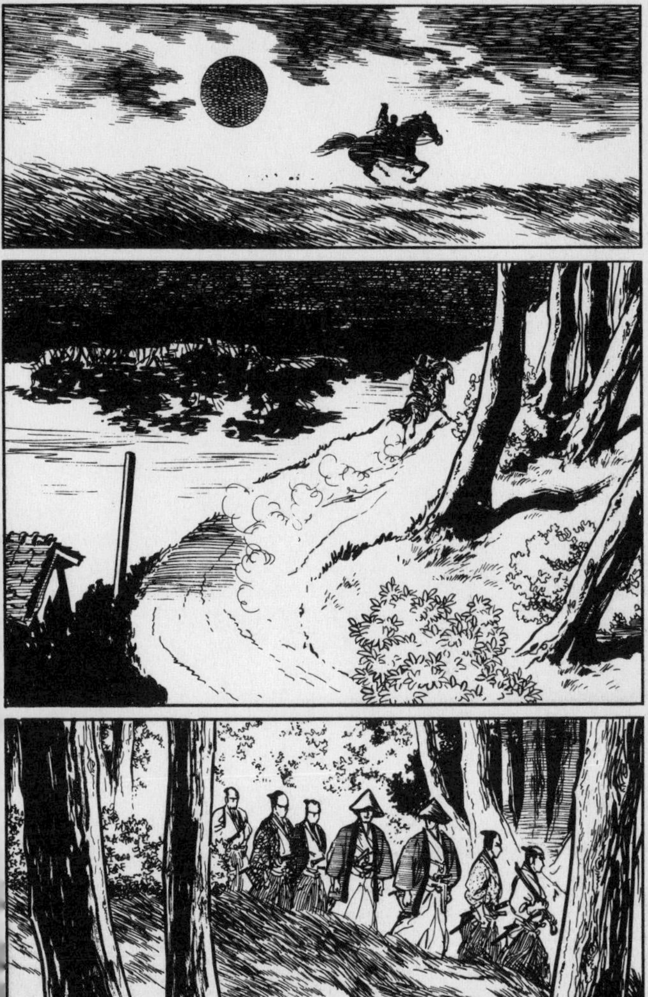

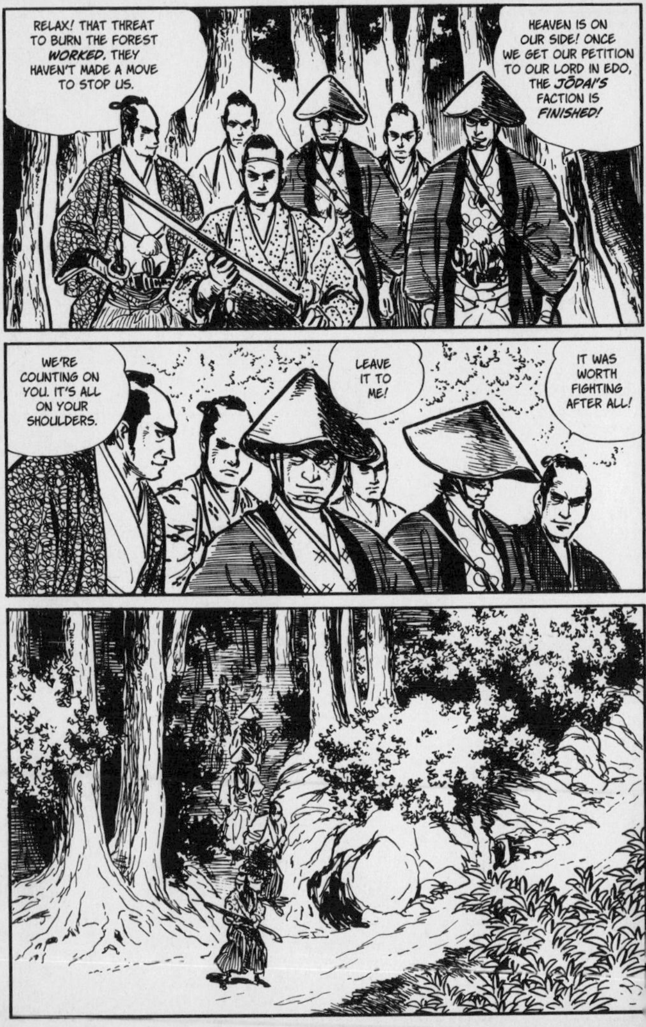
RELAX! THAT THREAT TO BURN THE FOREST **WORKED.** THEY HAVEN'T MADE A MOVE TO STOP US.
HEAVEN IS ON OUR SIDE! ONCE WE GET OUR PETITION TO OUR LORD IN EDO, THE ***JŌDAI'S*** FACTION IS ***FINISHED!***
WE'RE COUNTING ON YOU. IT'S ALL ON YOUR SHOULDERS.
LEAVE IT TO ME!
IT WAS WORTH FIGHTING AFTER ALL!

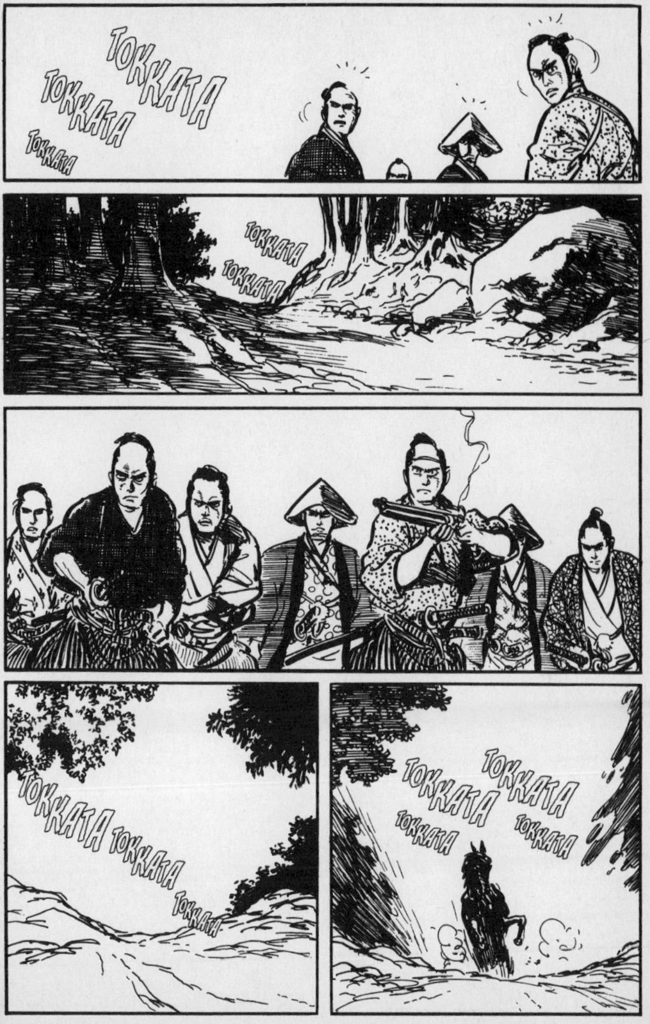
TOKKATA
TOKKATA
TOKKATA
TOKKATA
TOKKATA
TOKKATA
TOKKATA
TOKKATA
TOKKATA
TOKKATA
TOKKATA
TOKKATA

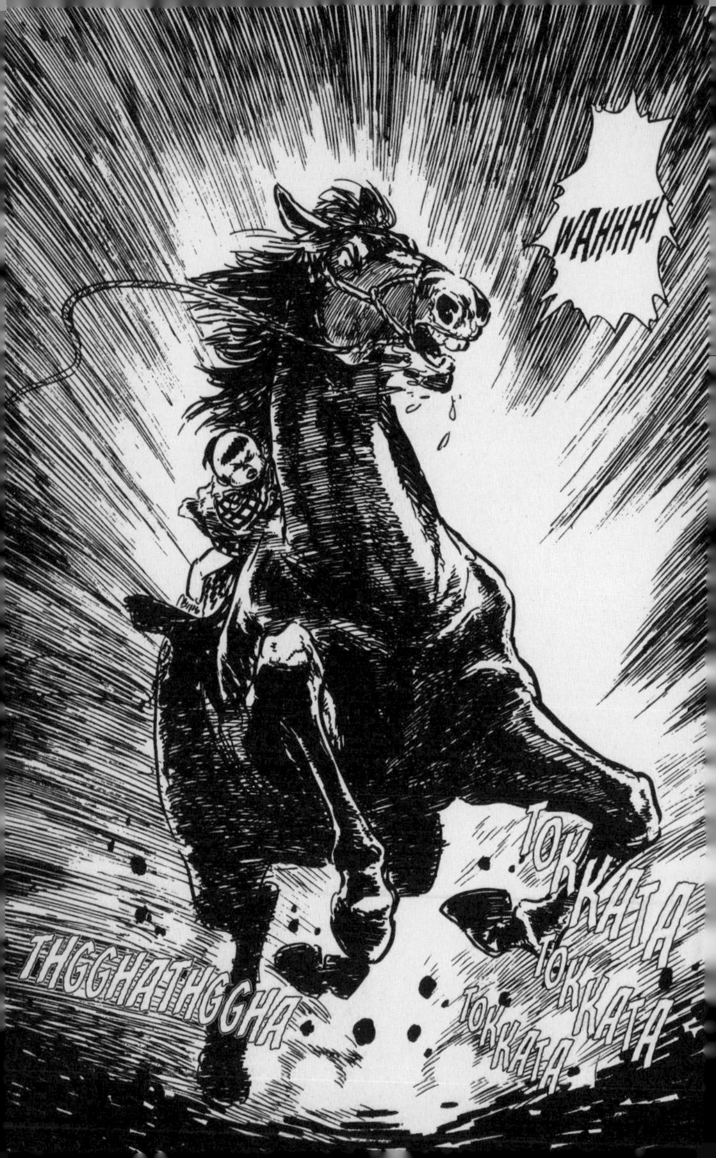
WAHHHH
THGGHATHGGHA
TOKKATA
TOKKATA
TOKKATA

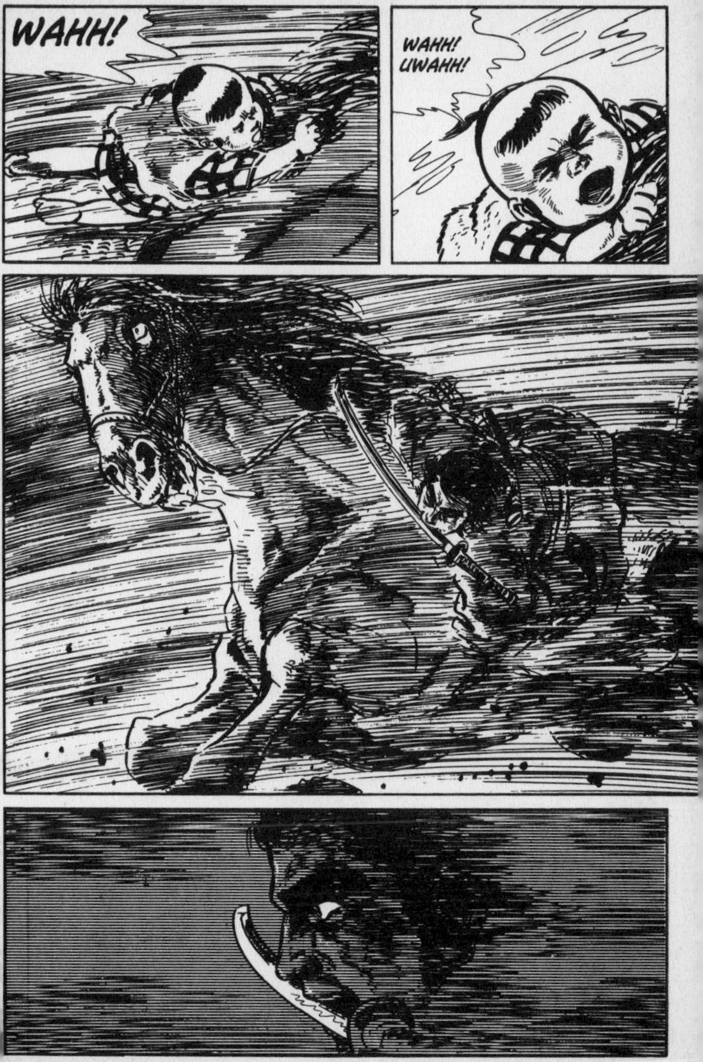
WAHH!
WAHH!
UWAHH!

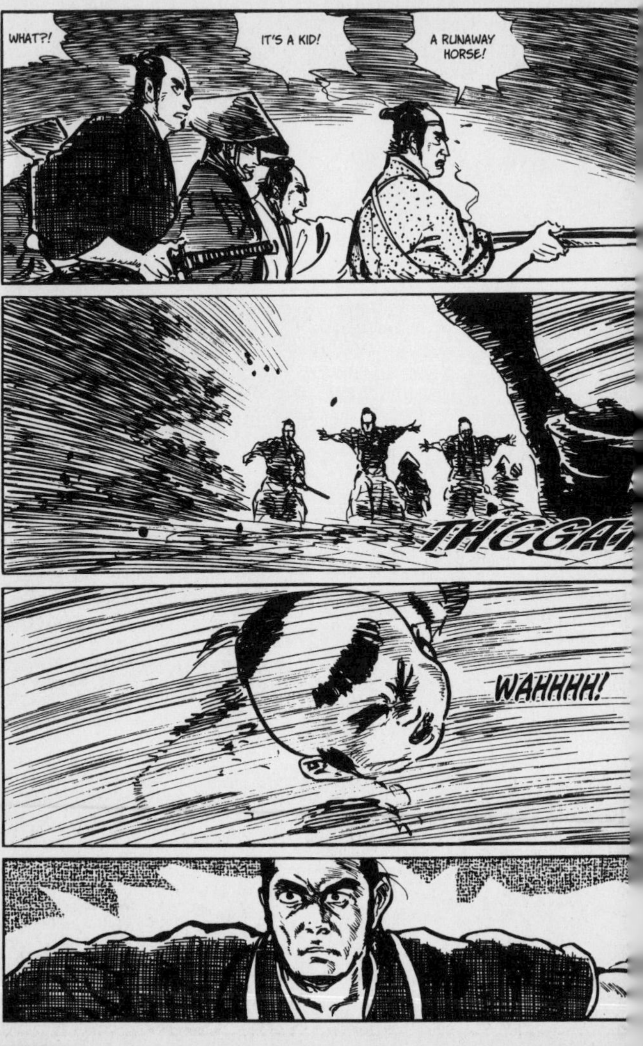
WHAT?!
IT'S A KID!
A RUNAWAY HORSE!
THGGA
WAHHHH!

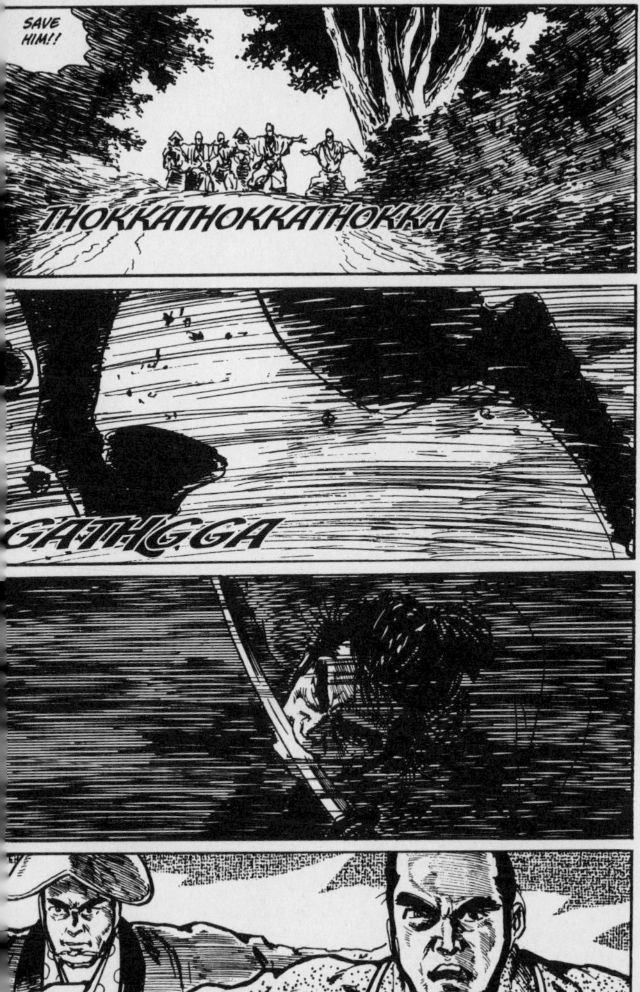
SAVE HIM!!
THOKKATHOKKATHOKKA
GATHGGA

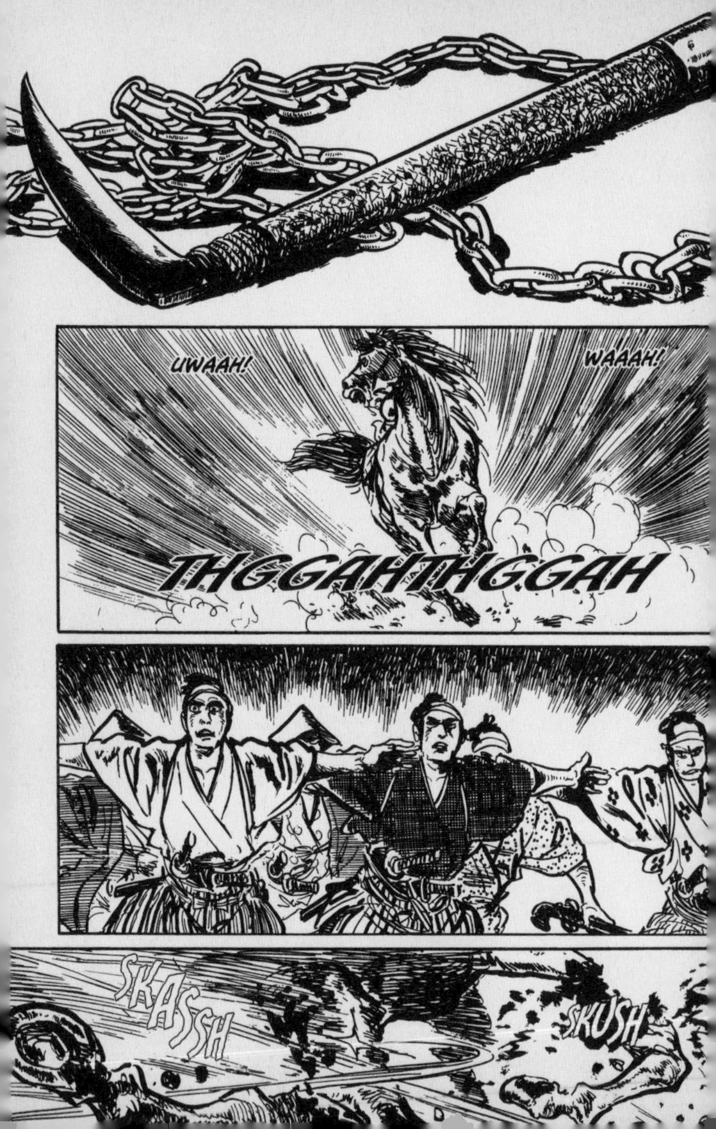
UWAAH!
WAAAH!
THGGAHTHGGAH
SKASSH
SKUSH

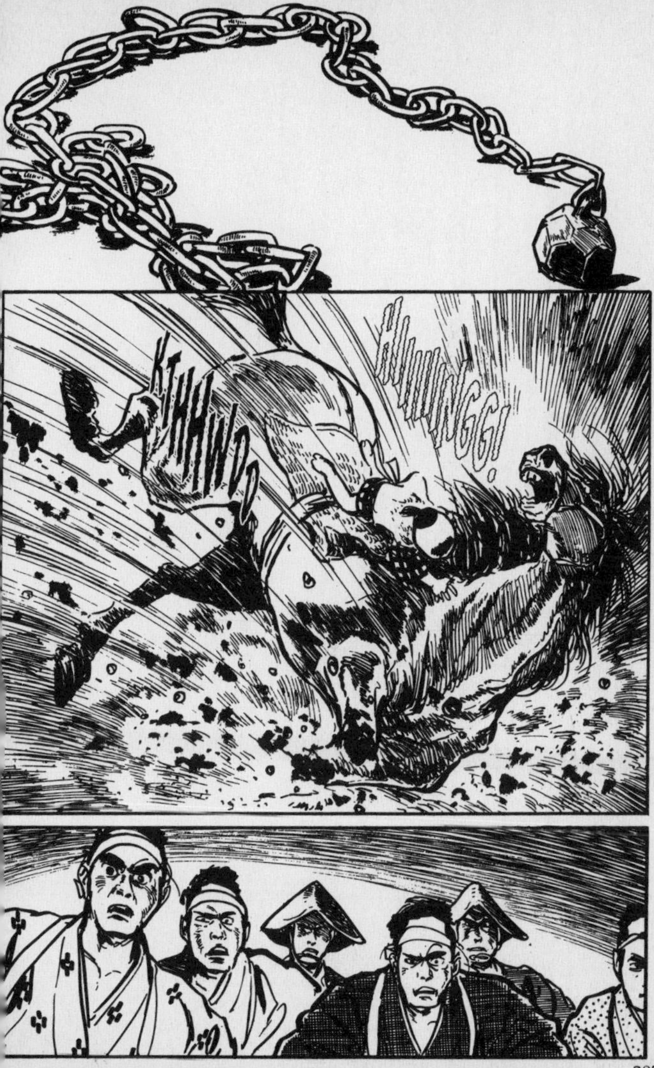
KTHHWOO
HIIIINGG!

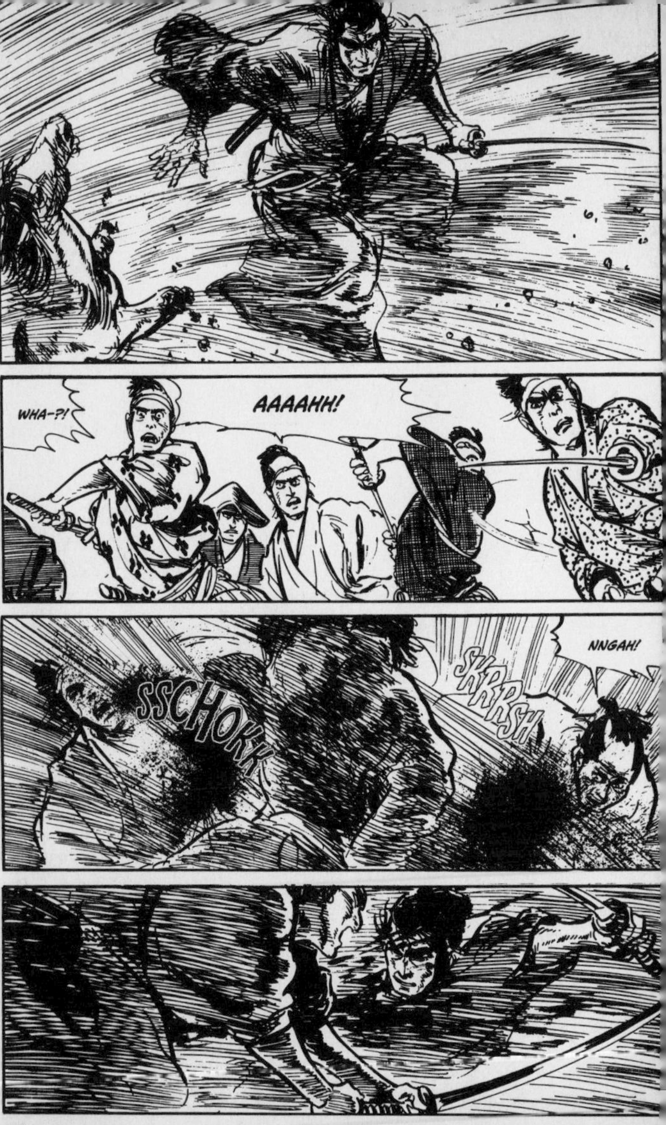
WHA-?!
AAAAHH!
SSCHOKK
SKRRSH
NNGAH!

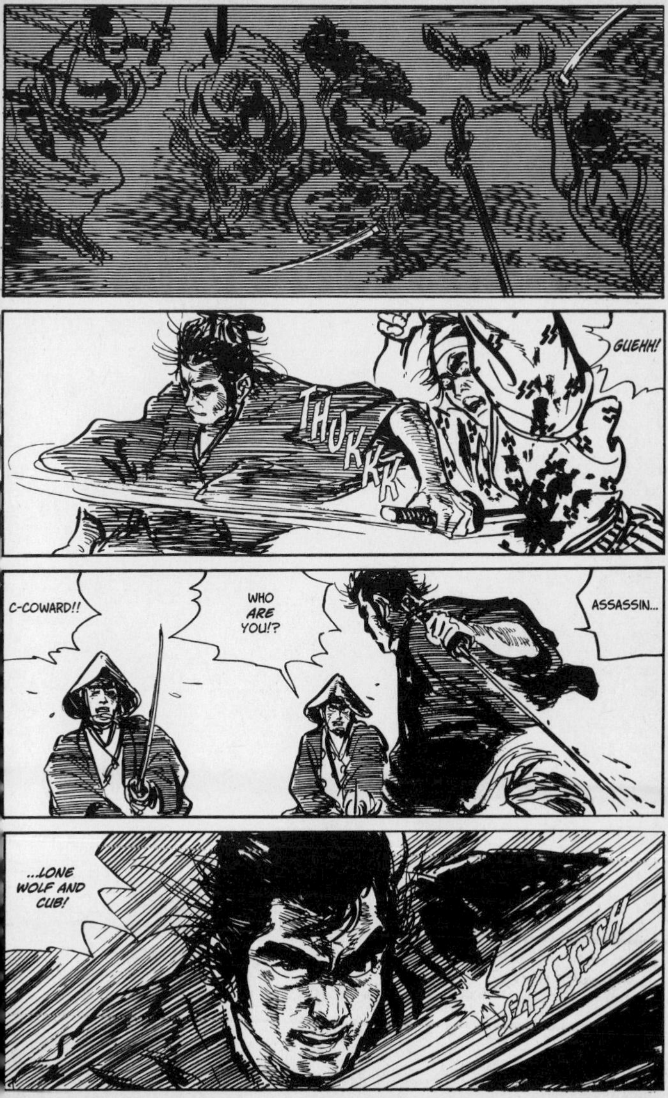
THUKKK
GUEHH!
C-COWARD!!
WHO ARE YOU!?
ASSASSIN...
...LONE WOLF AND CUB!
SKSSSH

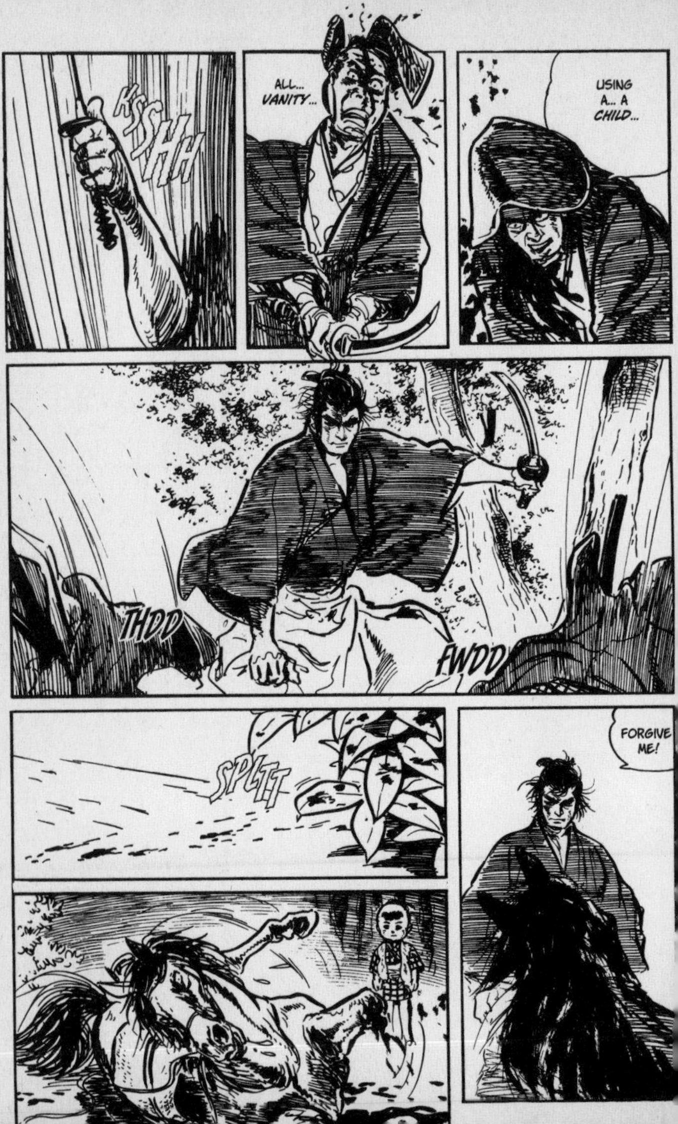
KSSHH
ALL... VANITY...
USING A... A CHILD...
THDD
FWDD
SPLTT
FORGIVE ME!

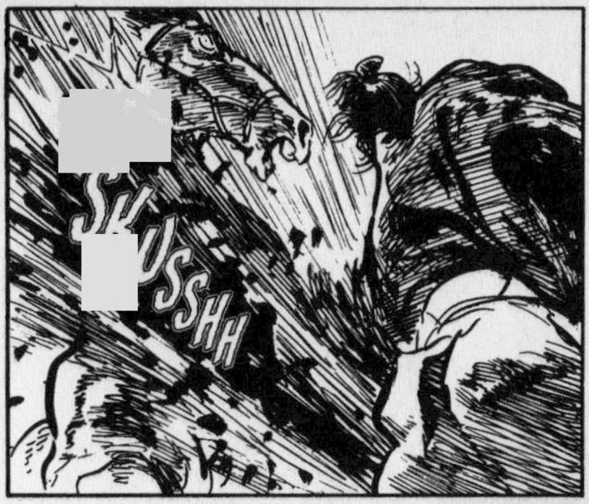
SHUSSHH
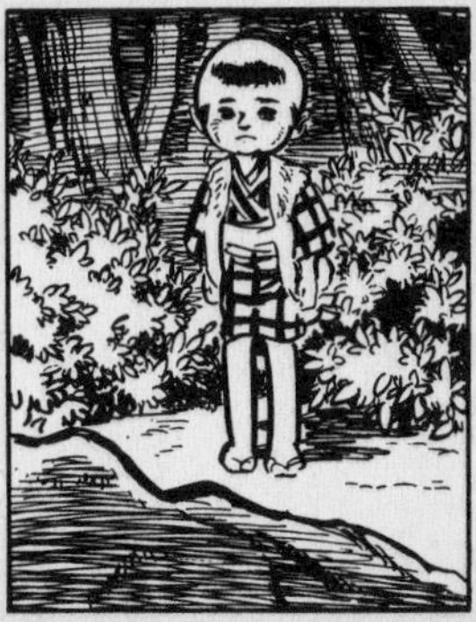
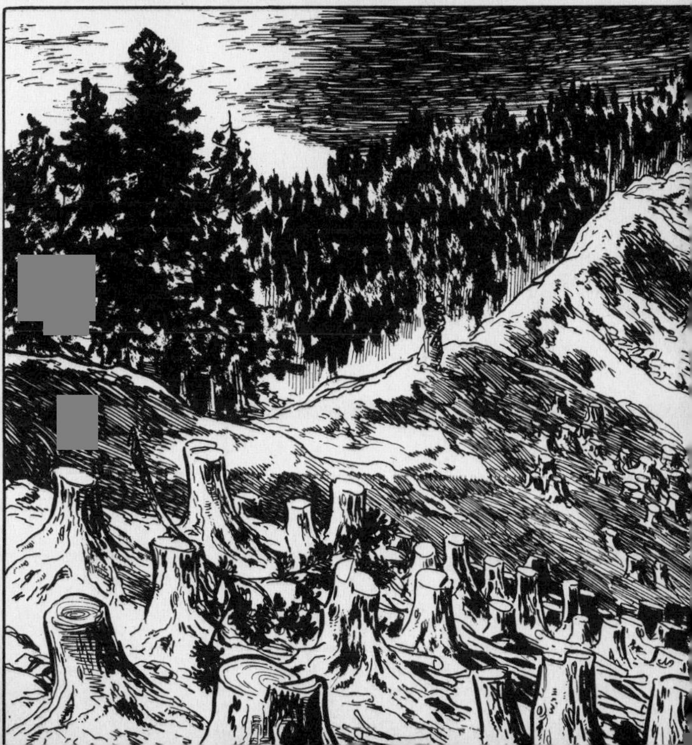

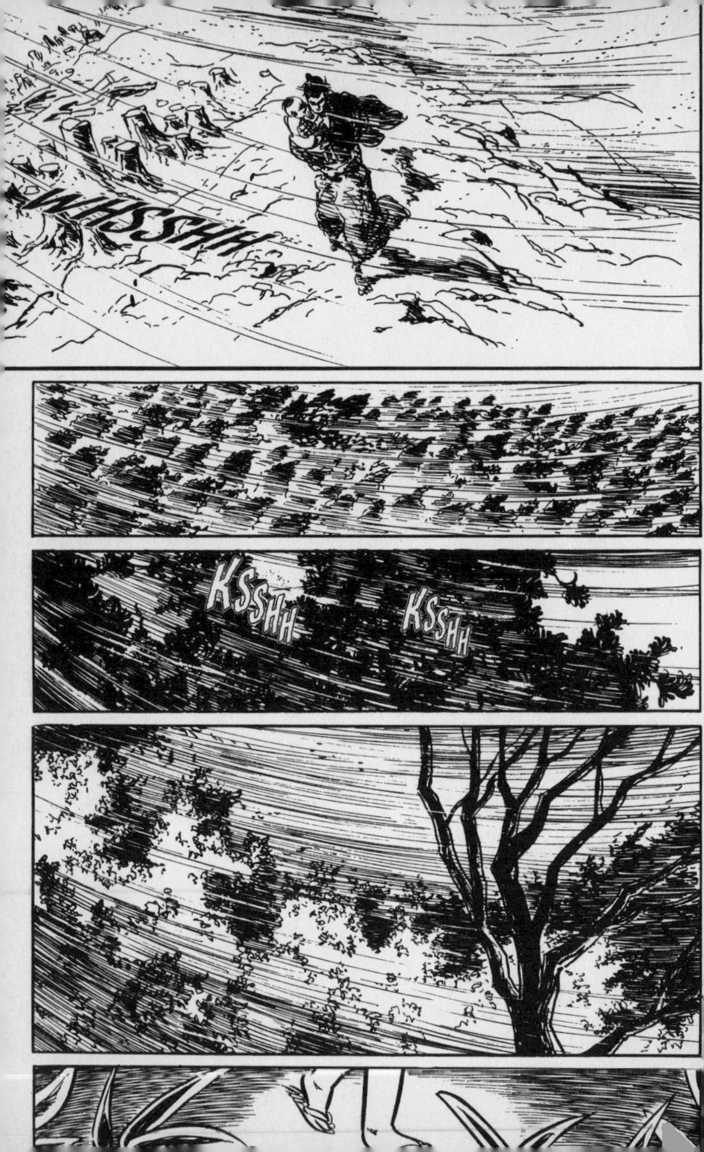
WHSSHH
KSSHH
KSSHH

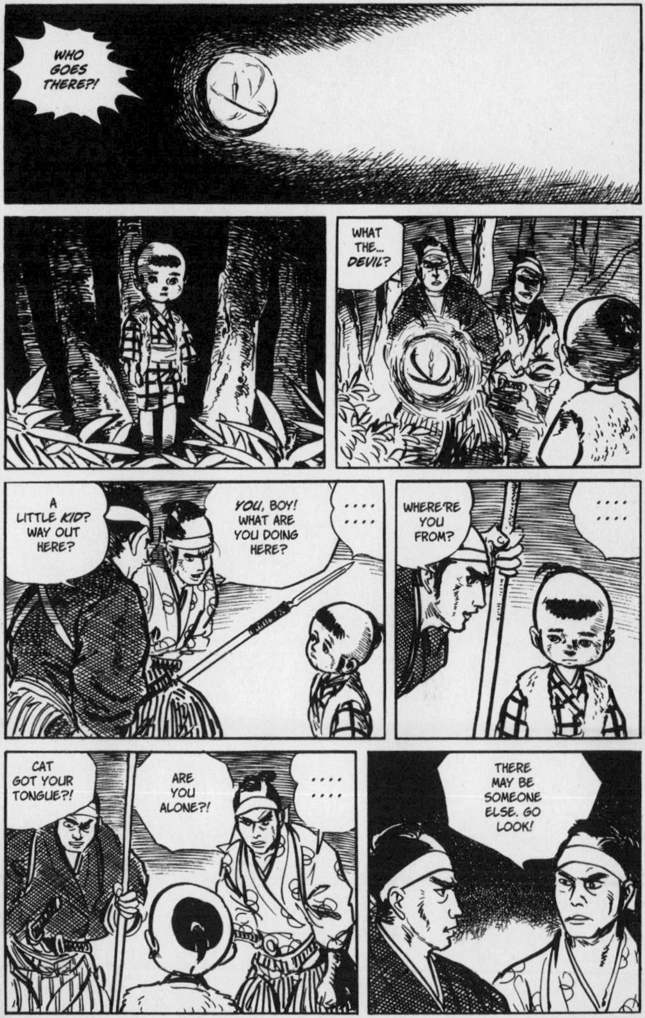
WHO GOES THERE?!
WHAT THE... DEVIL?
A LITTLE KID? WAY OUT HERE?
YOU, BOY! WHAT ARE YOU DOING HERE?
....
WHERE'RE YOU FROM?
....
CAT GOT YOUR TONGUE?!
ARE YOU ALONE?!
....
THERE MAY BE SOMEONE ELSE. GO LOOK!

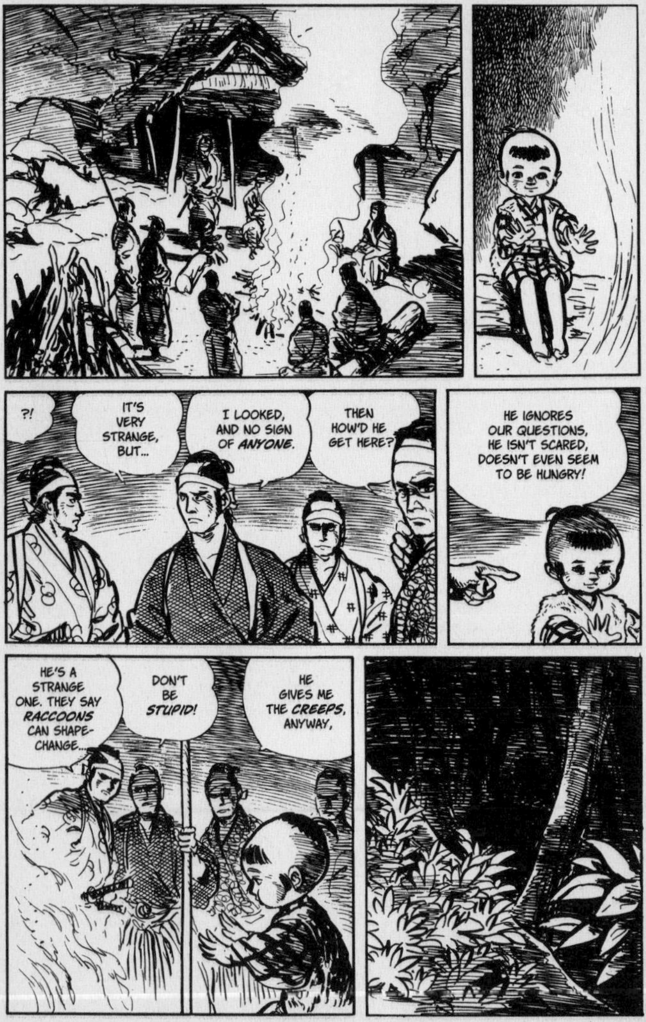
?!
IT'S VERY STRANGE, BUT...
I LOOKED, AND NO SIGN OF ANYONE.
THEN HOW'D HE GET HERE?
HE IGNORES OUR QUESTIONS, HE ISN'T SCARED, DOESN'T EVEN SEEM TO BE HUNGRY!
HE'S A STRANGE ONE. THEY SAY RACCOONS CAN SHAPE-CHANGE...
DON'T BE STUPID!
HE GIVES ME THE CREEPS, ANYWAY,

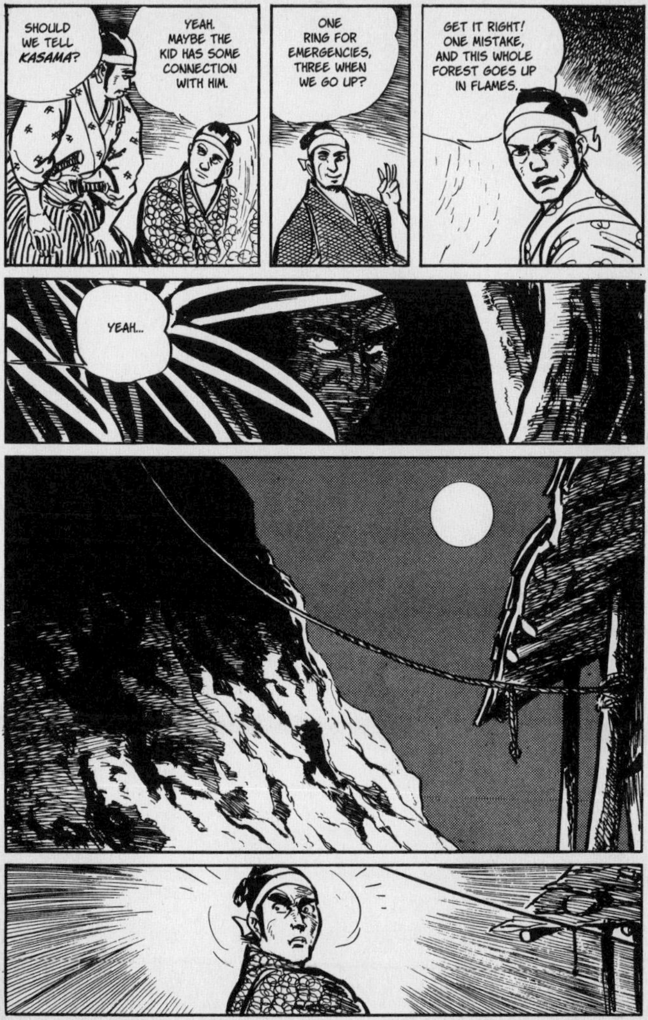
SHOULD WE TELL KASAMA?
YEAH. MAYBE THE KID HAS SOME CONNECTION WITH HIM.
ONE RING FOR EMERGENCIES, THREE WHEN WE GO UP?
GET IT RIGHT! ONE MISTAKE, AND THIS WHOLE FOREST GOES UP IN FLAMES.
YEAH...

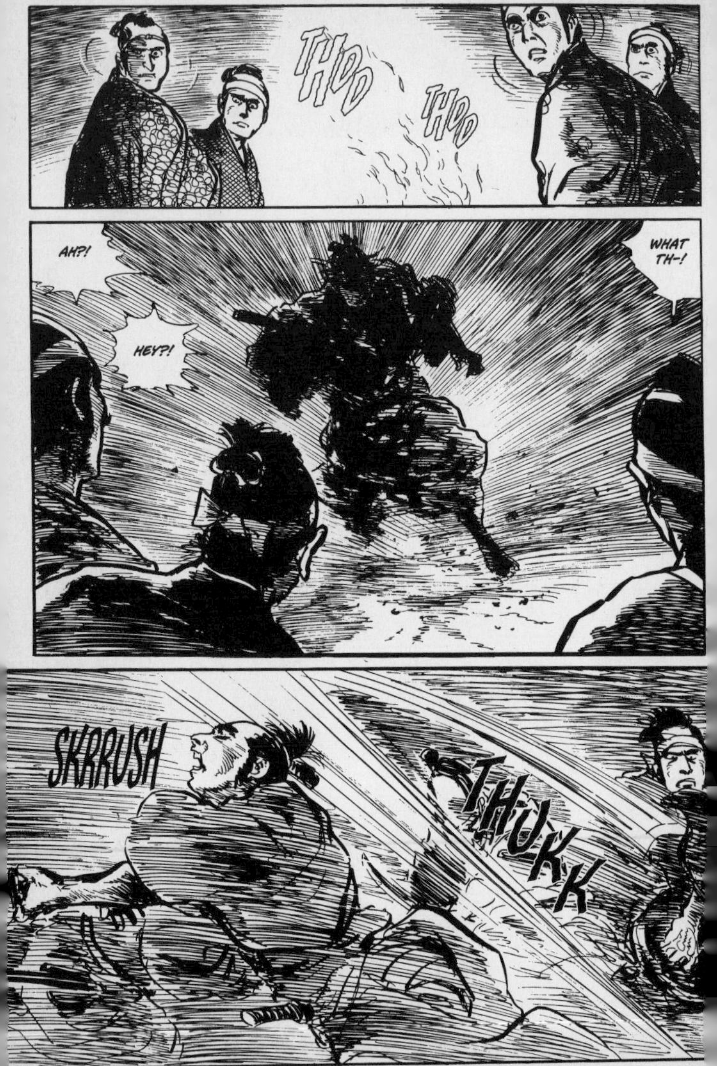
THOO
THOO
AH?!
HEY?!
WHAT TH-!
SKRRUSH
THUKK

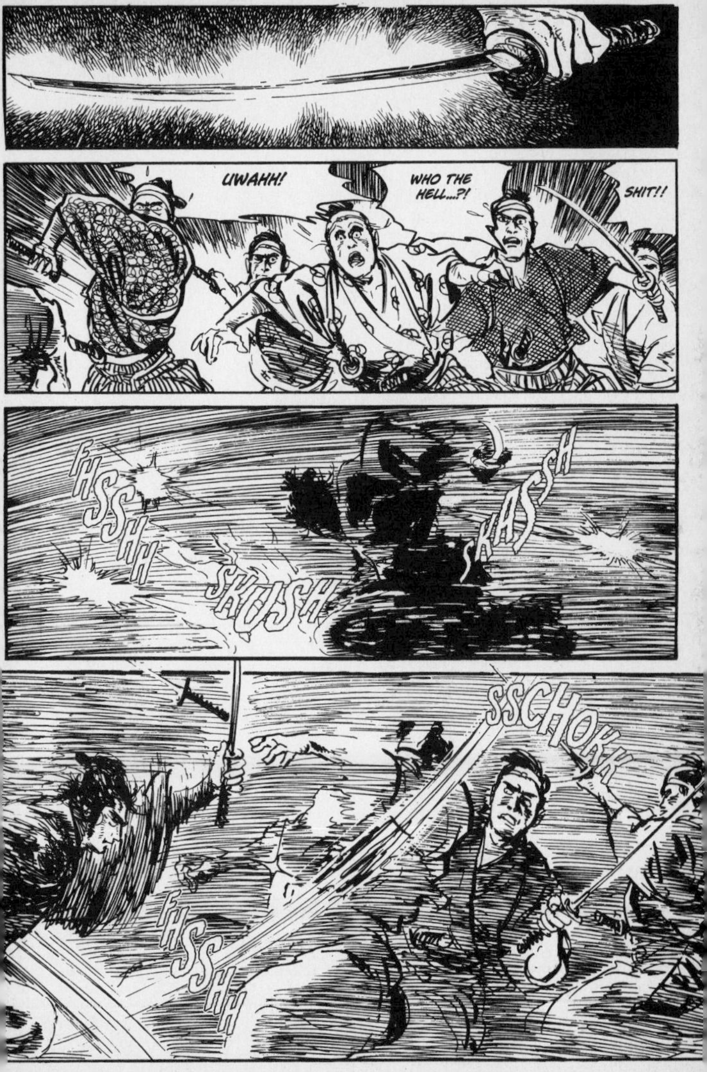
UWAHH!
WHO THE HELL...?!
SHIT!!
FHSSHH
SKUSH
SKASSH
SSCHOKK
FHSSHH

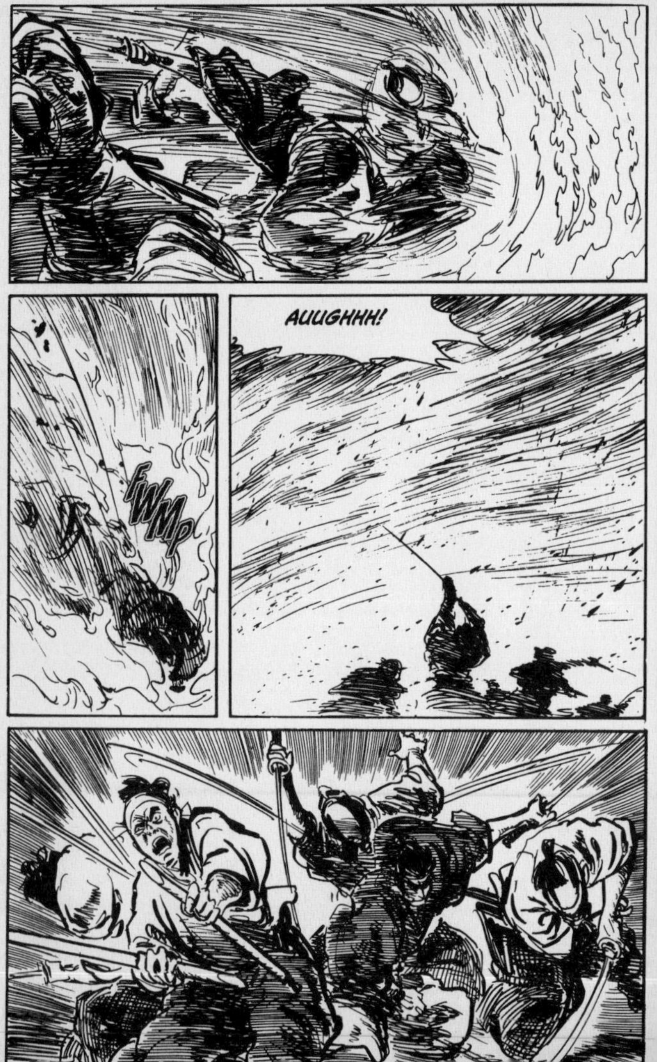
FWMP
AUUGHHH!

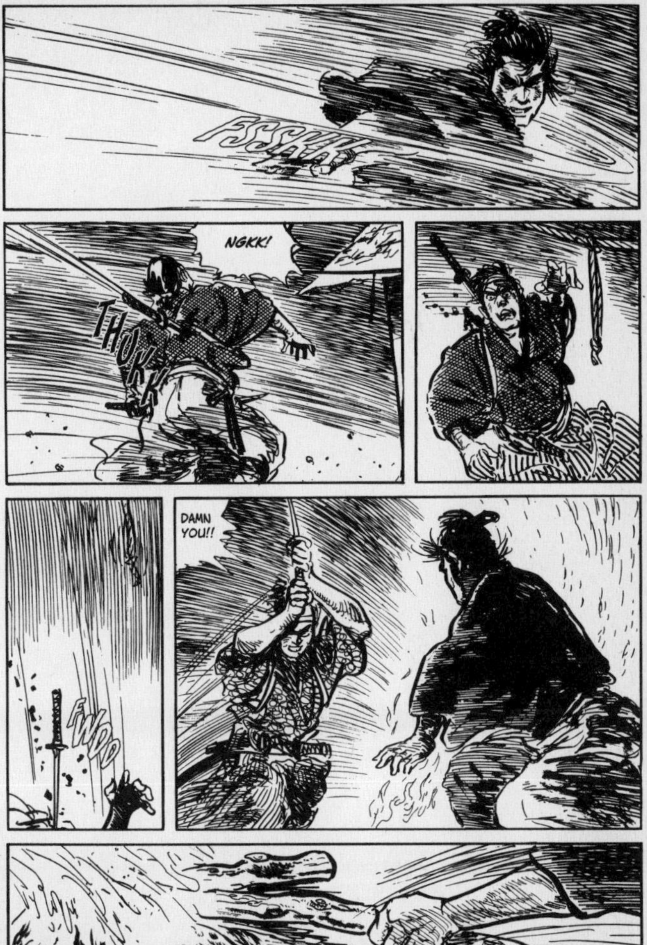
FSSHK
NGKK!
THUKK
FWOO
DAMN YOU!!

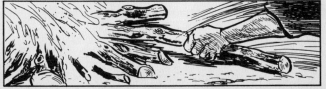

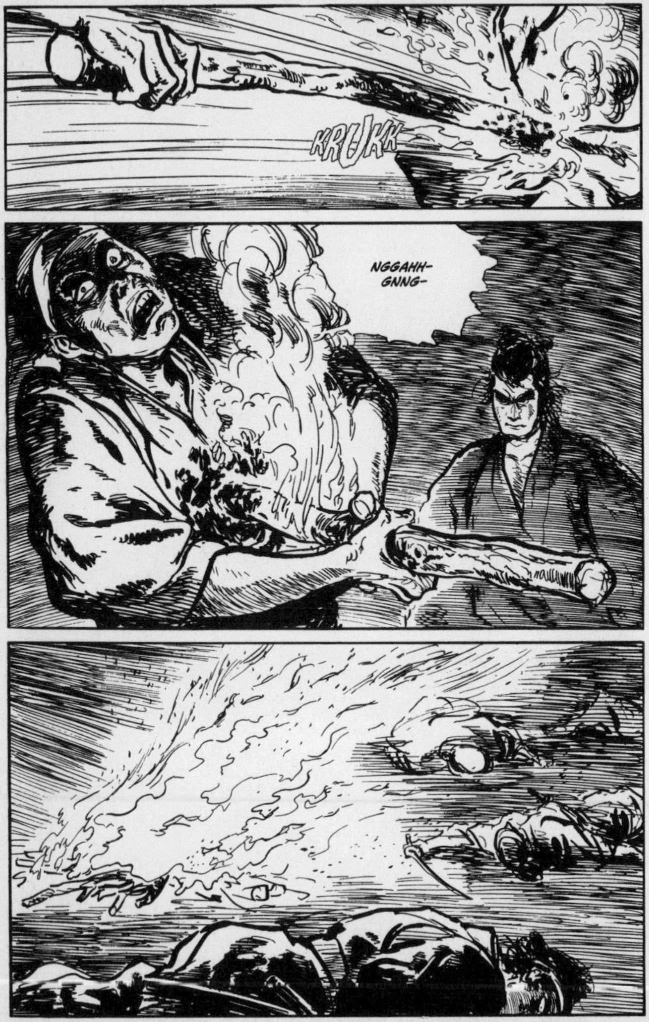
KRUKK
NGGAHH-
GNNG-

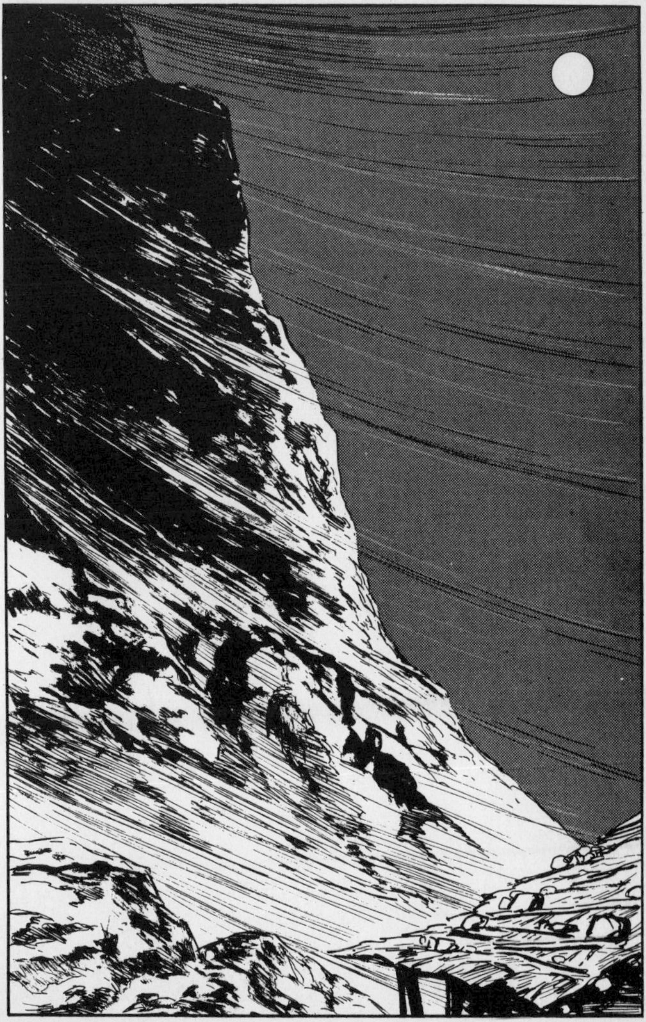

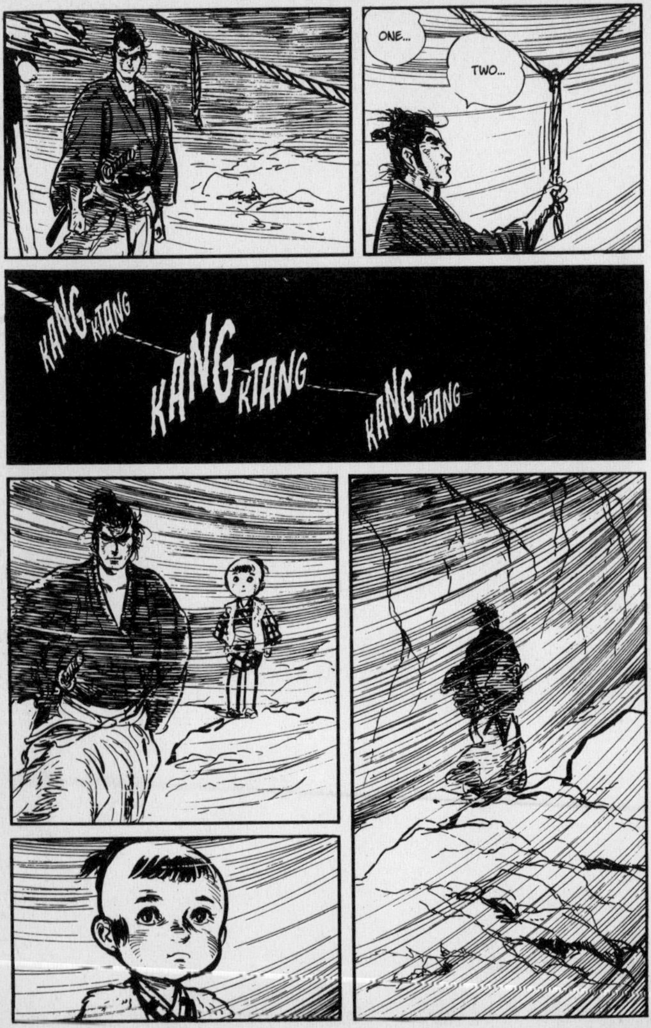
ONE...
TWO...
KANG KTANG
KANG KTANG
KANG KTANG

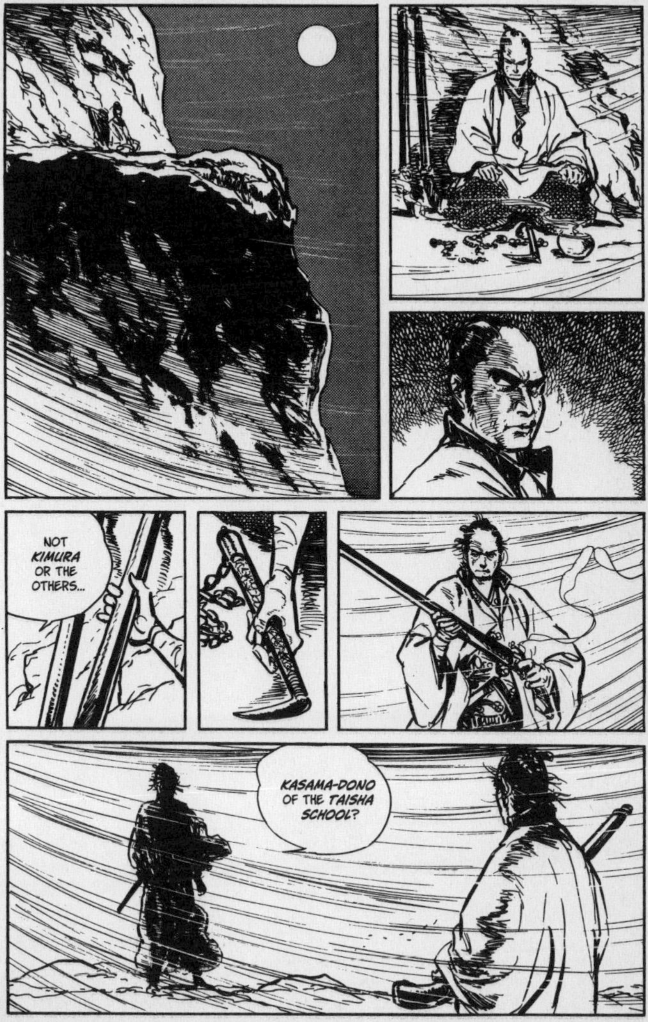
NOT *KIMURA* OR THE OTHERS...
KASAMA-DONO OF THE *TAISHA SCHOOL*?

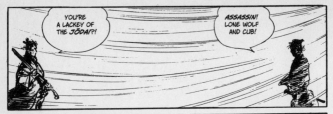

YOU'RE A LACKEY OF THE *JŌDAI?!*

ASSASSIN! LONE WOLF AND CUB!

LAUGHABLE! THIS IS A *SHISEKI-NO-CHI!* NO ROOM TO *MOVE!*

ONE WHO LIVES BY THE SWORD SHOULD KNOW BETTER.

KNOWING THAT, I SEEK A DUEL.

SO BE IT!

SHAKK

SUIŌ-RYŪP!

YET YOU CANNOT WIN ON *THIS* TERRAIN, NO *MATTER* HOW SKILLED.

302

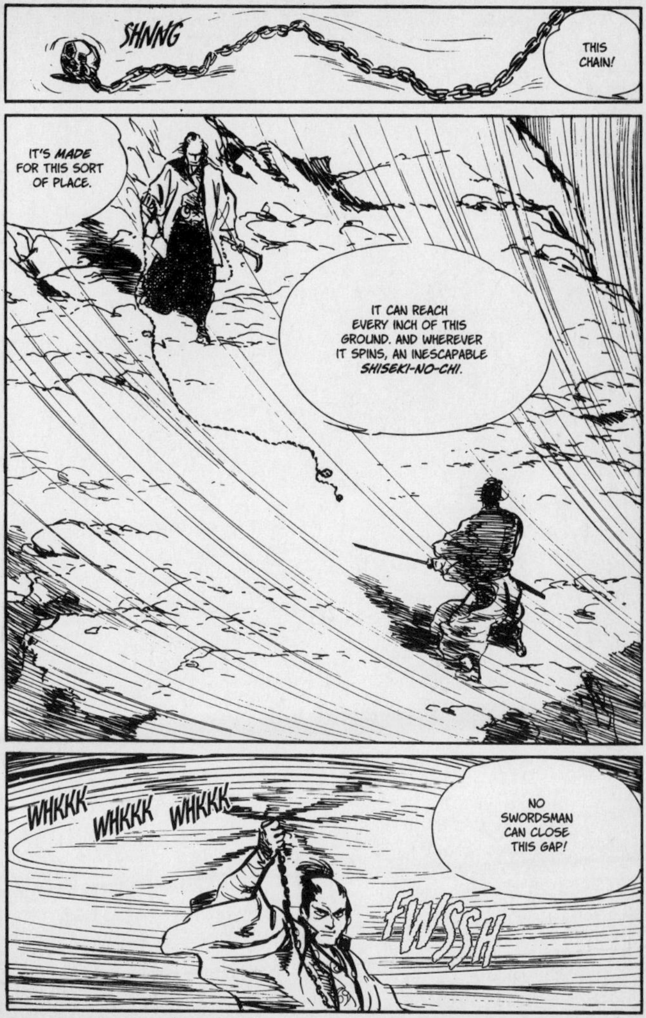
SHNNG
THIS CHAIN!
IT'S *MADE* FOR THIS SORT OF PLACE.
IT CAN REACH EVERY INCH OF THIS GROUND. AND WHEREVER IT SPINS, AN INESCAPABLE *SHISEKI-NO-CHI*.
WHKKK WHKKK WHKKK
NO SWORDSMAN CAN CLOSE THIS GAP!
FWSSH

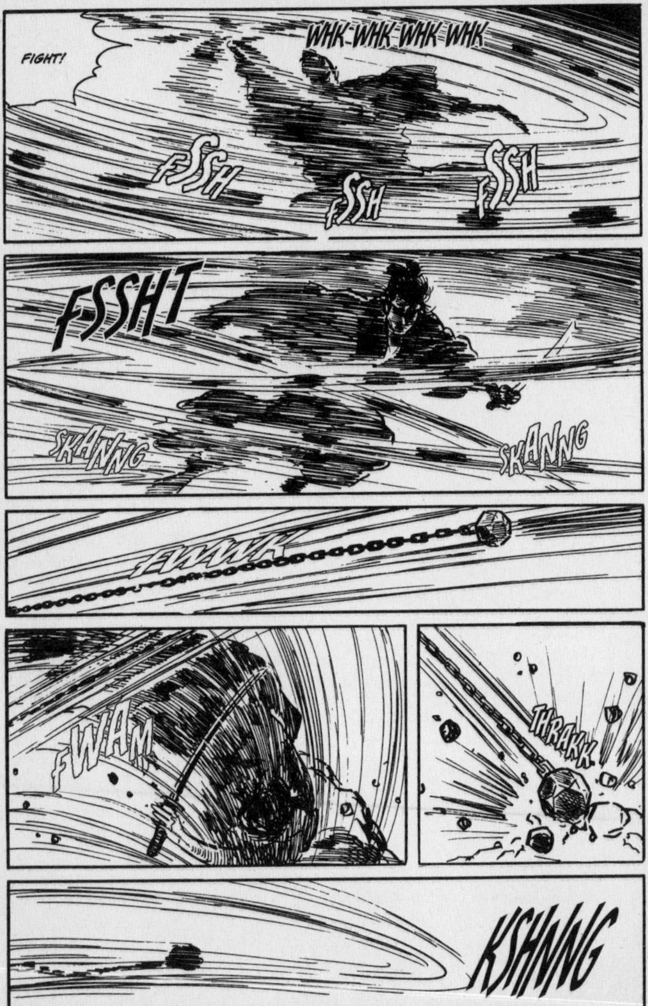

FIGHT!
WHK WHK WHK WHK
FSSH
FSSH
FSSH
FSSHT
SKANNG
SKANNG
FWWK
FWAM
THRAKK
KSHNNG

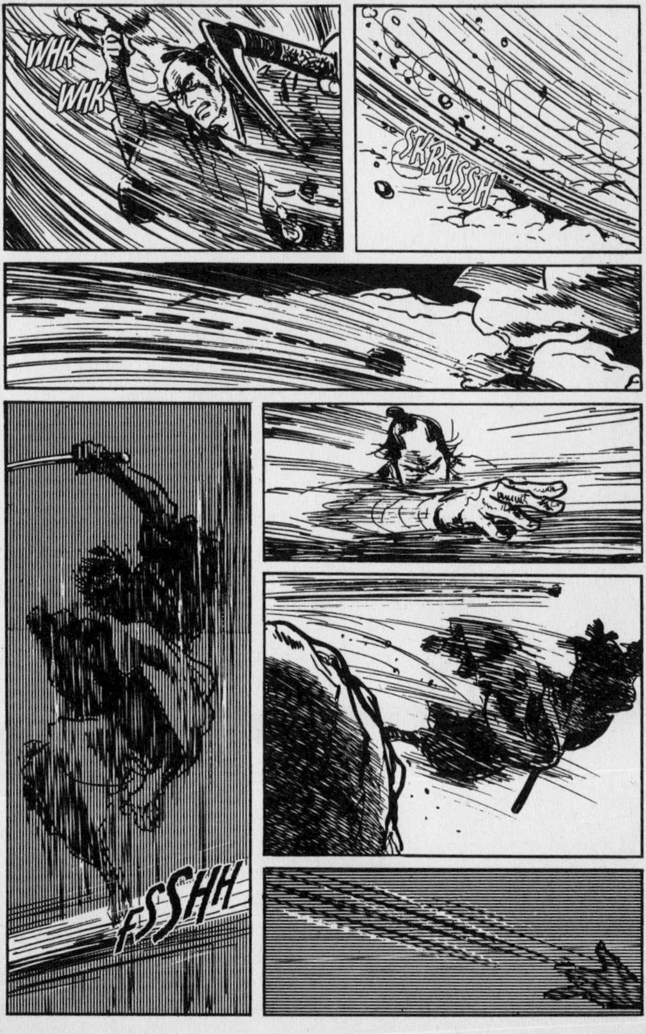
WHK
WHK
SKRASSH
FSSHH

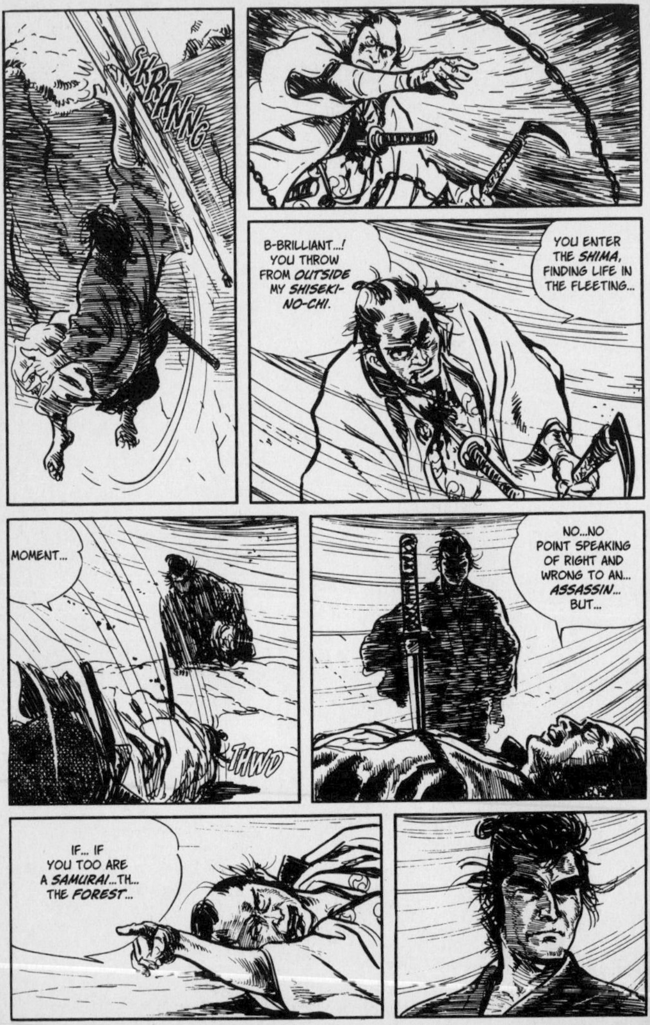
SKRANNG
B-BRILLIANT...! YOU THROW FROM OUTSIDE MY SHISEKI-NO-CHI.
YOU ENTER THE SHIMA, FINDING LIFE IN THE FLEETING...
MOMENT...
THWD
NO...NO POINT SPEAKING OF RIGHT AND WRONG TO AN... ASSASSIN... BUT...
IF... IF YOU TOO ARE A SAMURAI...TH... THE FOREST...

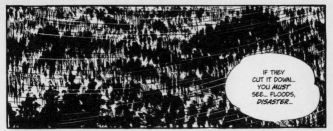

IF THEY CUT IT DOWN... YOU *MUST* SEE... FLOODS, DISASTER...

KUK... KRRK...

UHNGG... NGN!

THWD

307

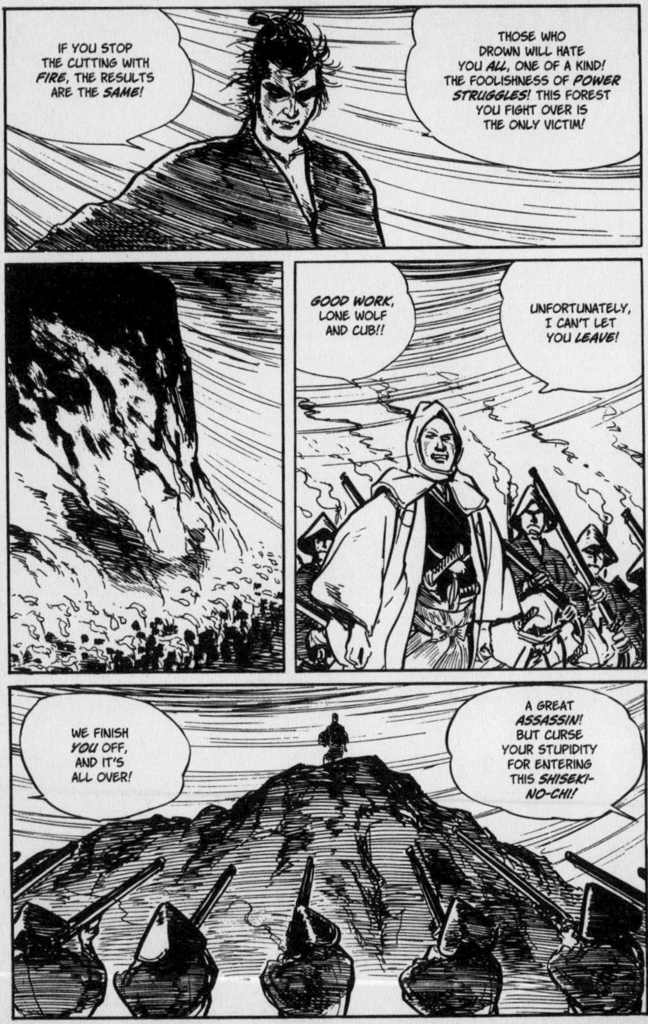
IF YOU STOP THE CUTTING WITH FIRE, THE RESULTS ARE THE SAME!
THOSE WHO DROWN WILL HATE YOU ALL, ONE OF A KIND! THE FOOLISHNESS OF POWER STRUGGLES! THIS FOREST YOU FIGHT OVER IS THE ONLY VICTIM!
GOOD WORK, LONE WOLF AND CUB!!
UNFORTUNATELY, I CAN'T LET YOU LEAVE!
WE FINISH YOU OFF, AND IT'S ALL OVER!
A GREAT ASSASSIN! BUT CURSE YOUR STUPIDITY FOR ENTERING THIS SHISEKI-NO-CHI!

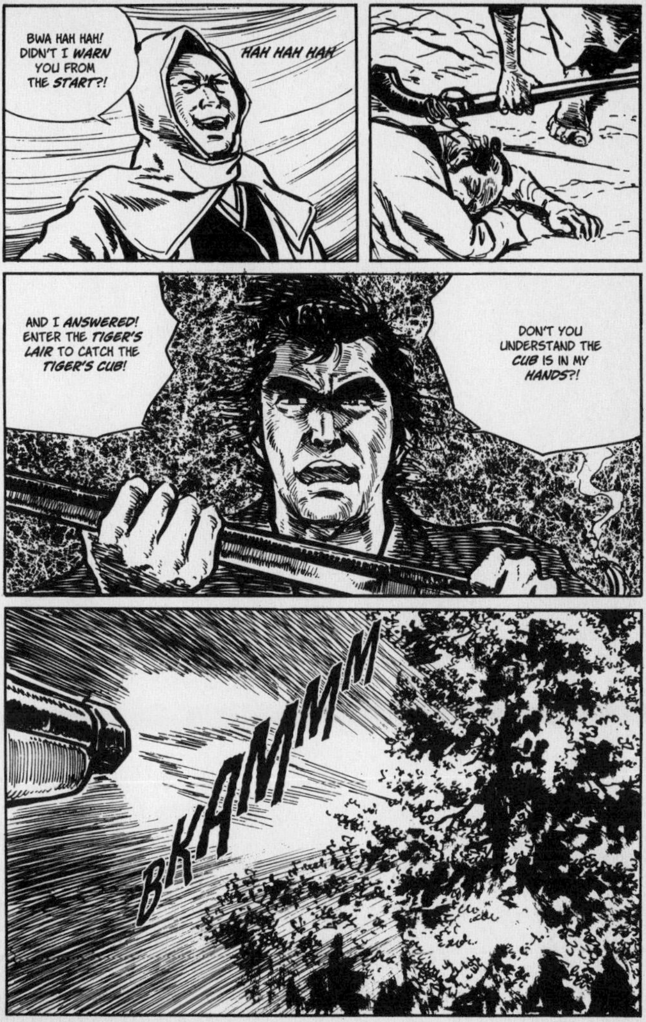
BWA HAH HAH! DIDN'T I *WARN* YOU FROM THE *START*?!
HAH HAH HAH
AND I *ANSWERED!* ENTER THE *TIGER'S LAIR* TO CATCH THE *TIGER'S CUB!*
DON'T YOU UNDERSTAND THE *CUB* IS IN MY *HANDS*?!
BKAMMM

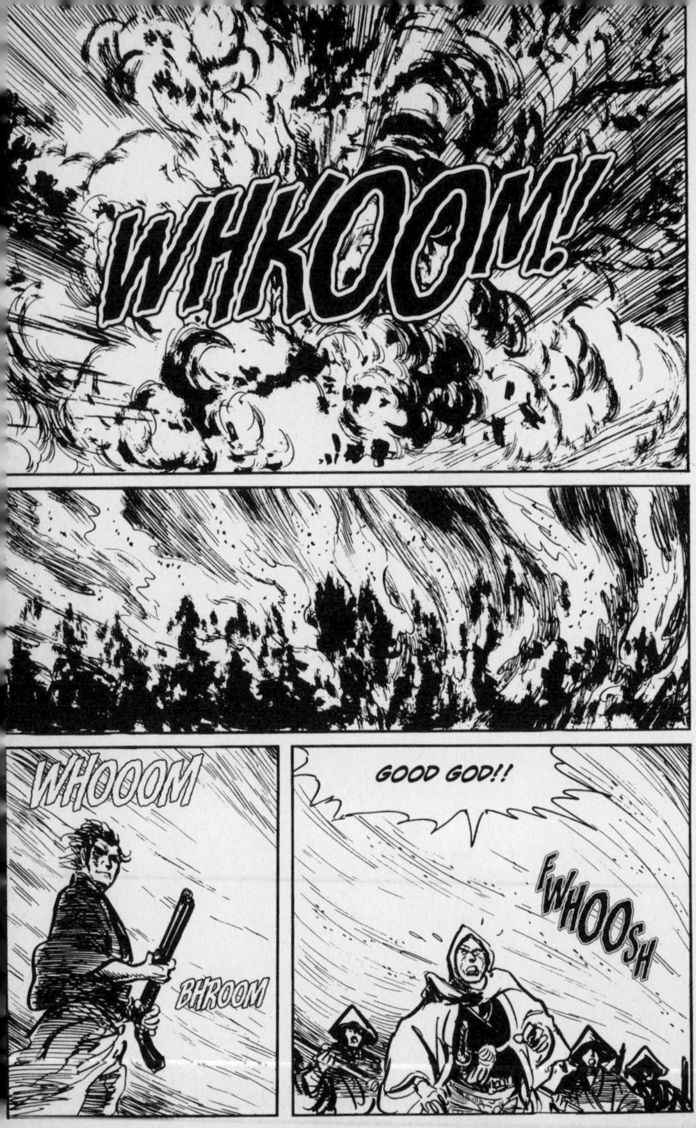
WHKOOM!
WHOOOM
BHROOM
GOOD GOD!!
FWHOOSH

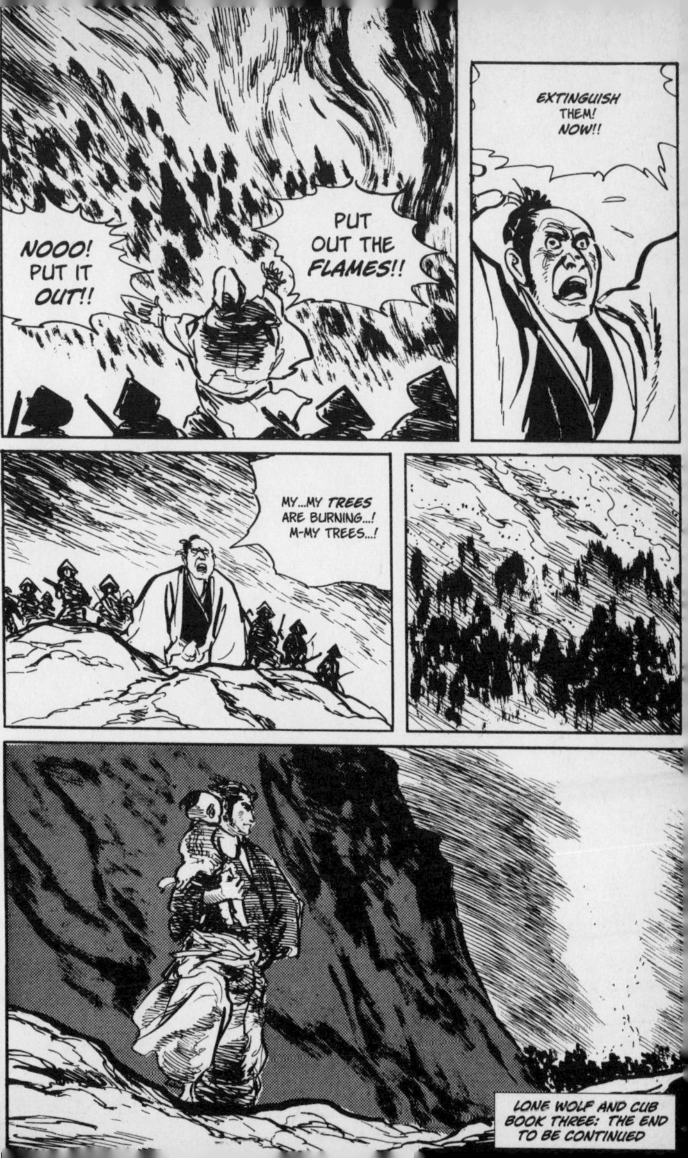
NOOO! PUT IT OUT!!
PUT OUT THE FLAMES!!
EXTINGUISH THEM! NOW!!
MY...MY TREES ARE BURNING...! M-MY TREES...!
LONE WOLF AND CUB BOOK THREE: THE END TO BE CONTINUED

GLOSSARY

annya
A working prostitute. There was a thriving sex industry in Edo-period Japan, and scores of different words to describe the different varieties of sex workers.

Benten
One of the seven gods and goddesses of good fortune popular among the common people, a folk version of Buddhist Boddhisatva, a manifestation of one aspect of the Buddha's nature. In this case, a Boddhisatva of mercy and compassion, usually depicted as female.

bōhachi, kutsuwa
The Japanese *yakuza* specialize in different underworld activities, from gambling and protection scams to prostitution. *Bōhachi* and *kutsuwa* were Edo-period terms for *yakuza* dealing in organized prostitution.

bugi
The martial arts, the arts of war. Restricted to the samurai class under the Tokugawa shogunate's strict social controls.

daimyō
A feudal lord.

dōtanuki
A battle sword. Literally, "sword that cuts through torsos."

Edo
The capital of medieval Japan and the seat of the shogunate. The site of modern-day Tokyo.

go-yō
Literally, "official business." Police and posses carried "*go-yō*" lanterns when searching for criminals, identifying themselves as law enforcers. A shouted "*Go-yō!*" could be the Edo equivalent of "Halt! Police!" for a *metsuke*, or "Make way!" for an official procession.

han
A feudal domain.

hanshi
Samurai in the service of a *han*.

haori
Half-coats.

hina
Elaborate dolls, traditionally displayed in the spring for the Girl's Day festival.

honorifics
Japan is a class and status society, and proper forms of address are critical. Common markers of respect are the prefixes *o* and *go*, and a wide range of suffixes. Some of the suffixes you will encounter in *Lone Wolf and Cub*:
chan – for children, young women, and close friends

dono – archaic; used for higher-ranked or highly respected figures
sama – used for superiors
san – the most common, used among equals or near-equals
sensei – used for teachers, masters, respected entertainers, and politicians

ihai

A Buddhist mortuary tablet. The death name of the deceased, given after they have passed away, is written on the tablet, which is kept at the family temple or altar. *No-ihai* were placed on the grave, *uchi-ihai* on household altars.

jōdai

Castle warden. The ranking *han* official in charge of a *daimyō's* castle when the *daimyō* was spending his obligatory years in Edo.

kannenbutsu

Literally, "cold prayers." There were many kinds of itinerant monks in Edo-period Japan, traveling the land as part of their religious discipline and relying on the handouts of the faithful. It was also a useful disguise for those with more than religion on their mind. *Kannenbutsu* were known for their penance in the chill of the coldest nights.

kōgi kaishakunin

The shogun's own second, who performed executions ordered by the shogun.

koku

A bale of rice. The traditional measure of a *han's* wealth, a measure of its agricultural land and productivity.

meifumadō

The Buddhist Hell. The way of demons and damnation.

metsuke

An inspector. A post combining the functions of chief of police and chief intelligence officer.

ri

Old unit of measurement. Approximately 4 kilometers (2.5 miles).

rōnin

A masterless samurai. Literally, "one adrift on the waves." Members of the samurai caste who have lost their masters through the dissolution of *han*, expulsion for misbehavior, or other reasons. Prohibited from working as farmers or merchants under the strict Confucian caste system imposed by the Tokugawa shogunate, many impoverished *rōnin* became "hired guns" for whom the code of the samurai was nothing but empty words.

ryō

A gold piece.

ryū

Often translated as "school." The many variations of swordsmanship and other martial arts were passed down from generation to generation to the offspring of the originator of the technique or set of techniques, and to any *deishi* students that sought to learn from the master. The largest schools had their own *dōjō* training centers and scores of students. An effective swordsman had to study the different techniques of the various schools to know how to block them in combat. Many *ryū* also had a set of special, secret techniques that were only taught to school initiates.

sakki

The palpable desire to kill, directed at another person. Sometimes called blood lust. Based on the concept of *ki*, or energy, found in spiritual practices and Japanese martial arts like Aikido. These body energies can be felt beyond the physical self by the trained and self-aware.

seisatsu yodatsu

Under the four-caste social system imposed by the Tokugawa shogunate, the samurai class had the unquestioned right to kill those in lower castes, often for the smallest of insults and infractions.

seppuku

The right to kill oneself with honor to atone for failure, or to follow one's master into death. Only the samurai class was allowed this glorious but excruciating death. The abdomen was cut horizontally, followed by an upward cut to spill out the intestines. When possible, a *kaishakunin* performed a beheading after the cut was made to shorten the agony.

shaba

Yakuza divided the world between the *shima* ("island"), the world of the *yakuza*, and *shaba*, the normal world.

shima

1. The zone of death.
2. See *shaba*.

sō-metsuke

Another name for "*ō-metsuke*." The senior law-enforcement officer of the shogunate, reporting directly to the *rōjū* senior councilors who advised the shogun.

tono

Lord, *daimyō*. Sometimes used as a form of address, as in *tono-sama*.

yakuza

Japan's criminal syndicates. In the Edo period, *yakuza* were a common part of the landscape, running houses of gambling and prostitution. As long as they did not overstep their bounds, they were tolerated by the authorities, a tradition little changed in modern Japan.

zankanjō

A confession. Vendettas were an accepted form of vigilante justice in the Edo period. While the killers knew the penalty for their act was death, they could exonerate their reputations after death with a *zankanjō* explaining their actions.

zegen

Procurer. Prostitution was legal in the Edo period, and the procurer was an essential link in the chain. Impoverished rural families would sell daughters to *zegen*, who sold them in turn to urban brothels.

KAZUO KOIKE

Though widely respected as a powerful writer of graphic fiction, Kazuo Koike has spent a lifetime reaching beyond the bounds of the comics medium. Aside from co-creating and writing the successful *Lone Wolf and Cub* and *Crying Freeman* manga, Koike has hosted television programs; founded a golf magazine; produced movies; written popular fiction, poetry, and screenplays; and mentored some of Japan's best manga talent.

Lone Wolf and Cub was first serialized in Japan in 1970 (under the title *Kozure Okami*) in *Manga Action* magazine and continued its hugely popular run for many years, being collected as the stories were published, and reprinted worldwide. Koike collected numerous awards for his work on the series throughout the next decade. Starting in 1972, Koike adapted the popular manga into a series of six films, the *Baby Cart Assassin* saga, garnering widespread commercial success and critical acclaim for his screenwriting.

This wasn't Koike's only foray into film and video. In 1996, *Crying Freeman*, the manga Koike created with artist Ryoichi Ikegami, was produced in Hollywood and released to commercial success in Europe and is currently awaiting release in America.

And to give something back to the medium that gave him so much, Koike started the *Gekiga Sonjuku*, a college course aimed at helping talented writers and artists — such as *Ranma 1/2* creator Rumiko Takahashi — break into the comics field.

The driving focus of Koike's narrative is character development, and his commitment to character is clear: "Comics are carried by characters. If a character is well created, the comic becomes a hit." Kazuo Koike's continued success in comics and literature has proven this philosophy true.

GOSEKI KOJIMA

Goseki Kojima was born on November 3, 1928, the very same day as the godfather of Japanese comics, Osamu Tezuka. While just out of junior high school, the self-taught Kojima began painting advertising posters for movie theaters to pay his bills.

In 1950, Kojima moved to Tokyo, where the postwar devastation had given rise to special manga forms for audiences too poor to buy the new manga magazines. Kojima created art for *kami-shibai*, or "paper-play" narrators, who would use manga story sheets to present narrated street plays. Kojima moved on to creating works for the *kashi-bon* market, bookstores that rented out books, magazines, and manga to mostly low-income readers. He soon became highly popular among *kashi-bon* readers.

In 1967, Kojima broke into the magazine market with his series *Dojinki*. As the manga magazine market grew and diversified, he turned out a steady stream of popular series.

In 1970, in collaboration with Kazuo Koike, Kojima began the work that would seal his reputation, *Kozure Okami* (*Lone Wolf and Cub*). Before long the story had become a gigantic hit, eventually spinning off a television series, six motion pictures, and even theme song records. Koike and Kojima were soon dubbed the "golden duo" and produced success after success on their way to the pinnacle of the manga world.

When *Manga Japan* magazine was launched in 1994, Kojima was asked to serve as consultant, and he helped train the next generation of manga artists.

In his final years, Kojima turned to creating original graphic novels based on the movies of his favorite director, Akira Kurosawa. Kojima passed away on January 5, 2000 at the age of 71.

THE RONIN REPORT

by Tim Ervin-Gore

In our fast and chaotic modern world, it is of increasing importance for one to choose and stay on a path. But what we might consider to be a central goal these days, such as monetary success or weight loss, falls far short of what a samurai considered in his life's path. A samurai's way, the "Way of the Warrior," was deeply entrenched in mastery of weapons and strategic tactics, but beyond common warfare was a depth of culture and awareness — the need to practice refined arts and social customs, the ability to negotiate risky alliances, and an acute perception of danger. This is the way of bushido.

Bushido, which literally translated means "the way of the military man" (hence, the Way of the Warrior), was a chivalrous code of conduct that defined the true soul of a samurai more than the swords on his waist. At the heart of *bushido* is death — not the act of dying or the violence that leads to it, but the concept that a samurai is prepared for death, ready to lay down his life for his master at any and all times, and to accept death gracefully. However, according to Miyamoto Musashi, a legendary samurai from the early 1600s who knew no equal in skill and concentration, the essence of the Way of the Warrior is "to believe that you cannot fail in doing anything."

Miyamoto wrote that line in the introduction of his *Book of Five Rings*, which explored *heiho*, his own version of the Way of the Warrior. Miyamoto lived at a time when war was waning, and long, peaceful periods allowed him to adapt his passions to art and culture, but the warrior's way was not always so refined. Approximately 700 years earlier, amidst furious battles against the indigenous Ainu peoples, the earliest samurai warriors began to evolve. As the samurai realized their power, the importance of a warrior's skill became an honored element and a quasi-religion. In these early times, the samurai's skills focused more on archery than swordplay, and samurai were judged upon their Way of the Horse and Bow or their Way of the Bow and Arrow, which signified a samurai's social bearing and position as much as his ability on the field of battle. This designation was central to the separation of samurai as an elite social class. As time passed like wind over the bloody battle plains, the role and importance of *bushido* to the warrior class increased with the importance of the samurai themselves. But eventually, as with Miyamoto, the time would come when the samurai became obsolete.

It is notable that the story of *Lone Wolf and Cub* is supposed to take place about twenty years after the death of Miyamoto Musashi. At this time, peace and control ruled the day, and samurai were forced to rethink their positions in the world. Many samurai settled into the arts, some writing the philosophy of *bushido* into books for future generations. Many samurai roamed across the landscape proving their mettle against other samurai, keeping the *bushido* in death a part of everyday life. And yet many other samurai learned to farm and ply other trades, all the while using lessons of *bushido* in their daily lives, and weaving the warrior arts into common life.

To learn the ways of *bushido* and bring it into your daily life, pick up *The Book of Five Rings* by Miyamoto Musashi, *The Art of War* by Sun Tzu, *Hagakure* by Tsunetomo Yamamoto, or *Code of the Samurai: A Modern Translation of the Bushido Shoshinsu* by Yuzan Daidoji and Thomas Cleary.

MANGA! MANGA! MANGA! DARK HORSE HAS THE BEST IN MANGA COLLECTIONS!